DESIGN FOR TRADE FAIR STANDS

GRAND STAND 4

FRAM3

Contents

INTERIOR PRODUCTS

LIGHTING

MOBILITY

SERVICES

SHOES AND ACCESSORIES

REL.

Antony Morato by PLS design

AN ENVIRONMENT OF HIGH IMPACT AND VISUAL INTENSITY FASHIONED FOR A TREND-DRIVEN MENSWEAR BRAND.

Trend-driven fashion brand Antony Morato participated for the first time in the winter edition of Bread & Butter in January 2012. Being true to the spirit of its design-oriented brand, the Antony Morato stand at the trade fair stood out by keeping alive its own chromatic concept of black, white and blue, thanks to the presentation realised by PLS design. Located in the Denim Base Area, the client sat alongside brands such as Levi's, Guess, Scotch&Soda and G-Star, thus strengthening the position of the Italian brand. Taking this into account, Antony Morato and PLS design wanted to produce an eye-catching environment that would immediately grab the attention of fair goers and draw people into the space. A joint idea developed into a communications and multimedia concept with a glowing blue cube that had a futuristic feel. A stunning and interactive choreography was created by a dynamic mix of neon lighting along with an eye-catching chequered floor. The stand was composed of four parts, one outside and three inside. On the outside, an entrance zone offered a welcome desk and seating for visitors to hang out. This area set the scene for the presentation and created an instant buzz around the brand. After a short walk through the booth's entrance hall, visitors found themselves in a black void with the two-storey illuminated cage-like structure ahead of them. Materials, details and technology harmonised to successfully shape a universe characterised by lights, reflections and strong contrasts. The interior space was divided into three areas dominated by the large, illuminated installation that showcased the winter collection. There was also a zone dedicated to catering, as well as a loft that accommodated a DJ booth.

TRADE FAIR **Bread & Butter**
WHERE **Berlin, Germany**
WHEN **January 2012**
DESIGNER **PLS design** ☒ **p.496**
STAND CONSTRUCTOR **Eurostands**
CLIENT **Antony Morato**
MARKET SECTOR **Denim fashion**
TOTAL FLOOR AREA **450 m²**
PHOTOGRAPHERS **Franz Brück, Sgaravato**

☒ The driving force of the season's mott• lured the clients into the stand.
☒ The facade of the stand had a grid-lik• skin of blue neon lights which framed th• reception counter.
☒ The glowing cage defined the centr• space and was a perfect backdrop fo• the featured collection.

Hilfiger Denim by Liganova

THE PRESENTATION OF A DENIM COLLECTION AMIDST A PLAYFUL WINTER LANDSCAPE.

A team of architects, marketers and point of sale specialists from Liganova conceived and implemented the 'Winter Adventures' exhibition stand for Hilfiger Denim at Bread & Butter in Berlin. The concept was based on playful winter experiences. The team sought to contextualise the idea of 'cool denim' in a booth that was a perfect dream world of abstract winter enhancements. The installation combined city and nature to represent the hustle and bustle of real life.

A glistening ice rink stood at the heart of the presentation, inspired by skaters all wrapped up for winter in New York's Central Park. The models that whizzed around the rink wore items from the Fall/Winter 2012/2013 collection. This feature was a real attention-grabber for passers-by at the fair, as was the 17-m-long and 7-m-high LED display wall that could be seen from across the exhibition hall. The ice rink dominated the presentation. A two-storey building on one side made space for further product display areas and meeting rooms. The layout meant the focus was always on the ice rink, with the white-stepped area acting as an auditorium so visitors had a great vantage point to watch the skaters modelling the latest collection. The timber and steel structure had an industrial vintage interior and was topped off with an open-air bar where visitors could chat and enjoy the wintery scene. Furthermore, the stunning view over the Denim Hall of Bread & Butter in the hangar at Tempelhof Airport added to the atmosphere and ensured the booth always exuded a super chilled buzz.

TRADE FAIR **Bread & Butter**
WHERE **Berlin, Germany**
WHEN **January 2012**
DESIGNER **Liganova** ☒ **p.494**
STAND CONSTRUCTORS **Liganova, The Brand Retail Company**
CLIENT **Tommy Hilfiger**
MARKET SECTOR **Denim fashion**
TOTAL FLOOR AREA **480 m²**
PHOTOGRAPHERS **Julia Nitzschke, Ugur Orhanoglu, Andreas Schöttke**

☒ The playful design was developed in common creative process to interpret th brief artistically.
☒ The LED wall was an ideal backdrop fo the skaters with its abstract impressior of winter scenes.
☒ Quirky decorations were chosen t complement the vintage-style interior.

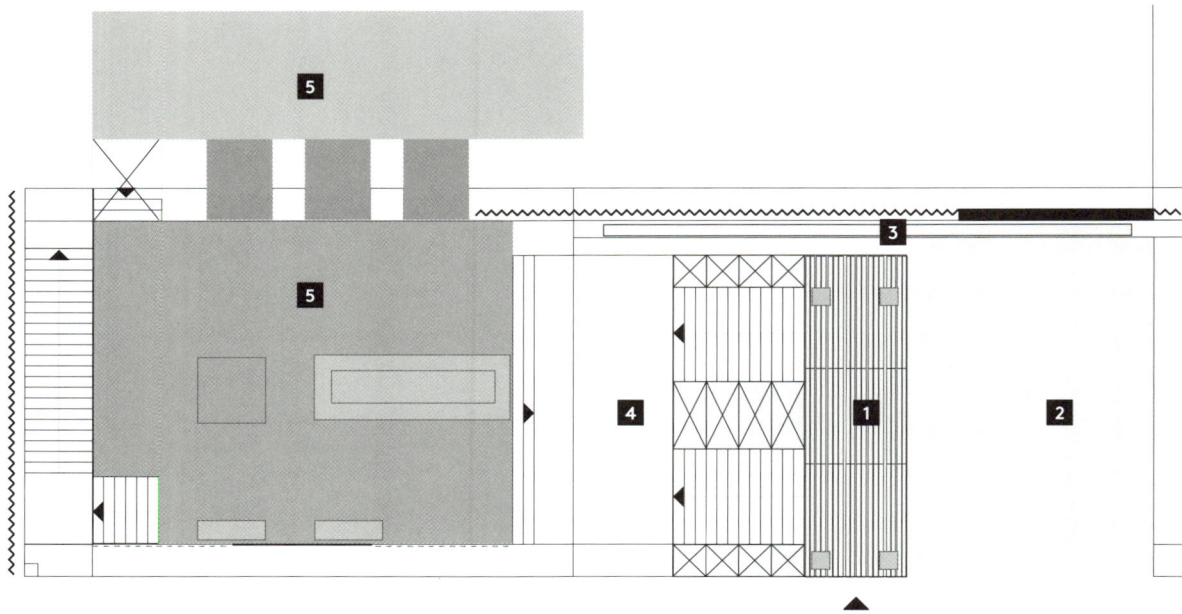

Floor plan

1   Reception deck
2   Ice rink
3   LED display wall
4   Viewing platform
5   Display area

Skaters all wrapped up for winter in New York's Central Park inspired the layout

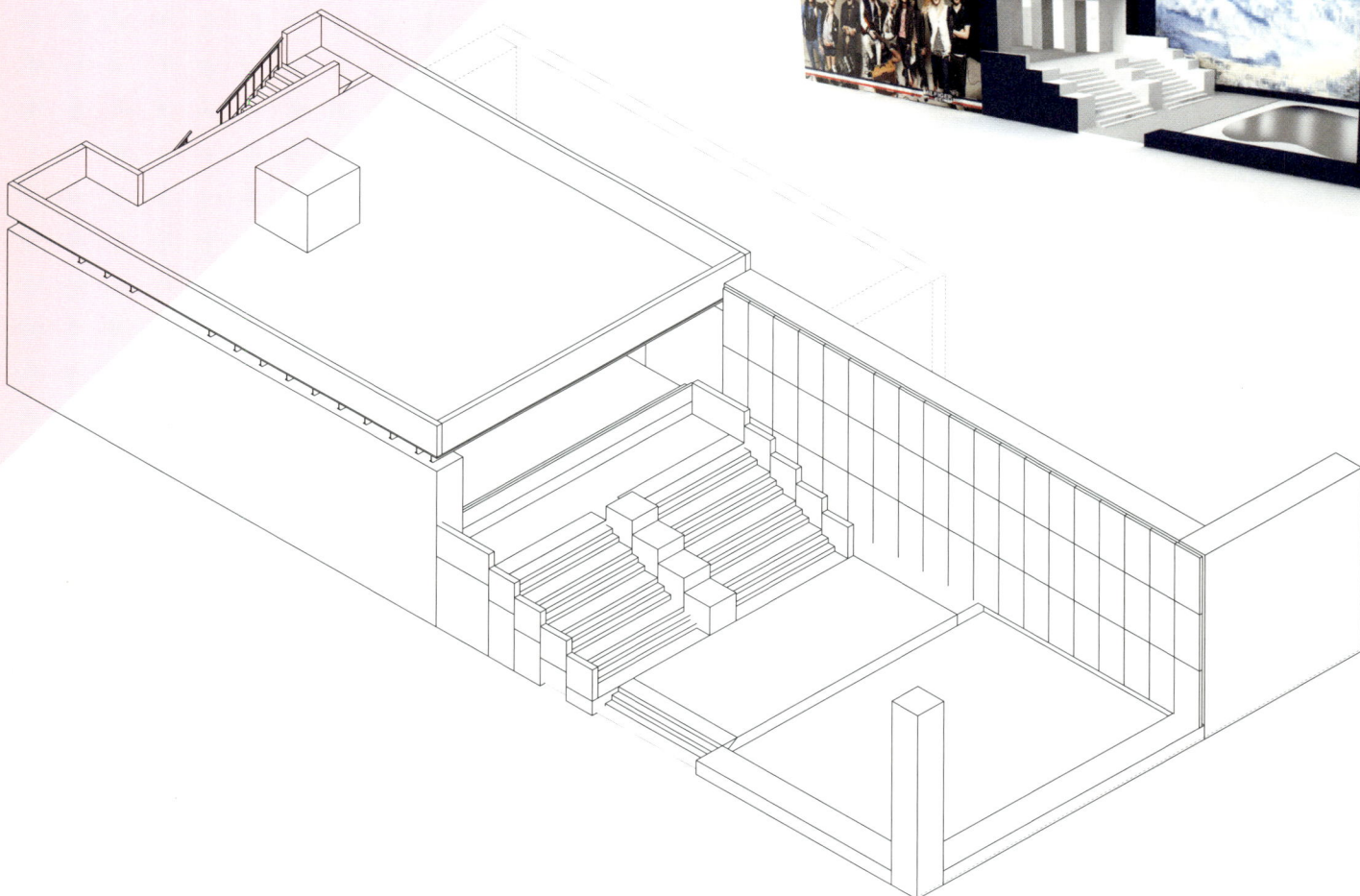

Technical drawing

Stunning views were afforded from the rooftop of the branded cube.
Renderings showing different views for the design concept of the stand.

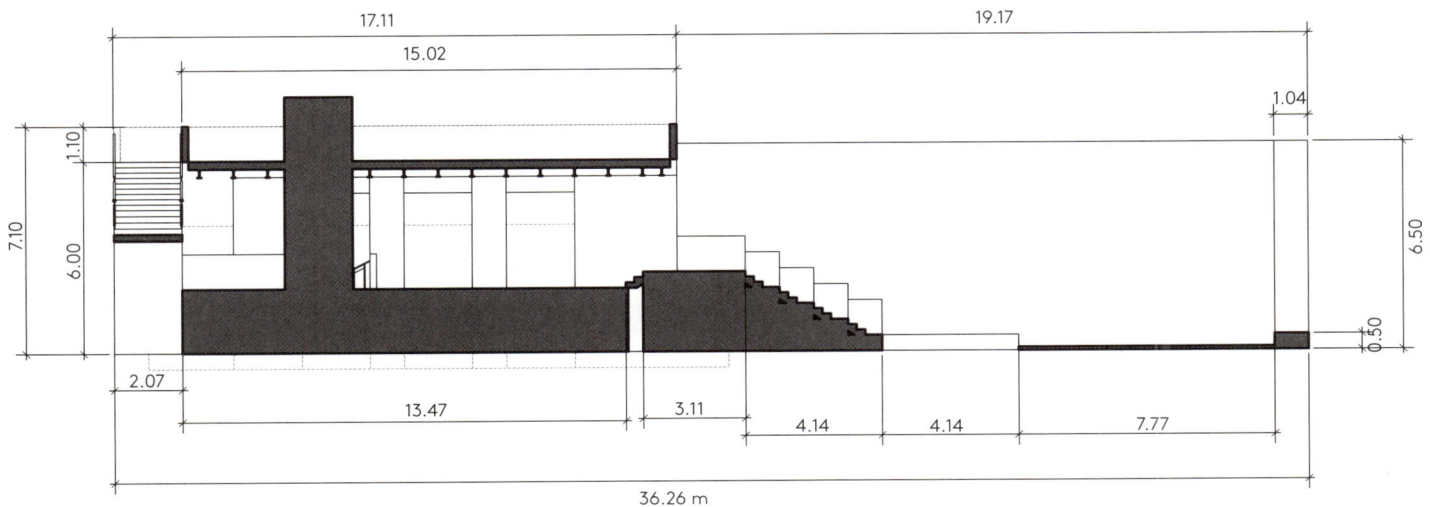

Longitudinal section

Jet Set by Arno Design

A SILVER-TINGED PRESENTATION SPACE INSPIRED BY ANDY WARHOL'S STUDIO.

TRADE FAIR **ISPO**
WHERE **Munich, Germany**
WHEN **February 2011**
DESIGNER **Arno Design** ◣ **p.488**
STAND CONSTRUCTOR **Arno Design**
CLIENT **Jet Set**
MARKET SECTOR **Sportswear**
TOTAL FLOOR AREA **420 m²**
PHOTOGRAPHER **Frank Kotzerke**

When Arno Design was tasked with job of creating a presentation at the winter sports fair ISPO, the team received an unusual request from the client: 'Please do not design a stand to represent our company'. Words to that effect were the basis of Jet Set's commission to Arno Design to construct a trade fair stand. After years of withdrawn silence, the brand – synonymous with luxury ski fashion, famous in the 1980s and headquartered in St Moritz, Switzerland – planned its stunning comeback at ISPO 2011 in Munich, Germany. With this order in mind, Arno refrained from including anything that one would expect from a conventional trade fair stand. No closed walls, no meeting booths, no branding to speak of, and no isolation from the hustle and bustle of the trade fair. Elitist, provocative and full of colour: this is how the sport fashion label was staged in the midst of the busy exhibition hall. The Factory, Andy Warhol's studio famous for its covering of tinfoil and silver paint, inspired the presentation. Approaching the stand, visitors could glimpse large-format, black-and-white images of New York, Swiss mountain scenes and silver foil panels subtly branded with the client's logo. In the interior, portraits and photographs by Michael Comte acted as a backdrop for the product showcases. There was much free space and shabby chic embellishments between the brass clothes racks, such as the bespoke seating elements in pink and silver, a 1970s leather sofa and bundles of shiny balloons. The 'Jet Set Racing' collection – designed in close cooperation with seven times Formula 1 champion Michael Schumacher and US downhill Olympic champion Lindsey Vonn – was situated on high silver pillars, a mode of presentation that underlined the product line's exacting requirements in terms of function and technology.

☒ The silver metallic decor was inspired by Andy Warhol's Factory.
☒ The high silver pillars were used to present the featured 'Jet Set Racing' collection.
☒ Silver foil ballons were suspended above the space.
☒ Juxtaposed with the futuristic silver decor were the retro furniture items, including the 1970s leather sofa.

Levi's by Como Park Studio

A GLOBALLY ACCESSIBLE URBAN METROPOLIS DESIGNED AS A PLAYGROUND FOR A NEW PRODUCT LINE.

TRADE FAIR **Bread + Butter**
WHERE **Berlin, Germany**
WHEN **January 2012**
DESIGNER **Como Park Studio** ⊠ p.490
STAND CONSTRUCTOR **Brandwacht & Meije**
CLIENT **Levi Strauss & Co.**
MARKET SECTOR **Denim fashion**
TOTAL FLOOR AREA **800 m²**
PHOTOGRAPHER **Zowie Jannink**

At the fashion trade show Bread & Butter in Berlin at the start of 2012, Levi's was to launch a new collection and Kenneth Jaworski at Como Park Studio had the job of creating an eye-catching branded space. The concept needed to show urban streets as a playground for the brand's first global product line. Inspired by installation art, scaffolding and temporary structures, the 800-m² space evoked the busy, human and industrial nature of city streets as part of the new Levi's global story. A city within the trade fair was created utilising static archetypes in an urban environment – vendors' cabins on street corners, city squares, etc. – versus elements that convey change and renewal, such as construction sites and regeneration areas. Shopping avenues around the edge of the space surrounded a central market place that formed the hub of the community. A long communal table was a focal point where fair goers could hold discussions, or just eat and relax. The square and streets informed the materials chosen for the distinct zones: unfinished scaffolding, raw wood, unfinished steel and rough paint all contributed to the idea of the world as a 'work in progress'. Working closely with Maurizio Donadi at Levi's, Jaworski – who also created the July 2011 Levi's stand – included multicoloured walls and the same oak herringbone flooring to ensure continuity between the two environments. Vital to the success of the space was the relaxed mood amidst the industrial framework, which came about thanks to dramatic lighting and attractive visual merchandising. Large city vistas blown up on a 6 x 5 m canvas enveloped the interior. All pictures were taken at street level so that visitors felt they were actually in the city. Attracting people to this urban metropolis was a simple and straightforward facade that created intrigue and encouraged visitors to enter the Levi's world.

⊠ Almost 1:1 scale street views were blown up to 6 x 5 m backlit visuals, with various familiar cityscapes presented.
⊠ Scaffolding was used to make up the structural framework of the stand.

Large city vistas gave visitors the sense of literally being 'in' the city

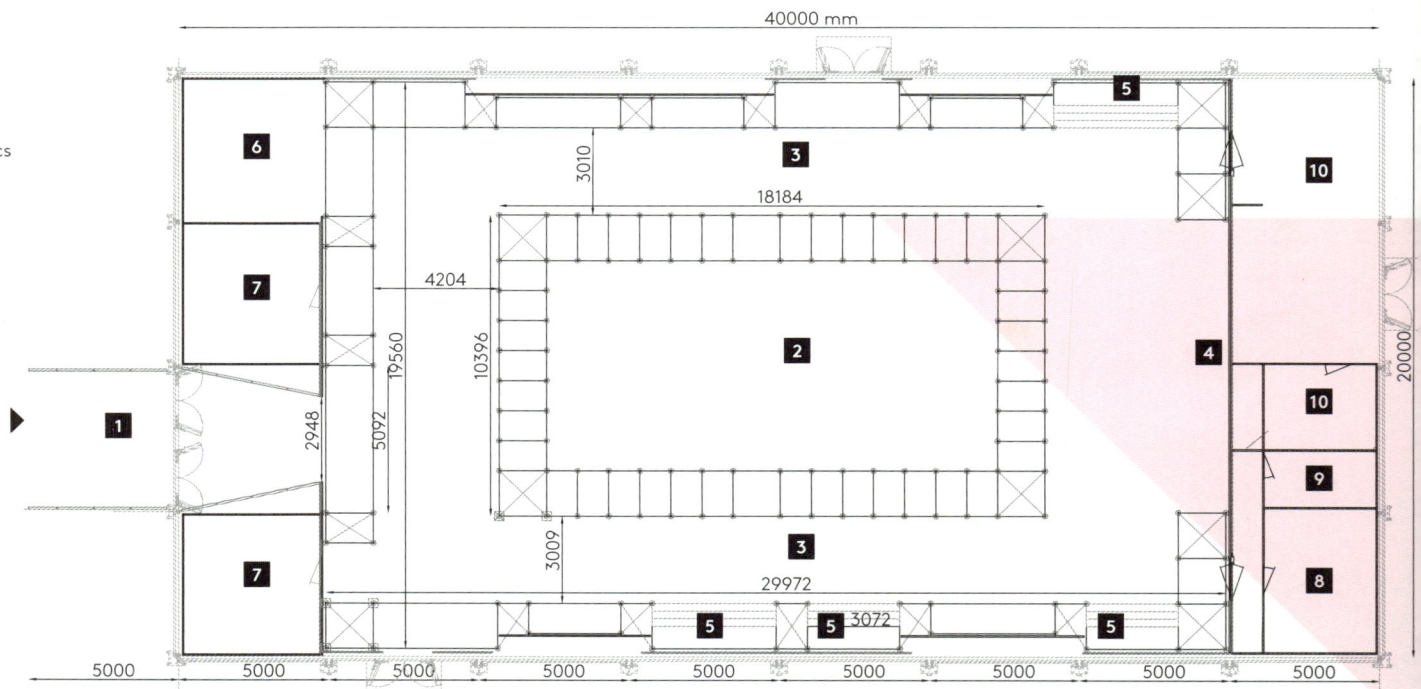

Floor plan

1 Tunnel
2 Market sqaure
3 Shopping street
4 Wall with cityscape graphics
5 Information desk
6 Chill area
7 Meeting room
8 Office
9 Cloakroom
10 Storage

Against the urban and industrial backdrop, the collection and product stories could be shown in a unique way without competing for attention.
Rendering giving a bird's eye view of the brand's unique metropolis at the fair.
Stacked TVs streamed a combination of Levi's ads and urban traffic content from streets across the world.

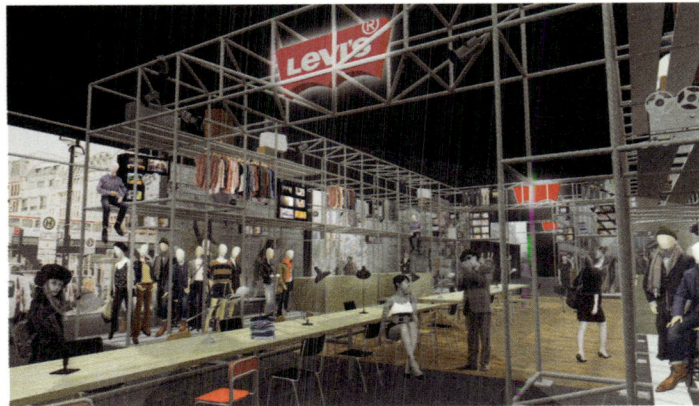

◪ Renderings of the central zone and the communal meeting area.

◪ The cities featured were Berlin, London, Moscow, New York, San Francisco, Sao Paulo, Tokyo and Los Angeles, with its Levi's Go Forth ad campaign.

◪ The four corners of the city market were reserved for Levi's more defined and refined clothing and tailoring.

A raw aesthetic contributed to the idea of the world as a 'work in progress'

Merrell by Laborrotwang

AUTUMNAL COLOURS IN A STAND
THAT RESONATED WITH A SENSE
OF THE GREAT OUTDOORS.

Merrell is an American brand focused on the outdoor footwear and clothing market. To underline its position in Europe, where it wished to expand the footwear side of its business, the firm decided to double the size of its usual booth at the 2011 Outdoor trade fair. Laborrotwang was commissioned to design the booth, with the brief asking for a modular and durable stand that was bold, surprising and open. When creating the concept, the designers kept in mind one phrase: 'The great wide open'. The team wanted to create a sense of adventure in the fair goers who visited the stand. Bold phrases written on the stand's walls inspired people to get outside and enjoy nature. As if visitors were walking through a canyon, tall and jagged walls lined a narrow path that opened up to reveal products grouped in a flexible manner. An additional highlight at the fair was the 'Barefoot ware' campaign. The key product presentations focused on the outdoor footwear product ranges, and large-format visuals reflected this. The design adapted colours, materials and patterns from the various product categories and retail solutions and united them formally under a 'Wide open sky' theme. Materials that created a natural decor across the Merrell platform included spruce planks and untreated wood benches, while rocks and stones created the feeling of a mountain hike. Design items also adorned the stand, including Miura bar stools by Konstantin Grcic, which picked out the vibrant orange that resonated around the space.

TRADE FAIR **Outdoor**
WHERE **Friedrichshafen, Germany**
WHEN **July 2011**
DESIGNER **Laborrotwang** ⊠ **p.494**
STAND CONSTRUCTOR **Stage Group**
CLIENT **Merrell**
MARKET SECTOR **Outdoor apparel**
TOTAL FLOOR AREA **325 m²**
PHOTOGRAPHER **Laborrotwang**

⊠ At the entrance, visuals of the 'Barefoot aware' campaign welcomed visitors.
⊠ The stand design was so successful that the client adapted the concept for its latest showrooms.
⊠ Furnishings and fittings were selected to create an earthy, natural decor across the booth.

Odlo by Laborrotwang

WINTER SPORTSWEAR WAS AT ONE
WITH NATURE IN THIS STAND AT ISPO.

Sportswear brand Odlo and design firm Laborrotwang have a long history of working together. In previous trade fair presentations for Odlo, Laborrotwang used a Burkhardt Leitner system for the stand framework. At the 2012 edition of ISPO, however, the team wanted a change. The orientation towards a more distinct stand design was a purposeful move in order to acknowledge the functional materials that Odlo uses in its product lines. These techno textiles respond very individually when worn by athletes; at the same time, they act as a layer between the wearer and the surrounding elements. The stand layout had natural features that evoked a woodland landscape. Spruce trees and piles of chopped wood were placed alongside the latest collections. A core concept welcomed fair goers as they entered the stand: greentec, a new form of sports underwear that can be recycled once worn out. This new fabric featured at the starting point of the Odlo experience to emphasise the company's eco tagline: 'Performance meets sustainability'. This key message also adorned surfaces at the entrance to the booth, where design elements tied in with the product presentation. Such elements included the floating ceiling and the forest of woven strings that represented the technical materials at a molecular level to explain the functionality of the materials. The vertical strings were fixed taut and resembled strands of tall grass, with large close-ups of leaf structures also alluding to the brand's green message. Huge visuals of alpine landscapes dominated the mainly white interior of the booth, and the large open space was divided up for different product categories. A focused lounge area served Swiss treats, and fair goers could perhaps briefly feel like they were in a mountaintop cafe, taking a break from skiing.

TRADE FAIR ISPO
WHERE Munich, Germany
WHEN January 2012
DESIGNER Laborrotwang ⊠ p.494
STAND CONSTRUCTOR mmd livedesign
CLIENT Odlo International
MARKET SECTOR Sportswear
TOTAL FLOOR AREA 480 m²
PHOTOGRAPHER Carsten Bauer

⊠ The Belux 'Cloud' pendant lights complemented the sleek, white furnishings of the hospitality zone.
⊠ The brief called for an open, flexible, natural and sustainable concept.
⊠ Odlo's eco approach to technical sportswear was outlined near the entrance of the booth.

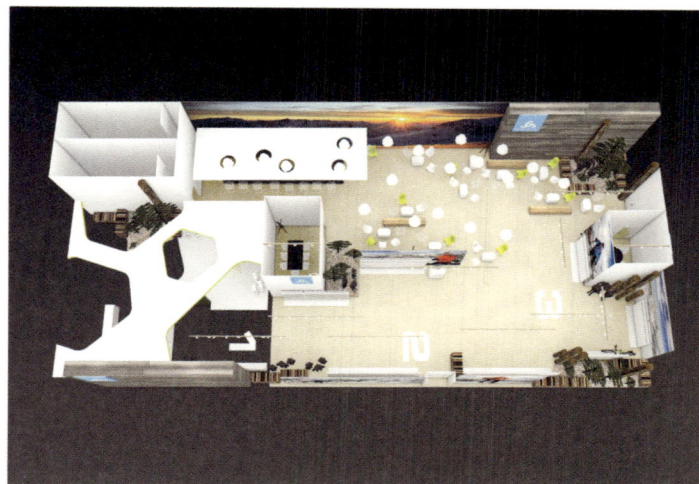

APPAREL

GRAND STAND 4

Molecular functionalities of 100% recyclable materials

☒ In the lounge were natural elements, such as the spruce tree in the corner and the wooden benches.

☒ White panels were used for the floor platform and ceiling at the entrance, as well the meeting room walls.

☒ In the renderings, the tall wall constructed from planks of timber is a prominent feature.

☒ Floor plan

1 Entrance zone
2 Display area
3 Lounge area
4 Bar
5 Meeting room
6 Storage

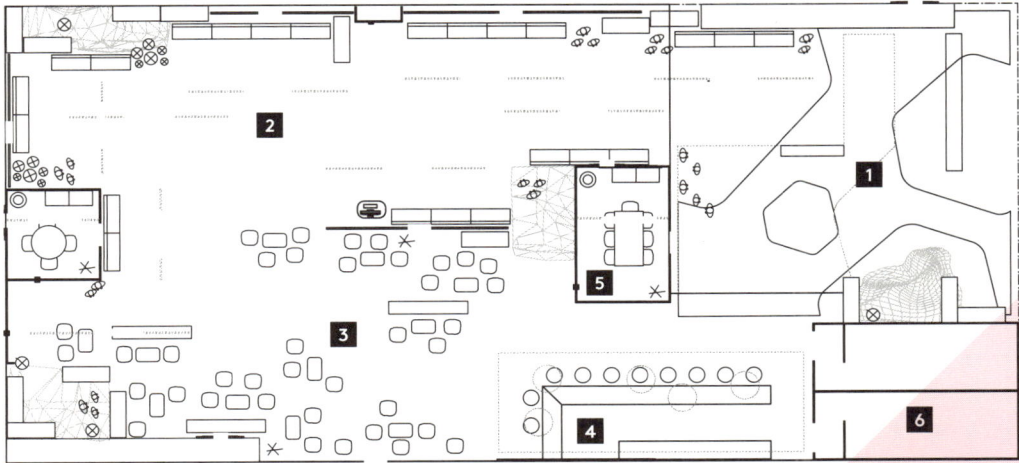

Rockford Mills by Como Park Studio

RECLAIMED MATERIALS CREATED A PERFECT ECLECTIC ENVIRONMENT FOR A DENIM BRAND'S LIFESTYLE CONCEPT.

Rockford, Illinois is a city located on the Rock River in the United States. It was this picturesque, industrial town that the client took as inspiration for both the name and story for his denim-based line known as Rockford Mills. Founder Kees Scholten visited Rockford and even got the blessing of the mayor to move forward with the name and concept. However, other than an American authenticity with a rock-and-roll flavour, the brand lacked a coherent 'lifestyle' concept. This is where Kenneth Jaworski at Como Park Studio came in, developing a concept for the brand and designing an attractive trade fair experience at the summer edition of Bread & Butter in 2011. The idea was to realise a totally free-standing structure in the open air of the fairground. Imagine a run-down shack that had been uprooted from the banks of the Rock River to take residence in Berlin, and that's what you got. The structure was a recycled framework with old corrugated steel and wooden panels as cladding. The interior was decked out with reclaimed furnishings – hanging lamps, tables, 1940s leather sofa and green enamelled storage cabinet – combined with vintage Eames chairs to create a mix that you might find in an industrial workshop or a riverside atelier, building on the story of the brand and its namesake location. As a final, and perhaps most unusual touch, the floor of the entire structure was paved with loose-laid slabs. For the design team, this was the final element needed to create a level of authenticity and finish the Rockford Mills story. In the end, the rugged, smart, industrial and eclectic environment proved a success, with a constant stream of visitors making their way into the Rockford Mills summer house over the course of the fair.

TRADE FAIR **Bread & Butter**
WHERE **Berlin, Germany**
WHEN **July 2011**
DESIGNER **Como Park Studio** ☒ **p.490**
STAND CONSTRUCTOR **Brandwacht & Meijer**
CLIENT **Rockford Mills**
MARKET SECTOR **Denim fashion**
TOTAL FLOOR AREA **68 m²**
PHOTOGRAPHER **Zowie Jannink**

☒ Reclaimed materials were used to create the exterior 'junkyard', which included a bespoke illuminated logo.
☒ The interior took on a relaxed vibe thanks to the positioning of select pieces of vintage furniture.
☒ Industrial lampshades and fans were affixed to the stand's corrugated roof.

Strenesse Blue by dfrost

THE CONCEPT INTRODUCED SOPHISTICATED, MARITIME FLAIR WITH A SUBTLE, MINIMALIST STYLE.

The first appearance of Strenesse Blue at the fashion trade fair Bread & Butter in 2011 was to introduce the brand and present the Spring/Summer 2012 collection. The brand commissioned dfrost to design its stand, and the tagline that the team worked from was: 'Feels like being on a cruise'. Inspired by a modern maritime way of living, the stand's overall concept embodied the look and feel of a contemporary yachting lifestyle. The sophisticated atmosphere on the stand had an uncomplicated air that matched the fashion brand's subtle, minimalist style. Emphasised in the design of the presentation was an overall application that was intentionally reserved in its appearance in order to allow the products to stand out. Simple and natural materials were refined in a contemporary manner. For the floor and walls, wooden panels were given a touch of glamour with a silver coating. The presentation had an open feel on its corner plot at the fair. There were no walls or enclosed areas. Passers-by might have imagined the stand as the extension of a yacht that had just berthed at a Mediterranean coastal town. The open sides of the booth were bordered on one side by a stony shoreline and on the other by a sandy beach. Visual merchandising was immediately visible across the fair thanks to the mannequins that danced on the pebbles and sand. Visitors accessed the interior along a diagonal path, akin to a passenger gangway, framed by metallic rails with white powder coating. Around the interior walls, OSB panels integrated storage and display units that were key in displaying accessories, showcasing with the collection with an urban and maritime flair.

TRADE FAIR **Bread & Butter**
WHERE **Berlin, Germany**
WHEN **July 2011**
DESIGNER **dfrost** ◫ **p.490**
STAND CONSTRUCTOR **dfrost**
CLIENT **Strenesse**
MARKET SECTOR **Fashion**
TOTAL FLOOR AREA **58 m²**
PHOTOGRAPHER **Dennis Orel**

☒ Maritime elements were at the heart of the design concept.
☒ The collection's name positioned on a bed of sand brought to mind thoughts of a Mediterranean blue sea.
☒ The simple display shelves were glazed with a silver coating.

Tom Tailor Denim by Dittel Architekten

A STRIKING STEEL GIRDER CONSTRUCTION DISPLAYED THE DENIM COLLECTION.

Dittel Architekten presented a young, urban image for the fashion and lifestyle company Tom Tailor in its stand design at the 2012 summer edition of the Bread & Butter fair in Berlin, Germany. For the brand's first appearance at the fair, the focus was on its established denim label. The brief requested a rough and industrial style booth that harmonised with the characteristics of denim. The team ensured that the denim apparel was put very much at the forefront of the design. Strong, complementary materials were used in the booth's construction, such as steel, metal, concrete and leather, which also blended with the architecture of the exhibition hall. The challenges that the design team faced included the height limitation zone, the inability to use ceiling lighting, and the need to create a clear entrance. Brick walls, industrial lamps, old factory windows and vintage furniture created a rough look that contrasted with the apparel. The front of the booth was open and accessible with an eye-catching feature – a large logo shaped out of weathered steel – positioned alongside the main promenade through the fair, which attracted visitors into the stand. The highlight of the stand was positioned at the very centre of the space: a steel construction weighing 20 tonnes that served as the main product carrier. The latest collection hung from the steel girders on leather straps, steel rails, nails, ropes and T-sections. The steel construction had to be stabilised by the right base and back walls. Bespoke display cases around the edge of the booth formed the side walls of the presentation. At the back of the stand, a small bar and a meeting place allowed fair goers to pause for a brief refreshment whilst discussing next season's collection.

TRADE FAIR **Bread & Butter**
WHERE **Berlin, Germany**
WHEN **July 2012**
DESIGNER **Dittel Architekten** ☒ **p.491**
STAND CONSTRUCTOR **Xplano**
CLIENT **Tom Tailor**
MARKET SECTOR **Denim fashion**
TOTAL FLOOR AREA **165 m²**
PHOTOGRAPHER **Rian Heller**

☒ The concrete and brick walls were white-washed with branded messages.
☒ Industrial materials were used to furnish the stand.
☒ The feature logo at the front of the stand was made out of Corten steel.
☒ Bespoke display tables were constructed from materials that were in keeping with the concept.

Wrangler by Wink

A CONCRETE BUNKER COMMUNICATED THE AUTHENTIC IDENTITY OF DENIM.

TRADE FAIR **Bread & Butter**
WHERE **Berlin, Germany**
WHEN **January 2012**
DESIGNER **Wink** ☒ **p.500**
STAND CONSTRUCTOR **Wink**
CLIENT **Wrangler**
MARKET SECTOR **Denim fashion**
TOTAL FLOOR AREA **330 m²**
PHOTOGRAPHER **Zowie Jannink**

For the January 2012 edition of Bread & Butter in Berlin, Wrangler turned to Wink to design and realise a stand to showcase its Fall/Winter '12 collection, based on its seasonal concept entitled: 'Keep true'. This is a key value for the brand and refers to its identity and its approach in creating authentic denim products. The concept combined the input of the seven iconic signature details featured in Wrangler's denim items to form the inspiration for the stand's overall design. A sturdy bunker with a concrete facade was created that boasted an ample terrace where fair goers could 'meet and greet', equipped with seating elements made out of bundles of Wrangler jeans. Bright, blue light shone through the peep holes drilled into the stand's frontage, enticing passers-by to enter the space along the darkened blue-tinged tunnel. Small open cubicles formed the entire perimeter wall, creating a clean, subtle backdrop for the merchandise. Each wall of the interior, individually panelled using concrete, acted as a canvas for campaign visuals that had been printed with beautifully atmospheric seasonal images. Islands, built up from wooden crates filled with granite blocks, acted as display pediums for the mannequins. A main focus came in the form of the towering back wall, finished with a smooth layer of concrete on which the themed and branded statement was emblazoned in bronze. Visitors' eyes were drawn down this vast wall to where illuminated pairs of jeans dangled behind the '7 icon' plinths. Inside each presentation case was a unique, identifying characteristic of the Wrangler brand. To reinforce their value, each item was handcrafted and individually cast in its very own white plaster mould. In a separate simple yet intimate space at the back of the booth, the premium collection was presented. Authentic materials proliferated, with copper piping shaped to created display rails, and steel ropes used to suspend the feature jeans models in front of the chalkboard backdrop.

☒ The stand's exterior, with its striking concrete facade, was inspired by the Canadian studio Castor Design.

☒ The pediums were a focal point of the stand, housing the seven signature icons of the Wrangler jean.

☒ Materials and detailing of the denim brand was the inspiration and creative vehicle to the stand's visualisation.

☒ The premium display space was the 'destination' for many visitors who spent time hanging out with the stand's stars: Buck, Eddy and Jim

BUCK E

Slim

Tapered

A

Regu

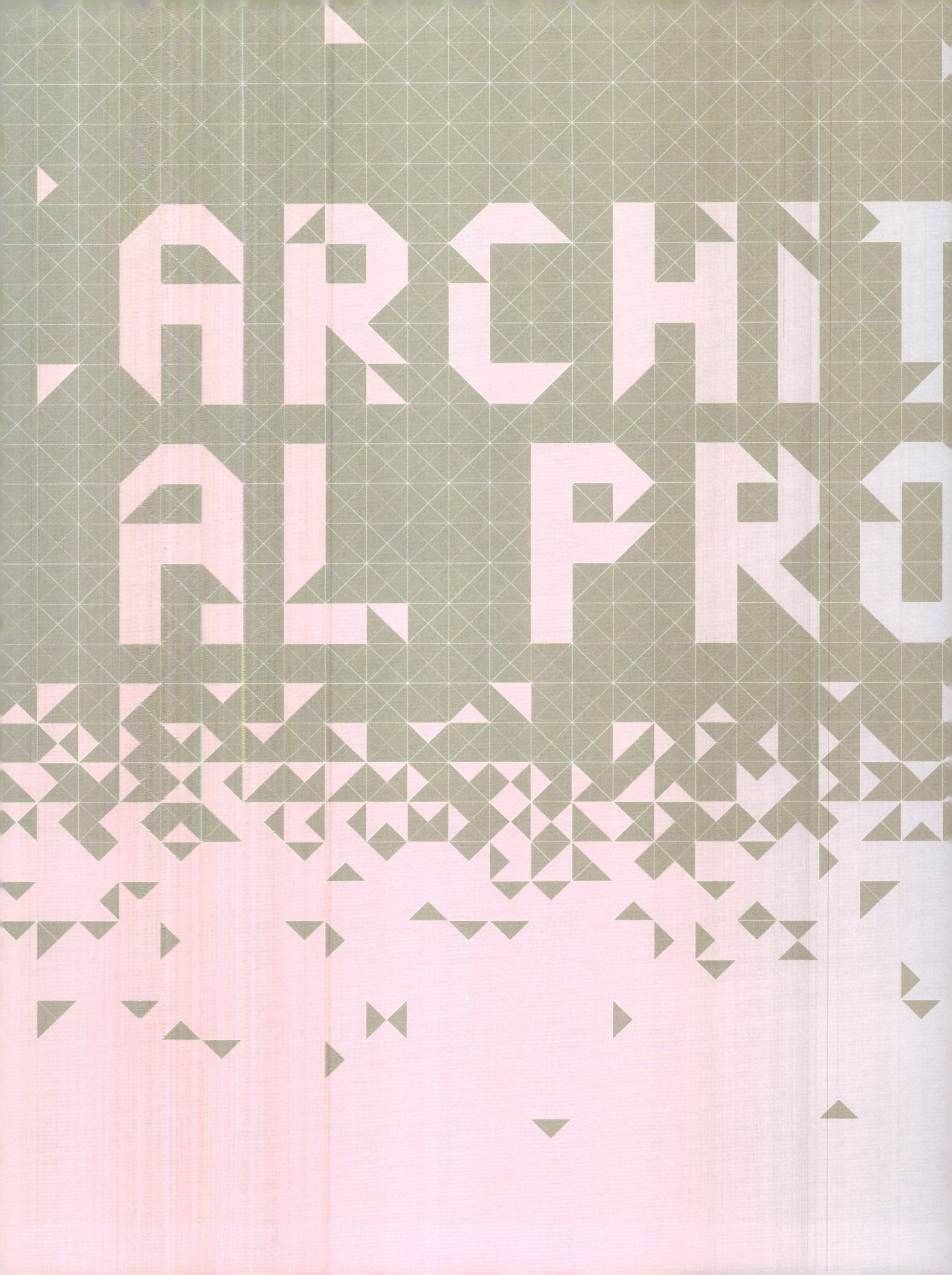

ARCHIT
AL PRO

ECTUR-
DUCTS

Billboard House by Apostrophy's the Synthesis Server

FOR ANYONE WHO EVER WONDERED WHAT LIVING IN A BILLBOARD MIGHT FEEL LIKE, THIS IS THE ANSWER.

The presentation that Apostrophy's designed for the annual Baan Lea Suan 2011 event in Bangkok was more three-storey house than conventional trade fair stand, albeit a house with a billboard attached. Baan Lea Suan is a major event for the Thai home decor and architecture industry, hosted by the magazine of the same name published by Bangkok-based company Amarin. In response to the fair organiser's 'House Prototype' competition, Apostrophy's presented the Billboard House. The design studio was inspired to create the house as an affordable and flexible housing solution for the city's inhabitants. By giving billboard spaces a dual purpose, the designers imagined a win-win situation for both local residents and advertising agencies faced with rocketing interest rates. The main architectural components of the Billboard House included: a trailer base, so the dwelling could be mobile; a kinetic facade with independent billboards on both sides of the house for added flexibility; white-painted latticework, with interchangeable panels; and a roof comprising solar cells as the main energy source for the building. The tall, narrow interior was arranged in the most efficient manner, with a linear alignment of storage and display units to afford the maximum use of space. The lower levels accommodated the living areas and bathroom, with the bedroom on the top floor. Each storey was linked with an open staircase that bypassed the mezzanine area, which doubled as an office. To expand the sense of space in the lower living area, a central void connected all the levels together, opening up the interior vertically. Although perhaps the Billboard House would be an ideal dwelling for an exhibitionist, a greater sense of solitude could always be garnered by swopping the attractive latticework sheets for some more privacy-inducing solid panels from time to time.

TRADE FAIR **Baan Lea Suan**
WHERE **Bangkok, Thailand**
WHEN **December 2011**
DESIGNER **Apostrophy's the Synthesis Server** ☒ **p.488**
STAND CONSTRUCTOR **Opulence**
CLIENT **Amarin Printing & Publishing**
MARKET SECTOR **Interior design and construction**
TOTAL FLOOR AREA **174 m²**
PHOTOGRAPHERS **Roongreangtantisook, Prayoon Tesprateep, Ketsiree Wongwan**

☒ The foundations were transportable, the form of a trailer base.
☒ The kitchen had an airy feel with vibrant yellow decor.

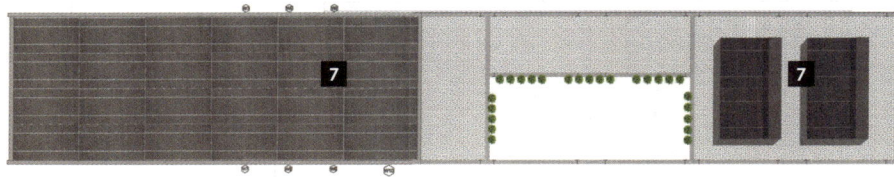

⊠ Floor plan

1 Terrace
2 Bathroom
3 Kitchen
4 Living room
5 Workspace
6 Bedroom
7 Solar panels

⊠ Second floor

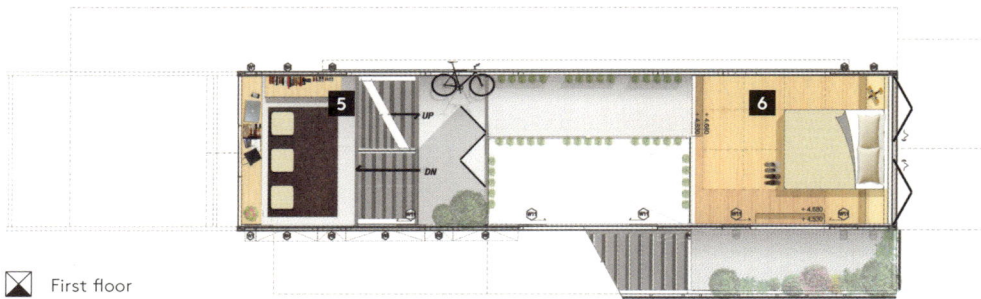

⊠ First floor

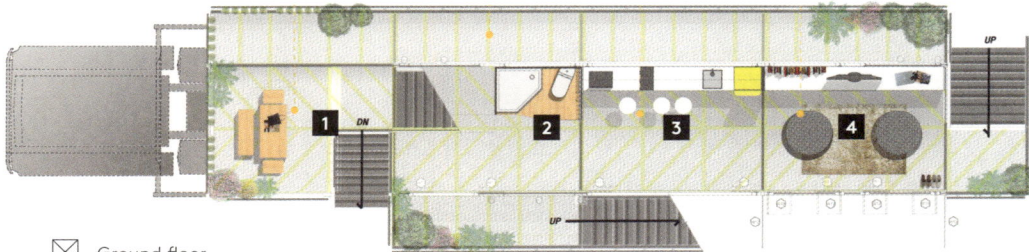

⊠ Ground floor

A central void connected all the levels

⊠ On the first floor, the mezzanine led visitors to the bedroom.
⊠ Railings found in houses and gardens in Bangkok were used in the decor.

Shutters were fitted to add privacy to the bedroom space.
Rendering showing the exterior of the Billboard House.
The 'ground floor' was designated as the living area and had a terrace at one end.

Perhaps the ideal dwelling for an exhibitionist

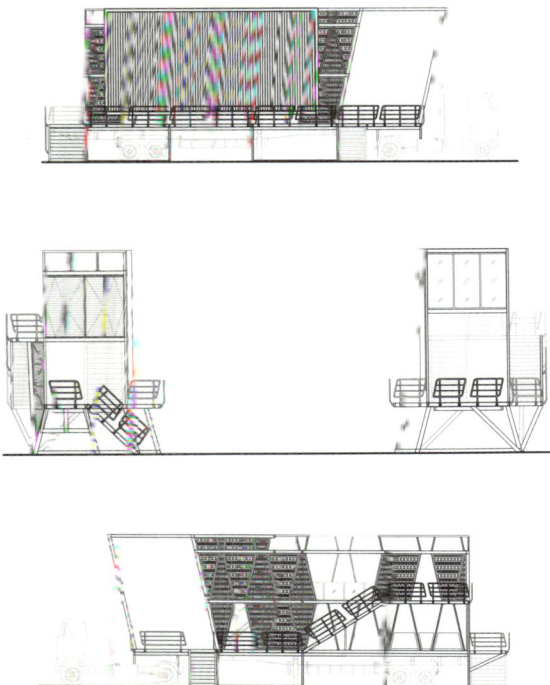

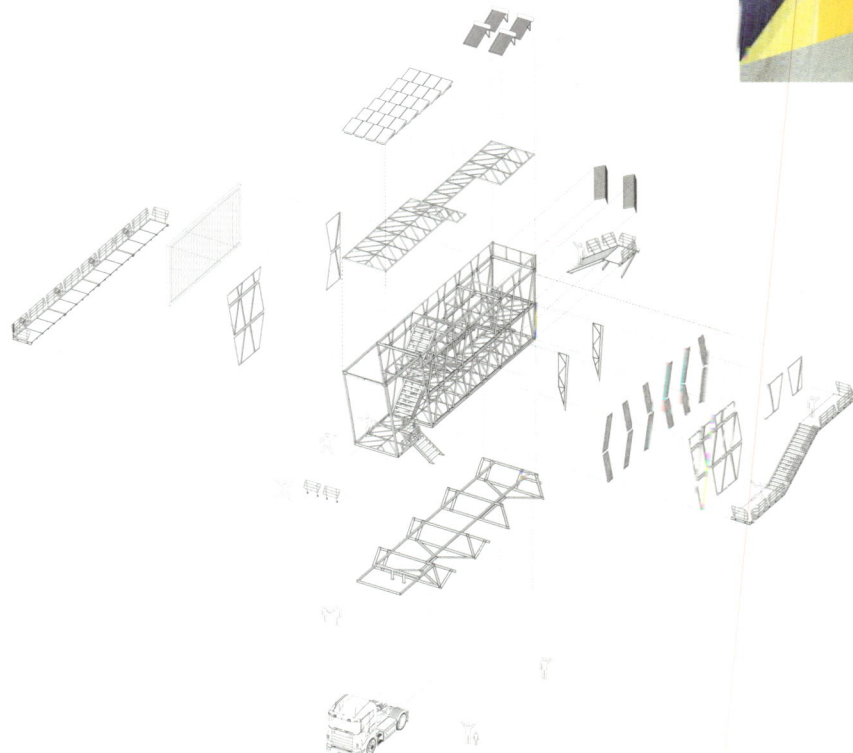

Technical drawings

Burkhardt Leitner constructiv by Ippolito Fleitz Group

SPATIAL SYSTEMS FORMED A PLAYFUL STAGE SET WITH A CONTEMPORARY AND CRISP LOOK.

TRADE FAIR **Euroshop**
WHERE **Dusseldorf, Germany**
WHEN **February 2011**
DESIGNER **Ippolito Fleitz Group** **p.493**
STAND CONSTRUCTOR **format Atelier für Messe + Design**
CLIENT **Burkhardt Leitner constructiv**
MARKET SECTOR **Interior design and construction**
TOTAL FLOOR AREA **182 m²**
PHOTOGRAPHER **Zooey Braun**

Burkhardt Leitner develops and produces modular architecture systems for temporary spaces. At the 2011 Euroshop retail trade fair, the company wanted its presentation to epitomise its corporate 'fantastic – systematic' slogan. Ippolito Fleitz Group's creative team set out to design a stand that would transform the minimalist functionality of the client's spatial systems and its core brand values – precision, lightness, sustainability, flexibility and mobility – into a playful and atmospheric stage set. The concept demonstrated the sheer multiplicity of options as a visually coherent feast, framed by an expanse of differentiated gauze displays around the edges of the booth. The treatments ranged from a grid of letters with core competences emerging as red bars, to a 3D facade made up of differently sized floral elements, producing a wall with an ornamental structure that changed appearance depending on the angle of view. This varied effect repeated in a concertina wall on the opposite side of the stand, where the client's slogan was spelled out in large white letters on a black background and vice versa. The stand interior featured a decorative language of cubic elements. The core connecting features of each of the spatial systems were integrated into display units, with interactive presentations on inset iPads showing different applications of the systems. The glass walls of the mobile conference room were adorned with leaf-shape motifs and plant boxes, transforming it into a hothouse of ideas. Positioned alongside the classic designer chairs in the seating area was a partly open, partly translucent 5-m-tall tower that functioned as a kitchen and storage space. Creating an atmosphere of contemporary crispness, the design details reached every corner of the stand, from the hanging black and white umbrellas that rotated and cast scintillating shadows on the scene below, to the wave-like fins creating contours on the ceiling like those found in a concert hall.

 The client's systems made an ideal spatial platform for creative brand staging.
 Floral ornamentation was used different elements of the stand.

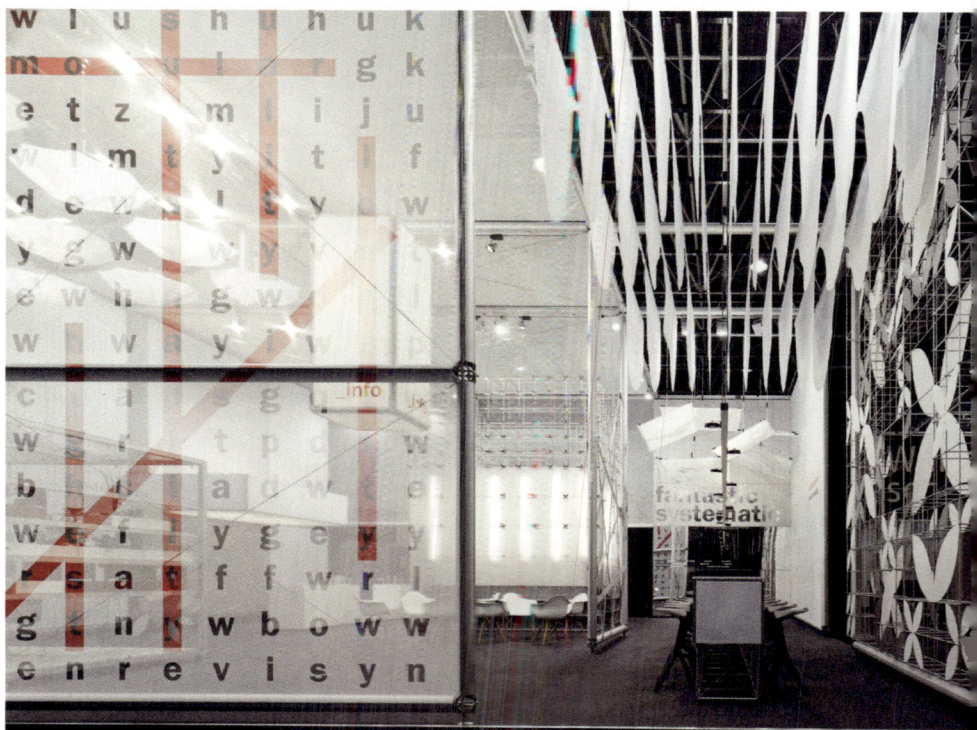

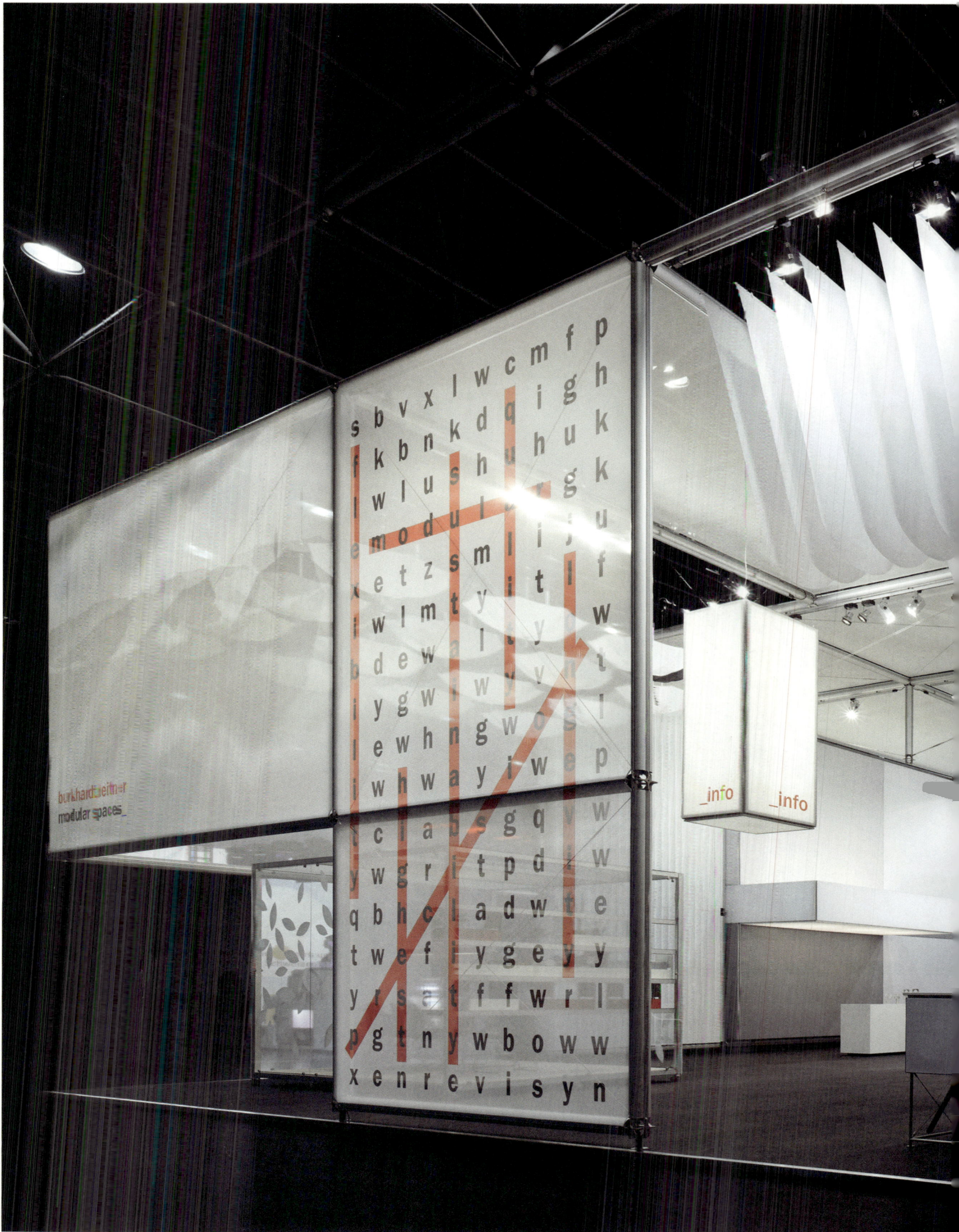

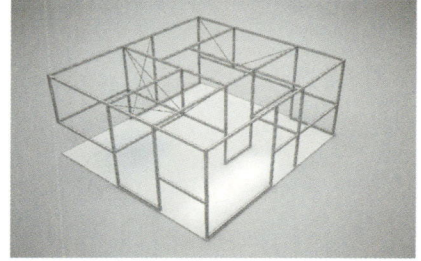

⊠ The red bars on the text-based panel brought to mind a word-search game.
⊠ The layout was based on a cubic system.

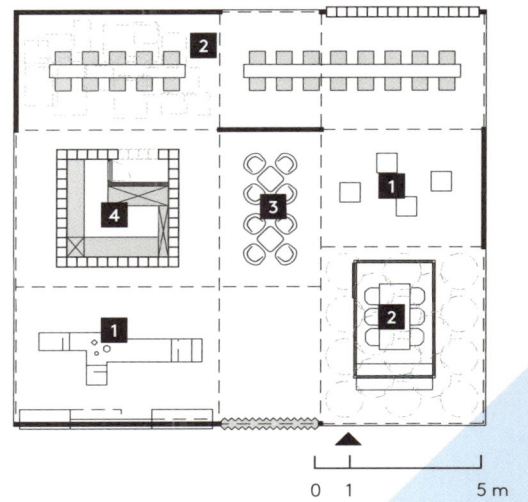

0 1   5 m

⊠ Floor plan

1   Product showcase
2   Meeting room
3   Seating area
4   Kitchen and storage

☒ Textile strips which formed a 3D network listed the client's sales partners.
☒ An array of textures and patterns abounded in the booth.
☒ Renderings show the white box concept and the different decoration details.
☒ A cloud of black and white umbrellas was positioned above the visitors' heads.

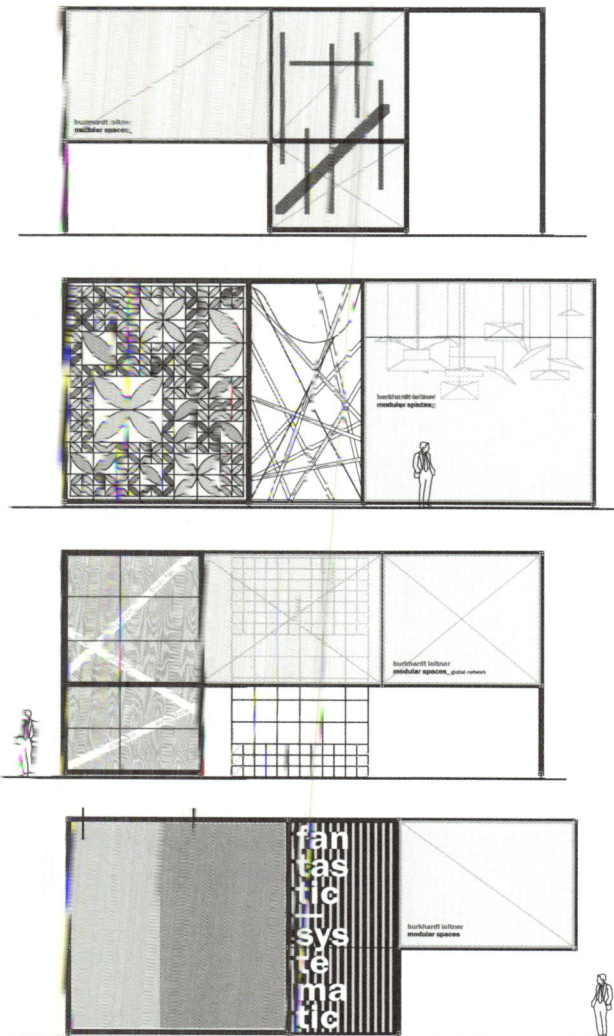

☒ Elevation Drawings

The sheer multiplicity
of options served up a
visually coherent feast

Desso by Tulp

A MANIPULATED ANGULAR STRUCTURE
CREATED UNIQUE ARCHITECTURE,
SCULPTED FOR CIRCULATION BETWEEN
ECO-CARPET TILES.

For the 2010 edition of the Interieur trade fair in Kortrijk, carpet manufacturer Desso commissioned Tulp to design its stand. The client had one proviso: the stand had to focus on EcoBase, a new carpet tile backing that fulfils its cradle-to-cradle criteria. The product's precept takes nature as a model and transfers it to industrial production – waste becomes nutrient in an endlessly continuing cycle – and Tulp took this idea to create a fair stand inspired by the never-ending stairs of Dutch artist M C Escher. The creative studio integrated the eco product into the overall design with a concept based on perspectives, dimensions and geometric forms. The idea started out with a flat plane folded into nine sections and then flattened again, with colours added between the resulting creases to form a multi-coloured, chequerboard effect. This configuration could then be manipulated into an angular structure that, when positioned upright, created a new form of architecture, composed of square segments that represented the shape of the EcoBase tiles, albeit oversized. The design team also played with perception: as visitors approached the presentation along the main thoroughfare, they got the impression that the stand was decorated only with shades of grey. Once inside they discovered the reverse side of each panel was tiled with a different hue of coloured carpet backing to create a vibrant array. With many of the panels interconnected overhead to create walkways, fair goers could circulate through the stand and experience the rainbow of colours on the walls while also discovering a simple selection of the product tiles displayed between the plinths.

TRADE FAIR Interieur
WHERE Kortrijk, Belgium
WHEN October 2010
DESIGNER Tulp ⚑ p.499
STAND CONSTRUCTOR Ulff & Ulff
CLIENT Desso
MARKET SECTOR Flooring
TOTAL FLOOR AREA 64 m²
PHOTOGRAPHER Oliver Jung

☒ The client's own collection of carpet tiles inspired the stand's design.
☒ The architecture of the presentation incorporated themes of perspective, mathematics and dimensions.
☒ Desso's vibrant red logo stood out clearly on the stand's exterior.

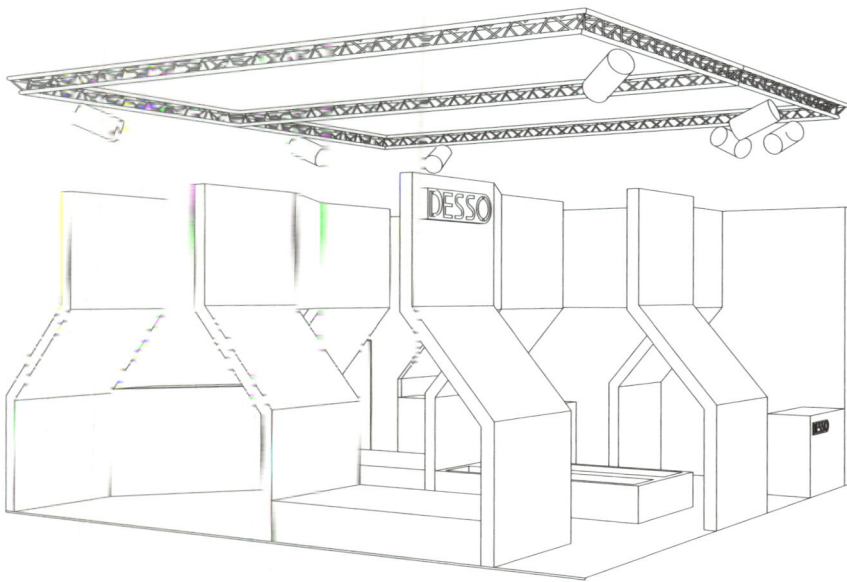

- The booth's illumination came from precisely positioned spotlights.
- The grey lining on the walls was made from actual carpet backing.
- The sheltered interior space within the stand had an open circulation.

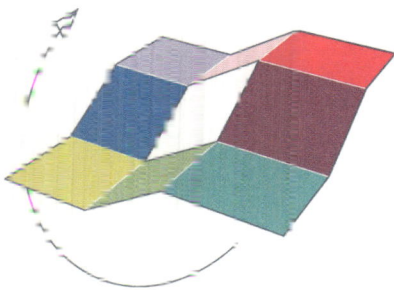

A folded plane was manipulated into an angular structure

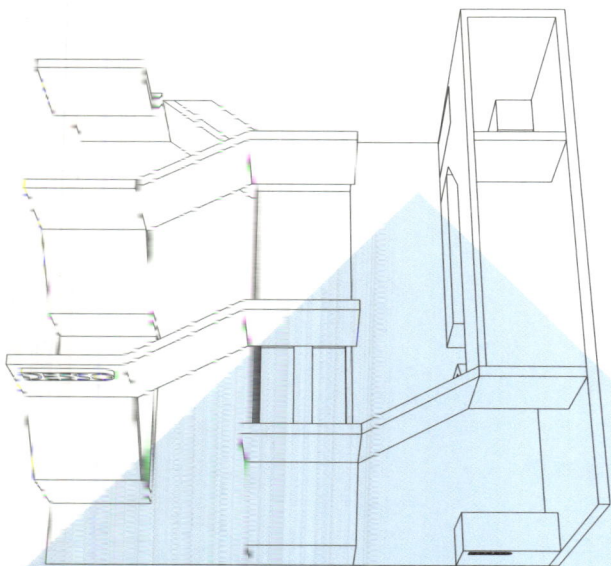

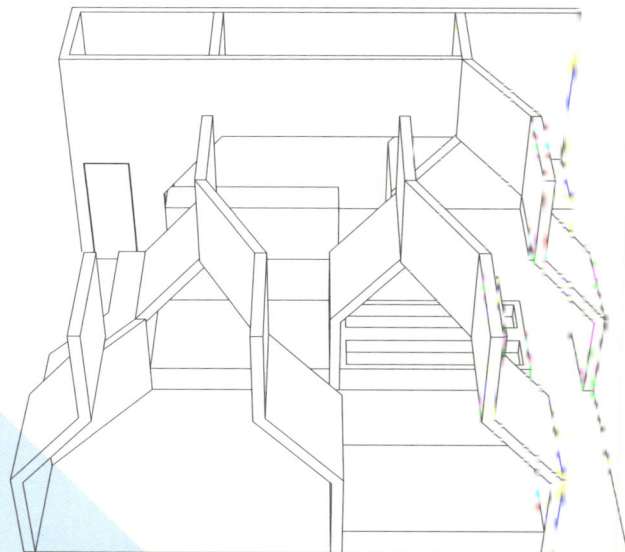

Top view.

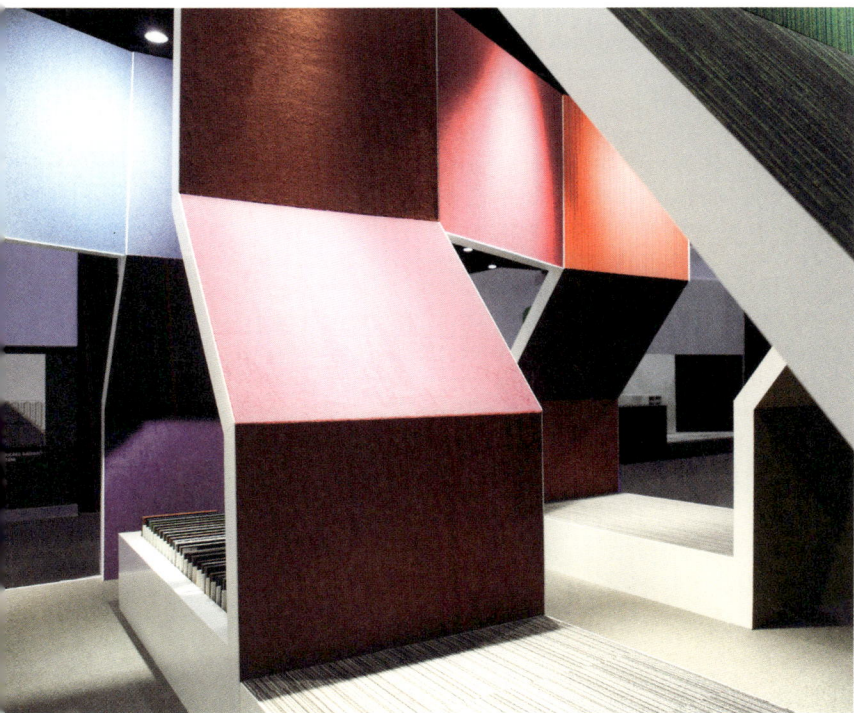

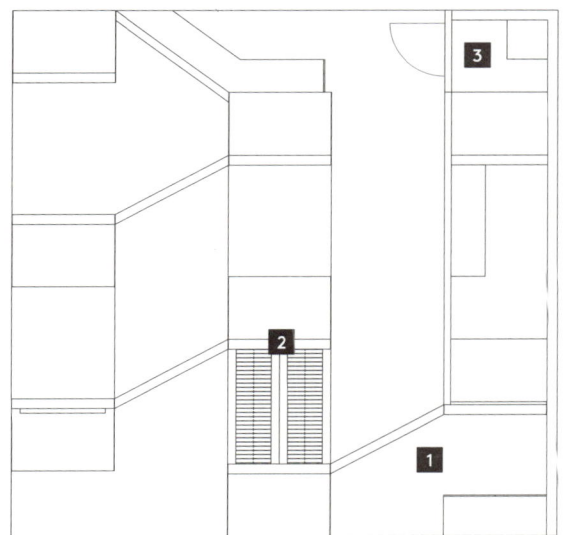

⊠ Floor plan

1 Information desk
2 Product display
3 Storage

Diamond Pavilion by Apostrophy's the Synthesis Server

ARCHITECTURAL AND ARTISTIC: A FUNCTIONAL ASPECT OF THE CLIENT'S FEATURE PRODUCT FORMED THE FRAMEWORK FOR THE BOOTH.

TRADE FAIR **Architect**
WHERE **Bangkok, Thailand**
WHEN **April 2011**
DESIGNER **Apostrophy's the Synthesis Server** ⊠ p.488
STAND CONSTRUCTOR **Apostrophy's the Synthesis Server**
CLIENT **Diamond Building Products**
MARKET SECTOR **Building products and solutions**
TOTAL FLOOR AREA **122 m²**
PHOTOGRAPHERS **Sirichai Luengvisutsiri, Pongsakorn Pongtawevira, Prayoon Tesprateep**

At the Bangkok Architect fair in 2011, Apostrophy's was commissioned to design a pavilion for Diamond Building Products. The client wished to focus in particular on Purlin, a line of hardware for roofing that would be launched at the fair. The concept for the pavilion was to create an artistic installation, with the client's products presented like bespoke works of art in a gallery. The team imagined fair goers walking into an aesthetic environment where they could sit leisurely and relax, surrounded by art objects made from durable-construction hardware products. Furthermore, the idea was to inspire visitors to create their own masterpieces at home. The completed space needed to have 360-degree accessibility with a friendly, welcoming vibe that newcomers and existing clients could equally appreciate as they approached the stand from afar. Transforming a functional aspect into the design element of the booth's construction – the joints and angles of the Purlin system – once assembled, formed the framework for the presentation. Architectural in shape, the matt-white Purlin towers added a rhythmic aspect to the space, whilst at the same time accommodating the pavilion's lighting. At the base of each stalactite-like configuration hanging overhead was a light box containing LED technology so that, at the flick of a switch, the atmosphere in the lounge could alter with different colours and dynamic patterns of lighting. The key aspects of the stand – reception, product display and bar – were positioned to enhance visitor circulation. By blurring marketing techniques, instead of focusing on 'direct-sale marketing and clients', the creative team took on the role of 'curators of house hardware for aspiring artists'.

⊠ The stand's angular architecture was constructed from the client's feature hardware product.
⊠ Visitors could take a seat at the heart of the stand, beneath the tall structure.
⊠ The changing colours within the space added a vibrant aspect to the booth.

Dyckerhoff Weiss by Ourstudio

A PLATFORM FOR CONTEMPORARY CONCRETE CREATIONS, PORTRAYING MONOLITHIC AS WELL AS DELICATE CHARACTERISTICS.

TRADE FAIR **BAU**
WHERE **Munich, Germany**
WHEN **January 2011**
DESIGNER **Ourstudio** ☒ p. 496
STAND CONSTRUCTORS **Zeiher, Saarbrücken**
CLIENT **Dyckerhoff Weiss**
MARKET SECTOR **Building products and solutions**
TOTAL FLOOR AREA **200 m²**
PHOTOGRAPHER **Joachim Hirschfeld**

At BAU, the Munich trade fair for building materials, Dyckerhoff Weiss asked Ourstudio to conjure up a presentation of its cement and concrete solutions that would be attractive and accessible to fair goers. The result focused on a spatial concept that steered clear of the standard product presentation found in hardware stores. Instead, the client's offerings were branded as a three-dimensional corporate design in a simple yet visually striking setting. The intention was to immediately capture the attention of passers-by, raising their level of interest and curiosity, and enticing them to stop, look, enter and interact. At this trade fair stand, the target group encountered suggestions, inspiration and advice for their own individual projects. The solution was to structure the presentation so that it resembled a garden featuring organic forms, curving paths and textured walls as exhibits, inspired by nature. All these elements were arranged in an ensemble that enticed visitors to approach and interact with the tactile material at the heart of the products – flowstone, a self-compacting concrete – which differed in form, colour and surface composition depending on whether it was used for walls or flooring. An eye-catching installation at the very front of the booth was the series of concrete-clad steps that led to nowhere, except perhaps 'down to the garden'. This innovative element, with its transparent balustrades, creatively represented the lightness of modern concrete constructions, as well as their contemporary characteristics. The glass plates installed on both sides of the prefabricated flight of stairs also communicated to customers a newly-developed adhesive bonding technique, outlining the latest cross-collaborations between the concrete and glass industries.

☒ White high-performance concrete was used to construct the stairs.
☒ The illuminated banner above the booth meant visitors could immediately connect with the brand.

Creative representation of the lightness of modern concrete constructions

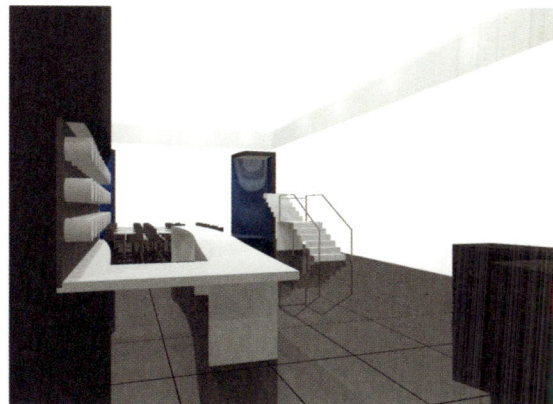

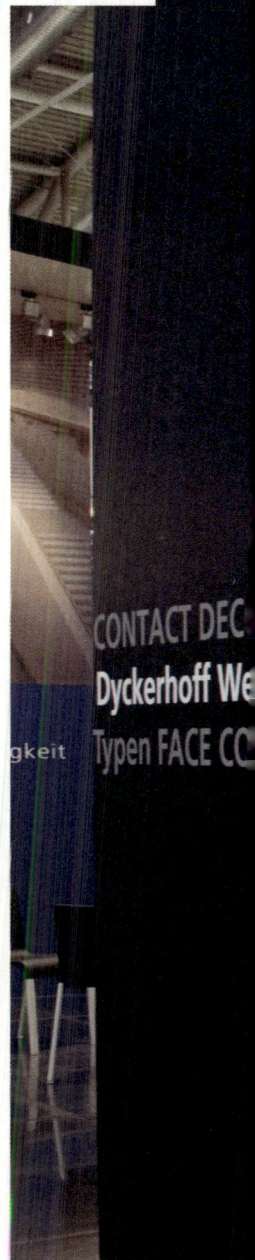

ARCHITECTURAL PRODUCTS GRAND STAND 4

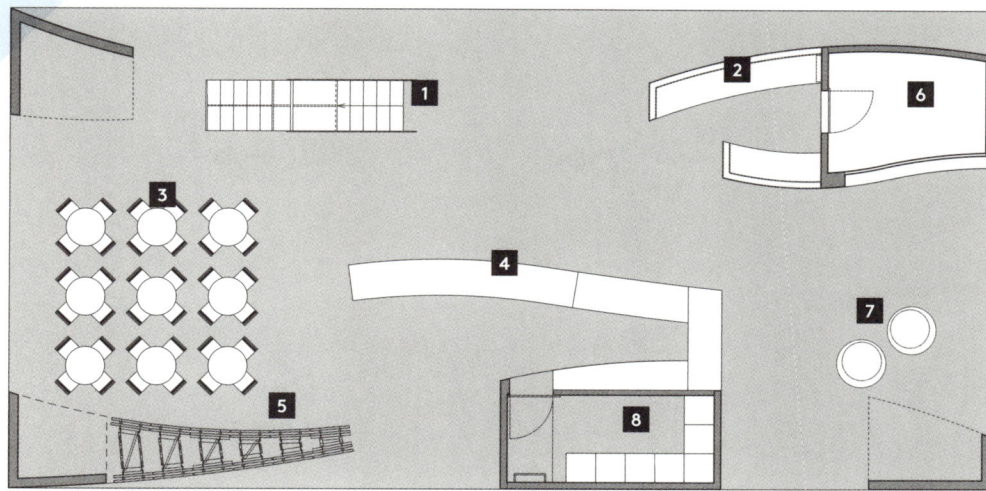

Floor plan

1   Flight of stairs
2   Information desk
3   Seating area
4   Bar
5   Feature wall
6   Cloakroom
7   Chill-out area
8   Kitchen and storage

0   100   500 cm

Fair goers gained a different perspective
when they climbed the stairs.
One wall had a concrete lattice
incorporating an organic pattern.
The stand had an overall corporate colour
palette of blue, black and white.

Munksjö by hw.design

PAPER TECHNOLOGY WAS COMMUNICATED
IN A UNIQUE ARCHITECTURE UTILISING A
THREE-DIMENSIONAL FOLDED MOTIF.

⊠ Rising to a height of 5.85 m, the angular sculpture was an eye-catching feature for passers-by.
⊠ The folded appearance of the feature wall resulted in an attractive reprise of light and shadow.
⊠ The corporate red logo stood out against the all-white furnishings.

At Interzum, the global event for suppliers to the furniture and interior construction industries, Swedish company Munksjö wished to make an innovative stand for both its products and its presentation. Munksjö commissioned hw.design to create an exhibition stand that highlighted the firm's expertise in pulp and paper technology and to translate its tagline – 'materials for innovative design' – into physical reality. The booth needed to reveal the full potential of the Munksjö products, embodying every aspect of the company's message: a premium service, a full product range, and an R&D zone focused on customer needs. To make paper tangible as an innovative material, the design team created a concept in which visitors could experience the brand within a unique architecture that appeared to utilise paper for its construction. Positioned on one side of a platform was a particularly eye-catching element: a large flat surface rising upwards, sculpted to form a circular enclave, enclosing a functional space and then opening up to a lounge area. It was designed to appear like a folded piece of paper, with a white surface naturally unravelling itself. On the other side of the stand was an angular structure – which doubled as a storage area or private meeting room – with its walls separated into triangular shapes that also looked like paper. The corporate motif 'Made by Munksjö' was positioned on a folded corner on the upper edge of the sheet. Of special design interest was the thinness of the walls, which were made using just 50-mm-thick end-grain sheets of balsa wood, painted white. During the course of the trade fair, dynamic illumination sequences and light projections bathed the presentation in red, blue and green light, creating different atmospheres and an architectural rhythm that distinguished the client in terms of the environment, technology and innovation.

TRADE FAIR Interzum
WHERE Cologne, Germany
WHEN May 2011
DESIGNER hw.design ⊠ p.492
STAND CONSTRUCTOR Design Productions
CLIENT Munksjö Paper
MARKET SECTOR Materials
TOTAL FLOOR AREA 200 m²
PHOTOGRAPHER Tobias Kern

expansion ———— to a new level

The unique structure appeared as a folded piece of paper unravelling

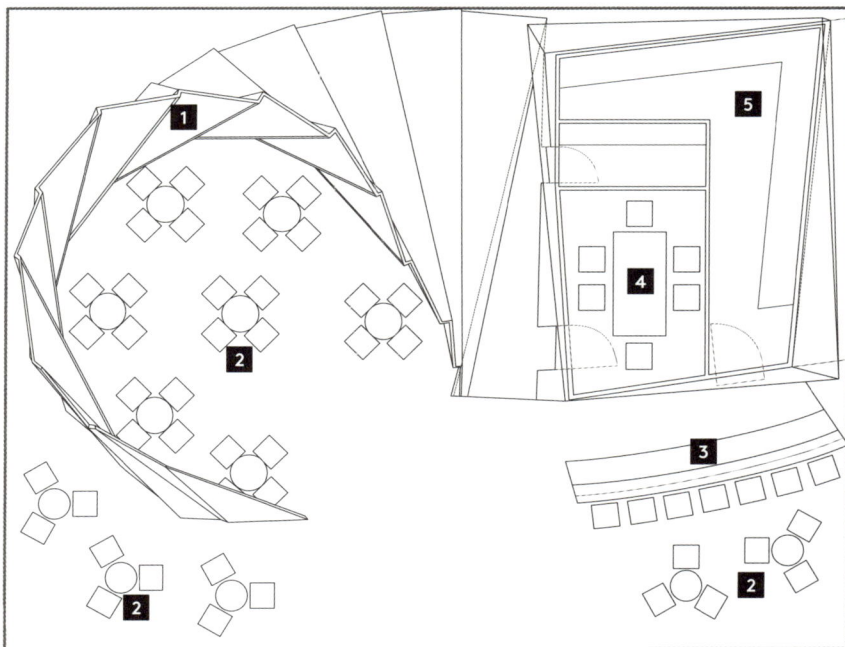

Floor plan

1 Sculpted wall
2 Seating area
3 Information desk
4 Meeting room
5 Storage

Different coloured lighting created a dynamic aspect to the stand.

A sheet folded with a constructive principle in a reverse rhythm developed into a space.

The stand's lounge area benefitted from superb acoustics.

Model of the curved structure.

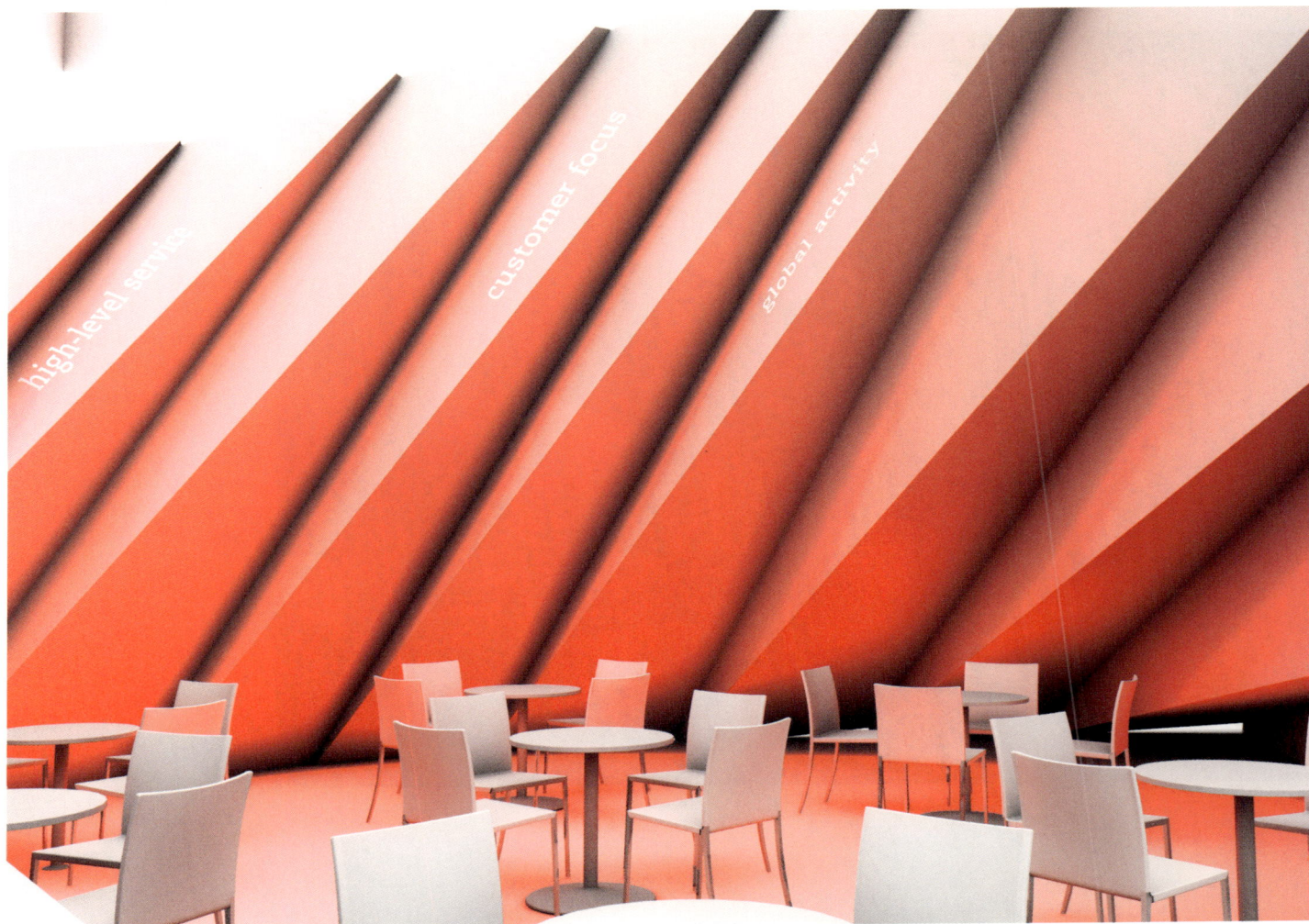

Parador by D'art Design Gruppe

MONOLITHIC ARCHITECTURAL STATEMENTS REVEALED NEW FLOORING BENEATH ELEVATED, ANGULAR ELEMENTS.

After 10 years, flooring company Parador returned to Domotex 2012 in Hannover, Germany with a monolithic new look. Designing the presentation of five new products was the job of the D'art Design Gruppe. A 6.5-m-high branded black canopy ensured that the company's presence was tangible from far across the exhibition hall. Within the stand, five architectonic panels tilted up from the dark tiled floor to reveal the new products beneath. Transparent gauze enveloped the stand's exterior steel structure, on the one hand to delimit it and on the other to enhance the open design. Wrapping the top of the stand, the fabric draped down to form the walls and was hoisted up at strategic points to allow access into the interior, turning the space within into an enclosed, cosy retreat. All attention focused on the product highlights, presented where the five panels were lifted up at an angle from the floor, equipped with backlit graphics, media streams and mirrors to reflect the displays. The angled panels were designed like lids that had been raised to reveal examples of laminate, parquet and vinyl floorings on the exposed floor beneath. A major focus stretching across the booth was the materials library, where product samples could slide horizontally out of a huge wall at the back of the stand, allowing visitors to view the vast array of products and materials. The basic illumination of all the Parador products on display corresponded to natural daylight in order to present the materials in their true colour shades, while warm illumination ensured that visitors felt comfortable in the booth's communication areas.

TRADE FAIR Domotex
WHERE Hannover, Germany
WHEN January 2012
DESIGNER D'art Design Gruppe ⊠ p.490
STAND CONSTRUCTOR viva Messe- und Ausstellungsbau
CLIENT Parador
MARKET SECTOR Home appliances
TOTAL FLOOR AREA 403 m²
PHOTOGRAPHER Tobias Wille

⊠ The black exterior was clearly branded with white lettering.
⊠ The materials library layout ensured numerous samples could be housed in a streamlined manner.

PARADOR

Edition Laminat
Edition Laminate flooring

Laminat
Laminate flooring

Parkett/Massivholzdielen
Engineered wood flooring/Solid wood flooring

Vinyl
Vinyl

Terrassendielen
Decking

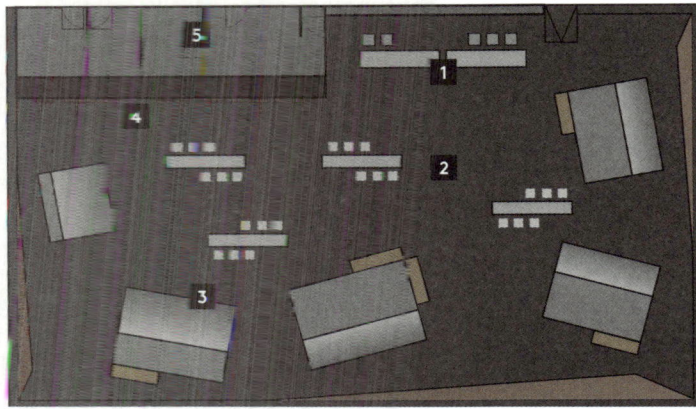

⊠ Floor plan

1 Information desk
2 Seating area
3 Product displays
4 Materials library
5 Storage

Architectonic panels rise up out of the stand's floor surface

⊠ The raised panels created a new dimension and an appropriate stage for the high-quality Parador products.

⊠ A monochromatic colour palette and steel surface treatment was used in the booth's decor.

⊠ The interior was visible to passers-by thanks to the draped gauze fabric around the stand.

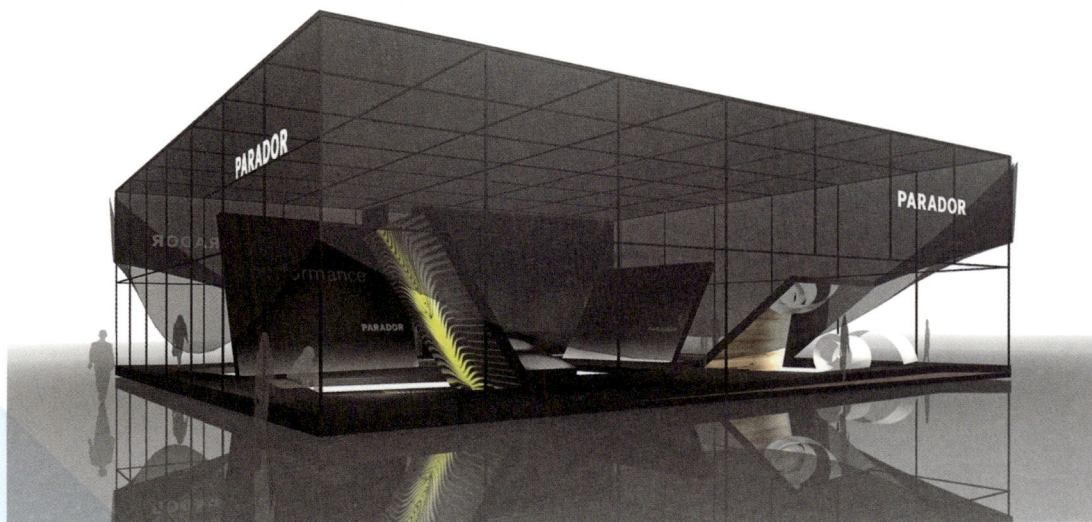

Pfleiderer by plajer & franz studio

ARCHITECTONIC CONSTRUCTIONS OF INNOVATIVE WOODEN PRODUCTS SYMBOLISED SUSTAINABILITY AND STRENGTH.

At BAU, the Munich trade fair for building materials, plajer & franz studio was commissioned to create a stand for wood products manufacturer Pfleiderer. Taking the brand motto of sustainability as the basis for the concept, the design team focused on the client's new 'green' biomass granulate product. The challenge in realising the design was to unify three elements – ecology, lightness and innovation – and translate them into a high-quality but individual concept. The Pfleiderer presentation exuded a sense of nature, with tall, angled fences rising up out of the stand to encircle benches, creating the outdoor feel of a parkland setting. Sheets of the featured green wood-based product were shaped into different lengths and positioned vertically in sweeping formations, which called to mind the strength and anatomy of the wings of a bird. The contours of the stand gave it a contemporary feel, with the overall white colour contrasting with the raw edges of the panels where the constituent natural wood chips could be seen. Each circular enclave formed a separate brand communication space, featuring either an information desk or sample boards of other key products. There was an open-plan feel to the booth, with the architectural structures creating a sense of height to catch visitors' attention from across the exhibition hall. Passers-by were given intriguing glimpses of the product presentations, but to discover more, they needed to enter the stand and investigate the various aspects up close, including the main seating cubicles in the centre of the stand. Here, a natural stripped-back feel offered another reference to the properties of Pfleiderer's newly developed highlight product. The integrated seating niches were constructed from raw plates stacked on top of one another, interspersed with different laminate options to emphasise the layering effect.

TRADE FAIR **BAU**
WHERE **January 2011**
WHEN **Munich, Germany**
DESIGNER **plajer & franz studio** ☒ p.49e
STAND CONSTRUCTOR **Firma Riedl**
CLIENT **Pfleiderer Group**
MARKET SECTOR **Wood products**
TOTAL FLOOR AREA **377 m²**
PHOTOGRAPHER **diephotodesigner.de (Ken Schluchtmann)**

☒ The height of the panels ensured the stand had long-range appeal.
☒ Product samples of the client's five sub-brands were located in each enclave.
☒ Overhead illumination came in the form of a white, branded lampshade that mimicked the curved shapes of the stand.

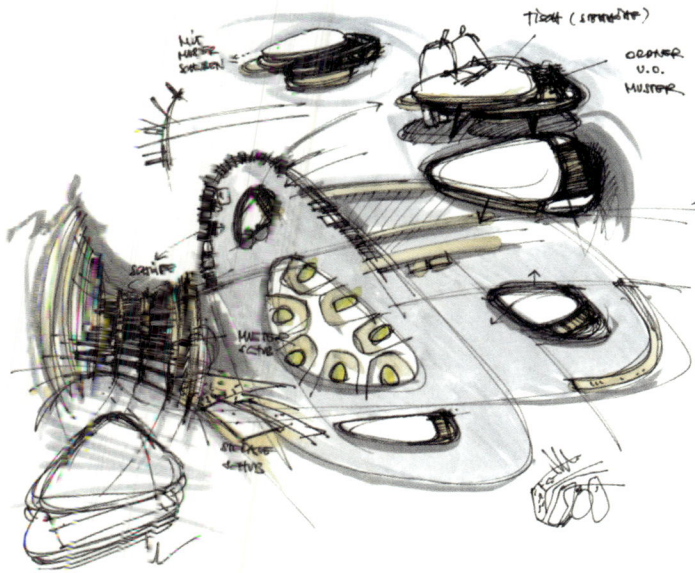

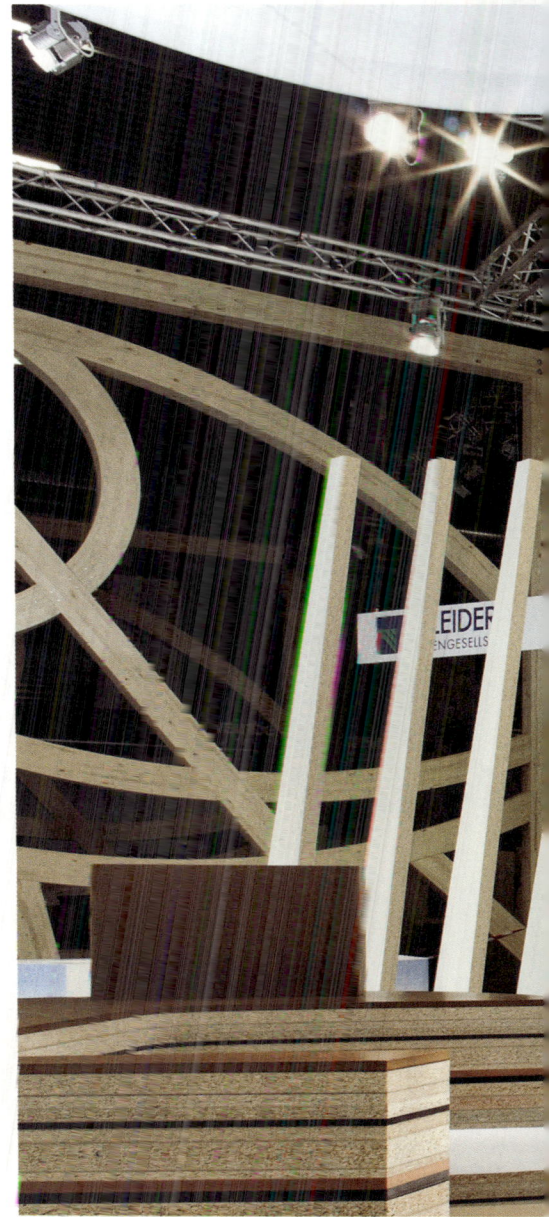

Floor plan

1 Information desk
2 Product display zone
3 Bar
5 Cloakroom
6 Storage

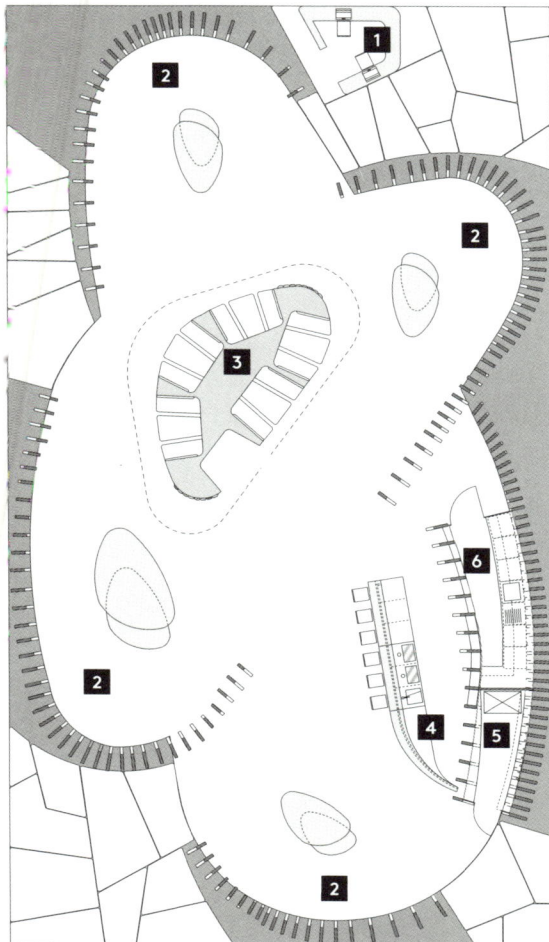

ARCHITECTURAL PRODUCTS

GRAND STAND 4

Architectural elements created an aspect of height

Initial sketches outlined the organic nature of the stand.
The design of the booth encapsulated lightness and innovation.
Raw wooden panels were piled up to create seating niches.
Renderings showing the eco product displayed in a natural setting.

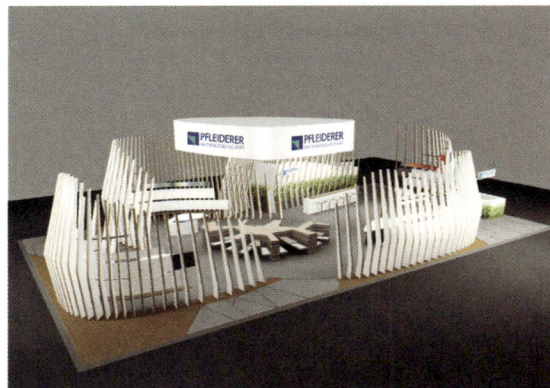

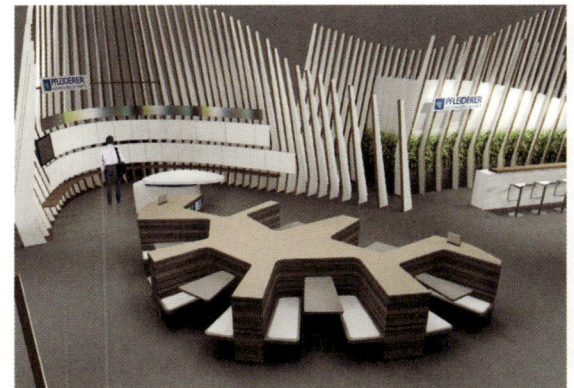

Remeha by The Inside and Via2V

A FUTURISTIC SETTING FORMED THE CREATIVE CONCEPT FOR A PRESENTATION OF INNOVATIVE HEATING SYSTEMS.

Remeha, a leading European manufacturer and distributor of innovative heating and hot water systems and services, introduced its new slogan along with its very latest boiler system during VSK 2012 in Utrecht. The stand concept needed to give this new slogan a prominent voice, clearly presenting Remeha to fair goers as 'comfort innovators' with a futuristic and innovative environment to display the product ranges. Michael Hermans and his team at The Inside answered the brief by ensuring the booth was open and user-friendly, with a clear use of new materials and innovative techniques – all values that the client stands for with its company ethos and also with its products. The first artist impressions of the stand were made by Hein Verberne, interior architect at Via2V, with The Inside team taking responsibility for realising the design. The idea of the presentation was for visitors to feel like they were walking into a futuristic spaceship, with their experience intensified by the arches at the entrance and the dome construction above the stand. The booth had a high-tech feel, with the metallic framework of the construction exposed like an outer skeleton. Corporate branding was positioned prominently, with the client's slogan wrapping around the circular dome overhead. The biggest challenge for the team was the construction of the dome, as it not only had to hang at a certain angle but also had to incorporate an existing column in the exhibition hall into its construction. The design team solved this by positioning the dome at the centre of the stand and using it as an impressive presentation of the latest product innovation: the new Tzerra boiler. The boiler was displayed as if it was the 'warp core' at the very heart of the Remeha world, with flashing LED strips ensuring it grabbed the attention of visitors. Other products were set on information panels that radiated from the centre of the stand.

TRADE FAIR VSK
WHERE Utrecht, the Netherlands
WHEN February 2012
DESIGNERS The Inside ☒ p.498 and Via2V ☒ p.499
STAND CONSTRUCTOR The Inside
CLIENT Remeha
MARKET SECTOR Heating systems
TOTAL FLOOR AREA 525 m²
PHOTOGRAPHER Martin Kuijper

☒ The entrance to the 'spaceship' led directly to the LED tower.
☒ The 20-m dome was a truss construction covered with fabric.
☒ Corporate yellow illumination was used across the stand.

Renolit by Von M and Projekttriangle

A FANTASY TYPOGRAPHICAL LANDSCAPE PEPPERED WITH TEXTURED PLASTIC-FILM RELIEFS TEMPTED VISITORS TO STOP FOR A WHILE.

Renolit, a leading manufacturer of high-quality plastic films for technical applications, presented its collection at Euroshop for the first time in 2011. The goal for the firm's presentation at the trade fair was to demonstrate the possibilities of the product by putting it to use in an aesthetically exciting and technically innovative way. In charge of the booth design was Stuttgart-based studio Von M. The team addressed the brief from a creative angle, inspired by illustrated fairy tales to create a fantasy world which fair goers could not resist stepping into to find out more. Populating the rich, dark environment were 3-m-tall plinths, differently sized white letters spelling out the client's name, and floating fluffy clouds to top it off. Stylised typography adorned surfaces in the form of reliefs – formed out of various deep-drawn plastic films taken from the product range – spelling out words that reflected the themes of 'nature' and 'city'. The design was inspired by the Lewis Carroll story *Alice Through the Looking Glass*, and acrylic-mirrored surfaces gave the presentation extra depth, distorting reality and playing with perceptions – just like in the story book. The intriguing three-dimensional landscape tempted visitors to stop for a moment and take the time to wander around and appreciate one of the many applications of the client's products. The stand had contemporary calligraphy as its focus, and the corporate lettering not only identified the brand to visitors but also doubled as flexible seating or podiums on which product information was placed.

TRADE FAIR Euroshop
WHERE Dusseldorf, Germany
WHEN February 2011
DESIGNERS Von M ⊠ p.499 and Projekttriangle ⊠ p.497
STAND CONSTRUCTOR Bluepool
CLIENT Renolit
MARKET SECTOR Plastic films
TOTAL FLOOR AREA 54 m²
PHOTOGRAPHER Zooey Braun

⊠ The stand's 3D landscape was created in collaboration with Projekttriangle.
⊠ One side of the panels visualised nature, the other showed motifs of the city.
⊠ The brown plinths were like trees in a fairy tale forest.

ARCHITECTURAL PRODUCTS GRAND STAND —

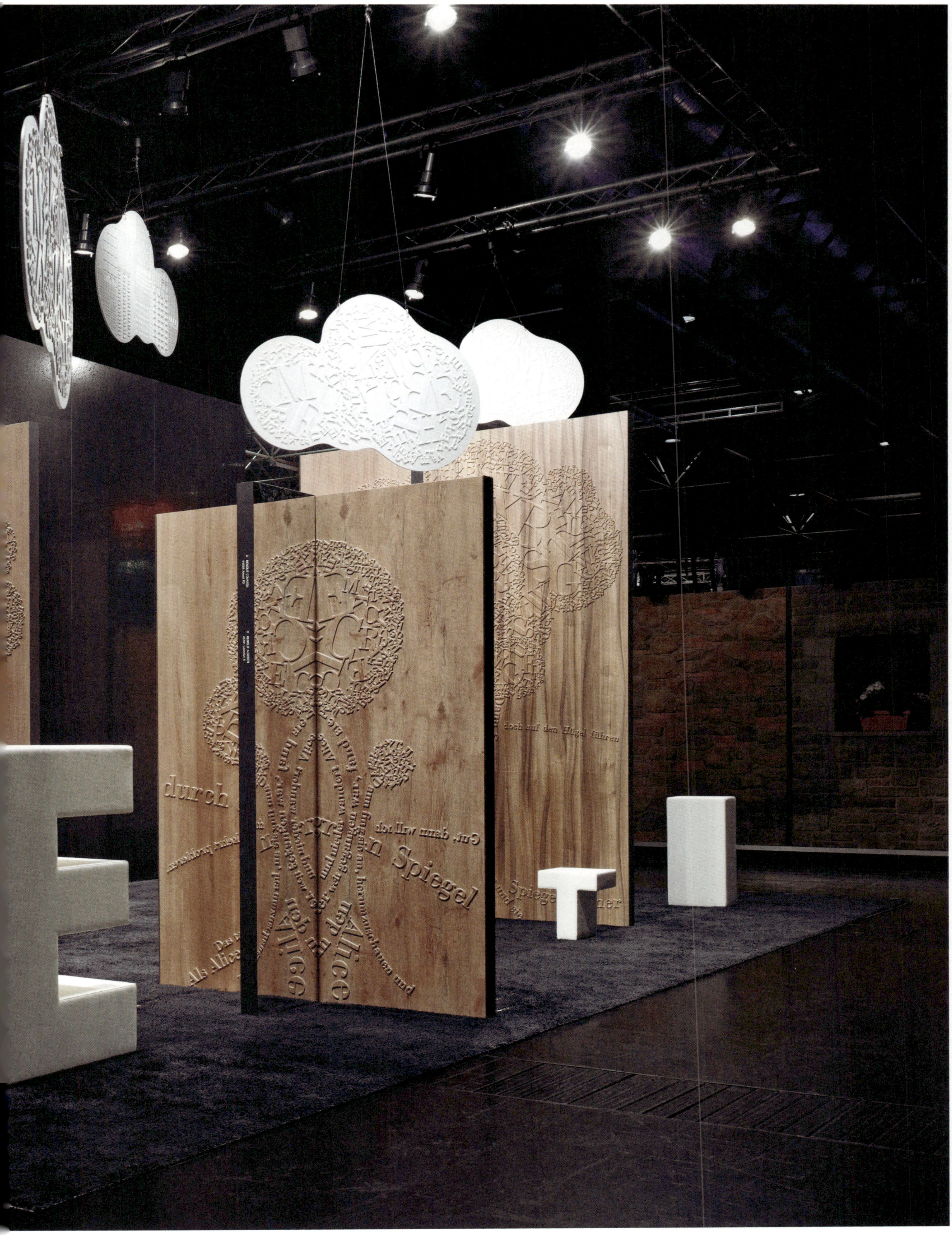
durch
Gut, dann will ich
Spiegel
doch auf den Hügel führen

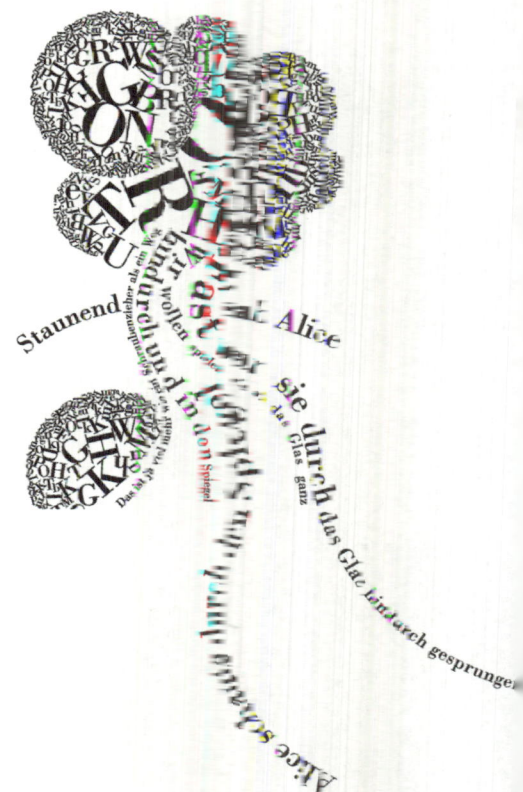

**Illustrated fairy tales that
create a fantasy world
inspired the concept**

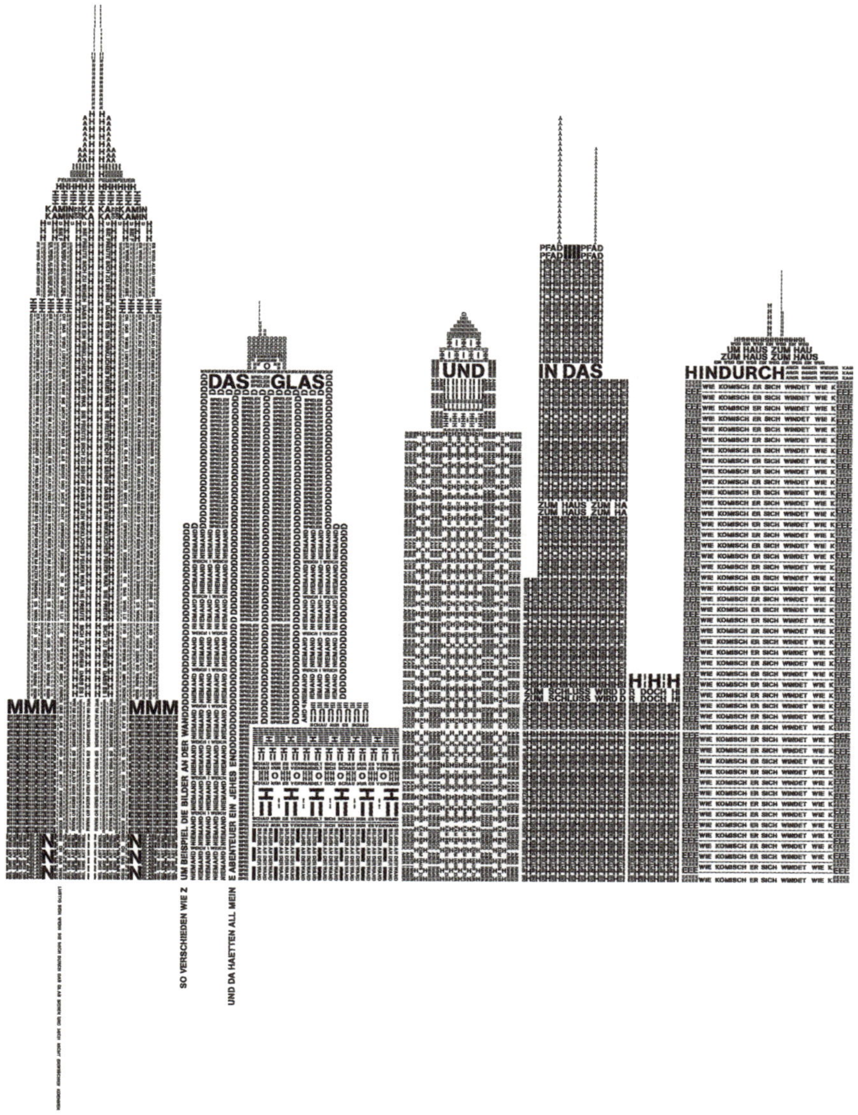

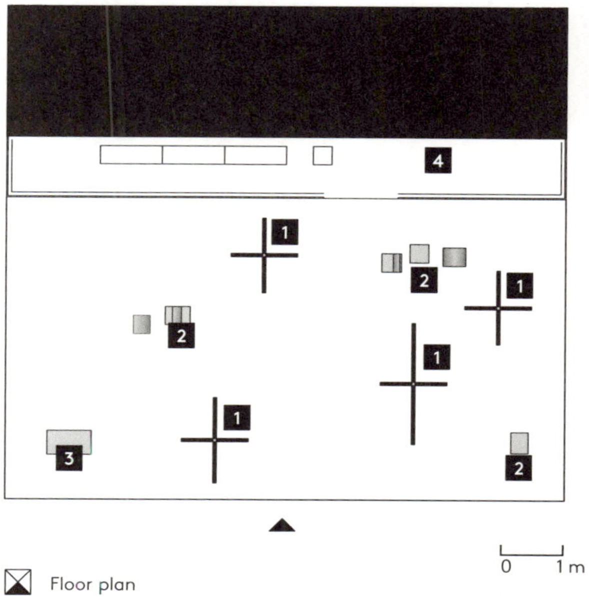

⊠ Floor plan

1 Columns
2 Stools
3 Table
4 Storage

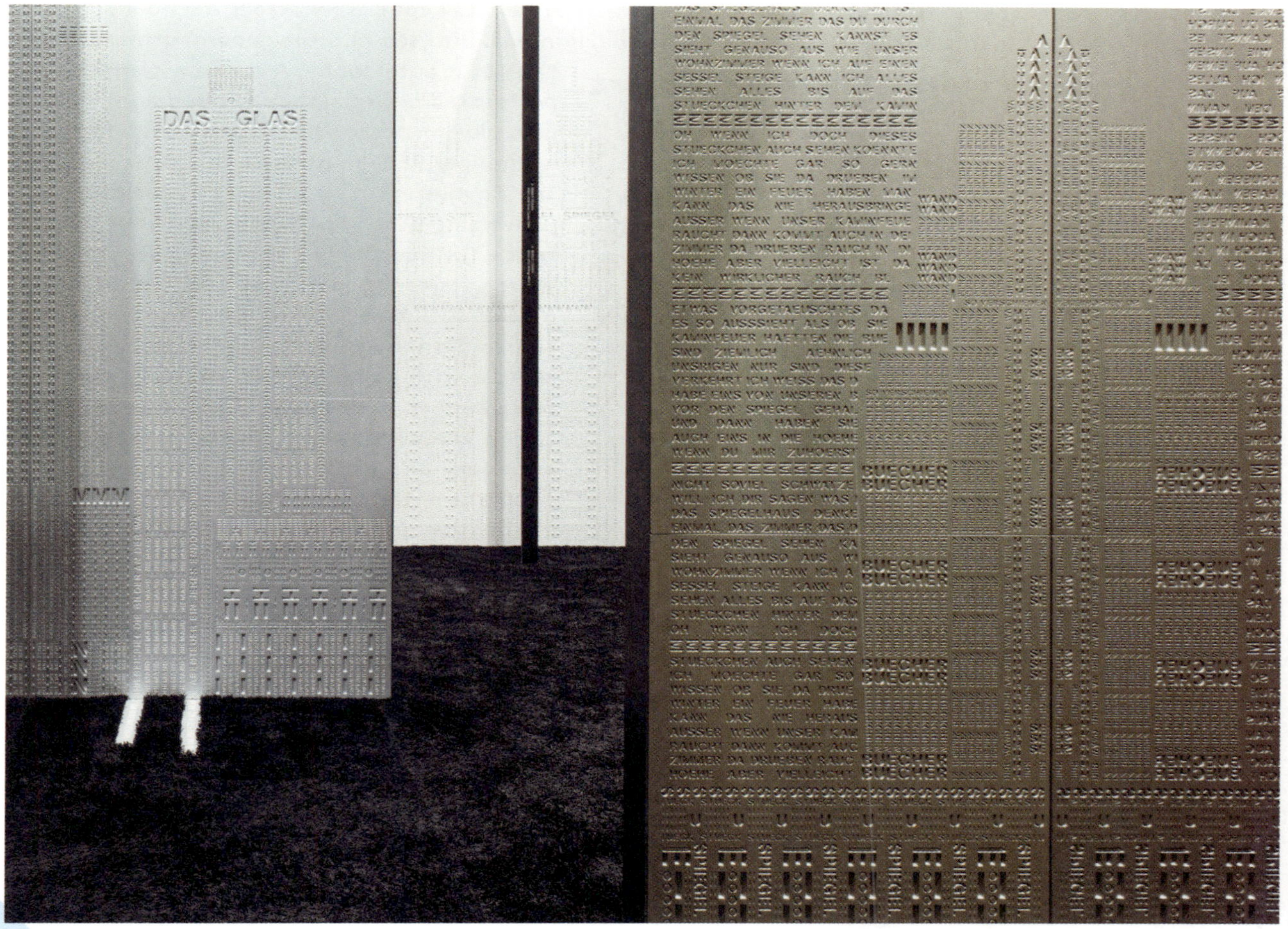

0   1 m

Prototyping of the plastic reliefs showing
the early stages of the project.
CAD was used in the creation of the
letter-filled skyline.
Swirls of letters formed the floral
illustrations in the 'nature' panels.
Pale, stone colours were used for the
panels depicting the 'city'.

Royal Ceramica by paolo cesaretti | architect

EASTERN PROMISE PERVADED THIS CONTEMPORARY CERAMICS PAVILION WITH A FUSION OF FINISHES, TEXTURES AND BRONZE HUES.

TRADE FAIR **Cevisama**
WHERE **Valencia, Spain**
WHEN **February 2012**
DESIGNER **paolo cesaretti | architect** ⊠ p.496
STAND CONSTRUCTOR **Olgiati**
CLIENT **Royal Ceramica**
MARKET SECTOR **Interior design and construction**
TOTAL FLOOR AREA **250 m²**
PHOTOGRAPHER **Estudio Julio Alonso Valencia (Sara Azorin)**

After establishing a good market share in the Middle East, Egyptian ceramics manufacturer Royal Ceramica took part in the Cevisama fair in Valencia with the aim of reinforcing awareness of its brand and collections in the overcrowded European market. With this intention, Paolo Cesaretti was brought on board to design a booth with a distinctive identity. The idea was to outline the philosophy of Royal Ceramica, a firm that produces European-style tiles based on Eastern themes and characterised by a multitude of decorative motifs. Interpreting this dual identity, the designer created a contemporary pavilion that fused the various finishes, textures and patterns, bringing to mind a grand and mysterious Arabic world. The concept engaged a sensibility that instilled in visitors the client's way of thinking, acting and manufacturing. A rich backdrop with a palette of dark browns, russets and golds was made possible through a careful selection of the client's key ceramic collections. Tiles with natural hues and textured finishes were chosen, interrupted by elegant yet luxurious details. Marble motifs with swirling patterns swept crisply across the floor surface and reflected in the stand's mirrored walls. The light was diffused and the general atmosphere was similar to that of a hotel lobby. A random composition of reflective perforated ceiling panels filtered light from above and set up a play of shadows with an oriental flavour. The agora – a gathering place in ancient Greece – is a strategic point in the Royal Ceramica world, and welcoming, meeting and conversing with clients were essential requirements of the space. In addition to the open aspects of the platform where visitors could view product offerings, there was a semi-secluded seating area that took the shape of an ellipsoidal lounge area, enveloped by a metallic-bronze curtain with its centre marked by a huge chandelier made from copper tubing. The curtain, made of 3 km of metal chain, was solid enough to create a clear and indisputable boundary and simultaneously light enough to encourage people to enter. From afar, the elegantly draping fringe-like installation acquired a solid form, characterised by shining and shimmering movement. The subtle sound produced from the curtain movement added a sensual highlight that visitors experienced within the space.

⊠ Detail of the display area framed in a glow of light and reflections.
⊠ A tubular light installation illuminated the reception desk.
⊠ Lengths of metal chain were draped to form an impressive installation.

Sistemi RasoParete by vc a | vannini+cesaretti

STREAMLINED INTERIOR ARCHITECTURE HOUSED IN A BLACK AND WHITE PRESENTATION WITH EYE-CATCHING BURSTS OF VIBRANT RED.

Sistemi RasoParete made a statement at Made Expo in 2011 – the emerging European fair for architecture and construction – with its totally renovated yet simply stated brand presentation. To communicate its tailor-made products for interior architecture, the company commissioned Milan-based studio vc a | vannini+cesaretti. The concept for the trade fair stand emphasised the client's vocation for producing perfectly engineered windows, doors and closets of the highest architectural quality. The major theme of the project was an archetypal symbol: the house. In addition to four walls and a gabled roof, the building featured interstitial spaces between its outer and inner layers, a minor theme that emphasised the interior. This theme also highlighted the client's streamlined product systems, which are specifically designed to exploit such spaces and cavities. The MDF construction was covered externally in black felt to give it a rough, textured surface that contrasted starkly with the purity of the smooth inner surfaces, with total crisp whiteness used to expand the perception of space. The open-ended character of the building's simple outline maximised the visibility of the central presentations. A solid volume positioned at the centre of the stand accommodated key products. Concealed storage systems and components that strongly characterised the Sistemi RasoParete portfolio also lined the inner surface of the house's perimeter. The iconic shape of the whole installation revealed three distinct perceptive elements: the dark outer skin, the white interior, and the startling bursts of red that symbolised the space enclosed between the first two elements. Visitors only noticed the red once they interacted with the presentation. Doors, cabinets and drawers, when opened, revealed the inner portions of the perimeter that vibrantly contrasted with the general all-white atmosphere. The dynamic interplay of glimpses of bright red that caught the eyes of passers-by enticed them into the booth to interact with the space, changing colours and configurations.

TRADE FAIR Made Expo
WHERE Milan, Italy
WHEN October 2011
DESIGNER vc a | vannini-cesaretti ⊠ p. 59
STAND CONSTRUCTOR Ricci Saoro
CLIENT Sistemi RasoParete
MARKET SECTOR Interio design and construction
TOTAL FLOOR AREA 48 m²
PHOTOGRAPHER Saveria Lombardi Vallauri

⊠ The interior space was stark, with a pristine white decor.
⊠ The booth took on the abstract form of a house.

ARCHITECTURAL PRODUCTS

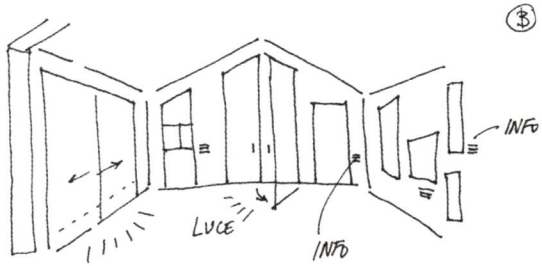

INFO
LVCE
INFO

The theme was an architectural and archetypal symbol: the house

☒ A 'slice' in each side wall created another access route into the stand for visitors.
☒ Streamlined storage was hidden in the stand's thick walls.
☒ Splashes of vibrant red awaited visitors once the doors were opened.
☒ The sketches conveyed the simplicity of the design.

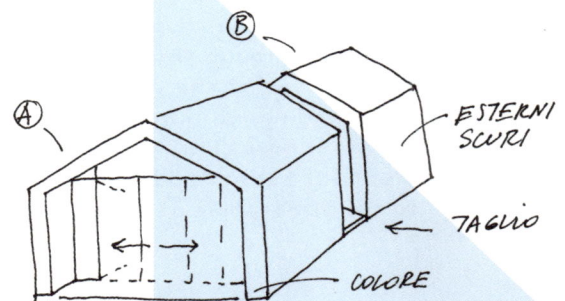

ESTERNI SCURI
TAGLIO
COLORE

Solon by Walbert-Schmitz and smd+partner

ENCAPSULATING THE ENERGY AND FLOW PATTERNS CREATED BY SOLAR STORMS, SWEEPING CURVES WRAPPED AROUND THIS STAND FOR A PRODUCER OF SOLAR-MODULE TECHNOLOGY.

Solon is a producer of solar modules and technology with a product portfolio that ranges from roof systems to full-scale power plants. For the Intersolar Europe fair in Munich in 2011, the company asked Walbert-Schmitz for a completely new and future-oriented stand. The concept called for a contemporary image that communicated the client's commitment to solar power. Moreover, the appearance had to be highly visible and inviting, standing out in the busy trade fair environment. The Walbert-Schmitz creative team, in cooperation with smd+partner design studio, visualised these requirements with the metaphor of solar flares. This natural spectacle became the symbol and common thread for the presentation. Solar winds are intensive, repetitive eruptions from the sun's surface in which high-energy matter forms huge loops of arching columns composed of glowing gases around sunspots. Drawing inspiration from such energetic processes Walbert-Schmitz turned spacious, white, curved and sweeping elements into the key features of the stand's architecture to imitate such dynamic movements. Tensioned fabric was manipulated into different shapes that depicted an unravelling ribbon as it hovered overhead, wrapped around the space and swept down to envelop the seating area before rising up again. This created an energetic sequence of motion that caught the attention of fair goers from across the exhibition hall, an effect enhanced by the illuminated corporate-blue branded signage positioned overhead. Open and transparent, the booth featured distinct spaces within its pure white environment that allowed for an exchange of ideas, technological aspirations and display of know-how. Visitors interacted with the client's products through the touch-screen and rotating information displays positioned at the front of the stand, and they 'operated' a futuristic palette window of solar modules to the music of their choice. This user-oriented engagement with Solon's innovations, as well as the media walls and monitor panels positioned around the stand's perimeter, all enhanced the high-tech environment and added to the atmosphere of information exchange.

TRADE FAIR Intersolar Europe
WHERE Munich, Germany
WHEN June 2011
DESIGNERS Walbert-Schmitz ☒ p.499 and smd+partner ☒ p.497
STAND CONSTRUCTOR Walbert-Schmitz
CLIENT Solon Energy
MARKET SECTOR Building products and solutions
TOTAL FLOOR AREA 360 m²
PHOTOGRAPHER Olaf Schiemann

☒ A curved reception desk fitted in with the flowing theme.
☒ The sweeping band wrapped around the lounge area.
☒ The high-tech space created a hands-on experience for visitors.

Thermopal by atelier 522

PRODUCT PLATES CREATED A DESIGN MOTIF IN A MODERN ARCHITECTURAL SETTING FOR LAMINATE MATERIALS.

At the 2011 Euroshop retail fair, atelier 522 was brought on board to create a contemporary stand for laminate materials manufacturer Thermopal. Using the tagline 'Designs, surfaces, technology' to encapsulate the client's expertise, the creative team worked on a concept that combined modern design with a traditional and recognisable architectural technique. The simple stand layout incorporated a 5.5-m-high back wall made of shingles, which not only was designed as an attractive detail and an eye-catcher for passers-by but also reflected the expertise of Thermopal and the diversity of its range of surface coatings. The backdrop incorporated almost 3000 model plates in various shades of red displayed as ornate elements. The individual laminates were artistically arranged so that they depicted a dynamic wave that swept elegantly across the length of the stand. The wall's surface was not strictly vertical but was slightly curved. This was most evident at its centre where a subtle opening sliced through it to provide access to a back office and storage area behind. The product presentation was one of simple restraint, with modern furnishings utilised to show the woodwork and laminates in detail. The placement of the furniture was purely functional: all product samples were arranged in a row along the front of the stand, immediately accessible to fair visitors; the next row back featured a series of meeting tables where staff and the public could interact. The result convinced fair goers who visited the presentation of the perfect setting for direct customer service related to the Thermopal products against a backdrop of modern architecture.

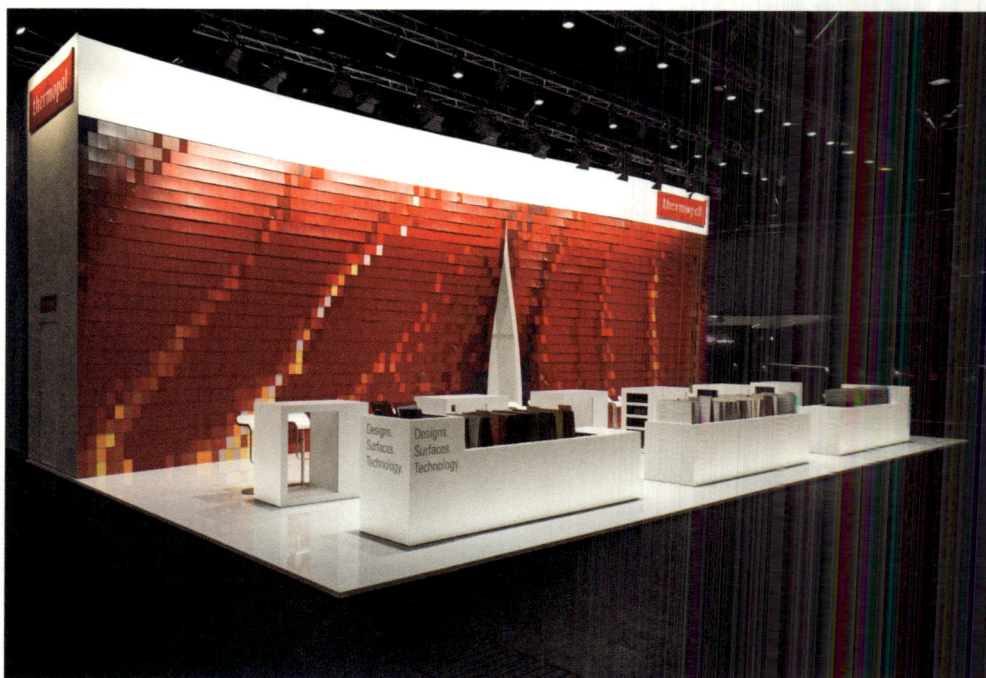

TRADE FAIR **Euroshop**
WHERE **Dusseldorf, Germany**
WHEN **February 2011**
DESIGNER **atelier 522** ☒ **p.489**
STAND CONSTRUCTOR **MBI Messebau**
CLIENT **Thermopal**
MARKET SECTOR **Interior design and construction**
TOTAL FLOOR AREA **112 m²**
PHOTOGRAPHER **atelier 522**

☒ The open booth was dominated by the red shingle installation
☒ A discrete entrance with architectural elegance was positioned in the back wall.

Velux by Atelier Seitz

Velux, the global producer of roof windows and skylights, has two core components at the centre of its business, as well as in its brand name: ventilation ('ve') and light ('lux'). For its presence at Dach & Holz, the trade fair for timber construction and interiors in Stuttgart in 2012, Atelier Seitz was commissioned to create the brand's presentation, which had light as the central theme. In keeping with the slogan 'Bringing light to life', the design team succeeded in counteracting the difficult lighting conditions found in many convention halls through the use of materials, form and above all illumination. An architectural outline of a Roman atrium was chosen as the basic inspiration for the trade fair stand, with the opening in the roof to bring light inside as the essential characteristic of this classical building form. Thus, the architectural symbolism of the atrium draws on precisely those corporate values that distinguish the brand: comfort, quality of life, daylight and fresh air, in combination with sustainability through energy-optimised products. The booth purposefully had a transparent appearance and played deliberately with contrasts of light and shade. Slots similar to those in Velux venetian blinds framed the sides of the presentation area and integrated the product displays as a corporate white-branded background, providing a clear delineation to the booth whilst still offering tantalising glimpses of the interior to passers-by. Creative side-entrances took the shape of roof-shaped vestibules alongside specially constructed cubes that presented the Velux systems in room-like settings, allowing visitors to experience the essence of the products at first hand. Strategically placed spotlights simulated the effect of daylight, which demonstrated the function of the sunscreen products. Within the fully modular concept and integrated design, forest imagery suggested a breath of fresh air, as did a real-life tree positioned in the centre of the stand – another visual contrast between household interiors and exteriors.

WITH A LAYOUT INSPIRED BY ROMAN ARCHITECTURE AND THE VENETIAN VERNACULAR, THIS TRANSPARENT STAND PLAYED WITH LIGHT AND SHADE.

☒ Geometrical forms were a key element of the design.
☒ The open facade created the atrium space for the product presentations.
☒ The stand concept underlined the contrast between light and shade.

TRADE FAIR Dach & Holz
WHERE Stuttgart, Germany
WHEN JANUARY 2012
DESIGNER Atelier Seitz ☒ p.489
STAND CONSTRUCTOR Atelier Seitz
CLIENT Velux Deutschland
MARKET SECTOR Building products and solutions
TOTAL FLOOR AREA 400 m²
PHOTOGRAPHER Olaf Schiemann

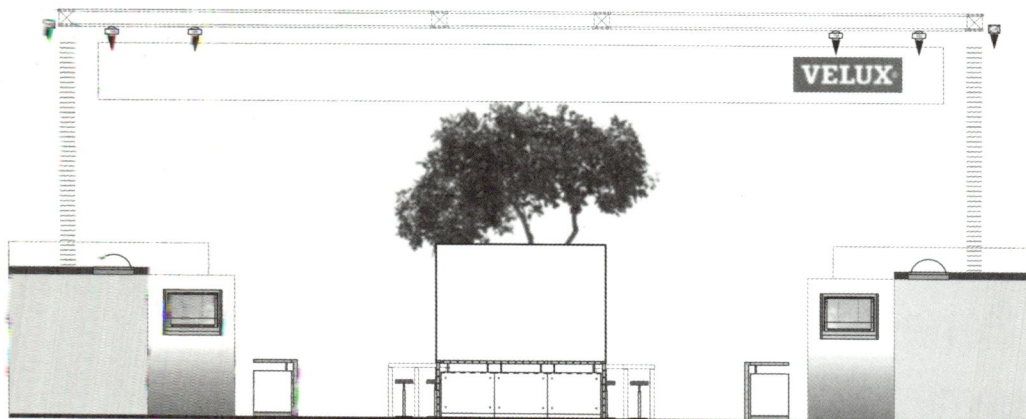

Bringing light to life was the basis of the concept

☒ The forest imagery represented the
    giving qualities of light.
☒ The roof-shaped vestibules incorpora
    spotlights that simulated daylight.
☒ The modular concept allows for sta
    from 15 to 400 m².

☒ Side elevations

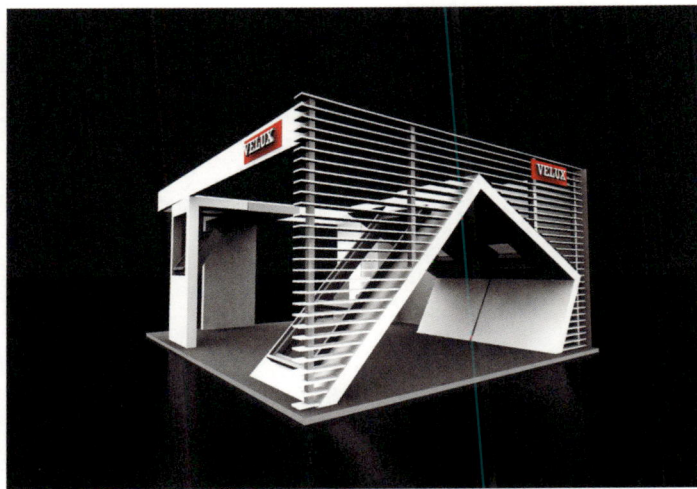

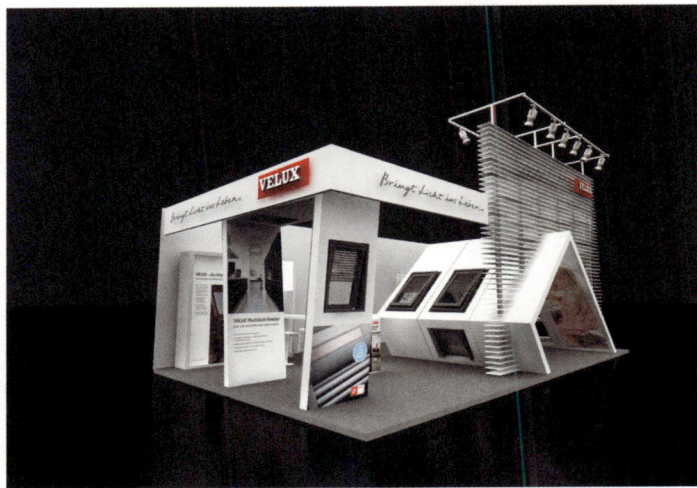

ATELIER SEITZ

VELUX

CONS.
PROD

MER
JCTS

Afa by studiomfd

STAND FOR A DISPENSING SYSTEM THAT
INCORPORATED FLUID AND FLOWING
FACETS WITH A CLINICAL AIR.

Afa Dispensing Group is a world leader in technologically advanced liquid dispensing systems. The firm planned to launch its latest propellant-free spraying technology for its new product, Flair, at the 2011 Interpack. Afa commissioned studiomfd to design a platform at the fair for this product and the accompanying technology. The brief requested an affordable, outstanding and easy-to-build stand that reflected the company's personality. The design team came up with a concept of 'fluent shapes that meet the innovative world of Afa'. A clinical exhibition stand with white curtains created a mystical installation that was light and flowing. The stand decoration referred to hygiene and product innovation. Visitors could measure the progressive level of Afa's product innovations at specially designed testing displays. Product samples were used as key display items, not least in the columnar installations. An attention-grabbing spectacle was the spiral of sprayer bottles positioned at ever-decreasing heights above a circular stage. Suspended in a curve with weighted bottom hems, the bottles trembled softly, swaying as visitors walked past. The swathes of crisp, white, wipe-clean fabric also embodied the fluid concept by the wave-like movement of the graphics and texts projected onto the cloth. The 'wave' action symbolised the fluids for which Afa develops its dispensing products. The flowing curtains enhanced the routing for fair goers through the stand, enveloping the central, more colourful, column as well as defining two separate rooms at the back.

TRADE FAIR **Interpack**
WHERE **Dusseldorf, Germany**
WHEN **May 2011**
DESIGNER **studiomfd** ☒ **p.498**
STAND CONSTRUCTOR **Gielissen Interiors and Exhibitions**
CLIENT **Afa Dispensing Group**
MARKET SECTOR **Dispensing systems**
TOTAL FLOOR AREA **65 m²**
PHOTOGRAPHER **Marcus Schwier**

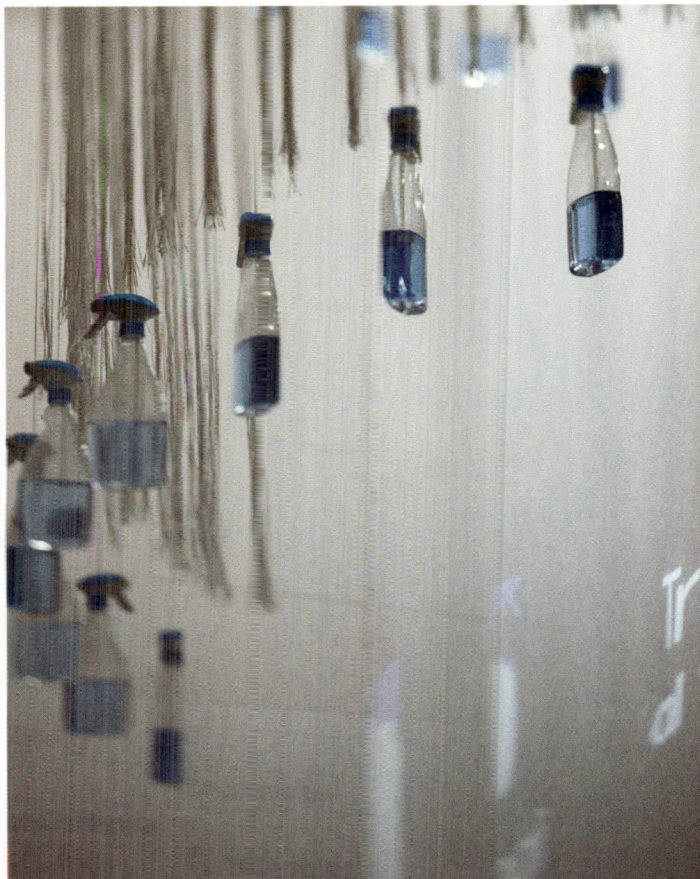

☒ The fringed curtain incorporated dispensing bottles, suspended as if they were an art installation.
☒ Spherical, flowing forms were a key aspect of the design.
☒ Branded text was projected onto the white curtain.

Bangma Verpakking by Pubblik

ORDINARY PACKAGING MATERIALS
STOOD OUT AS EXTRAORDINARY
PRODUCTS WHEN PRESENTED IN
A CONTEMPORARY SETTING.

Bangma Verpakking is an all-round packaging specialist, selling basic packing materials as well as custom-made cardboard boxes. The company asked Pubblik to design its stand for Macropak, a biennial packaging fair in the Netherlands. The design challenge was to make an ordinary product extraordinary without ignoring the brand's wide range of basic products that also needed to be displayed. Pubblik came up with the concept to show both the raw materials and the products in a contemporary and almost-homely setting. The design of the stand was like a large, open cabinet that was full of coloured boxes and striking patterns, which caught the eyes of visitors to the fair from a distance. For optimal exposure of the products, the basic structure of the booth was painted dark grey, constructed with slats to define the different sections of the stand whilst also providing sight lines across the booth. The parallel wooden beams which ran up and over the space, cleverly converted every surface into a storage potential or shelving aspect, or acted as a plinth from which to affix spotlights. Walls were stacked high with rows of boxes of one type or colour, allowing for an attractive visual pattern emerge. Another striking design was seen in the custom-made carpet on which the client's logo was printed in corporate colours. This acted as a pathway that led the visitors around the space. The layout of the stand allowed for niche meeting areas and information zones where key product details were graphically written on the walls. A full-size 'bespoke box making' machine was also snuggly fitted into the space, alongside the designer furniture and fittings. The stand also featured a large white hospital to counter, to attract visitors and informally do business.

TRADE FAIR Macropak
WHERE Utrecht, the Netherlands
WHEN October 2010
DESIGNER Pubblik ▶ p. 497
STAND CONSTRUCTOR DPM Expo
CLIENT Bangma Verpakking
MARKET SECTOR Packaging
TOTAL FLOOR AREA 80 m²
PHOTOGRAPHER Pubblik

☒ The stand was open and accessible from two sides.
☒ Products were packed high within the building blocks of the booth.
☒ The coffee counter was set prominently for an informal atmosphere.

BANGMA verpakking

INDUSTRIE

BANGMA VERPAKKING IS EEN ... VERPAKKINGSSPECIALIST
MET ALS SPECIALITEIT GOLFKARTONNEN VERPAKKINGEN.
HET BEDRIJF RICHT ZICH ONDER MEER OP DE ADVISERING EN VERKOOP AAN
GEBRUIKERS IN DE INDUSTRIE SECTOR.
ONZE KRACHT LIGT IN DE COMBINATIE VAN KWALITEIT, ADVIES OP
MAAT EN EEN UITSTEKENDE SERVICE.

ZOETWAREN

BANGMA VERPAKKING LEVERT DIVERSE SOORTEN TRAYS AAN
BIJVOORBEELD SNOEPFABRIKANTEN, PATISSERIËN EN BANKETBAKKERIJEN.
DEZE TRAYS WORDEN INGEZET ALS DISPLAY VERPAKKING EN HEBBEN DOOR
DE FLEXO LAK BEDRUKKING EEN HOGE PRESENTATIEWAARDE.
WIJ DENKEN MET U MEE ALS HET GAAT OM SERIE-VERPAKKINGEN EN
... ZETCENTRA DOOR HEEL NEDERLAND KUNNEN WE SNEL

VISSERIJ

DE DOZEN VOOR DE VISINDUSTRIE WORDEN GEMAAKT VAN
ZOWEL MASSIEF- ALS GOLF KARTON. DE DOZEN HEBBEN EEN UITSTEKENDE
STAPELWAARDE DOOR DE KRAFTKWALITEIT VAN HET KARTON. DOOR
OP MASSIEF KARTON PE COATING TOE TE PASSEN IS HET NIET
MOGELIJK DAT DE BEVROREN VIS ZICH AAN HET KARTON HECHT.
OMDAT DE DOZEN HANDOPZETBAAR ZIJN, ZIJN ZE GEMAKKELIJK IN HET
GEBRUIK.

AUTOLOCK DOZEN

Bild by Miks Konzepte

A WELL-KNOWN PLAYER IN THE NEWSPAPER WORLD MADE ITS MOVE INTO THE BOOK MARKET WITH A CLASSIC YET CONTEMPORARY STATEMENT.

The owner of the popular German tabloid newspaper *Bild* chose the Frankfurt Book Fair as the ideal location to present its exclusive book collection in 2011. This was the first appearance at a European trade fair for the brand and it wanted to mark its expertise in the literary field. Miks Konzepte was in charge of realising the stand design, opting to emphasise the products by displaying them in a library setting, the most typical place to read and experience books. With a grand gesture of portraying the space with the air of a classic library, a contemporary feel was instilled which also underlined the newspaper's individuality. This concept was clearly visible at one end of the stand in the design of the tall bookshelves, which were not classic pieces of furniture made of dark wood, but fine line drawings on the walls themselves. This illusion was contrasted by the presentation of the books placed on real shelves that protruded at intervals of different heights. The colour palette was light and understated, an overall white design with splashes of corporate red – from the brand logo clearly evident overhead to the classic reading lamps on the walls. The booth was also equipped with state-of-the-art technology consisting of a flat-screen TV on one wall and mobile end-devices at the opposite end of the stand in the information zone. Discretely integrated into the design was the multifunctional stage area so that the library could also be transformed and used for different public relations events, such as author meet-and-greets, readings and forums with testimonials and guests.

TRADE FAIR **Frankfurt Book Fair**
WHERE **Frankfurt, Germany**
WHEN **October 2011**
DESIGNER **Miks Konzepte** ☒ **p.495**
STAND CONSTRUCTOR **Miks Konzepte**
CLIENT **Axel Springer**
MARKET SECTOR **Books and media**
TOTAL FLOOR AREA **48 m²**
PHOTOGRAPHER **Martin Hasse**

☒ The design was reminiscent of the actual library at the client's headquarters in Berlin, Germany.

Capri Sun by Miks Konzepte

FUN AND FUNCTION: THIRST-QUENCHING ORGANIC FRUITINESS REALISED AMIDST A GREEN PLAYGROUND SETTING.

TRADE FAIR Internorga
WHERE Hamburg, Germany
WHEN March 2012
DESIGNER Miks Konzepte ⊠ p. 495
STAND CONSTRUCTOR Miks Konzepte
CLIENT Deutsche Sisi-Werke
MARKET SECTOR Food and beverage
TOTAL FLOOR AREA 21 m²
PHOTOGRAPHER Martin Hasse

A refreshing stand design was created by Miks Konzepte for the new Capri Sun drink when it was revealed to the world at Internorga 2012. For the first organic fruit drink of its type from the brand, the design team jumped at the chance to present the product on a green playground where, true to the brand philosophy, visitors could have lots of 'natural fun'. An outdoor air was given to the small stand by decking it out with tufts of green grass both underfoot – with a carpet of artificial turf – and rising up the walls surrounding the stand in terms of illustrations and graphics. The main attraction was a game based on a pulley system that was positioned along the back of the stand. With a brief tug on any of the juice drink pouches that dangled from the ceiling, the benefits of the fruity thirst quencher would be hoisted up to appear in the windows, either in the form of a fruit basket or an information panel. With this playful product experience, the design team successfully combined the two central brand elements – fun and function – in an effective manner to create a homogeneous end concept. Another eye-catching aspect of the stand was the innovative display system, which stood at almost 2 m in height and was designed in the shape of the product. This key visual attracted visitors to try one of the new organic drinks and was also large enough to be noticeable from some distance away, increasing the playground's long-range effect inside the exhibition hall. Every detail used at the Capri Sun booth exuded naturalness and created an atmosphere of authenticity and credibility of the concept. The natural MDF materials further enhanced the eco feel and natural finish of the stand, which convincingly reflected the organic qualities of the fruit drink.

⊠ A playful and interactive approach represented the central brand elements of 'fun and function'.

⊠ The product-shaped display system fitted to the natural look and feel of the booth.

Coca-Cola by Pinkeye

A GRAPHICAL RED THREAD WAS RESPONSIBLE FOR GUIDING THE VISITOR THROUGH A VISUAL STORY OF COCA-COLA'S 125 YEARS IN DESIGN.

TRADE FAIR Coca-Cola 125 Years of Design Expo
WHERE Gent, Belgium
WHEN December 2011
DESIGNER Pinkeye ☒ p.496
STAND CONSTRUCTORS Ber Meersman, Claerhout, De Muur
CLIENT Coca-Cola
MARKET SECTOR Food and beverage
TOTAL FLOOR AREA 400 m²
PHOTOGRAPHER Greg Smolders

To commemorate its 125-year anniversary, the global drinks brand Coca-Cola organised a series of celebrations worldwide. The creative force behind the expo that was held in Gent, Belgium was the Pinkeye studio. The brief was to illustrate how Coca-Cola's design – from packaging to marketing – has changed over time. The team was inspired by the brand's logo and this was implemented as a key visual across a white backdrop. In the recognisable red colour, large graphics spelled out the corporate story as a thread running through the space, flowing over the room's walls and across the ceiling. Visitors were guided through the expo which showed the evolution of the Coca-Cola brand through the graphic design of the logo, industrial design of its coolers, various communication campaigns over the decades and, primarily, the design of its bottles and packaging. A major focus was the central box podium dedicated to the story of recycling the plastic bottles to transform them into a special edition designer chair – the 111 Navy Chair. This product had been first manufactured the year before by Emeco in a unique collaboration with the drinks brand. Based on Emeco's original aluminium chair designed in 1944 for the US Navy, this version of the chair is made from at least 111 recycled plastic Coca-Cola bottles along with a special combination of other materials, including pigment and glass fibre for strength. It is estimated that more than three million plastic bottles are repurposed annually for the production of these chairs, a reflection of the Coca-Cola's commitment to sustainability, constant innovation and originality in design.

☒ As visitors walked through the space, an optical illusion based on the Coca-Cola logo fragmented and recomposed itself.
☒ The vertical columns showcased the different manifestations of the Coca-Cola bottle
☒ A striking display of recycling in real life: from waste product to shiny new object of beauty.

Coca-Cola
Het aantal Coca-Colaflesjes dat reeds gerecycleerd is tot 111 Navy Chairs
6100571 ×
111
START!

Glocal Design Station by ROW Studio

VISITORS WERE ATTRACTED INTO THE COLOURFUL, COCOON-LIKE ENCLOSURE WHERE THEY COULD REST A WHILE AND READ THE MAGAZINES ON DISPLAY.

For *Glocal* magazine's stand at Habitat Expo 2011, the annual design and furniture fair in Mexico City, ROW Studio was commissioned to create a space that people would want to enter, explore and, above all, stay for a while. The concept for the booth was a resting station, where visitors could take respite from the surrounding noises, lights and agitation of the fair. Once inside, they could take a seat and read the magazines enveloped within a cosy, cocoon-like environment that sheltered them. The construction and material for the booth was supplied by Masisa, a leading manufacturer of MDF panels in Latin America. ROW Studio worked closely with Masisa, responding to the brief that the structure should showcase a range of MDF finishes as a way to portray the possibilities of the material. The team chose two colour sequences, one from black to white including some wood texture materials and the other – along the length of the stand – ranging from dark green to orange. A flowing space was sought and since the MDF panels could not be bent to generate curves, it was decided to use them as a sequence of parallel planes cut with a CNC router to generate a complex, curved skeletal surface. Where the planes intersected, they formed a grid of shelves that served as display and storage space for the magazines and other products. What was realised was a vibrant, undulating booth that stood out as an island of simplicity and communication within the busy fair. Encapsulating the essence that anyone entering would indeed take the time to rest there for a while, from one end of the stand visitors could spy a large clock face just in case anyone got so ensconced that they forgot the time.

TRADE FAIR Habitat Expo
WHERE Mexico City, Mexico
WHEN May 2011
DESIGNER ROW Studio ⊠ p.497
STAND CONSTRUCTOR Masisa
CLIENT Glocal Design Magazine
MARKET SECTOR Media and publishing
TOTAL FLOOR AREA 24 m²
PHOTOGRAPHER Sóstocles Hernández

⊠ The exterior signage was reminiscent of the magazine's own masthead.
⊠ The versatility of the MDF panels allowed for curved contours to shape the booth.
⊠ The appeal of the stand came from its simplicity, with its bare skeleton of colourful hues creating an inviting space.

CONSUMER PRODUCTS   GRAND STAND 4

Lego by Arno Design

LARGER-THAN-LIFE LEGO PIECES WERE USED AS THE BUILDING BLOCKS IN AN INTERCONNECTED 3D EXPERIENCE.

For its stand at the 2011 toy fair in Nuremberg, Germany, Lego requested a presence that would represent its motto: 'Off into a new decade'. Arno Design responded to the brief with a configuration that combined a confident corporate statement in the form of emotion-evoking and eye-catching brand signals. The scene was set with a 1000-m² presentation area consisting of modular elements, which meant it was flexible and could be adjusted to accommodate diverse programme requirements. A larger-than-life Lego figure was illuminated near the entrance, welcoming visitors to the stand and directing them down the corridor where the company founder's motto adorned one wall, 'The best is just good enough'. The interior – playfully decorated with light fixtures made to look like giant Lego pieces hanging overhead – was divided up into distinct worlds. The product showcase area had a crisp white decor and made use of modular tables, round turning plates, free-hanging shelves and light boxes to display the latest toys, figures and models. An angular path of lights on the floor and a corresponding break in the ceiling seamlessly led visitors through the product worlds into the lounge area. Here, the space had a bright and airy feel, decorated with the materials, colours and shapes of the legendary Lego pieces. Surrounding the central seating area were glass-walled meeting rooms, providing a mixture of enough privacy to allow for the required discretion with as much openness as possible. The concept of immersing visitors into a three-dimensional Lego world was sustained throughout the stand – from the reception area right through to the interior lounge and the meeting rooms.

TRADE FAIR **Spielwarenmesse International Toy Fair**
WHERE **Nuremberg, Germany**
WHEN **February 2011**
DESIGNER **Arno Design** ☒ **p.488**
STAND CONSTRUCTOR **Raumtechnik Messebau**
CLIENT **Lego**
MARKET SECTOR **Games and toys**
TOTAL FLOOR AREA **1000 m²**
PHOTOGRAPHER **Frank Kotzerke**

☒ A large, illuminated figure welcomed fair-goers to the Lego world.
☒ The logo wall at the end of the entrance pathway was made of 1200 Lego pieces.
☒ The stand consisted of modular displays of the latest product offerings.

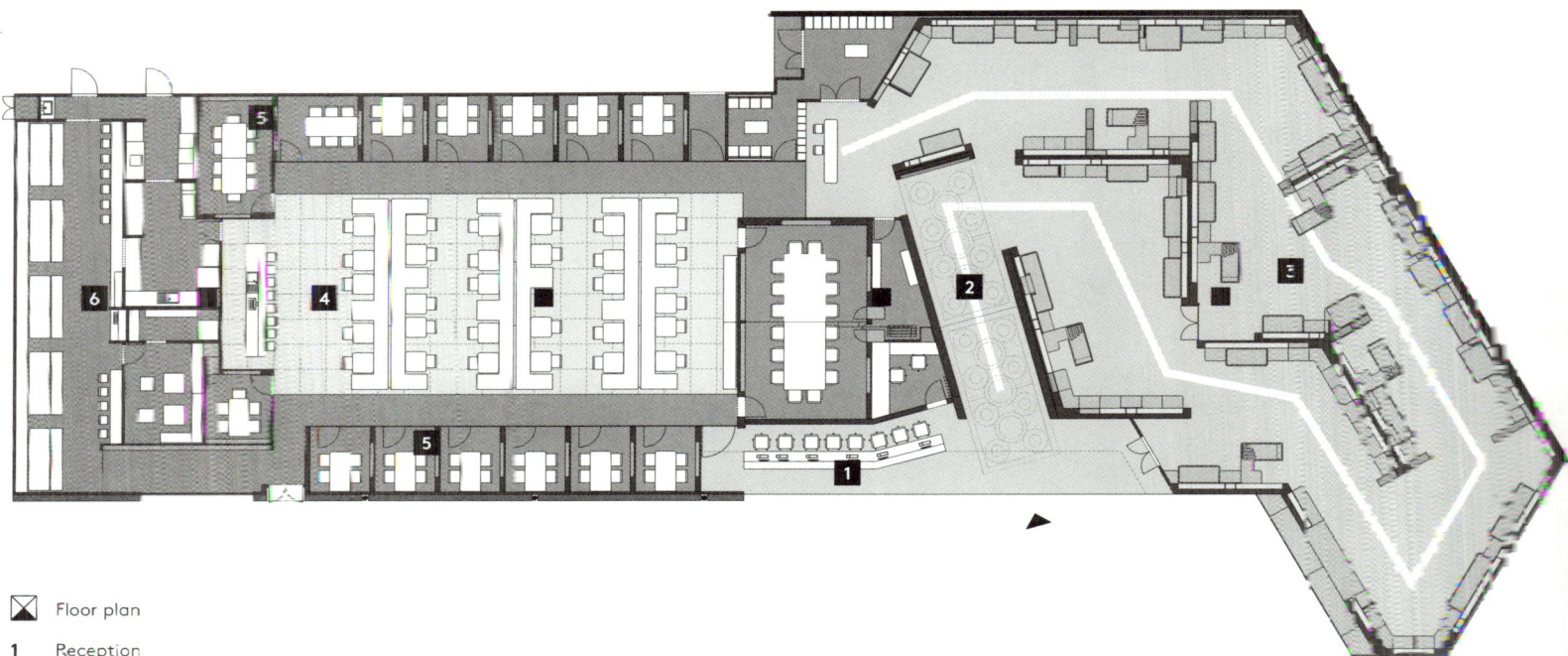

⊠ Floor plan

1 Reception
2 Entrance hall
3 Product showcase
4 Lounge area
5 Meeting room
6 Back office/storage

The glass walls had coloured foils affixed that could be adjusted at any time to fit the changing requirements of the space. Facade under construction (project manager, Ulrich Bauler of Arno Design). Renderings by Konrad Waltl of Arno Design showing the entrance and product presentation.

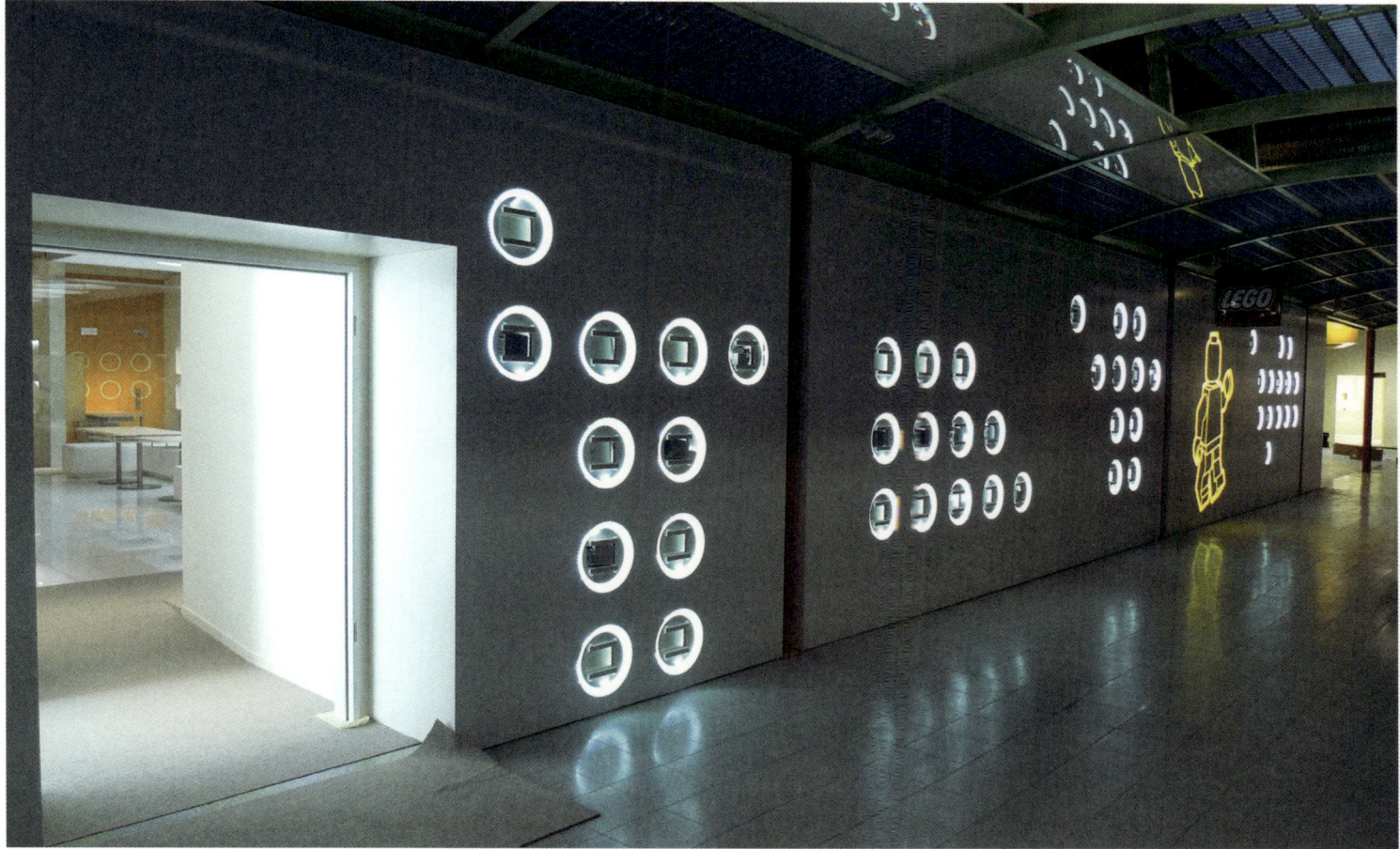

Visitors were immersed in a three-dimensional Lego world

Sony PlayStation by Uniplan

INTERACTIVE GAMERS WERE TRANSPORTED FROM A CORNER OF COLOGNE TO A FUN-FILLED AND SUN-KISSED STRETCH OF THE CALIFORNIAN COASTLINE.

TRADE FAIR **gamescom**
WHERE **Cologne, Germany**
WHEN **August 2011**
DESIGNER **Uniplan** ☒ **p.499**
STAND CONSTRUCTOR **Uniplan**
CLIENT **Sony Computer Entertainment**
MARKET SECTOR **Games and toys**
TOTAL FLOOR AREA **1638 m²**
PHOTOGRAPHER **Stefan Schilling**

The international trade fair gamescom is one of the biggest in the world for interactive gaming and entertainment. Thousands of young people throng to the fair's exhibition halls in Cologne every year in August to discover what is new in this field. From the exhibitor's perspective, if you want to get noticed here, you need to come up with a good idea. Sony PlayStation's ambition was to tempt guests in the midst of this turbulent atmosphere with some light-hearted, easy-going summer entertainment. Uniplan's creative team devised a fun scenario that would attract visitors onto the stand to spend some quality time, with the motto being to create 'your own summer'. The destination for this sun-kissed escape plan was Venice Beach, California. Fair goers were invited to stroll down the Ocean Front promenade with sun, sea and sand on one side and both urban and green spaces on the other. This cohesive PlayStation world was divided up into four zones as a key element of the architectural design, each filled with the many originally-shaped gaming stations – in the form of a shark, a telephone booth, a series of wooden rowing boats and a backstreet garage to name but a few. The world premiere of the 'PlayStation Vita' was celebrated on the large plaza, with plenty space also incorporated into the stand for guests to chill out in the lounging areas. Colourful, bright graphics and graffiti-clad walls decorated the distinct areas, amidst such props as surfboards and battered Volkswagen vans.

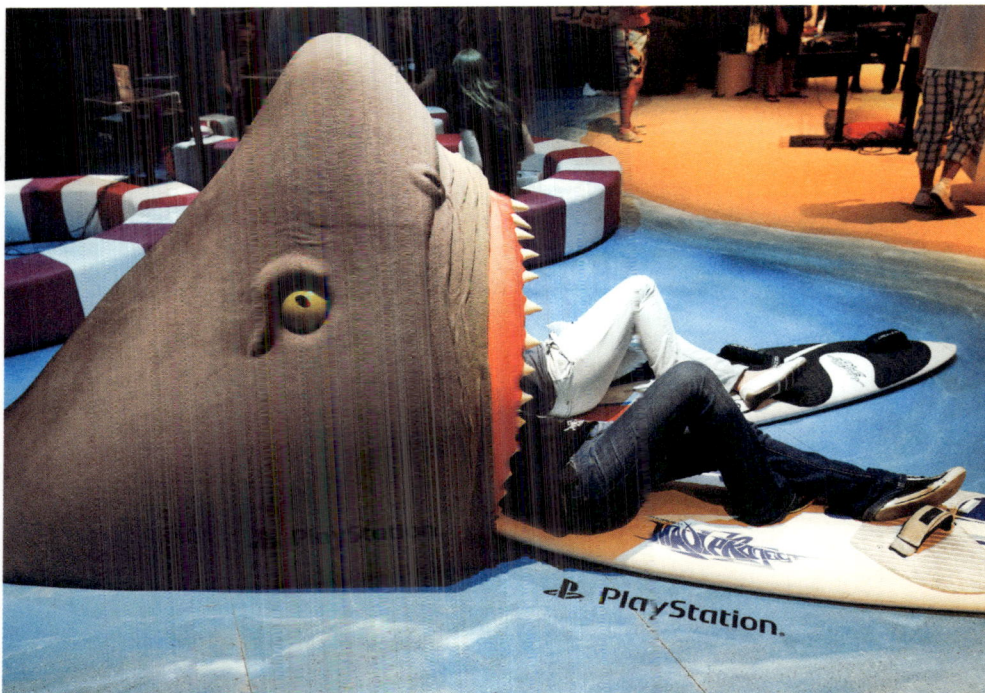

☒ The stand exuded a fun vibe and energetic buzz.
☒ The 'Ratchet & Clank' zone engaged gamers as they sat in colourful boats.
☒ A cloud of distinct brand icons hung suspended overhead.

Vedett by Pinkeye

PIXELLATED SPACE WAS TURNED INTO OUTER SPACE, WITH A BEER BOTTLE AS A ROCKET SHIP.

The Belgian beer brand Vedett states that it does not take itself too seriously except where the quality of its beer is concerned. For its stand at the 2011 edition of the Belgian bar show Venuez, the beer brand wanted to make an immediate and positive impression on visitors and commissioned design studio Pinkeye to realise a visually-striking booth. The colourful design was inspired by arcade games of the 1980s, with pixellated images and static animations. Pinkeye's team opted for a quirky 'out of this world' concept, positioning a Vedett bottle as a space rocket being boosted through the atmosphere into the depths of outer space. The dynamic pixellated pattern was created thanks to more than 8000 beer coasters that were specially printed for the occasion in a palette of red, green and black, with some other splashes of colour thrown in for good measure. A burst of fiery yellows and oranges propelled the bottle upwards, whilst the pixel effect also gave the impression of an exploding star which reached out across all the surfaces of stand, from the bar counter to the drinks podiums in the centre of the booth. Illumination of the stand came in the form of ceiling spotlights positioned overhead. On the wall behind the bar, the Vedett logo shone brightly in the form of a bespoke light box which was custom-made in the familiar pixel art fashion.

TRADE FAIR **Venuez**
WHERE **Antwerp, Belgium**
WHEN **February 2011**
DESIGNER **Pinkeye** ⊠ **p.496**
STAND CONSTRUCTORS **PN, Tint Graphics**
CLIENT **Vedett**
MARKET SECTOR **Food and beverage**
TOTAL FLOOR AREA **40 m²**
PHOTOGRAPHER **Pinkeye**

⊠ The giant Vedett bottle was depicted lifting off and seemingly exploding into thousands of colourful fragments, creating a visually arresting booth.
⊠ The graphical tapestry of the design was a perfect fit for Vedett's tongue-in-cheek identity and eclectic style.

Wargaming by Walbert-Schmitz and smd+partner

REALISING A LANDSCAPE OF TANK TURRETS, AMMO BOXES AND OIL DRUMS THAT WAS MORE BATTLEGROUND THAN BOOTH.

Wargaming.net is an online game developer that has been operating since 1998. The company specialises exclusively in online military-strategy games. For gamescom 2011, the client tasked Walbert-Schmitz with showcasing in a martial setting its newest game, the 'World of Tanks'. With a specific brief to target the visitors' hunger for authenticity and intensity, the concept was to be more battleground than booth. The Walbert-Schmitz creative team, in cooperation with smd+partner design studio, realised a stand that encapsulated the genuine aesthetics of the game itself whilst maintaining a corporate sophistication. A suspended, expressive steel enclosure riddled with punctures – made out of translucent fabric that looked like a battle-hardened, minimalist tank – enveloped the space above the stand. This vast canopy with its rusted brown camouflage-like feel, actually did anything but disguise the booth; instead it was a key aspect in attracting attention from afar. The fabric curtain was adorned with splotches of ochre-coloured paint and then perforated with 815 imitation bullet holes using an industrial laser. Beneath this imposing structure, visitors walked into their very own game simulation, welcomed by five turrets – each depicting a different period in tank design – which functioned as individual game stations. Further laptops atop 30 ammunition boxes were available for more gaming tactics and military manoeuvers. After they were done skirmishing, visitors could relax on khaki-coloured sandbags that were strewn over the floor and watch scenes from the game and other trailers on two large high-definition rear-projection screens.

The fabric canopy substantiated the brand through high visibility and recognition.
The expressive stage in the interior of the stand formed an emotional hub.

TRADE FAIR **gamescom**
WHERE **Cologne, Germany**
WHEN **August 2011**
DESIGNERS **Walbert-Schmitz** p.479 and **smd+partner** p.497
STAND CONSTRUCTOR **Walbert-Schmitz**
CLIENT **Wargaming.net**
MARKET SECTOR **Games and toys**
TOTAL FLOOR AREA **215 m²**
PHOTOGRAPHER **André Loessel**

300 CARTRIDGE
7.162MM - M82
CARTONS
LC-97 F256-209

300 CARTRIDGE
7.162MM - M82
CARTONS
LC-97 F256-209

300 CARTRIDGE
7.162MM - M82

The props located inside the stand w
used as game stations.
The canopy, which weighed in o
deceptively light 80 kg, was also use
a projection screen.

Under a canopy perforated with 815 imitation bullet holes, visitors walked into their own game simulation

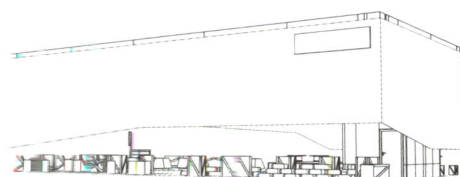

Elevations

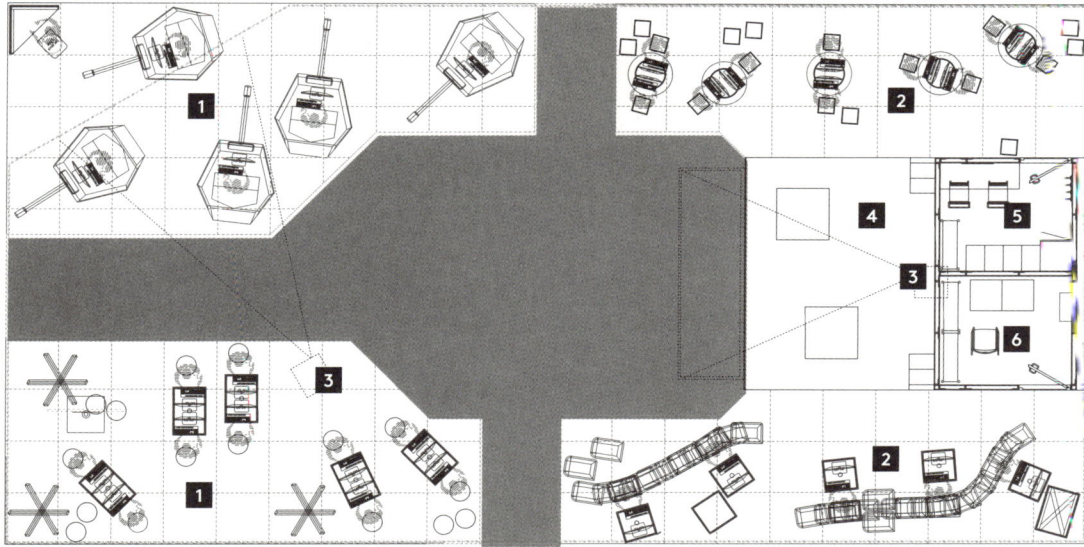

Floor plan

1 Product stations
2 Seating
3 Screen projector
4 Stage
5 Storage
6 Office

ELECT

Baumüller by Atelier Seitz

STEP-BY-STEP, VISITORS WERE TAKEN ON A RELAXED JOURNEY INTO AN AUTOMATED REALM.

TRADE FAIR SPS IPC Drives
WHERE Nuremberg, Germany
WHEN November 2011
DESIGNER Atelier Seitz ☒ p.48?
STAND CONSTRUCTOR Atelier Seitz
CLIENT Baumüller Nürnberg
MARKET SECTOR Control systems technole
TOTAL FLOOR AREA 304 m²
PHOTOGRAPHER Olaf Schiemann

At the 2011 SPS trade fair for electric automation technology, the design of Baumüller's stand was realised by Atelier Seitz. The studio was commissioned to devise a versatile, modular concept that could easily be translated into other fair environments whilst delivering a consistent brand message. The client's product offering – a range of system solutions for all sectors of electrical and mechanical engineering – needed to be delivered within a systematic and coherent configuration of design elements. The stand was given a modern and technical look, which underlined the aims and tradition of the client. The colour and graphic concept used represented succinctly the brand's corporate identity, whilst the numerous complex products were laid out as if on a time line. A yellow ribbon-like banner overhead weaved its way across the ceiling, whilst a white pathway on the floor connected the different zones, leading visitors through the different product realms. The neutral grey backdrop applied elsewhere allowed the product presentations to stand out on the various vertical modules. Highlighting the technological aspects of the products was a multimedia screen, placed at the front of the stand to give it maximum visibility. This area also doubled-up as a presentation podium, which attracted people's attention to entice them onto the stand and to explore the space. Enclosing the booth on one side were grey-painted walls that rose up and over the lounge area at the back of the booth, thus creating a 14-m-wide archway overhead. The seating area therefore gave visitors a feeling of being secluded, providing them with an oasis of quiet in the busy and noisy atmosphere of the trade fair. It also created a relaxing space for informal meetings and hospitality for guests.

☒ The grey archway separated the lounge area from the technical side of the stand.
☒ The time line structured the stand; it led visitors sequentially through the product groups on display.

Dell by Standard Studio

SYMBOLISING THE BUILDING BLOCKS OF INNOVATION, A GRAPHICAL ELEMENT WAS THE CHARACTERISTIC CONTEXT FOR A HARMONIOUS EXPERIENCE.

TRADE FAIR **Dell World**
WHERE **Austin, United States**
WHEN **October 2011**
DESIGNER **Standard Studio** ⊠ **p. 93**
STAND CONSTRUCTOR **GES**
CLIENT **Dell**
MARKET SECTOR **IT and telecommunicatic**
TOTAL FLOOR AREA **1675 m²**
PHOTOGRAPHER **David Magnusson**

The inaugural Dell World event held 2011 in Austin was aimed at IT industry professionals and had a theme of 'unlocking innovation in a virtual era'. The goal of the three-day event, which hosted Dell's high-level public and large enterprise customers, was to position Dell as a 'thought leader' in services and solutions. Standard Studio was responsible for the design of the executive lounge area at the fair, collaborating with Embarcadero Partners. The concept was to create a unique temporary environment that would stimulate conversations about innovation and opportunities in new technologies, computing services and social media. The starting point for the team was to establish an identity system specific to Dell World in the form of a distinctive graphic that could be applied across all mediums, from promotional literature to the environment space itself in order to ensure a harmonised and homogeneous experience. The characteristic symbol – a series of hexagonal shapes in vibrant hues – was repeated across the temporary space so that the client's presentation was conceived as a seamless whole, from the suspended shapes which formed 'clouds' over the stand, to the animated sequences projected onto surrounding screens which gave the impression of angular 'thought bubbles'. It was also significant that the floor plan of each individual space incorporated the six-sided shape. Large-scale printed graphics on fabric, stretched on customised aluminium frames, were positioned to cordon off the different seating areas, thus giving visitors ample relaxed opportunities for exchange and discussion. Additionally, the hexagonal pattern was applied in the distinctive colours and treated as various identity markers to accompany the presentation, including an information system, a visual framework for the web and mobile app, and even a social planning element.

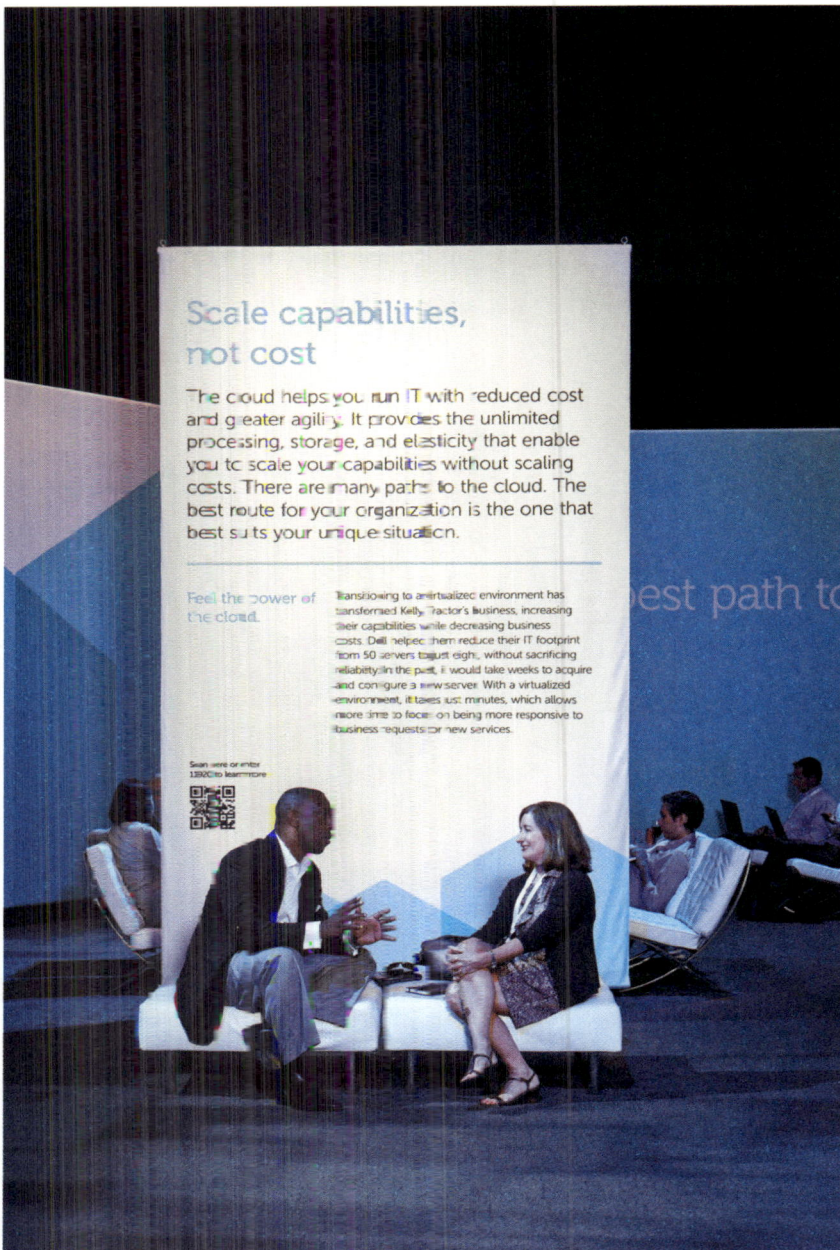

Scale capabilities, not cost

The cloud helps you run IT with reduced cost and greater agility. It provides the unlimited processing, storage, and elasticity that enable you to scale your capabilities without scaling costs. There are many paths to the cloud. The best route for your organization is the one that best suits your unique situation.

⊠ Product offerings were sorted by co and content.
⊠ The fabric panels printed with grap were used to create an intimate separate experience from the rest of show floor.

Floor plan

1 Graphic panel
2 Suspended panel
3 Seating area

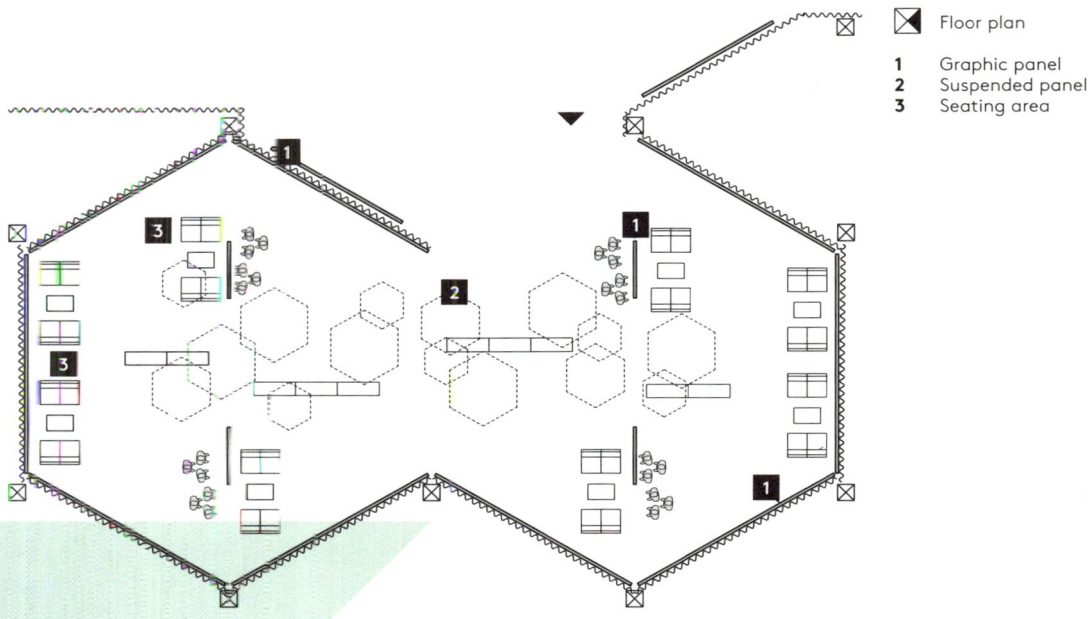

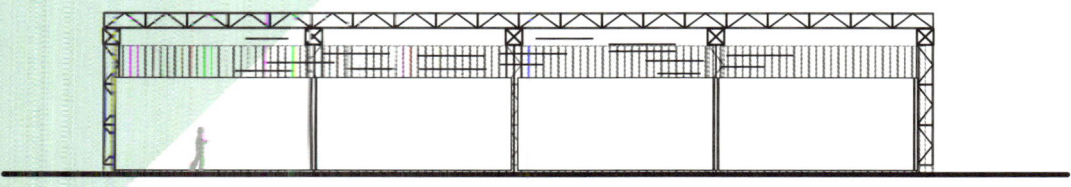

Side elevation

Fair goers could relax on the white eat
furniture in the lounge area

Rendering indicating the differ
hexagonal aspects.

The entrance to the Dell World had
LED wall with motion graphics.

The graphic identity system gave the impression of angular 'thought bubbles'

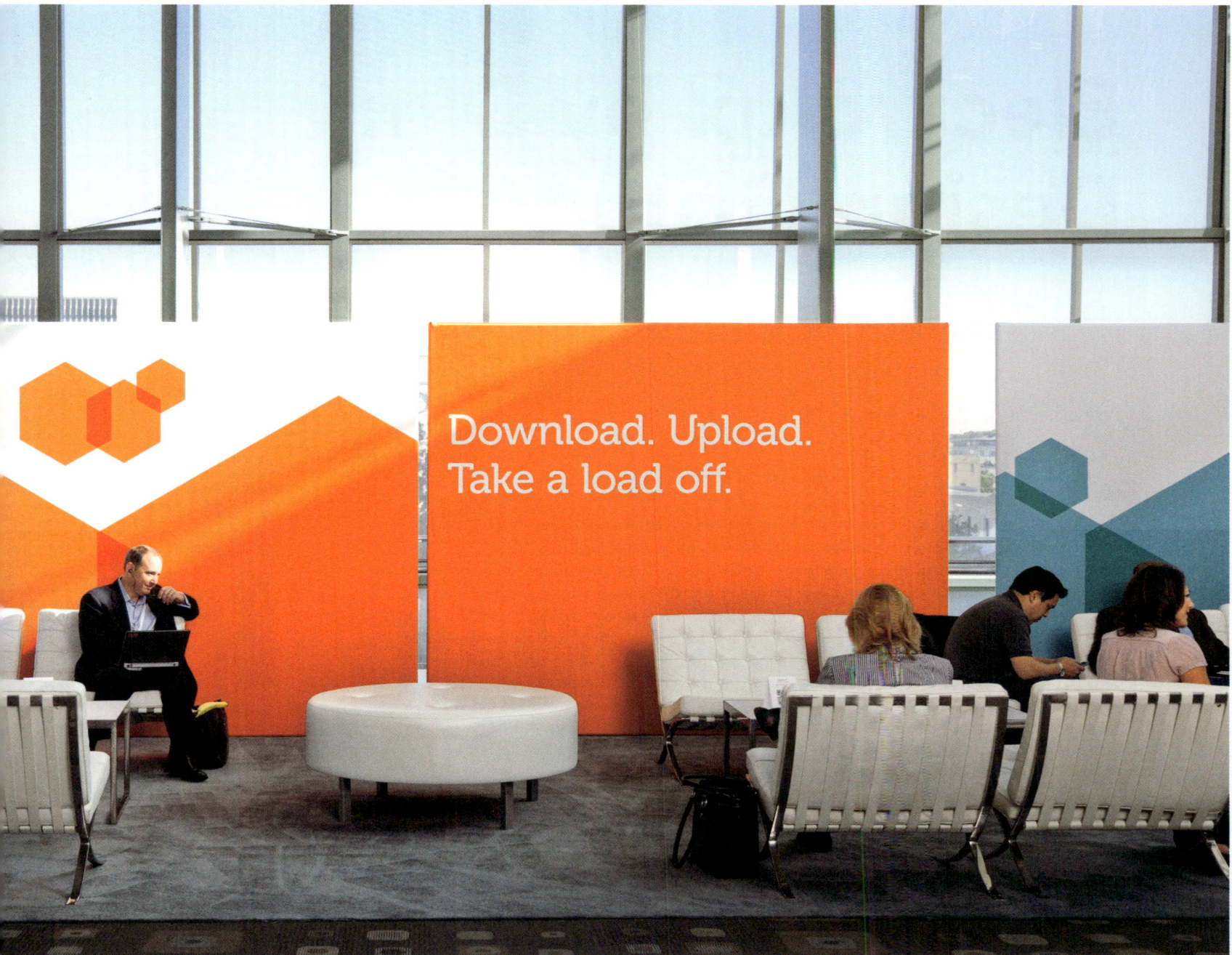

Download. Upload.
Take a load off.

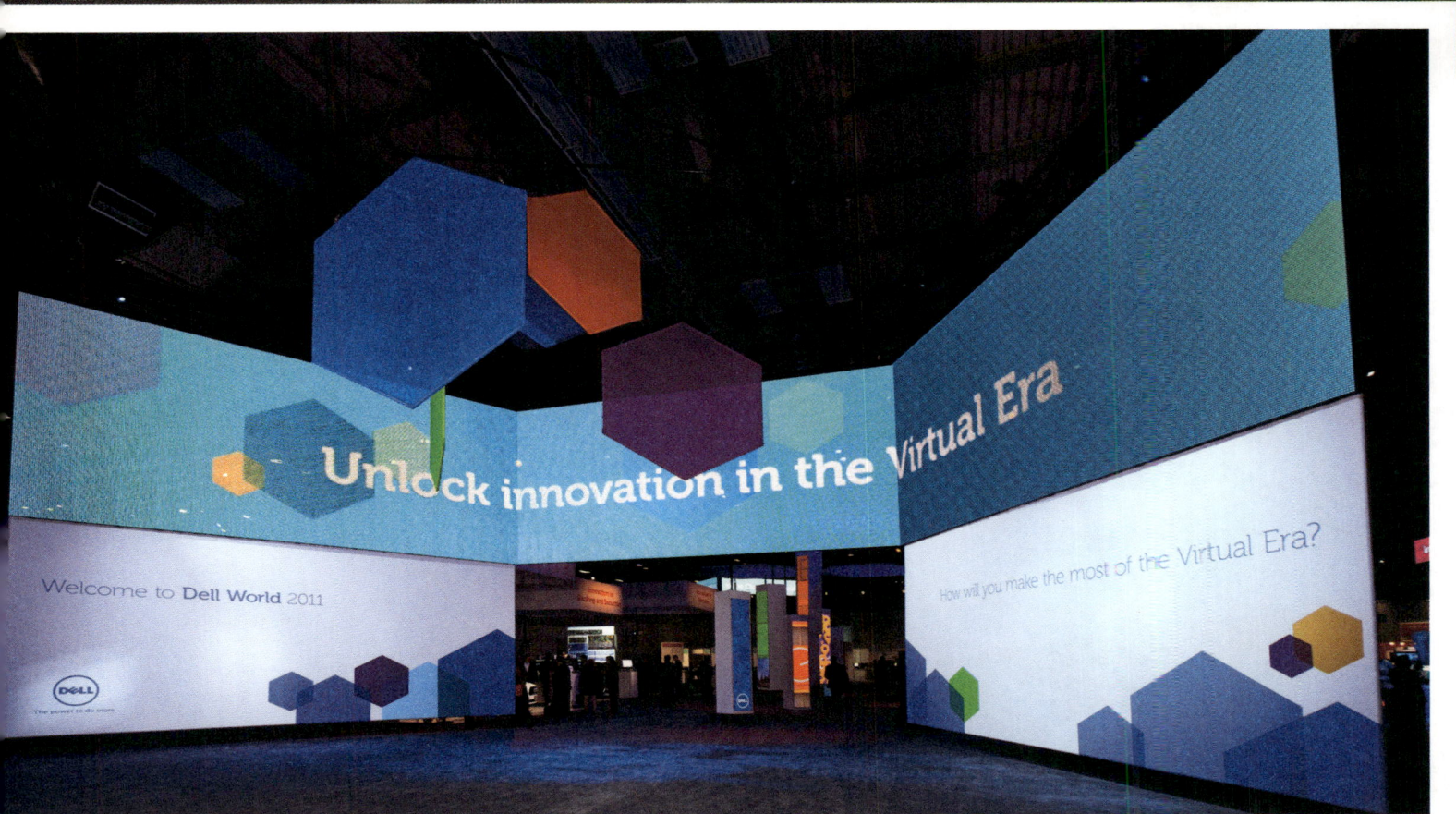

Welcome to Dell World 2011

Unlock innovation in the Virtual Era

How will you make the most of the Virtual Era?

Electrolux by D'art Design Gruppe

INSPIRATION WAS ON THE MENU WITHIN THIS ARCHITECTONIC SPACE FOR COOKING APPLIANCES.

Electrolux launched its new Inspiration Range at Eurocucina in April 2012. The range comprises modern appliances that were originally developed for professional chefs and have now been adapted for use in household kitchens. D'art Design Gruppe was in charge of creating the Electrolux presentation at the fair, which needed to highlight the exclusiveness of the appliances. The creative concept essentially fused a number of fundamental components: light and space in order to communicate the products' high quality; and multimedia and interaction to convey the appliances' innovations. Visitors were invited to have hands-on experiences with the technology, both to be inspired and to learn by doing. Alongside interactive touch screens were also visual images and audio sounds, ensuring visitors enjoyed an all-round sensory experience within the stand. The atmosphere imbued by the design of the space was one of a relaxed journey of exploration. A combination of bright, spacious and rectilinear structures with warm woods conveyed the Scandinavian flair of the client and matched the elegance of the products on show. An appealing aspect incorporated into the architecture was the seemingly floating walls, which added to the sense of discovery as visitors walked around the stand; if they were lucky enough, they even got to taste the professional chefs' offerings which were served up in the 'live cooking area'. On the exterior of the booth, the floating walls were combined with 3D-layering aspects to incorporate a textured panel which wrapped around the stand. This was subtly branded with the client's logo in a simple, yet effective, design statement. Passers-by could glimpse into the space from all angles, being enticed inside not only by the product displays but also from the aroma of culinary delicacies being cooked-up inside the stand.

TRADE FAIR **Eurocucina**
WHERE **Milan, Italy**
WHEN **April 2012**
DESIGNER **D'art Design Gruppe** ⊠ p.490
STAND CONSTRUCTOR **Holtmann Messe & Event**
CLIENT **Electrolux**
MARKET SECTOR **Home appliances**
TOTAL FLOOR AREA **1000 m²**
PHOTOGRAPHER **Tobias Wille**

⊠ Infotainment, multimedia and interaction conveyed the contents and innovations with direct experiences.
⊠ The light, spacious stand was a prominent stage for the high-quality products.
⊠ Chefs prepared food using the appliances in the spaciously arranged kitchen.

Ericsson by Jack Morton Worldwide

A VISION FOR A NETWORKED SOCIETY WAS REALISED WITH AN ELEGANT YET INDUSTRIAL INTERCONNECTIVITY.

For the fifth consecutive year, Jack Morton was commissioned to create an innovative and engaging brand presence for Ericsson at the Mobile World Congress. The brief asked for a space where customer relationships could be nurtured and where the industry could be inspired with Ericsson's vision of 'the networked society'. The challenge for the design team was two-fold: to communicate the client's continuous innovation by surprising and delighting its audiences at the fair, and to illustrate the brand's evolution, so that the experience supported a journey to change perceptions, without alienating existing customers. The creative concept put the networked society at the very heart of the design so that it felt tangible and fully incorporated into the client's way of working, with two architectural elements being critical in shaping this. Firstly, 'the spine' was the physical representation of the concept's connectivity, forming a dynamic pathway leading visitors to the different zones within the space. Secondly, radiating out from this, was a series of 'fragments' carrying constantly changing corporate imagery to bring together all of Ericsson's content across the presentation and aligning it with the strategic vision. 'Elegant industrial' was the design language instilled across the stand, juxtaposing raw finishes with concentrated moments of elegance. The vibrancy of the brand was encapsulated in the booth's decor by the use of corporate hues picked out in the eye-catching, illuminated installations and angular structures positioned around the stand. Incorporating textures, finishes and shapes that instilled a wit and charm into the product platforms ensured the experience was brought to life, differentiating the distinct elements whilst retaining the sense of a unified, integrated brand experience.

TRADE FAIR **Mobile World Congress**
WHERE **Barcelona, Spain**
WHEN **February 2012**
DESIGNER **Jack Morton Worldwide** ⊠ **p.493**
STAND CONSTRUCTORS **Display International, Nicholas Alexander**
CLIENT **Ericsson**
MARKET SECTOR **IT and telecommunications**
TOTAL FLOOR AREA **8000 m²**
PHOTOGRAPHER **Xavier Vila**

⊠ Visitors entered into a technology-inspired world through a luminous gateway.
⊠ The immersive experience wove together nine content areas including demo areas, an auditorium, meeting rooms and various vibrant hospitality spaces.
⊠ Overhead media screens captured the brand's signature identity through animated imagery.

- Stainless steel fixtures and wooden farm tables in the cafe encapsulated the 'elegant industrial' aesthetic.
- The space was designed to create intrigue, stimulate conversations and maximise social interactions.
- The interactive, 3D display articulated Ericsson's holistic vision across industry, geography and communication pathways.
- The exposed light bulbs and distinctive colour palette in the gathering space brought Ericsson's personality to life.

The creative concept put 'the networked society' at the very heart of the design

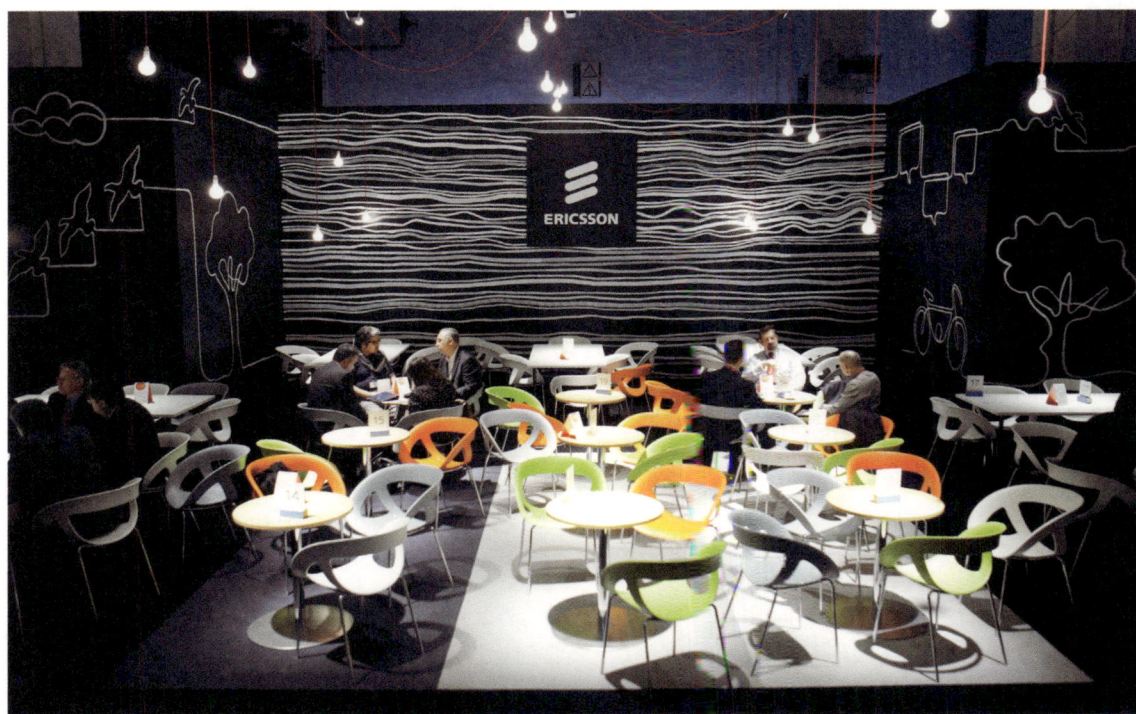

Gaggenau by eins:33

ALL THE INGREDIENTS TO TRANSFORM RAW
MATERIALS INTO CULINARY MASTERPIECES
WERE LAID OUT IN AN ARCHITECTURAL SETTING
COMPRISING ORGANIC AND INORGANIC ASPECTS.

TRADE FAIR Eurocucina
WHERE Milan, Italy
WHEN April 2012
DESIGNER eins:33 ⊠ p.491
STAND CONSTRUCTORS Altmann
Laden- und Innenausbau, Serviceplan
CLIENT Gaggenau Home Appliances
MARKET SECTOR Home appliances
TOTAL FLOOR AREA 300 m²
PHOTOGRAPHER Bodo Mertoglu

At Eurocucina 2012, Gaggenau presented itself against a bold backdrop thanks to the design team of eins:33 who created an uncluttered booth with a sculptural aesthetic. The client's brief called for its professional-standard technology for the home kitchen to be showcased in an expressive architectural setting. The concept for the design saw a strong emphasis on raw materials, inspired by the brand's core values: extraordinary, authentic and uncompromising. The blueprint for the stand comprised two diagonally-positioned cubes – one constructed of steel and one of wood – presented on an open platform; what was realised was a stand with a dark and imposing ambience. The steel cube's surface of hot-rolled steel sheets demonstrated the raw materials used for the production of the high-quality appliances. Built into this structure were two cooking modules, aimed to give visitors an insight into the level of precision used in the manufacture of the appliances. In the opposite corner, the organic zone was presented in the form of a wooden cube constructed from layered oak boards. Through the slatted panels, passers-by could catch a glimpse of the interior with its walls lined with bunches of fresh herbs and clusters of carrots. Here also, other ingredients could be stored that would be used in the culinary masterpieces prepared periodically on the stand for the delectable delight of fair goers. Flanking the two cubes was an arrangement of architectural pieces displaying Gaggenau's appliances in an abstract yet sculptural layout. In the sleek, solid furniture pieces made of black MDF, various product sequences were demonstrated, from the hobs in the central counters to the ovens in the beam-like cantilevering elements. Both the organic (wood) and the inorganic (steel) worlds successfully expressed the brand's innovative and technical side on the one hand and its emotional and involving side on the other.

⊠ Steel products were presented in the inorganic cube to demonstrate precision in manufacturing and quality management.
⊠ The minimal design of the stand focused on the product itself.
⊠ A scenography of fresh ingredients decorated the layered wooden cube.
⊠ Architectural shapes, such as blocks, bars and cubes, gave a minimalistic platform to showcase the appliances.

Gas cooktop VG 491.
Grill elettrico VR 414
Gas cooktop VG 491.
Forno cottura a gas VR 414
Electric grill VR 414.
Teppan Yaki VP 414
Induction cooktop VI 491.
Forno cottura ad induzione VI 414,
Steamert VK 414.
Forno cottura a vapore VK 414,
Teppan Yaki VP 414
Induction cooktop VI 491.
Teppan Yaki VP 414

ne

Vario 400.

Piano cottura ad induzione VI 461.
Induction cooktop VI 461.

Friggitrice elettrica VF 414.
Deep fryer VF 414.

Piano cottura a gas, wok VG 415.
Gas wok VG 415.

Piano cottura a gas VG 425.

The concept was inspired by raw materials: steel and wood

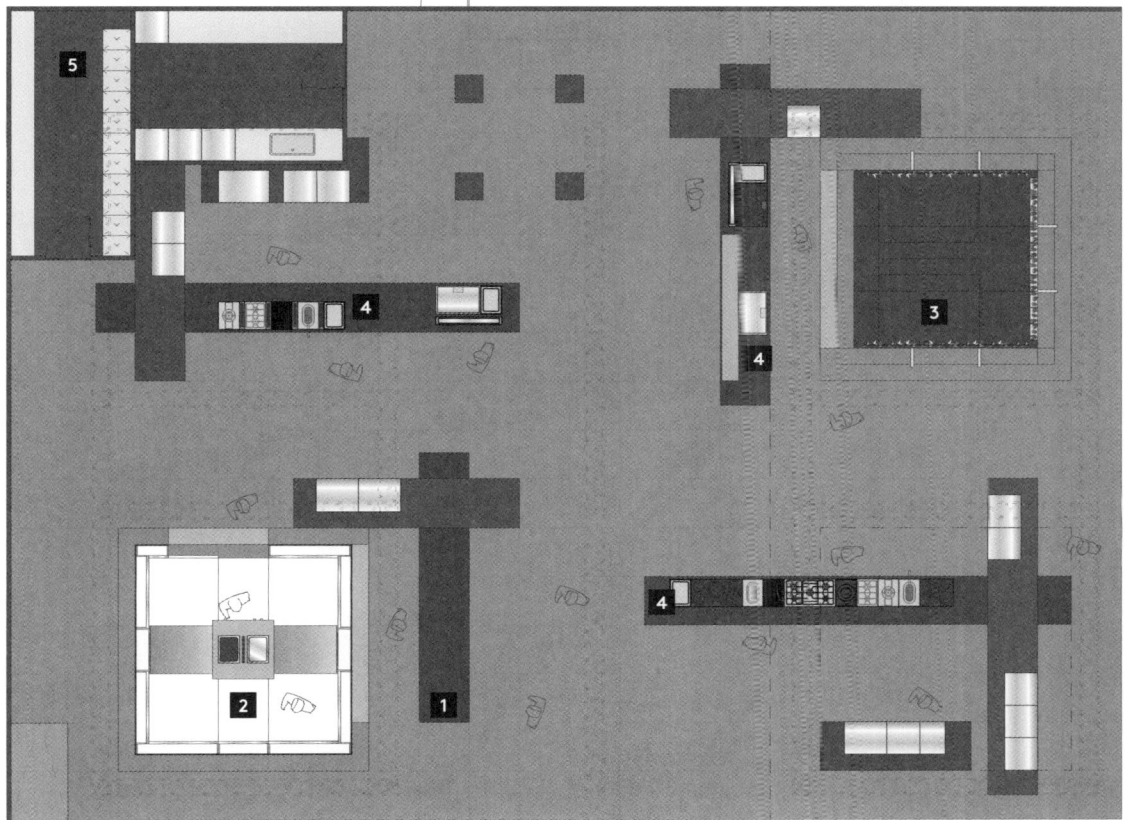

Floor plan

1 Reception
2 Steel cube
3 Wood cube
4 Product display counters
5 Storage

The sculptural essence of the stand was strengthened by the use black MDF, compatible to the surrounding materials. Within the elongated black volumes, a combination of kitchen appliances could be displayed.
Sketch indicating the positioning of spotlights as viewed from the front of the stand.

Hewlett-Packard by Standard Studio

CLEAN AND INTUITIVE TECHNOLOGY WAS POSITIONED IN A STRAIGHTFORWARD SETTING OF RADICAL SIMPLICITY.

TRADE FAIR **HP Embark**
WHERE **San Francisco, United States**
WHEN **February 2011**
DESIGNER **Standard Studio** ⊠ **p.498**
STAND CONSTRUCTORS **FNTech, SEDI**
CLIENT **Hewlett-Packard**
MARKET SECTOR **IT and telecommunications**
TOTAL FLOOR AREA **1200 m²**
PHOTOGRAPHER **David Magnusson**

At the HP Embark event in San Francisco in February 2011, Hewlett-Packard announced a new line of mobile webOS-powered products, including its innovative HP TouchPad. The aim of this event was to position Hewlett-Packard as a viable contender in the smartphone and tablet market, with Standard Studio responsible for creating an environment that was a complete departure from the company's typical events. In order to realise this, Standard worked closely with HP's own creative team. Seeking to create a space that was 'optimistic, fresh, bright, creative, fun, witty, inspiring and sophisticated', the end result was a new way of thinking about the HP brand. An ethos of radical simplicity was instilled into the space. The environment needed to be clean and intuitive, echoing HP's hardware and the new webOS technology. The design concept saw all unnecessary elements stripped away in order to create an honest and straightforward experience. The location – an industrial warehouse – was transformed for this high-tech showcase with plush carpet laid over the concrete floor and fabric drapes wrapping around the walls to soften the space. Corporate blue was the primary colour backdrop, teamed with theatrical lighting to create a dynamic atmosphere. A number of bespoke furniture pieces made from natural dark wood were designed to have simple yet sleek silhouettes. Long tables and counters were positioned so that visitors could freely engage with the technology, or else they could be guided through the webOS features by an HP expert at the specially-designed demo booths. Witty aspects were incorporated in the graphic images which lined the walls, as well as in the seating zones. Decking out one such area as a natural rock formation was certainly a quirky and fun idea, and perhaps it was also an attempt to subliminally get the message across that 'HP rocks'.

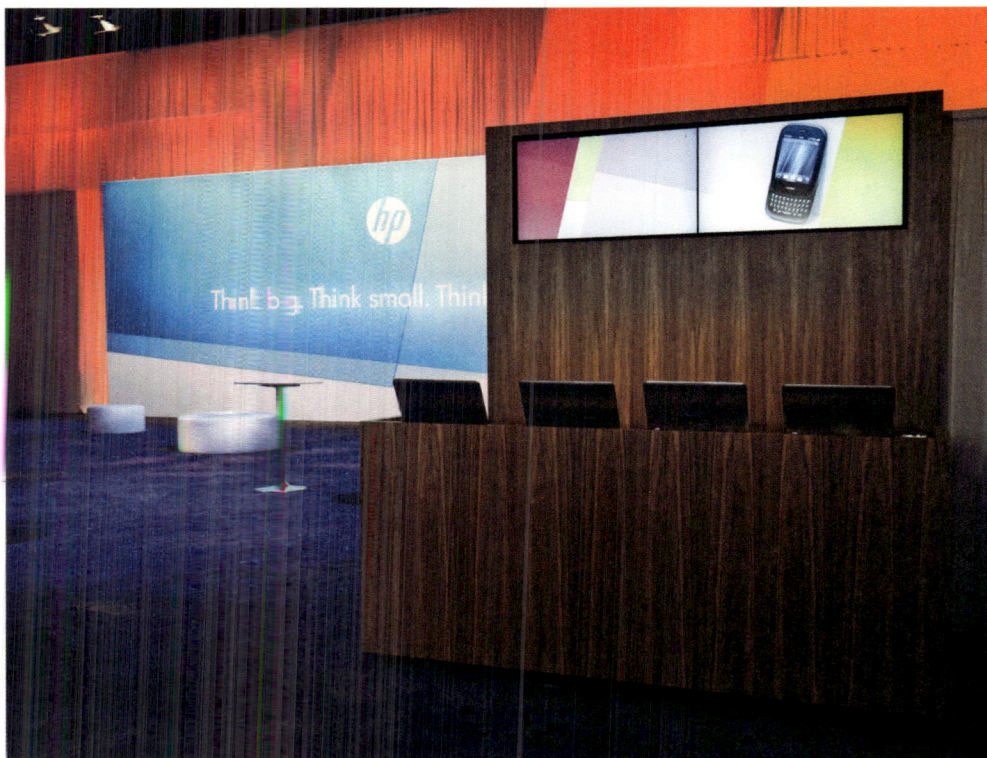

⊠ Bespoke welcome desks with integrated monitors played product teaser videos for attendees as they checked-in.
⊠ Large-scale banners lined the walls of the lounge area, bringing the mobile devices to life.

webOS, across your universe.

Demo booth drawings

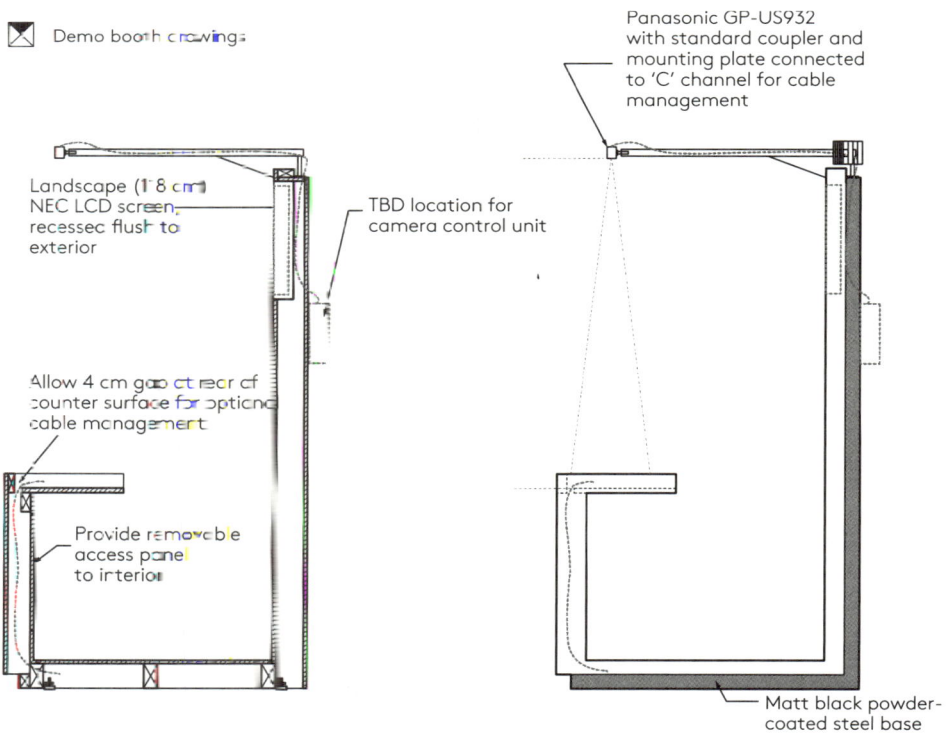

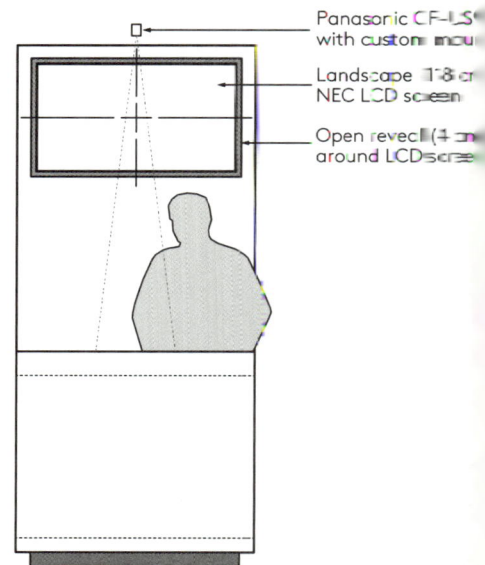

Panasonic GP-US932
with standard coupler and
mounting plate connected
to 'C' channel for cable
management

Landscape (118 cm)
NEC LCD screen,
recessed flush to
exterior

TBD location for
camera control unit

Allow 4 cm gap at rear of
counter surface for optional
cable management

Provide removable
access panel
to interior

Panasonic CF-LS
with custom mou

Landscape 118 cm
NEC LCD screen

Open reveal (4 cm
around LCD screen

Matt black powder-
coated steel base

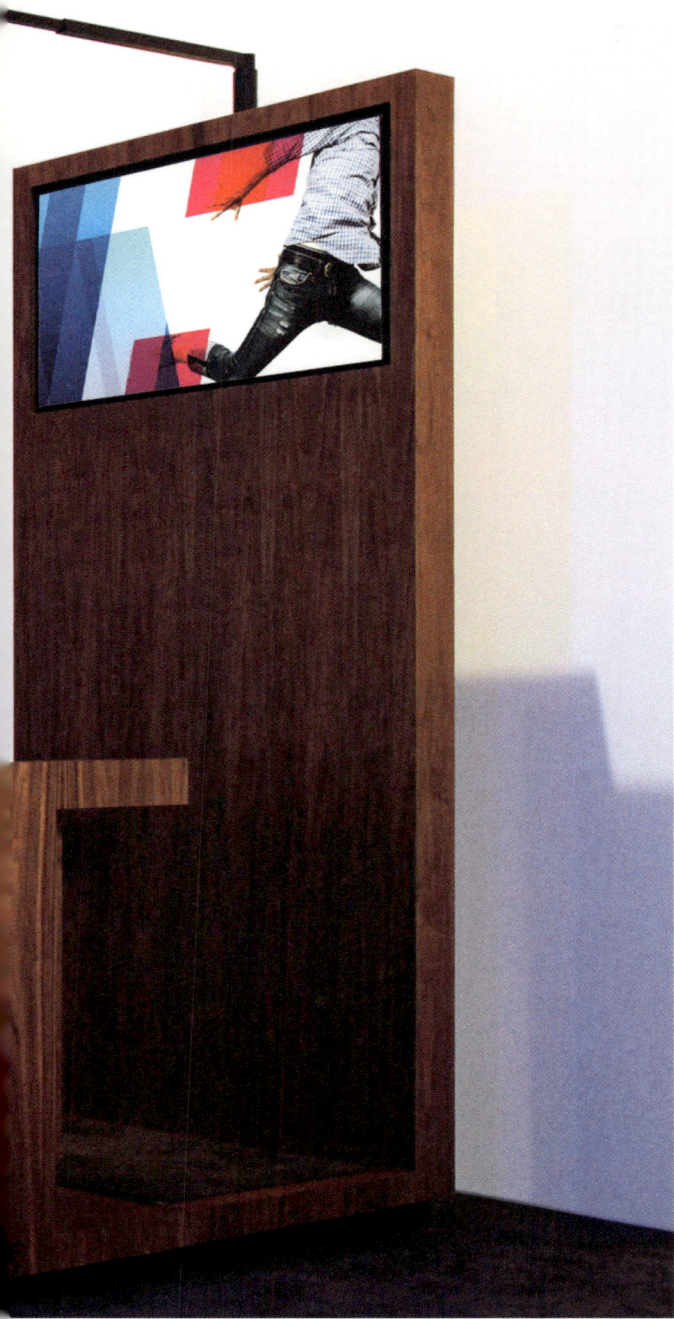

Bespoke furnishings had simple yet sleek silhouettes

Custom-made demo booths allowed real-time videos to be projected via a camera and monitor.
The overhead screen allowed many people at once to view the demo.

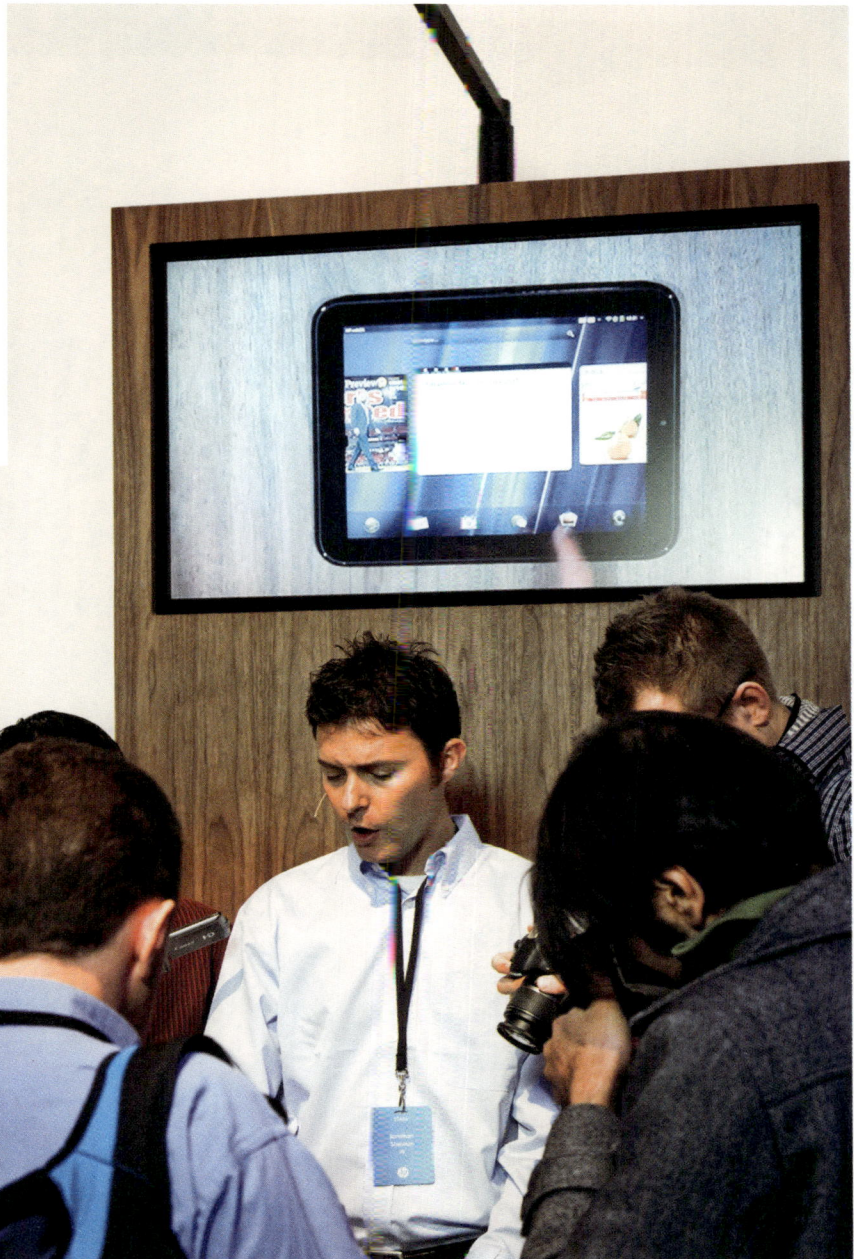

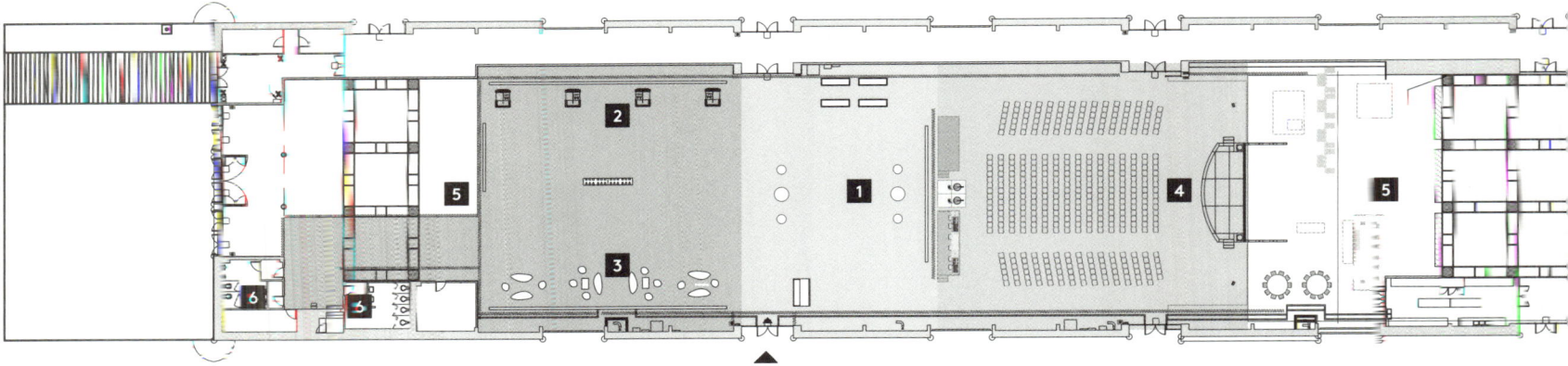

◩ Floor plan

1   Registration lounge
2   Product showcase
3   Seating area
4   Auditorium
5   Back of house
6   Lavatories

☒ Dark wood panelling was also used to frame the keynote presentation area.
☒ The product bar allowed mobile devices to be tethered and powered while still being fully accessible to visitors.
☒ Fair goers were ensured a hands-on experience testing out the products.
☒ Renderings of the proposed layout within the warehouse setting.

An ethos of radical simplicity was instilled in the space

Intel by 2LK Design

A WAVE OF VIBRANT ILLUMINATION – ROLLING OVER AN INTERACTIVE WORLD OF TECHNOLOGY AND CONNECTIVITY.

The Intel Corporation used its annual appearance at CES, the world's pre-eminent consumer electronics show, to launch the Ultrabook™. Also promoted was the Intel Technology used in smartphones, tablets and a variety of other innovation proof points, such as in the automotive and retail industries. Working with the Intel brand values, its Die'namic signature style and the Intel theme for the show 'Connect to Life', 2LK Design created this flagship Intel exhibit. Portraying the theme as a bold, organic form, the key element of the design was 'The Wave'. Concurrently a wall, ceiling and display surface, this eye-catching structure dominated the booth and created a unique environment to house the display and demonstration areas. The structure demanded visitors' attention and was highly visible from all approaches. Its constantly-changing theatrical lighting and projected interactive 'eco system' images became the talking point of the show, visually connecting Intel with visitors as they entered the exhibition hall. A key feature was 'The Spotlight' presentation/storytelling space, where invited guests from all walks of life could share their passion for how Intel Technology enabled them to excel. This area was adjacent to the Ultrabook™ feature, a combination of bar-height counters and sculptural and vertical screens that allowed visitors to experience the new product at first hand. 'Flower beds', consisting of fibre optic grass and Intel microprocessor 'flowers', ran through both these spaces creating a magical environment and constantly connecting back to Intel Technology. The demonstration areas flanked these central features. The majority of the demo stations were designed to be 'visually porous', minimising their architectural impact whilst maximising their workability as interactive spaces. The meeting and hospitality spaces were hidden and enveloped by 'The Wave', which completes this unique environment.

TRADE FAIR **CES**
WHERE **Las Vegas, United States**
WHEN **January 2012**
DESIGNER **2LK Design** ⊠ p.488
STAND CONSTRUCTOR **The Taylor Group**
CLIENT **Intel Corporation**
MARKET SECTOR **IT and telecommunications**
TOTAL FLOOR AREA **1115 m²**
PHOTOGRAPHER **Line 8 Photography (Michel Guyon)**

⊠ 'The Spotlight' was a storytelling zone where special guests shared their passion for Intel technology.

⊠ The demo stations were minimised structures enveloped under the illuminated canopy.

⊠ The feature wall was constructed from a white soft-knit fabric stretched over a tubular steel frame.

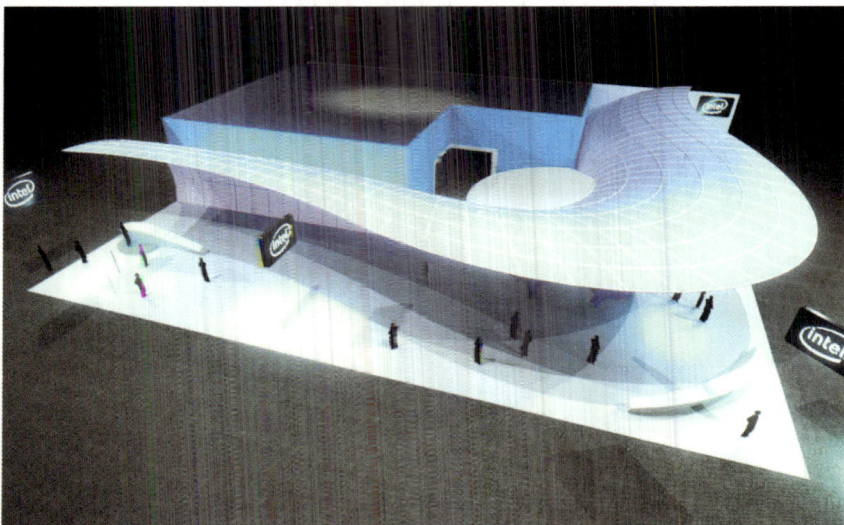

⊠ Floor plan

1 Feature product showcase
2 Interactive modules
3 Product presentations
4 Demo area
5 Audience arena
6 Stage
7 VIP reception
8 Hospitality area
9 Storage

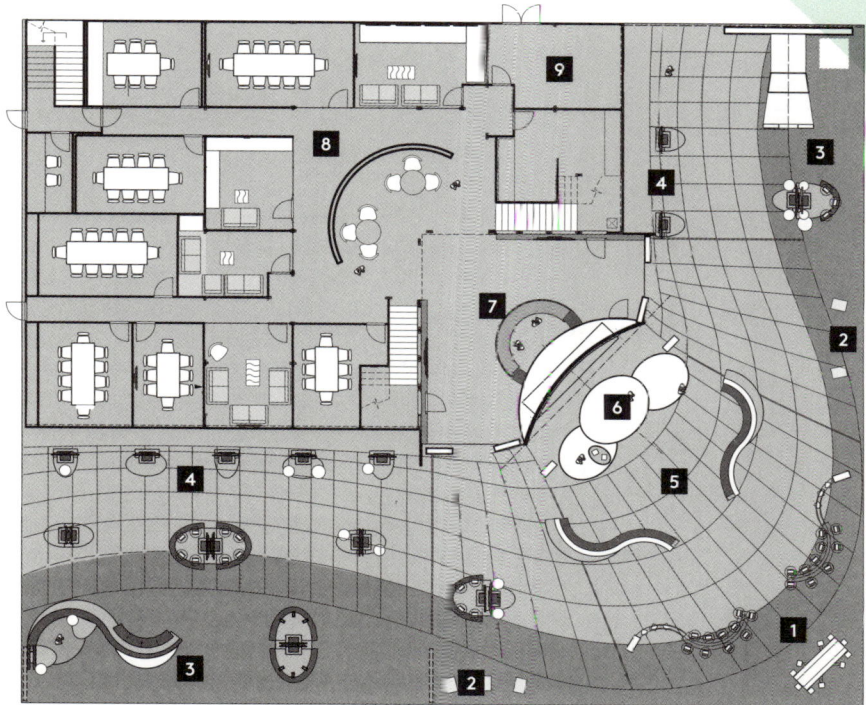

Theatrical lighting was used with projected 'eco system' images

Curvaceous interactive stations allowed visitors to create their own virtual life-forms.
Renderings showing how the idea of 'The Wave' was developed.
The colourful structure dominated the space, rising up above the crowded exhibition environment.

Priva by Confetti

A LIVING AND BREATHING STAND WAS CRAFTED AS A FRESH AND MODERN MICROCLIMATE FOR AUTOMATED PROCESS CONTROL.

Priva works in the field of automated climate and process control in the horticultural and building intelligence markets. Ready for the roll out of its new corporate identity, the firm teamed up with the design studio Confetti to create a new stand for VSK 2012. The brief called for a modern and captivating presence, with an additional requirement that the booth should be reusable and applicable to future international trade shows. The client states that its products are 'at the heart of living and working environments' and the Confetti team, led by designer Janne Koppenaal, was inspired by the heartbeat graphic that can be seen in the Priva branding. Using a white base and corporate blue LED lighting for maximal reflection to illuminate the space, a booth was created that was a breath of fresh air in the busy trade fair environment. In one aspect of the stand, an imposing framework was constructed with fabric stretched overhead. On the fabric was printed images of a blue sky with white fluffy clouds, beneath which visitors could stand whilst they checked out the products or discussed particulars with Priva staff. The environment felt very 'alive' thanks also to the white wooden crates suspended at different heights that were planted with real foliage with ivy leaves trailing over the sides. Amidst this setting, visitors could also relax on the wooden seats which appeared to hang from rope, as if they were swings in a garden. A natural air was imbued throughout the stand, not only due to the surrounding plant life, but also the bamboo flooring and oak details which contrasted, as well as complemented, the contemporary design and high-tech products. Display modules were custom-made for the project, many of which were made from wood including the information desk with blue lighting emanating from between each of the oak planks.

TRADE FAIR VSK
WHERE February 2012
WHEN Utrecht, the Netherlands
DESIGNER Confetti ☒ p.490
STAND CONSTRUCTOR Confetti
CLIENT Priva
MARKET SECTOR Control systems technol...
TOTAL FLOOR AREA 308 m²
PHOTOGRAPHER Hans Zijffers

☒ Plant life was a key decorative aspect positioned around the booth.
☒ The blue sky over the stand added to its fresh and airy feel.
☒ Each wooden plank appeared to float on a bed of blue light.
☒ The brand's heartbeat graphic was translated into a 3D wooden structure.

Sony 3D World by FreeState

Sony showcased its global offerings in 3D technology within an impressive '3D world' at the consumer electronics trade fair IFA in 2010. For the design of its presentation, the company commissioned FreeState calling for an engaging and inspiring brand experience. The design studio answered the brief with an exciting and immersive destination. Inspiration came from the historic streets of 16th-century Rome: a place expertly woven with the intensity and focus of medieval streets that gave way to the wonder and awe of St Peter's Square. Such a historic starting point may seem out-of-sync with Sony's futuristic 3D world but the aim was to draw on some important learning points from these classical clues, albeit updated to accommodate the fluidity of today's technology-driven culture. The idea was to create a curious pull for visitors, enticing them around corners and playfully engaging them in a game of discovery. At the fair in Berlin, FreeState's custom-designed streets within the vast space were home to thousands of Sony's most cutting-edge technologies and visitors could wander around this world with their senses constantly bombarded. Reverberating from the centre of the stand's very own 21st-century piazza was a sonic heartbeat thanks to the musical performances which were hosted throughout the duration of the fair. In this centre courtyard, visitors had plenty of space to lounge on the bespoke furniture and witness screenings specially prepared to demonstrate the capabilities of the entire 3D-production process. Leading off from the central hub were promenades and distinct zones where visitors could have hands-on experience of the latest games and high-tech activities. The steel framework construction of the stand was decorated with spray-painted MDF and Plexiglas in a branded, colourful palette to complement the fun, lively energy of the presentation.

> VISITORS WERE IMMERSED IN A FUTURISTIC WORLD OF ENTERTAINMENT WHEN THEY STEPPED INTO THIS 3D SPECTACLE OF CUTTING-EDGE TECHNOLOGIES.

TRADE FAIR IFA
WHERE Berlin, Germany
WHEN September 2010
DESIGNER FreeState ☒ p.492
STAND CONSTRUCTORS Studio Babelsberg, Limelight, Gielissen
CLIENT Sony
MARKET SECTOR Consumer electronics
TOTAL FLOOR AREA 6063 m²
PHOTOGRAPHER James McCauley

☒ Fair goers were enticed along wide walkways, following the pulsating beat
☒ Hands-on experiences awaited visitors in the gaming zones, emblazoned with bold, colourful graphics.
☒ The 30-m-long projection screen illuminated the central courtyard.

Sony Connected World by FreeState

MIXING MULTI-SENSORY EXPERIENCES WITH ORDER AND SYMMETRY WAS VITAL IN ORDER TO COHERENTLY PRESENT AN INTERCONNECTED WORLD OF HIGH-TECH PRODUCTS.

TRADE FAIR **IFA**
WHERE **Berlin, Germany**
WHEN **September 2011**
DESIGNER **FreeState** ⊠ **p.492**
STAND CONSTRUCTORS **Studio Babelsberg, Limelight, Gielissen**
CLIENT **Sony**
MARKET SECTOR **Consumer electronics**
TOTAL FLOOR AREA **6063 m²**
PHOTOGRAPHER **James McCauley**

At the consumer electronics fair IFA in 2011, Sony was to launch a number of key new products and commissioned FreeState to design its stand – the largest at the fair covering an area of over 6000 m² – for the fourth year in succession. The space needed to showcase the converging complexity of the client's content, online services and integrated projects in such a way as to be understood immediately from the perspective of all the fair goers. For the creative team, the task of providing visitors to the Sony stand with a cogent, multi-sensory experience, with all the implied audio-visual complexities, required a design that was as simple as it was organised. Ordered and symmetrical, the realised stand design took inspiration from the Plaça Reial in Barcelona. The vast space of this interconnected world, with its 7.5 km of cabling throughout, was a series of squares within squares which had a total of six entrances. The outer courtyard was broken into rows of clearly laid-out avenues with distinct content categories, all of which were spaces in themselves but combined to lead towards the inner court. This was a curtained-off garden of electronic delights, with full-height backlit screens – or clouds – which were used to portray dynamic images, messages and pulses of content. Behind the scenes, much like Barcelona's secret passageways, there was a restaurant hidden from view along with 38 meeting rooms. In the central area, illumination was an important element in setting the atmosphere: the light show was synchronised with an accompanying soundtrack. Many of the stand's more secluded areas had a quieter ambience and so for visitors to experience a successful transition from the randomised pockets of activity, a perfect cohesion of loud versus quiet was called for within the vast shell of the presentation.

⊠ In the outer courtyard avenues, visitors were assured a content-rich experience.
⊠ The inner garden of electronic delights showcased the convergence of content, service and device.
⊠ The space was an ensemble of live happenings, with over 2000 interactive products displayed throughout.

FREESTATE

INTS
PROD

RIOR
JCTS

Artek by
Meiré und Meiré

FINNISH FURNITURE STAGED ON A
BRIGHT PLATFORM WITH A SIMPLE
SCANDINAVIAN AESTHETIC.

Artek has presented its vision of connecting modern visual arts, rational furniture production and popular education steadily over the years, ever since its foundation in Finland in 1935. This has made the company an omnipresent opinion leader among the creative class of Nordic design. Brand agency Meiré und Meiré – responsible for the design of the Artek stand at the 2012 furniture fair in Milan – wanted to encapsulate this vision. In the Finnish firm's presentation, the design team instilled a sense of gentle happiness.

The concept was a charming celebration of the everyday object that would not overpower fair goers. The completed stand was open, friendly and welcoming, with a light touch. By reflecting upcoming fashion trends such as the palette of fresh colours, the design referenced Artek's core values through accessible and timeless materials in a contemporary way. The uncomplicated architecture merged into a collaged storytelling, which in turn encapsulated an entertaining dialogue and a bold statement. The sculptural simplicity complemented the brand's furniture designs and gave each piece a coordinated staging – from the central zone at the front of the stand to the raised podiums and the staircase that led visitors to an elevated area at the back of the booth. Simple geometric, coloured lines on the floor demarcated the different product families and highlighted product placements. The client's logo adorned each wall of the stand, tying the architecture together succinctly through chromatic relationships. The whole structure was made out of birch plywood except for a yellow handrail, which sliced the scene in two. Intensifying the colour impulse was the storage room painted entirely yellow, which passers-by could glimpse through the open door.

TRADE FAIR Salone Internazionale del Mob
WHERE Milan, Italy
WHEN April 2012
DESIGNER Meiré und Meiré ⊠ p.495
STAND CONSTRUCTOR Kubix
CLIENT Artek
MARKET SECTOR Furniture
TOTAL FLOOR AREA 150 m²
PHOTOGRAPHER Achim Hatzius

⊠ Colour played an important role in concept, emphasising the products t were displayed.
⊠ The installation was envisioned 'classics with a contemporary twist'.
⊠ The booth design appeared to be from one mould, with all the flo walls, platforms and counters mad birch plywood.

Autoban
by Autoban

SOLID LUXURY
IN A TEMPORARY
EXHIBITION SPACE.

Autoban exhibited the first of a series of four unique interactive installations at the International Contemporary Furniture Fair (ICFF) in May 2012. The Istanbul-based architecture, interior and product design studio showcased its furniture range and launched four new products at the fair. The installation, specifically designed by the brand for the presentation in New York, spread over 100 m² and consisted of a series of interconnected heptagonal modules. Accessible from three sides, the light and airy stand featured a spatial organisation that promoted a sense of discovery as fair goers wandered around. A white plastic framework formed four 'rooms' with open sides, and white fabric panels with monochromatic Autoban imagery created the backdrop to the booth. The space had a temporary, tent-like feel but with a solid and luxurious interior thanks to the designer products. New products launched at the event included the Throne Series, consisting of a bar stool, a lounge chair and a sofa. The pieces combined traditional and contemporary elements with materials such as rattan, walnut, oak, leather and fabric. Metallic glints also caught the eyes of passers-by from another new product, the Flying Spider pendant lamp, based on Autoban's iconic Spider lamp, available in gold-plated or chrome-plated steel. The new products were exhibited coherently alongside existing items from the Autoban range, including the award-winning Suite Bed with its dramatic wraparound timber headboard.

TRADE FAIR **ICFF**
WHERE **New York, United States**
WHEN **May 2012**
DESIGNER **Autoban** ☒ **p.489**
STAND CONSTRUCTOR **De La Espada**
CLIENT **Autoban**
MARKET SECTOR **Furniture**
TOTAL FLOOR AREA **100 m²**
PHOTOGRAPHER **De La Espada**

☒ The four modules were interconnected, allowing visitors to freely wander from one side to the other.
☒ Geometric shapes made up the stand architecture, as well as the network of white lines on the floor.
☒ The white temporary space had a touch of golden glamour.

blomus by Ueberholz

A PRISTINE WHITE PRESENTATION OF
DESIGNER HOME WARE PRODUCTS
PORTRAYING 'PURE LIFE'.

During 2010, the design company blomus revealed to the world its new corporate branding, with the 'pure life' tagline coined to encapsulate the firm's commitment to creating lifestyle products of timeless beauty inspired by the natural world. For Ambiente 2011, the brand's philosophy – underpinned by solid materials, clear lines and intuitive communication – was translated into a spatial experience by the German studio Ueberholz. The concept for the booth was to create a presentation that had an authentic radiance, which left visitors experiencing 'pure life' with all their senses. The design consisted of semi-transparent, as well as opaque and white surfaces, that structured the space and provided a platform on which to play with light, shade and projections. Large pendant lampshade-like mobiles with dynamic shadow art portraying key products attracted people's attention from across the exhibition hall. Distinct product scenarios akin to shop windows were positioned around the periphery of the stand, viewable to passers-by. The booth's boundary was interrupted by openings that were indicated by large grey floor tiles that led visitors to the interior of the presentation, past some of the 700 home ware products on show. Communication zones afforded room for exhibition talks and gave direct visual contact between the themed environments. The products were not only a key part of the setting, but also actively integrated into the concept. They were used in the dedicated hospitality area at one end of the stand for serving food and drinks, thus giving fair goers the ultimate experience of using the products first hand.

TRADE FAIR Ambiente
WHERE Frankfurt, Germany
WHEN February 2011
DESIGNER Ueberholz ☒ p.499
STAND CONSTRUCTOR Ueberholz
CLIENT blomus
MARKET SECTOR Home ware products
TOTAL FLOOR AREA 336 m²
PHOTOGRAPHER Frank Dora

☒ Fresh green foliage on the stand ties with the natural 'pure life' theme.
☒ Many of the featured ranges were displayed as concise collections.
☒ Beneath each giant lampshade was a singular business segment.

Platforms for playing with light, shadows and projections

☒ The light mobiles, with their dynamic 2D shadow art of key products, attracted the attention of fair goers.
☒ Products were positioned along the length of the stand for visitors to try out.
☒ Meeting areas were available at one end of the booth.
☒ Strips of fabric panelling were used to create the booth's boundary.

Brunner Milan 2011 by Ippolito Fleitz Group

A COLOURFUL AND ACROBATIC ARRAY
OF SUSPENDED CHAIRS EMPHASISED
THE LIGHTWEIGHT CHARACTER OF
A NEW ITEM OF FURNITURE.

For furniture manufacturer Brunner's presentation at the Milan Furniture Fair in 2011, the company sought to establish a presence in the design sector with the launch of its new 'twin' plastic chair. Ippolito Fleitz Group, the studio behind the concept for the Brunner stand, placed the lightweight and weather-resistant chair at the heart of the presentation. The result: a whole world constructed around the slogan 'See/Reflect/Act', in which the furniture was not simply a display item but a vibrant protagonist in a scene that resembled an art installation. An acrobatic display of the colourful chairs set in front of curved walls faced with mirrored, polystyrene shingles created a kaleidoscopic effect. The display began with a loose grouping of different 'twin' models on the right of the entrance to the stand. A single chair from the midst of this group was elevated to eye level, and this formed the starting point for a dynamic whirl made up of dozens of chairs suspended in a cloud above the visitors' heads. These chairs then appeared to execute a backwards somersault in which each adjacent section was rotated through 45 degrees. Visitors could thus view the chairs from every conceivable angle in the overhead swarm. The surrounding mirrors added dramatic impact to the scene, seemingly increasing the already large number of chairs. Their colourful palette cascaded down the walls, mixing with the whole plethora of reflections. The honeycomb structure of the mirrored tiles shattered the reflected images of both chairs and visitors into pieces, rendering individual forms unrecognisable and recomposing them into a pixellated mosaic of colour. Islands of white artificial grass, which formed surfaces for key displays as well as lounge chairs towards the back of the space, underscored the stand's non-linear layout. This area doubled as a meeting point furnished with other Brunner products.

The stand became a stage, wholly encapsulating visitors and drawing them into the spatial experience.
The shiny walls reflected colourful hues of the vibrant product display.

TRADE FAIR Salone Internazionale del Mo
WHERE Milan, Italy
WHEN April 2011
DESIGNER Ippolito Fleitz Group ✉ p.493
STAND CONSTRUCTOR Hospes Team
CLIENT Brunner
MARKET SECTOR Furniture
TOTAL FLOOR AREA 70 m²
PHOTOGRAPHER Thomas Libis

Brunner Milan 2012 by Ippolito Fleitz Group

A TEXT-BASED LANDSCAPE SPELT THE WORDS OF A STORYLINE AND SET THE SCENE FOR NEW FURNITURE PRODUCTS.

The Milan Furniture Fair in 2012 saw the unveiling of not one but two new products from furniture manufacturer Brunner: its 'hoc' stool and its 'plot' modular seating system. Ippolito Fleitz Group was commissioned to create a presentation installation, which needed to offer an intense spatial experience that showcased Brunner's latest products in a contemporary setting. Inspiration for the concept came from the 'plot' system itself, with the intertwining words of story as a key visual element of the design. From a distance, the black and white backdrop of the booth seemed just that: a perfect setting for the seating products with their colourful yet muted hues. The eye-catching space immediately drew passers-by inside to test the furniture. It was only on closer inspection that the backdrop revealed itself as a textual narrative that took fair goers on a poetic voyage of discovery and inspired them to stop and linger awhile. The configuration of seating elements positioned at different heights resulted in an orthogonal landscape framed by black walls. White plastic letters – once used in information boards that have all but vanished from hotel lobbies, bars, airports and conference facilities – set in black, grooved panelling created associative figures and scenarios. Further scrutiny revealed that the imagery was composed of lines of text, from descriptions of the new products to sequences of dialogue, song lyrics, quotations and meditations, all related to the theme of sitting. The presented scenario was succinctly set off by the brightly illuminated 'sky' of white, contoured textile fins suspended overhead. The entire scene conjured up a fantastic world, transforming the experience of testing new products at an exhibition into a contemplative moment of relaxation.

The simple space was decorated with a total of 54,000 white plastic letters.
Amidst images and text based on the theme of sitting, one product tumbles from the hand of God.
The contoured panes of fabric gauze on the ceiling alluded to clouds.

TRADE FAIR **Salone Internazionale del Mobile**
WHERE **Milan, Italy**
WHEN **April 2012**
DESIGNER **Ippolito Fleitz Group** ⊠ **p.493**
STAND CONSTRUCTOR **Hospes Team**
CLIENT **Brunner**
MARKET SECTOR **Furniture**
TOTAL FLOOR AREA **90 m²**
PHOTOGRAPHERS **Francesco Di Loreto, Ippolito Fleitz Group**

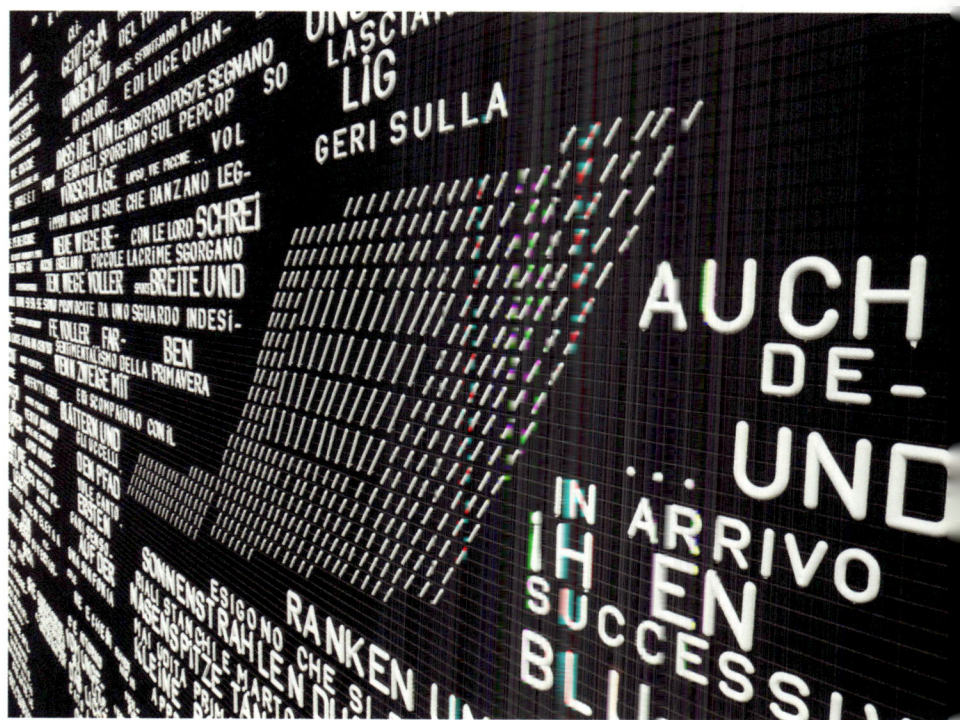

THE TREES ARE GOD'S GREAT ALPHABET: WITH THEM HE WRITES IN SHINING GREEN ACROSS THE WORLD HIS THOUGHTS SERENE. - LEONORA SPEYER
OF ALL THE WONDERS OF NATURE, A TREE IN SUMMER IS PERHAPS THE MOST REMARKABLE
TREES ARE YOUR BEST ANTIQUES. ALEXANDER SMITH
FOR IN THE TRUE NATURE OF THINGS, IF WE RIGHTLY CONSIDER, EVERY GREEN TREE IS FAR MORE GLORIOUS THAN IF IT WERE MADE OF GOLD AND SILVER.
THE TREES THAT HAVE IT IN THEIR PENT UP BUDS TO DARKEN NATURE AND BE SUMMER WOODS ROBERT FROST
SCHLAUCHBOOT
UNA CUNETTA SCAVATA
SEDIA NOIOSA IN UNA SALA
LEGNO DI QUERCIA
UN CLUB FINOMATO: SIT DOWN YOUNG
VECCHIO: THE DOG SITS ON THE TUCKER-
UNA CASA DA TEA UN APPUNTAMENTO AL BUIO:
CHIARO IN LEGNO DI PINO AL TAVOLO DELLA CUCINA
SOTTOBOSCO DINANZI A UN
BELLO IN UNA TAVERNA
BELLO DA BAR TREMEN-
ROSA CON
CHINA IN LEGNO
SELVAGGIO SUL TERRENO
DON'T SIT DOWN VELLUTA-
LIAM SITS IN AVALON POLTRON-
SOLE: I'M GONNA SIT ON THE PORCH SEDIA
THE RIVERSIDE. PICCOLA POLTRONA CUBO
HOC

Campana by Stefan Zwicky

DESIGNER FURNITURE ITEMS SHOWCASED AS IF THEY WERE ARTWORKS IN A SCULPTURE PARK.

The international home and furniture exhibition Neue Räume is an annual event in Zurich. For the 2011 show, the organisers commissioned Stefan Zwicky to present the work of Fernando and Humberto Campana in a modest-sized space. The central presentation within the fair was dedicated to 'green design', with the work of the Brazilian sibling duo constituting a special attraction. The work that has come out of the Campana studio since the 1980s has often been of an experimental slant, such as the projects for Alessi, Oluce and Corsi Design Factory. It was the duo's long-standing work with Italian furniture manufacturer Edra, however, that first attracted attention on a larger scale. The Campana brothers often work with nature-oriented or recycled materials, such as old wood, coconut fibres, wire, waste fabric or plastic tubing, and the Stefan Zwicky design team decided to feature these aspects in the Neue Räume presentation, the geometry and structure of which was inspired by the sculpture park next to Aldo van Eyck's sculpture pavilion in Arnhem, the Netherlands. The rectangular stand measured 14 x 7 m and was divided into five distinct sections along its length of equal dimensions but with differently positioned openings in the interior walls, creating a route for visitors past the expressive items on display. This gave the interior a clear-cut structure and delineated the space in a way that gave each product a clearly defined platform to fully capture its forms and features. These were also emphasised thanks to the mirror-like quality of the material applied to the dividing surfaces inside and at the end walls of the space. Draped from the ceiling, the partition elements were made of 5-m-long lengths of synthetic gauze with metallic film that provided animated reflections of the furniture and fair goers alike.

TRADE FAIR Neue Räume
WHERE Zurich, Switzerland
WHEN November 2011
DESIGNER Stefan Zwicky ▷ p.495
STAND CONSTRUCTOR Strickler Reklame
CLIENT Neue Räume
MARKET SECTOR Furniture
TOTAL FLOOR AREA 48 m²
PHOTOGRAPHERS Michael Sieber, Christine Wolf, Stefan Zwicky

The gauze material allowed visitors a tempting glimpse of the product displays, enticing them to step inside.
The draped mirrored foil placed around the booth created interesting and distorted reflections.

Floor plan

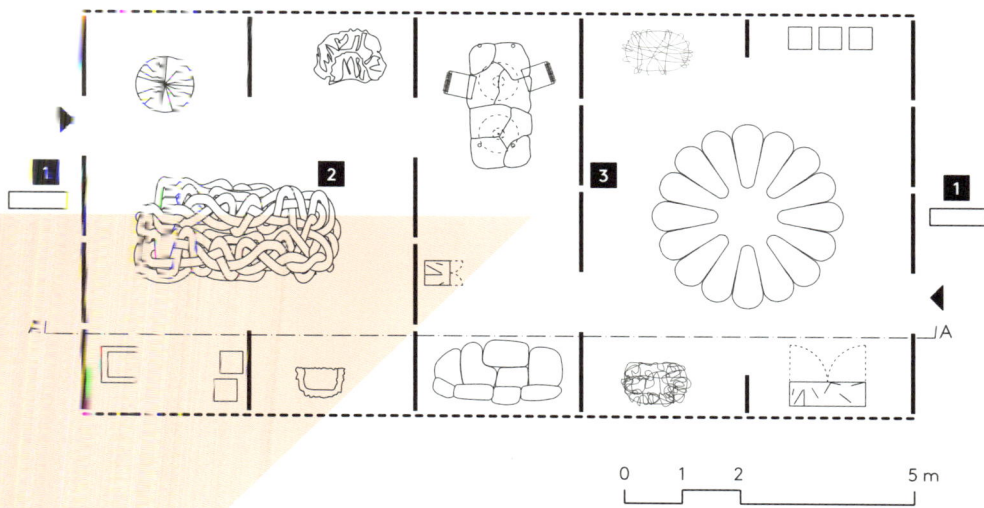

1   Signage graphic
2   Product presentation
3   Dividing wall

Section A

A clearly defined platform to capture forms and features

The exhibition's geometry and structure was inspired by a sculpture park.
The metallic foil acted as a mirror giving the impression there were two Favela Chairs on display.
Every wall surface treatment in the stand served to distort reality.

INTERIOR PRODUCTS

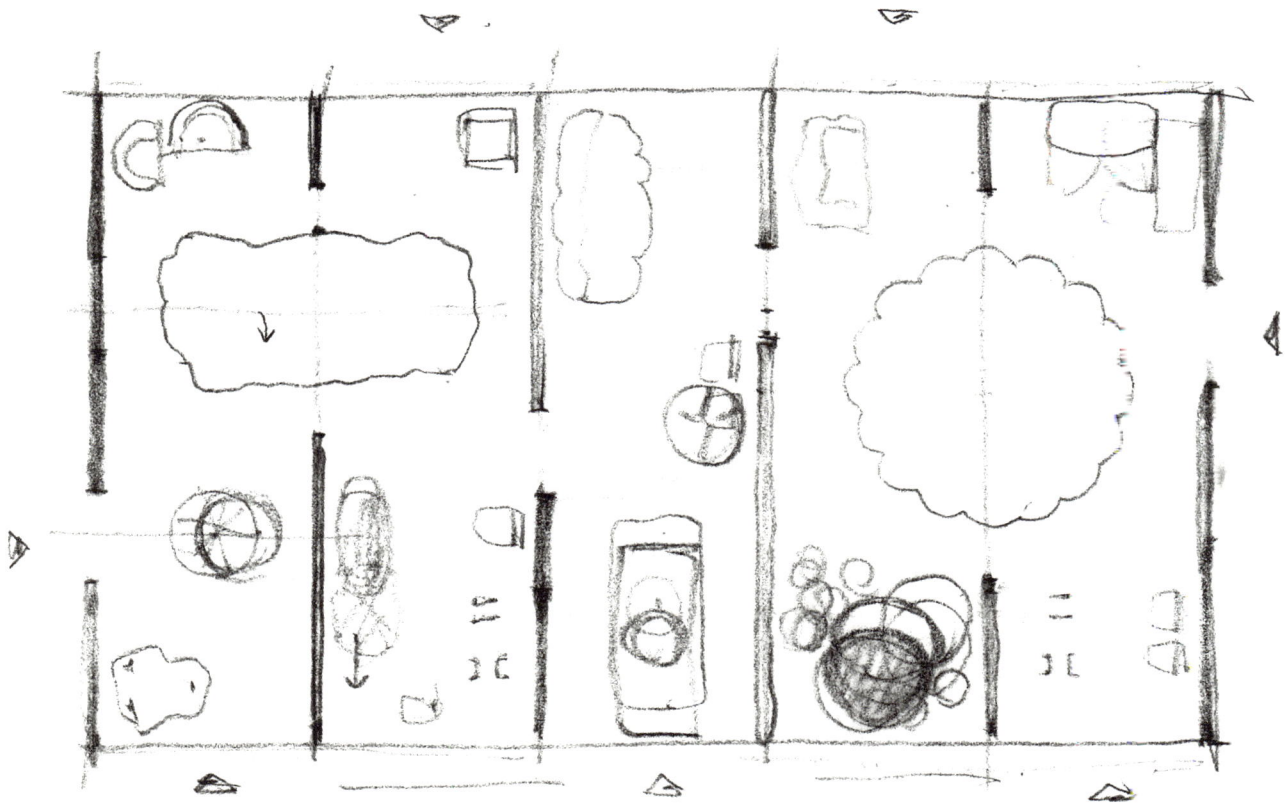

- Draped from the ceiling were 6-m lengths of the metallic material.
- Initial sketch of the design indicating the route that visitors might take through the stand.
- The floor was covered with a luxurious white wool carpet.
- The materiality of the concept was in keeping with the Campana approach.

Lengths of metallic film provided animated reflections

Das Haus by Doshi Levien

DEFINING THE IMAGE AND VISION OF A HOME BY DRAWING ON A FRAGMENTED COLLAGE OF MEMORIES, BOTH REAL AND IMAGINED.

The design team Doshi Levien was responsible for the feature presentation at imm cologne 2012. As guests of honour, Nipa Doshi and Jonathan Levien were invited by the organisers of the international furniture fair to design 'Das Haus – Interiors on Stage'. The imm creative director Dick Spierenburg, worked with the concept of Frank A Reinhardt (Far Consulting), which focused on creating an artificial living situation within the trade fair: in effect, a very public yet very personal living space. The project gave the designers a chance to formulate a creative statement on modern interior culture using up-to-the-minute products. Doshi Levien realised their own individual and lively home under narrowly defined architectural conditions. In every part of the house, different areas connected with one another and redefined what they could be and how they could be used. The designers experimented with colours and materials, integrating water and nature into the living area and putting technologies old and new to the test as models for a sustainable household. All the elements of the presentation complemented one another to form a harmonious whole – from the furniture, multimedia, bathroom fixtures and kitchen design to the solid open-structure and transparent walls of the living spaces. Even artistic elements seemed like an integral part of the architecture. A multilayered glass wall by London graphic design studio Pony, for instance, doubled as privacy screening for the kitchen as well as a projection surface for overlapping pictures of the house, symbols and reminiscences of domestic life. The furniture designed specifically for the project by Doshi Levien referenced both classic Western design traditions and elements of Indian culture, reconciling formal opposites and different functions. The platform also displayed something that could be described as humorous distance.

TRADE FAIR imm cologne
WHERE Cologne, Germany
WHEN January 2012
DESIGNER Doshi Levien ☒ p.191
STAND CONSTRUCTORS Koelnmesse, Schnaitt International-Messe- und Ladenbau
CLIENT Koelnmesse
MARKET SECTOR Furniture
TOTAL FLOOR AREA 80 m²
PHOTOGRAPHER Constantin Meyer

☒ The stand's low facade allowed visitors to catch glimpses of the colourful interior.
☒ The project manager for Das Haus was Rüdiger Sprave (Koelnmesse).

A creative statement on modern interior culture

The spaces were interconnected: top sketch shows one perspective of strip. Charpoy daybed and the ph indicates its proximity to the bedroom. Fair goers could get an impression what it would be like to live in suc networked and multi-faceted space.

Focused on an artificial living situation within the trade fair

Design São Paulo by Atelier Marko Brajovic

THE DOME-SHAPED BUILDING CREATED AN ARCHITECTURAL ENVELOPE TO HOUSE A DESIGN CITY WITH A TRANSPARENT URBAN SPRAWL.

Design São Paulo Salon is a commercial and cultural fair that positions the Brazilian city of São Paulo on the major international design calendar. The inaugural event was held in 2011 in the Oca building, the distinctive dome-shaped structure in Ibirapuera Park, designed by Oscar Niemeyer in the 1950s. Atelier Marko Brajovic was commissioned to design the architecture of the fair. In the research phase of the project, a need was identified to address some basic issues of a classical 'spartan' set-up. It was decided that the fair's spatial organisation needed a new type of urbanism with some key requirements. It had to be a permeable, democratic and adaptable space that highlighted encounters, surprises and coincidences. And it had to stimulate an 'aesthetic and multi-sensorial experience'. The main concept of the project was based on the paradigm of 'the city' and, in particular, the city that is not defined by a master plan but by parameters of relations between the functions, the public, and the architectural envelope of the building. The layout included private and semi-private spaces that were articulated as piazzas and streets, organising the functions of the fair and spontaneous circulation through the event. The city (i.e. the urbanism of the fair) was complex, articulated and sensual: it surrounded the public as a sensorial experience of contents and forms, relating the whole scenography to the visitors through an intimate and emphatic journey. The city's 'houses' (the stands of the fair) boasted a deformed geometry derived from a classical house paradigm, with a simple and stripped-down decor of natural wood and bare light bulbs. The different stands were not sharply separated from one another. Instead, exhibitors could communicate with fair goers through the simple windows cut out of the walls and through the corner openings of the stands, thereby relating their products to one another and to the 'public spaces' of the fair.

TRADE FAIR Design São Paulo Salon
WHERE São Paulo, Brazil
WHEN June 2011
DESIGNER Atelier Marko Brajovic ☒ p.489
STAND CONSTRUCTOR Ponto Sec
CLIENT Luminosidade
MARKET SECTOR Furniture
TOTAL FLOOR AREA 2250 m²
PHOTOGRAPHER Bruno Fernandes

☒ Outside on the Oca facade, blue LED lighting was evident.
☒ The vertical ramp acted as a street, connecting the various levels of 'the city'.
☒ Each stand was unique mutation of a 'house', adapted to the product exhibition format.

ATELIER MARKO BRAJOVIC

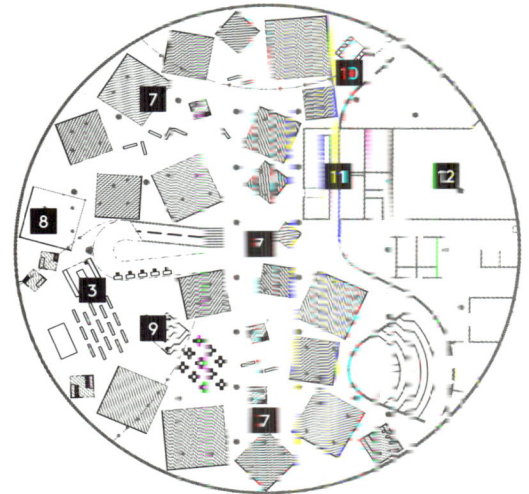

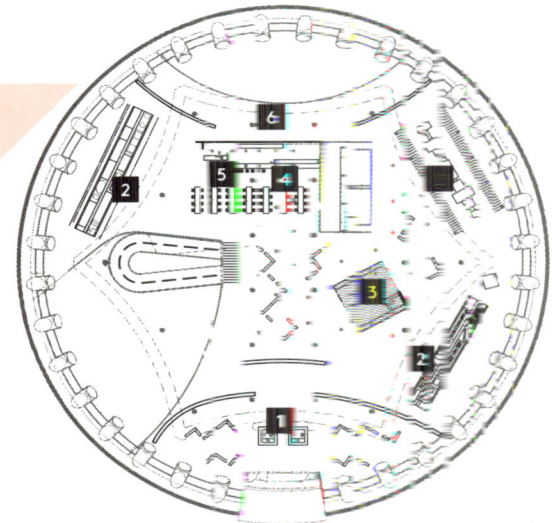

- 'Eclipse' scenographic elements were created using natural light and the RGB LED system.
- Tree lights lined the 'borders of the city' (the walls of the Oca building).
- All the furniture, lightning and visual communication details were design exclusively for the fair.
- The winding street had road markings and a zebra crossing.
- Bare pendant light bulbs illuminated the cafe area.

First floor

Floor plan

1 Reception
2 Special exhibition zones
3 Shop
4 Restaurant
5 Kitchen
6 Lounge
7 Exhibition stands
8 Workshop
9 Cafe
10 Lockers
11 Toilets
12 Back of house

Ground floor

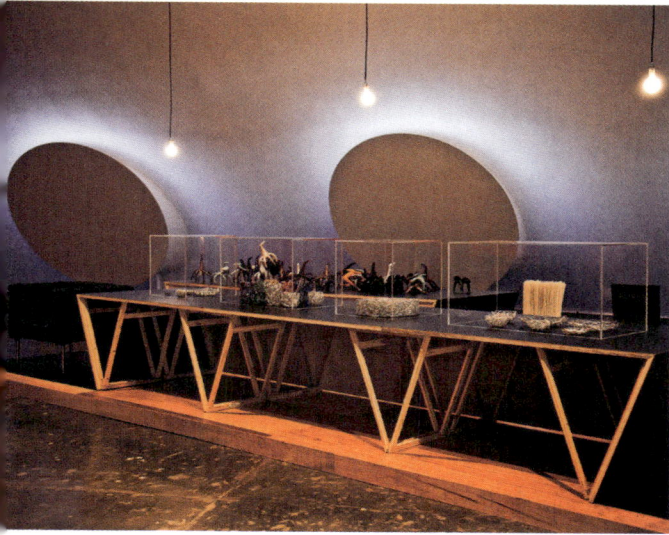

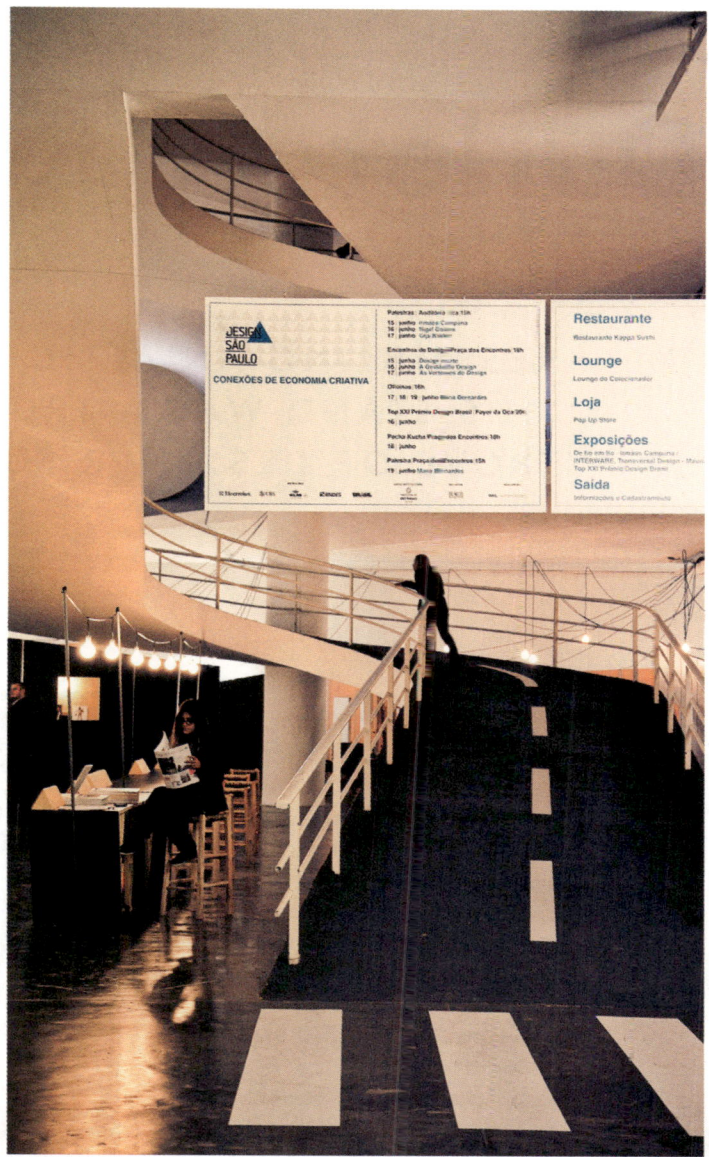

The main concept was based on the model of a city

Durlet by Rotor Group

RESEMBLING AN ATTIC SPACE,
THIS STAND WAS A TRUE TREASURE
TROVE OF DESIGNER FURNITURE.

Treasures from the attic was the core idea behind the Durlet stand at Interieur 2010. The Belgian furniture brand commissioned the team at Rotor Group to come up with a catchy and unique concept for the display of its latest ranges of contemporary furnishings. Rotor translated the idea of an old attic into a huge wooden rooftop space to create a nostalgic and cosy atmosphere for design fanatics in search of a genuine Durlet leather sofa. The booth structure featured uncoated wood in the form of a house from a bird's eye perspective. As if getting a glimpse into the attic of an old timber dwelling, visitors enjoyed their first impression of the stand. Rotor Group opted for an open space along the main passageway without losing the intimacy of a mysterious attic. With one completely open side at the gable-end of the 'house', the roof timbers were immediately visible, but this was no fusty attic with long-forgotten and cobweb-laden chairs and trunks laid out before fair goers. Set against the simple wood-panelled backdrop was a collection of designer furniture that shone in the stylish attic beneath the spotlights. Many new customers could discover what the furniture brand had to offer, with the seats, sofas, tables and chairs all arranged on the open stand, alongside a couple of storage items and old picture frames that set the scene. The stand could also be accessed from the main thoroughfare of exhibition hall via side entrances that took the form of gaps in the angled walls. Rumour has it that, due to the open space, many of the spiders and big-eared bats used as decoration in the eaves escaped from the attic stand and are probably still inhabiting the fair building.

TRADE FAIR Interieur
WHERE Kortrijk, Belgium
WHEN October 2010
DESIGNER Rotor Group ⊠ p.45
STAND CONSTRUCTOR Rotor Group
CLIENT Durlet
MARKET SECTOR Furniture
TOTAL FLOOR AREA 1680 m²
PHOTOGRAPHER Jean Godecharle

⊠ The attic was completely open along one side, immediately revealing its beams and rafters to visitors.
⊠ Wooden planks and panels were used to cover all the surfaces of the stand.

Graff by dcube

VIBRANT ILLUMINATION AND REFLECTIVE MATERIALS CREATED AN AQUATIC WORLD FOR CONTEMPORARY BATHROOM PRODUCTS.

Bathroom manufacturer Graff presented a new image to the world at the Cersaie trade fair in 2011. Swiss design company dcube was brought on board to showcase the company's latest collections and opted to use the key products themselves as the basis for the scenography of the stand. The approach to visual merchandising enabled the brand to stand out from the other fair exhibitors thanks to a clear architectural harmony that complemented the communication media deployed. Realised by Davide Oppizzi the owner of dcube, in collaboration with Jean-Marc Salemi, the design was inspired by capillarity and the distinctive appearance of oil on water. The team created intimate areas of presentation as raised islands that stood out in the darkened space thanks to key aspects of yellow backlit illumination. A curvilinear design and an organic atmosphere pervaded the stand, incorporating an aquatic feel and a suggestion of movement. Ceiling-mounted spots projecting light through a narrow focus illuminated all products, rendering a theatrical atmosphere. Some key products were presented on matt-black platforms, which ensured a dramatic contrast with their white surfaces. Highly reflective ceramic materials adorned the floors and walls of the rest of the stand and gave a feeling of lightness. In addition, the white laminate floors reflected the surrounding presentation modules like the water of a calm pond. Two pools of water covered with volcanic stones allowed showers to operate as a closed loop for demonstrations. Flat-screen monitors positioned at intervals on the main wall played promotional films that relayed corporate information and news to visitors.

TRADE FAIR Cersaie
WHERE Bologna, Italy
WHEN September 2011
DESIGNER dcube ☒ p.490
STAND CONSTRUCTOR Anonima Eventi
CLIENT Graff
MARKET SECTOR Sanitary ware
TOTAL FLOOR AREA 198 m²
PHOTOGRAPHERS dcube (Davide Oppizzi), Zerotremedia (Walter Monti)

☒ The contours of the ceramic washbasin were emphasised by yellow illumination
☒ Reflections were seen across the floor of the stand and in the water in the pool with volcanic stones.
☒ The bathtub was featured on a podium made of dark wood and backlit glass.

Renderings and 3D images showing the ceiling was structured in vibr translucent materials.

A yellow line rose up and along the len of the stand marking the entrance.

The baths illuminated base made it s like a star on a sleek, dark stage.

Illumination caused reflections t animated and enlivened the wh architecture contrasted by light dark areas.

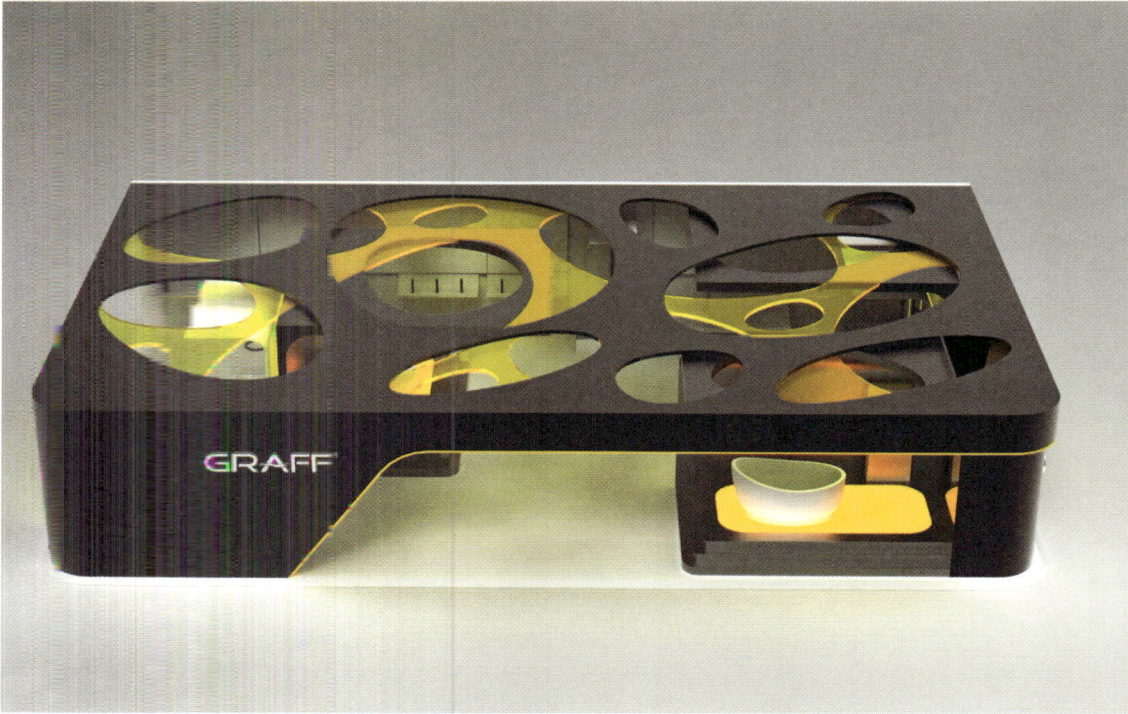

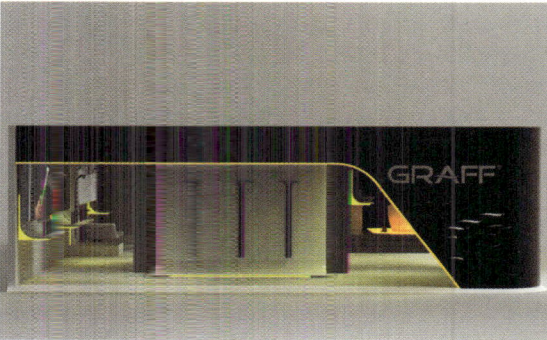

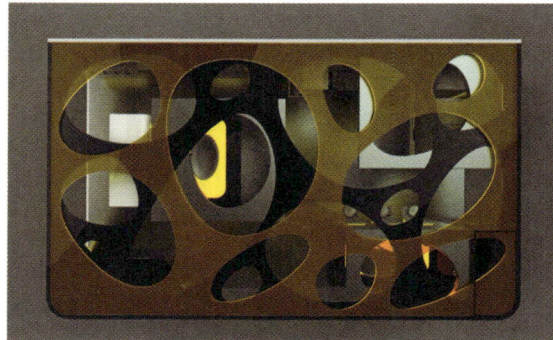

Key products comprised the scenography of the stand

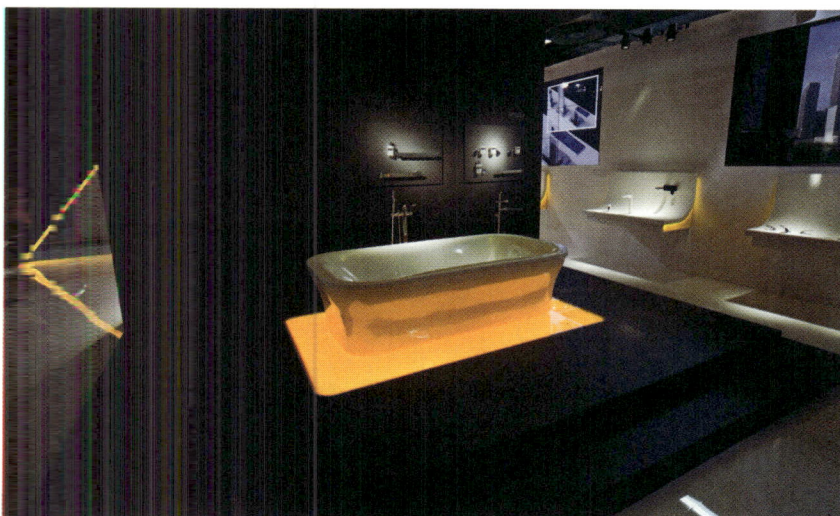

Grohe by Schmidhuber

AN URBAN VILLAGE EMBODIED
THE SUSTAINABLE SCENARIO
FOR THIS COLLECTION OF
PREMIUM BATHROOM FITTINGS.

'Enjoy Water' was the title of Grohe's brand and product presentation at the SH 2011 trade fair in Frankfurt. The brief from the luxury bathroom fittings manufacturer called for an intricate interplay between design, technology, quality and – most importantly – sustainability. The Munich-based studio Schmidhuber was in charge of the stand design. The challenge was not only to present 350 novel products coherently but also to unite the individual areas of bath, shower, sanitary systems and kitchen, as well as the first-ever international presentation of the Grohe Spa collection. The concept gathered these diverse product areas to form one 'urban village' in such a manner that they could be presented as separate modules at future trade shows. The community of different product collections was defined and emphasised under a brand umbrella that delineated the booth. Panels constructed from multilayered, semi-transparent fabric wrapped around the space above the presentation area on which the brand values were highlighted. These integrated screens, with their dynamic projections, conveyed corporate messages to passers-by and to fair goers across the expanse of the exhibition hall. Within the stand, similar illuminated branded banners defined individual presentation areas. The length and breadth of the exhibition booth was decked out in the corporate colours of white and blue, with splashes of grey and silver to tie in with the metallic hues of the bathroom fittings on show. There were also display modules that highlighted the client's sustainable technologies, while a 'shower pool' attracted a lot of attention from visitors. Natural materials also featured throughout, from the oak wood used for the floor and information counters to the woven linen used in the lounge seating area – another nod to the key brand value of sustainability that played a pivotal role in all the product areas.

TRADE FAIR **ISH**
WHERE **Frankfurt, Germany**
WHEN **March 2011**
DESIGNER **Schmidhuber** ▣ p.497
STAND CONSTRUCTOR **Messebau Tünnissen**
CLIENT **Grohe**
MARKET SECTOR **Sanitary ware**
TOTAL FLOOR AREA **1200 m²**
PHOTOGRAPHER **Joerg Hempel**

▣ Modular product areas formed a singular urban village, defined by the Grohe brand umbrella.
▣ The charcoal grey and dark blue presentation modules had a top surface made of white Corian.
▣ The shower pool was a hit with visitors.

Holzmedia by Von M and Projekttriangle

Manufacturer of multimedia furniture, Holzmedia is dedicated to design details that ensure true aesthetics. The firm wished to emphasise its modern approach to design at the Orgatec trade fair in Cologne in 2010 by encompassing its ethos of 'stepping out of the ordinary but keeping the familiar' within its presentation. The Von M team, working in close collaboration with Projekttriangle, was responsible for the stand's design. The booth gave a solid impression of the brand to passers-by within the exhibition hall and was intriguing enough to tempt them inside to find out more. The stand presented itself as brilliant white, reduced to the essentials, with perfectly placed graphics and only a few vertical openings to allow glimpses of the interior. The decor was emphasised by purple accents. A strong shade was chosen as a 'purple cow' – a phrase that means something remarkable, eye-catching and unusual. However, the eye-catching element that intrigued fair goers was not a cow but the image of a hog positioned on the glass wall of a 3-m-high cube at the very centre of the

SMART OFFICE FURNITURE SAT COMFORTABLY ALONGSIDE A CURLY-HAIRE HOG IN THIS CUBIC SPACE.

stand. The curly haired hog was the brainchild of artist Martin Grothmack and referred to Holzmedia's headquarters, located in a former pigsty in the countryside just north of Stuttgart. Entrances to the stand itself and to the ancillary rooms were aligned to set up exciting perspectives, and it was only when visitors entered the stand that the variety of products featured was revealed. Inspired by the intelligent solutions of the media furniture on show, the storage space and technical rooms disappeared into the cavity within the chunky exterior walls, with the overall design vocabulary for the booth revealing itself as solid and cubic – references to key visuals of the company.

TRADE FAIR Orgatec
WHERE Cologne, Germany
WHEN October 2010
DESIGNERS Von M ☒ p.479 and Projekttriangle ☒ p.497
STAND CONSTRUCTOR bluepool
CLIENT Holzmedia
MARKET SECTOR Multimedia furniture
TOTAL FLOOR AREA 220 m²
PHOTOGRAPHER Ericida González

☒ The artwork *Borste* (translation: 'bristle') decorated the glass wall.
☒ The cubic concept was applied to the furnishings and fittings.
☒ The stand was presented in brilliant white with deep purple accents.

Home Office by Stefan Zwicky

WITH THE RECOGNITION OF EVERYDAY ITEMS PLACED IN ANOTHER CONTEXT, COLOURFUL RING BINDERS CREATED A VIBRANT BACKDROP FOR A SERIES OF WORKSTATIONS.

At the 2011 edition of Neue Räume, the Zurich-based trade fair for home furnishings, the organisers wished to inform visitors with a stand dedicated to the advent of the 'home office'. The architecture studio of Stefan Zwicky was brought on board for the project. Nowadays, with desktop computers, laptops and the internet, tasks that were previously tied to a specific location may be performed virtually anywhere, allowing many people to work from home if the opportunity arises. Thus, the modern home office brings with it new types of furniture. To communicate this story, the design team opted for a simple setting that served a dual purpose for visitors: first, to offer them an overview of this type of workplace; and second, to enable them to experience specific home office items from a number of specialist Swiss furniture retailers. Ten workstations were placed on anthracite-coloured carpet in the exhibition entrance area, arranged one after the other to allow for a rapid comparison. Each workstation had an interactive aspect thanks to the presence of a solitary item on top of the table – an iPad – that encouraged fair goers to sit at the desk and fully experience the set-up. The title of the special display, with white typography in outsize lettering placed on black wooden panels, formed a connecting background on the wall directly behind the workstations. Instead of positioning the text high up on the wall, the designers chose to set the lettering flush with the floor. This created room for the prime positioning of an office-inspired installation by Swiss artist Beat Zoderer, well known for his vibrant and geometric artworks. His multicoloured, chequerboard effect defined the presentation. Only on closer inspection could fair goers see that the source of the coloured pattern stretched above the desks along the length of the stand was, in fact, 226 ring-binder files.

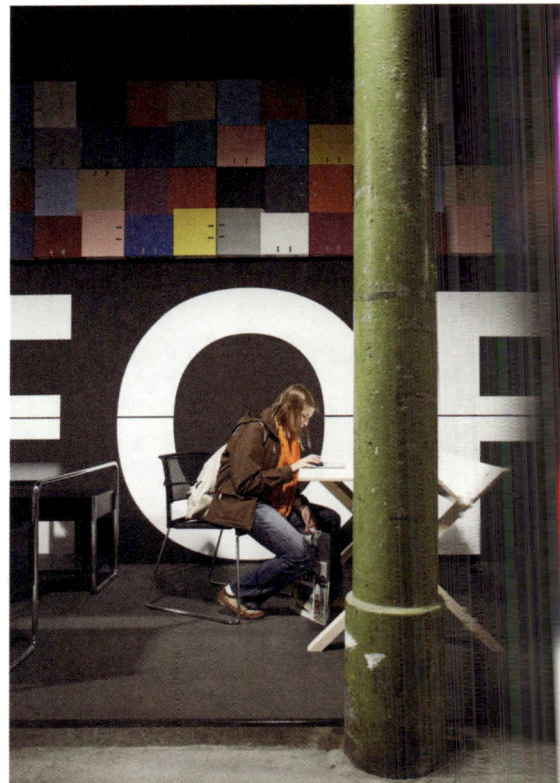

TRADE FAIR Neue Räume
WHERE Zurich, Switzerland
WHEN November 2011
DESIGNER Stefan Zwicky ☒ p. 478
STAND CONSTRUCTOR Stricker Reklam
CLIENT Neue Räume
MARKET SECTOR Furniture
TOTAL FLOOR AREA 38 m²
PHOTOGRAPHERS Michael Sieber,
Stefan Zwicky

☒ The simplicity of the stand meant visitors felt at ease to take a seat and make use of the iPads on display.
☒ The long, narrow space was highly visible to visitors near the entrance of the fair.

HOMEOF

HOMEOFFICE

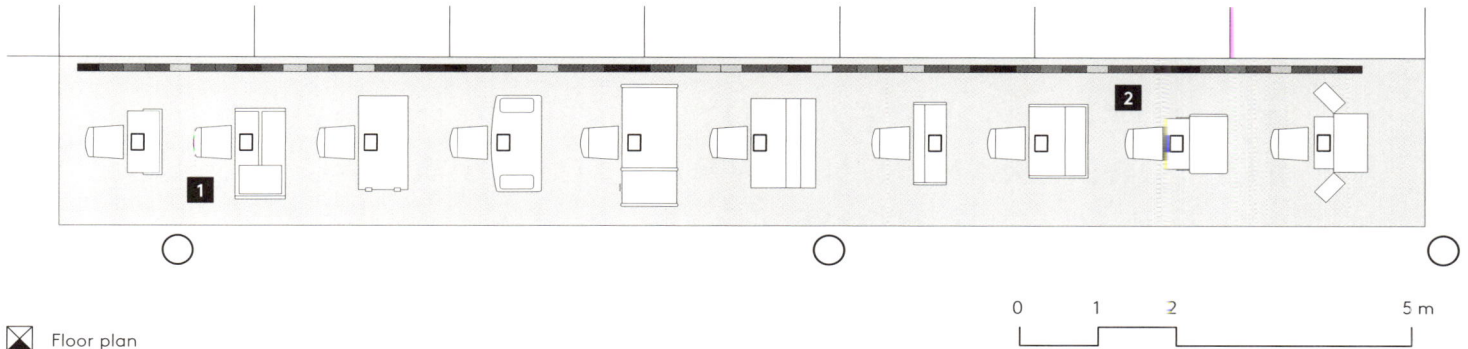

0   1   2   5 m

A multitude of ring binders created a pixellated pattern

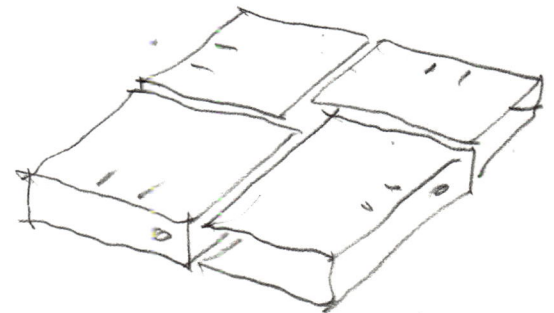

⊠ Drawing showing the scale of the letters compared to the binders.
⊠ The final design (opposite) stayed true to the initial concept sketch.
⊠ Selecting the exact positioning of each of the coloured ring binders was a major part of the process.

Hyundai Mostra Black by Estudio Guto Requena

AN INTERACTIVE EXHIBITION THAT INVOLVED VISITORS EXAMINING WHAT TURNS A SÃO PAULO HOUSE INTO A HOME.

For the first edition of Hyundai Mostra Black – a much-anticipated interior design exhibition in São Paulo – the organisers commissioned Estudio Guto Requena to realise an interactive environment that would capture the imagination of visitors. At the city-wide event, the location for this presentation was a house in a neo-classical style of architecture, which aptly related to the project theme. For the basis of the concept, the design team asked one question: what turns a residential space into a home? Is it its decoration, its objects, the people sharing the space, or memories stored within it? The interactive exhibition reflected on the significance and subjectivity associated with people's homes. The ambient space featured a red volume, with its form generated by the extruded contours of a traditional house. The basic question was asked of visitors throughout the course of the exhibition, with real-time responses collected via social media and presented in the form of an interactive wallpaper as one of the space's main features. As visitors entered the interior they encountered the red-tinged volume decorated with framed items that recalled the history of both the property itself and the previous occupants. These forgotten objects sparked memories and were fundamental pieces of the installation's narrative. The corridors were lined with red-painted panels, and rooms within rooms traced the outline of a child's playhouse and contained further fragments of recollections. At the top of the flight of stairs, digital wallpaper featured recurrent words with those that gained special relevance being displayed larger than the other words. The narrative ended in the women's public bathroom, where the finishing of the entire ceiling and of parts of its tiled wall and floor was removed to reveal the structure behind. The room took on a dream-like – perhaps even spooky – atmosphere with a central light source providing illumination composed of original lamps taken from other rooms of the house.

TRADE FAIR **Hyundai Mostra Black**
WHERE **São Paulo, Brazil**
WHEN **June 2011**
DESIGNER **Estudio Guto Requena** ⊠ p.491
STAND CONSTRUCTOR **AGR Construções**
CLIENT **Hyundai Mostra Black**
MARKET SECTOR **Decoration and home equipment**
TOTAL FLOOR AREA **63 m**
PHOTOGRAPHER **Fran Parente**

⊠ A key part of the project was that visitors could also take part via social media.
⊠ The objects on show were found abandoned in the house and purposefully positioned to spark recollections.

The red volume incorporated the extruded contours of a traditional house

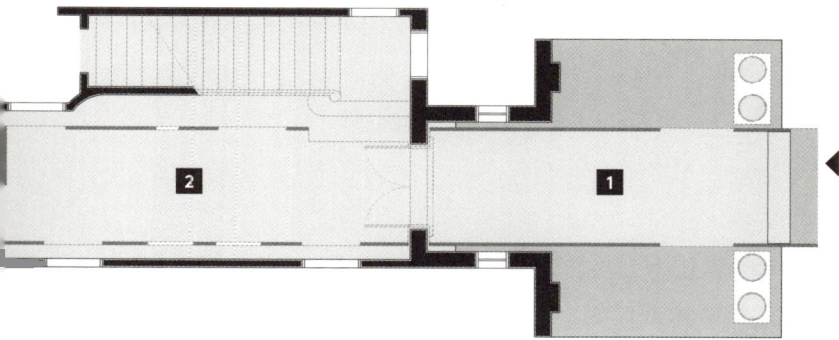

Ground floor

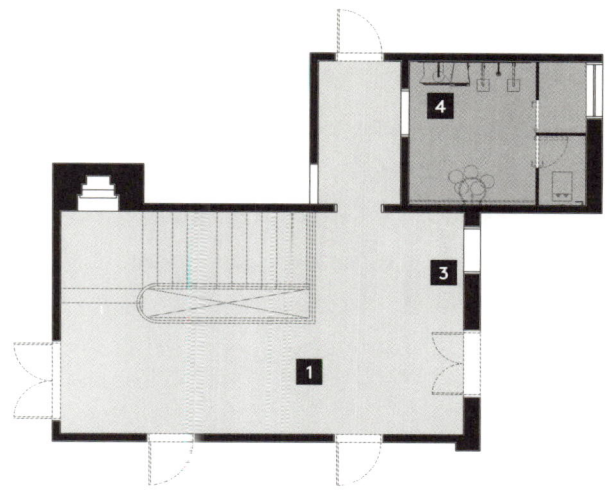

First floor

Floor plan

1 Entrance hall
2 Exhibition area
3 Digital wallpaper
4 Bathroom

Sensors in the floor detected the arrival of visitors and stimulated the digital wallpaper to spur into action.

Precise illumination of the interior was key to creating a contemplative atmosphere throughout.

There was a dream-like quality in the bathroom with its multitude of lights.

On one wall, an installation of taps and shower heads was displayed.

Mattiazzi by Studio Nitzan Cohen

CONTEMPORARY FURNITURE PUT UNDER THE SPOTLIGHT ON A SIMPLE STAND WITH MAXIMUM IMPACT.

Qubique was conceived as the next generation trade fair for furniture and design that unites trade and marketing with communication and entertainment. At the 2011 event in Berlin, Studio Nitzan Cohen realised a simple, succinct and eye-catching presentation for furniture brand Mattiazzi. The great challenge for this project was to create maximum impact with minimum resources. The design team opted for a sole construction material in the decor of the entire installation. Flame-retardant raw chipboard covered the floor and wall surfaces, and it formed plinths for the designer chairs. Radical changes to its character and image lent this cost-effective material a touch of class. The entire installation was painted pristine white and illuminated with bare red light bulbs placed in a single row around the edge of each low product platform. A large circular raised display area formed the central feature of the stand, while other elements created an unobtrusive perimeter around the booth. An added highlight of the presentation was the contemporary take on the Italian brand's well-established logo. This consisted of standard neon tube lights affixed to form the outline of a letter 'M' on a giant branded panel. Mounted on a backplate and simply positioned to lean against the rear wall, this created an illuminated backdrop for the product installation. The installation was stylish and clean yet very playful and light.

TRADE FAIR Qubique
WHERE Berlin, Germany
WHEN October 2011
DESIGNER Studio Nitzan Cohen ⊠ p.498
STAND CONSTRUCTOR Mattiazzi
CLIENT Mattiazzi
MARKET SECTOR Furniture
TOTAL FLOOR AREA 60 m²
PHOTOGRAPHER Gerhardt Kellermann

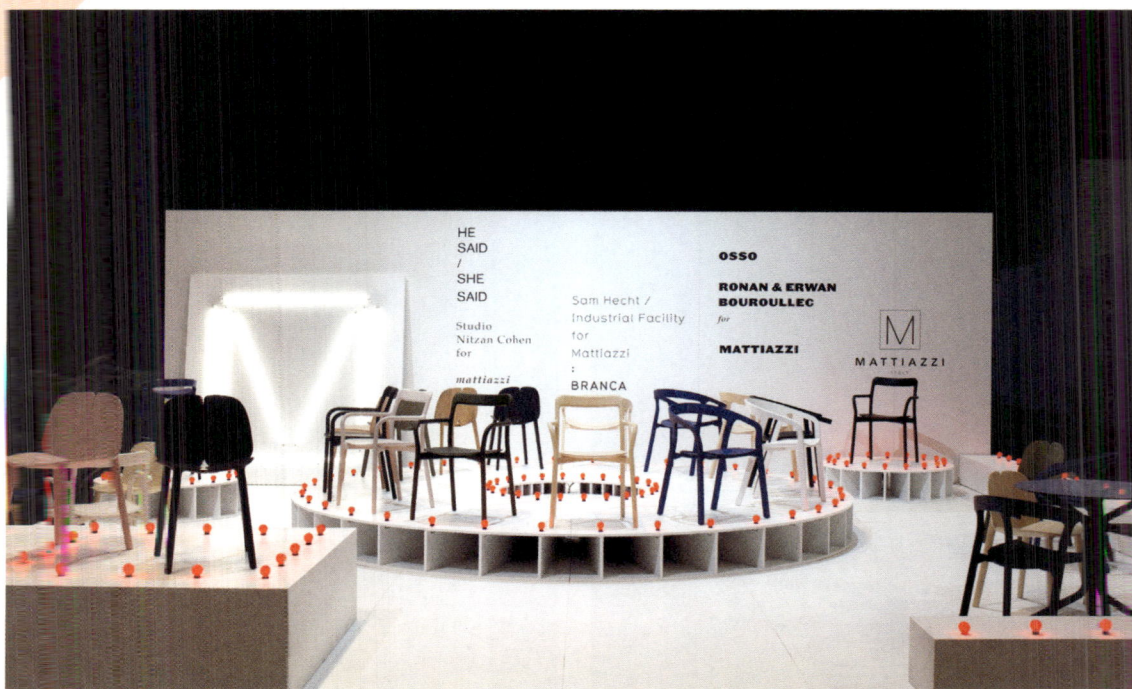

⊠ The playful, pristine white presentation had elevated platforms with flashes of red illumination marking the perimeters.
⊠ The bright branded panel created a clean, crisp backdrop for the bar stool pedestal.

Object of Desire by hippos design architecture

PRODUCTS POSITIONED ON A PLAYFUL PLATFORM INSPIRED BY THE ATMOSPHERE OF THE PRAGUE LOCATION OF THE STUDENT DESIGNERS.

TRADE FAIR Salone Internazionale del Mobile
WHERE Milan, Italy
WHEN April 2011
DESIGNERS hippos design architecture ⊠ p 492
STAND CONSTRUCTOR AAAD in Prague
CLIENT AAAD in Prague
MARKET SECTOR Decoration and home equipment
TOTAL FLOOR AREA 50 m²
PHOTOGRAPHER hippos design architecture

Hippos design architecture was commissioned to realise the presentation of the Academy of Arts, Architecture and Design (AAAD) in Prague at the Salone Internazionale del Mobile in Milan in 2011. Entitled 'Object of Desire', the exhibition showcased products by students from various departments within the academy, ranging from industrial design all the way through to work bordering on fine art. While creating the concept for the AAAD booth, the hippos team wanted to reproduce a somewhat abstract atmosphere full of fairy tales, dreams and games, translating that which can found at the academy on the banks of the River Vltava, where meanings, definitions and scale are so often challenged. It soon became obvious that this dreamy landscape would have to have a few inhabitants, who were brought to life with the help of graphic designer Stepan Malovec. The curved, contemporary display tables had a charming appeal owing to the shapes, circles and creatures that were laser-cut to create interesting and eye-catching contours. Incorporating outlines of characters such as bunnies and birds into the storyline helped to ensure a playful feeling in the stand. At the same time, great emphasis was placed on the practical aspects. Since the installation was to be used in several other locations after Milan, the team created a structure that could be erected with only a few simple tools. All the elements of the booth were designed to be light and packed flat for ease of transport. Assembled from aluminium composite panels that gave the designers creative freedom in the vertical plane, the stand was held together horizontally by an unobtrusive construction grid of threaded metal rods. Faced with over 100 white slats, 20 rods and several hundred bolts, the production crew successfully managed the challenge of labelling everything correctly and packing all the parts in the right order.

⊠ The bespoke display system was designed with ease-of-packing in mind.
⊠ The laser-cut slats were made from aluminium composite panels.
⊠ The charming design created a contemporary platform for the showcased work.

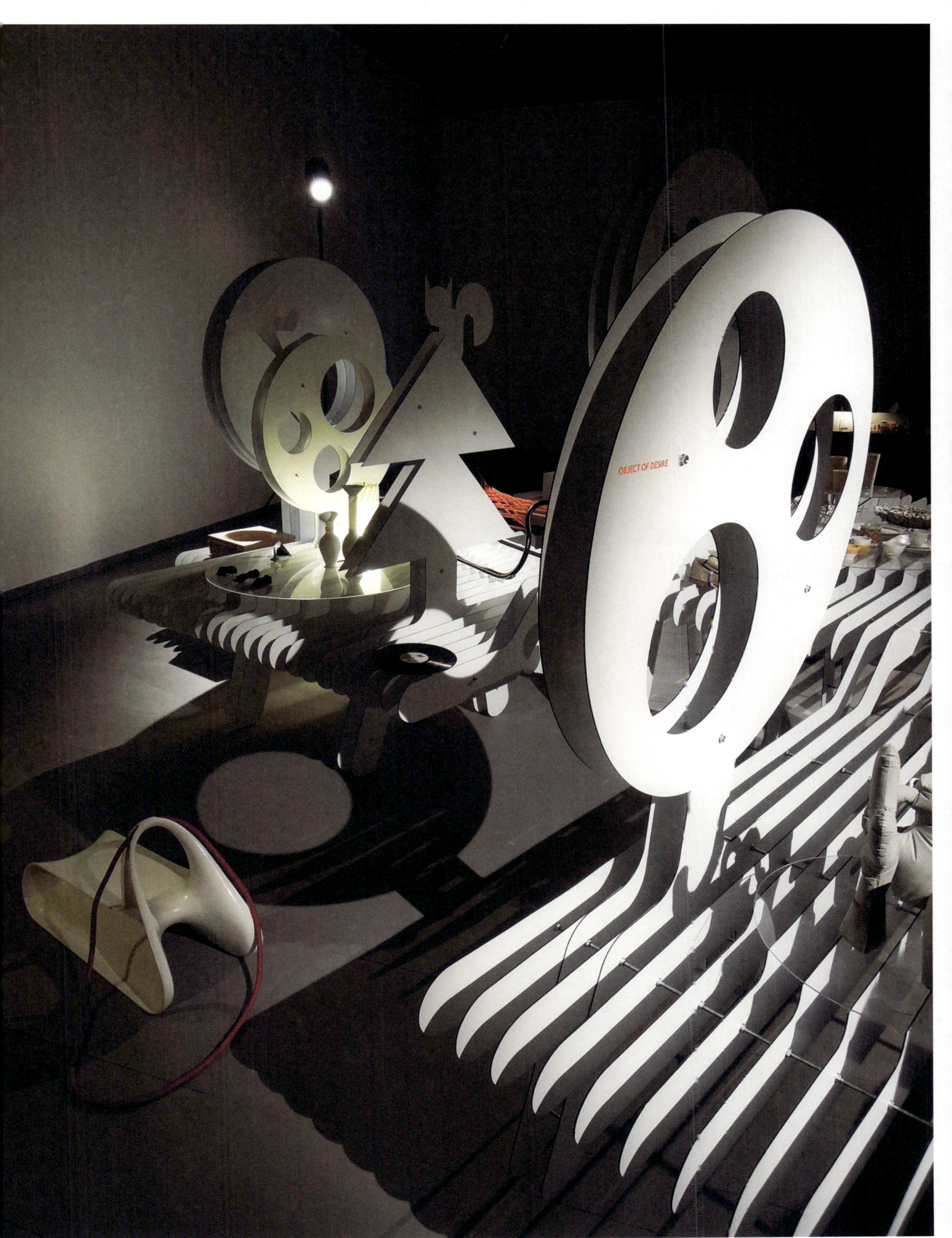

INTERIOR PRODUCTS GRAND STAND

Past, Present and Future for Kusch+Co by Atelier Brückner

CLASSIC TO CONTEMPORARY CHAIR
COLLECTIONS SET A STUNNING SCENE
AS A CELEBRATION OF 75 YEARS OF
FURNITURE DESIGN.

Furnishing a stand at Milan Design Week for German furniture manufacturer Kusch+Co was the task of design studio Atelier Brückner. The presentation amounted to a spectacular scenography befitting a celebration of the company's 75-year history. The design team chose to answer the brief with an eye-catching setting with a visual tagline of 'Past, present and future'. Awaiting visitors was an installation in the form of a stage, furnished in an artistic manner to place the treasures of design history in a contemporary context alongside new products. A completely black surrounding space ensured that the products stood out as the stars of the show. Composed of 50 historical and current chair models presented chronologically under spotlights, the design classics from Kusch+Co were enhanced by red accents and suspended in front of a mirrored wall. This 'gallery of ancestors' was complemented by rows of chairs placed on the parquet. Some of the chairs on the floor appeared to float upwards, giving the impression that the current designs were turning into design classics right before the fair-goers' eyes. Visitors themselves took part in the performance, standing amongst the chairs as they viewed the collection and even taking a seat. The stage also doubled as an auditorium, with the seats facing a large video screen that adorned the opposite wall and showed films that tied in with the furniture presentations. The 7-m-high mirror positioned next to the collection of chairs suspended from the ceiling reflected the visual narrative into the installation, enhancing the impact of the presentation even further.

TRADE FAIR Salone Internazionale del Mobile
WHERE Milan, Italy
WHEN April 2012
DESIGNER Atelier Brückner ◄ p. 185
STAND CONSTRUCTOR Mada Exos
CLIENT Kusch+Co
MARKET SECTOR Furniture
TOTAL FLOOR AREA 180 m²
PHOTOGRAPHER Michael Jungblut

- The title of the show was displayed dangling from lengths of string.
- A total of fifty products were displayed, with classic chairs positioned alongside new designs.
- The design classics from Kusch+Co, featured by red accents, were suspended in front of a mirror wall.
- Visitors experienced the chairs as tangible protagonists.

SERIES 1010 BINA
DESIGNED BY FRANK PERSON

SERIES 2000. 2000 UNI VERSO
DESIGN BY NORBERT GEELEN

SERIES 8000
DESIGN BY PORSCHE DESIGN STUDIO

Project Kyo-to by Little

JAPANESE ARTISAN CRAFTS WITH MODERN DESIGN SENSIBILITES WERE PRESENTED IN A SERENE SPACE.

The Tokyo International Gift Show is the largest international trade show in Japan, with exhibits of personal gifts, consumer goods and decorative accessories. In August 2011, the Kyoto Chamber of Commerce and Industry invited designer Sachio Hihara to launch 'Project Kyo-to' – a major enterprise that brought together 20 traditional artisans in an attempt to tie traditional techniques from Kyoto to the future. The 20 new craft products that were realised over the course of 6 months were brought to a global audience at the fair in Tokyo in February 2012. They were presented within a booth designed by Saori Miwa of design firm Little. The concept behind the spatial expression of the stand was a revision of the elements that make up the collective vision of Kyoto traditions, leading to a revelation not of the city's sense of design – colours, shapes, etc. – but of its 'sensitivity'. The products were displayed as artworks on presentation tables set in a crisp white environment that married brightness with calmness – attractive enough to show the items at their best, yet delicate enough to support their sobriety. Intriguing images of the individual craft items were symbolically positioned alongside. These adorned the interior walls of the booth, with a contemporary graphic motif in fresh and contemporary colours that incorporated hexagonal shapes made to look like folding screens. All these elements combined to create a ceremonial atmosphere, conducive to storytelling in the Japanese tradition. Another subtle splash of colour came from the translucent noren curtain that hung at intervals over the entrances to the booth. These marked the boundary of the space and, as the curtain was purposefully positioned at eye level, the products on the tables inside caught the attention of passers-by. The gentle swaying and fluttering of the fabric caused by the movement of people walking past, or into the booth, added to the serenity of the space.

The graphic on the wall was designed by Jun Ishigura.
The simple space had an accurate ambience for the craft products.
Noren curtains are used traditionally in the entrances to Japanese shops.

TRADE FAIR **Tokyo International Gift Show**
WHERE **Tokyo, Japan**
WHEN **February 2012**
DESIGNER **Little** ◪ **p.494**
STAND CONSTRUCTOR **D-9**
CLIENT **Kyoto Chamber of Commerce and Industry**
MARKET SECTOR **Craft products**
TOTAL FLOOR AREA **72 m²**
PHOTOGRAPHER **kentahasegawa**

Rosenthal by Bachmann.Kern und Partner

TABLEWARE PRESENTED IN AN OPEN SPACE DEFINED BY CRISS-CROSSING ELEMENTS, FROM CATWALKS TRAVERSING THE FLOOR TO WOODEN BEAMS SOLIDLY SURROUNDING THE SPACE.

Tableware manufacturer Rosenthal commissioned architecture firm Bachmann. Kern und Partner to create its stand for Ambiente 2012, following two previous successful exhibition collaborations in 2010 and 2011. The primary challenge for the team was to design a coherent multi-brand concept without affecting the individuality of each of the five brands featured across the presentation: Rosenthal, Sambonet, Versace, Thomas and Hutschenreuther. The first impression of the stand was an impressive facade of solid white beams criss-crossing the booth and holding the structure together, without forming barriers. Striking views and perspectives provided insight into the brand presentation inside the space. Orthogonal axes separated two distinct exhibition areas into five zones, one for each brand. The design concept deliberately moved away from harsh boundaries and instead relied upon open architecture, allowing visitors to cast their eyes freely in all directions. On the exterior of the stand, black panels with simple white graphics marked the location of each brand. Optically levitating walls, which could be used modularly, not only provided the perfect backdrop for displaying products, but also served as partitions between the individual sectors. Black catwalks on the floor, which also appeared to wrap up and over the stand as 'sails' on the ceiling, functioned as additional connecting elements between the different booth zones. Detached from the product presentation, emotionally charged installations on the catwalks conveyed the identities of the different brands to fair visitors.

TRADE FAIR **Ambiente**
WHERE **Frankfurt, Germany**
WHEN **February 2012**
DESIGNER **Bachmann.Kern und Partner** ⊟ p.489
STAND CONSTRUCTOR **kohlhaas messebau**
CLIENT **Rosenthal**
MARKET SECTOR **Tablewear**
TOTAL FLOOR AREA **830 m²**
PHOTOGRAPHER **Volker Neumann**

☒ Cloud-like lampshades produced a soft and diffuse lighting effect.
☒ Branded black panels provided a perfect backdrop for the products.
☒ The client and the individual brands were clearly represented.

The design deliberately moved away from harsh boundaries

White beams were used to define the edges of the booth.
The hybrid space served as display areas as well as providing an impression of living space.
A multi-tiered table presented the tableware, emphasising the different heights of the displayed product.

Serafini by atelier 522

AN ANGULAR, ASYMMETRIC LANDSCAPE CARVED OUT TO MAXIMISE DISPLAY POSSIBILITIES.

TRADE FAIR Euroshop
WHERE Dusseldorf, Germany
WHEN February 2011
DESIGNER atelier 522 ☒ p.489
STAND CONSTRUCTOR John USW
CLIENT Serafini
MARKET SECTOR Furniture, fixtures and shopfitting systems
TOTAL FLOOR AREA 140m
PHOTOGRAPHER atelier 522

Slanted walls, asymmetrical edges and unusual angles were all architectural elements that welcomed visitors to the Serafini stand at the Euroshop trade fair in 2011. For its presentation of modern design products for both indoor and outdoor display systems, Serafini commissioned the design talents of atelier 522 to carve out a creative concept. The continuous, sculpted Serafini world consisted of a cluster of five cube-shaped vestibules that utilised to full advantage both the interior and exterior walls for display options. The uneven-sided booths were not closed-in or restrictive in any way but formed a network of angled archways and interconnecting paths to logically lead visitors around the stand to discover the full range of product offerings. With a complementary neutral palette of greys, taupes and creams, there were many special features that atelier 522 included as decorative elements made from natural materials, such as cardboard, wood and felt. Some walls were also embellished with white graphics in origami-like shapes alongside detailed product information. Illumination came from a multitude of sources, from downlighters and spotlights to simple pendant bulbs. The slanted concept was also embedded in bespoke furniture pieces that the design team created to harmonise with the angled geometry of the landscape. A highlight was the reception counter in matt black MDF, which impressed with its simple elegance. Irregularly-shaped seating elements and standing table furniture invited visitors to take a moment and relax in a contemporary environment with a friendly atmosphere. Whilst the lopsided structures looked out of balance, this was far from the truth since they were all solid and sturdy. The wonky world in essence was a well-rounded presentation with a touch of quirkiness that was a talking point amongst fair goers.

EASY

☒ The white wall graphics had an origami-like appearance.
☒ Each display system was assigned its own asymmetric space.

serafini®

CLIPS LED

Suzanne Goodwin Design Studios by Lucille Clerc

CONTEMPORARY TEXTILES ADORNED A SPARSE SPACE WITH COMPLEMENTARY FLORAL SILKSCREEN PRINTS THAT CLIMBED THE WALLS.

TRADE FAIR **Tent London**
WHERE **London, United Kingdom**
WHEN **September 2011**
DESIGNER **Lucille Clerc** ☒ **p.494**
STAND CONSTRUCTOR **Lucille Clerc**
CLIENT **Suzanne Goodwin**
MARKET SECTOR **Interior textiles**
TOTAL FLOOR AREA **5 m²**
PHOTOGRAPHER **Lucille Clerc**

Suzanne Goodwin is a London-based designer passionate about colour and pattern. Producing fabrics that combine modern technology with handcrafted techniques, she finds her inspiration in paper (folded, crushed and crinkled) and metallic materials, utilising the techniques of pleating, smocking and digital printing in the production of her fabric collections. For her presence at Tent London in 2011 – part of London Design Festival – Goodwin commissioned friend and fellow CSM graduate Lucille Clerc to design the small booth. The two had previously worked together on developing projects, since Clerc's approach also incorporates hand-printing processes, textures and folding techniques, and these harmonise well with the textured fabrics and patterns of Goodwin's soft interior products. With an open brief, the aim was to realise an environment that would complement the product patterns and invite people to stop and take stock of the small stand and the products on display. The challenge was to create a strong visual intervention that would leave a trace in people's minds so that they would remember Goodwin's collection. The idea was to imagine that the patterns on the fabric would spread and climb the walls as if coming to life. Clerc reinterpreted the floral textile patterns as CMYK silkscreen prints on paper to create seven different designs with a colour palette ranging from yellows and oranges to blues and purples. Elongated strips of folded paper were then assembled to create the 'living wall'. A simply decorated space that complemented the products was thus established, incorporating an entirely hand-printed installation that was directly assembled on site. To match this folded-paper installation, a brochure with folded pages also invited people from all over the fair to come to the stand and discover the whole collection of interior designs.

☒ The printed paper was layered in strips around the top of the small booth.
☒ The silkscreen patterns echoed the designs of the textiles on display.

The H&M Dollhouse by Knock

A SETTING FOR HOME FURNISHING PRODUCTS THAT MIXED STYLE AND SCALE WHILST CONJURING UP CHILDHOOD MEMORIES.

The Stockholm-based concept, design and brand experience agency Knock was in charge of designing a product presentation for international fashion brand H&M. In 2009, the Swedish firm launched H&M Home and has since made its mark on the world of 'fashion for home furnishings'. The brand was planning to launch its Autumn 2012 Collection and required a media event for 300 top international interior and fashion journalists. The collection was divided into six distinct styles, and the main challenge for Knock's design team was to display all product styles simultaneously in an effective, creative and authentic way. The answer: 'The H&M Dollhouse'. But this wasn't to be a toy-sized doll's house. It needed to have the dimensions of a real house, only with the appearance of a doll's house – i.e. a gaping hole where the facade should be – so that onlookers could enjoy an instantaneous overview of the products on show. An old cinema in central Stockholm was used as the display space. One of the theatres was turned into a contemporary household presentation, replete with distinct living areas and rooms represented in different styles. Pieces from the collection were carefully selected and displayed in the different rooms as if they formed a real house. The playfulness of reliving a childhood memory in a surreal setting created an experience that the invited guests appreciated greatly. This was a presentation not only to be admired but also explored. Visitors were invited inside the house to investigate the home textile products in the different settings. After walking around all the rooms, they could then take time to relax in the tiered 'garden' space, where they could sit and enjoy lunch, with a perfect view of the collection.

TRADE FAIR **H&M Home**
WHERE **Stockholm, Sweden**
WHEN **April 2012**
DESIGNER **Knock** ☒ **p.493**
STAND CONSTRUCTOR **Independent Studios**
CLIENT **H&M Home**
MARKET SECTOR **Home textile products**
TOTAL FLOOR AREA **420 m²**
PHOTOGRAPHER **Jens Andersson**

☒ The setting for the presentation was an old cinema.
☒ The tiered levels acted as an auditorium from which visitors could view the house and its contents.

An instantaneous overview, in an effective, creative and authentic way

Renderings

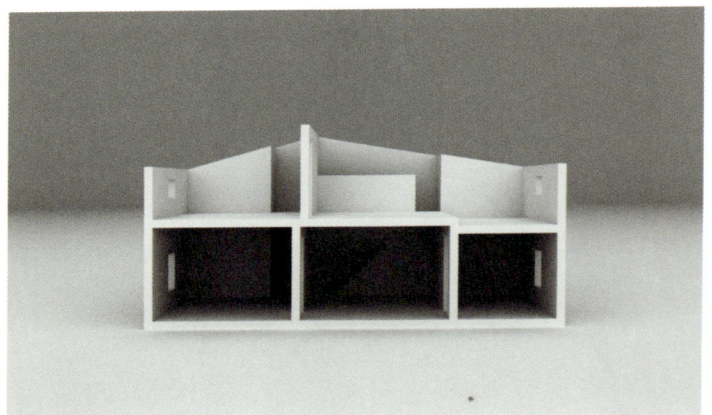

Sketch labels: COAST, 5METERS, WOOD, VINTAGE, BARRIERS BRASS, LIGHTS, BOOKSHELF, WHITE, WINDOWS, SOFA, BEDROOM, PATHTUB, SLIDE, KIDS, STAIRS, WOODEN PANELS, SHOWER SOFA, LAMP, LIGHTS, BEDS, CLEAN, STEPS, KITCHEN, PUNCH, DOOR, EXIT, DOOR, 10 METERS, CARPET, FENCE

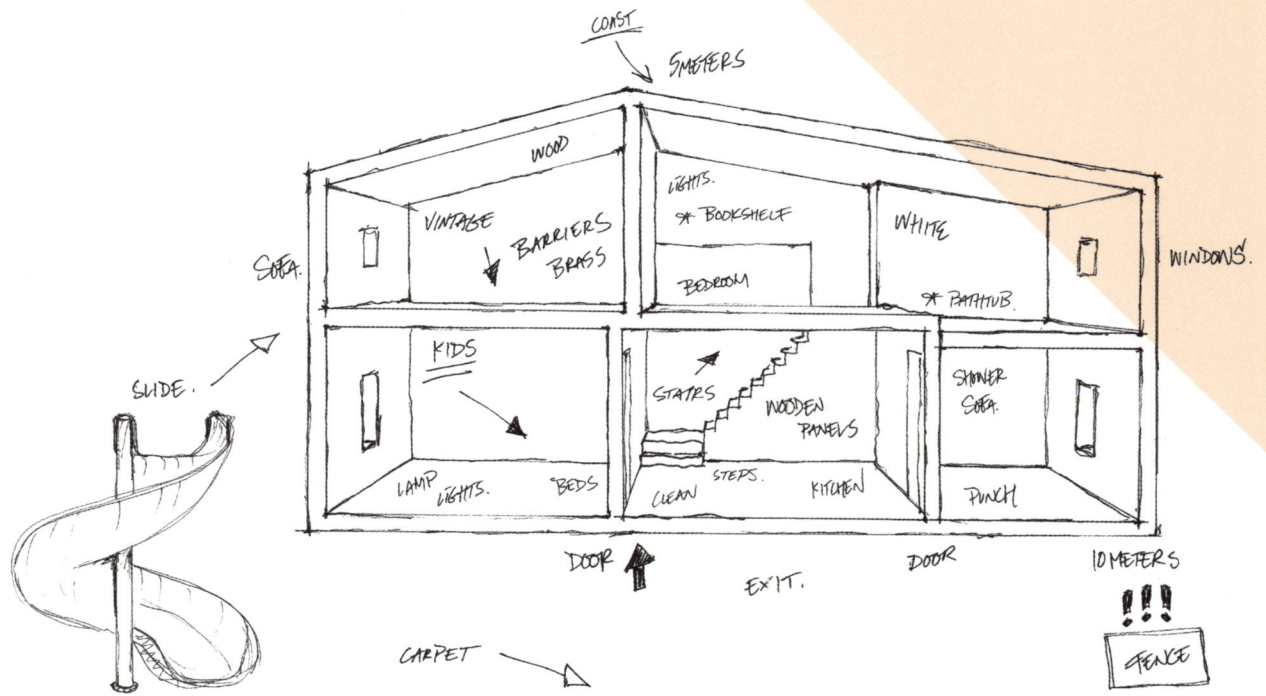

⊠ Sketch of the house, indicating its open and playful character.
⊠ Customers entered into the main hallway, from where all zones in the house were accessible.
⊠ Each room took on a personality of its own, depending on its purpose.

The playfulness of reliving a childhood memory in a surreal setting

Authentic building materials were used in the construction with worn, wooden floorboards adding character.
Through the windows, it seemed like night time outside.
H&M Home textile products from the featured collection really made the house feel like a home.
Lighting was important to set the perfect ambience in each space.

Toto by Mach Architektur

THE PEACEFULNESS OF A JAPANESE GARDEN PERMEATED THE PRESENTATION AMIDST A BACKDROP OF NATURAL MATERIALS.

TRADE FAIR **ISH**
WHERE **Frankfurt, Germany**
WHEN **March 2011**
DESIGNER **Mach Architektur** ◻ **p.494**
STAND CONSTRUCTORS **GMOD Design, Walbert-Schmitz**
CLIENT **Toto**
MARKET SECTOR **Sanitary ware**
TOTAL FLOOR AREA **1300 m²**
PHOTOGRAPHER **Fotodesign Schiemann**

Mach Architektur was assigned by the Japanese firm Toto to design a trade fair booth to represent the company at the sanitary fair ISH 2011 in Frankfurt. In order to reflect the brand's eco-friendly philosophy, the Mach team designed a natural space as a suitable framework in which to exhibit the latest products. Encapsulating a calming atmosphere, the booth consisted of a garden area surrounded by three open pavilions, which invited fair goers to relax and experience the various products and technologies. The pavilions divided the vast stand into separate themed areas. Visitors could take a journey through the entire world of Toto, starting with the luxurious bathroom collections before moving on to the technology zones, which explained details of the company's 'clean and green' and water-saving technologies. Natural materials blended with modern architecture and high-tech products with high-end quality, forming a harmonious and peaceful presentation. Rustic grey stone tiles alternated with light wood terrace planks as complementary flooring materials throughout the booth. They combined with the screen-like panels and wood-slat walls that separated the different areas to evoke images of traditional Japanese bathhouses. With this visual backdrop, the ceramic products and clear-lined furniture stood out and also effectively presented Toto, which was established in 1917, as a firm with tradition and historical roots. The stand design embraced the Japanese origins of the company whilst also catering to the requirements of the European market. This was the source of the idea to present individual modern bathroom suites in the ambience of a Japanese garden.

⊠ The central garden was at the heart of the natural environment.
⊠ Strips of illumination around the floor edges gave the impression that the platforms were floating.
⊠ The reception area's back wall and welcome desk was given a bamboo finish.

VitrA by Neo International Design & Communications

SETTING THE SCENE OF BATHING IN FOREST WOODLAND, THE DESIGNERS ENCAPSULATED THE CLIENT'S RESPECT FOR NATURE.

VitrA is a Turkish brand offering a range of products for complete bathroom solutions with sanitary ware, taps, bathtubs, furniture and tiles. Neo International Design & Communications was commissioned to create the brand's space at the Unicera trade fair in Istanbul in 2012. Neo worked closely with VitrA's design team on the project. With a brief to reflect the client's advertising campaign tagline – 'Reborn every day' – the design team decided to focus on VitrA's three main agenda items: design, sustainability and innovation. The concept highlighted the client's respect for nature as well as the inspiration that VitrA designers draw from the natural world. Emanating a simple and pure essence, a pristine white backdrop framed the stand that housed the product range. Invited to enter the booth through a white metal archway, fair goers first passed a series of flat-screen TVs lining the walls. As they made their way into the stand, they were welcomed by branded imagery as well as a film that featured a VitrA bathroom – the same bathroom that appeared at the end of the pathway at the heart of the presentation. Here, a refreshing and natural atmosphere dominated thanks both to real tree trunks – employed as design elements and as supports for the double-height ceiling – and a waterfall feature that added an acoustic touch, calling to mind the sound of a stream running through a forest. A simple shell surrounded the stand. An expanse of glass along the full length of each exterior wall formed a strip window that offered passers-by enticing glimpses into the interior. Inside, grey porcelain tiles covered the floor throughout, while natural dark wood features from benches to stairs added to the natural ambience of the stand.

☒ A waterfall connected the different elevations of the booth.
☒ Natural wood was a prominent feature in the presentation.
☒ Wide walkways in the interior created a relaxed atmosphere for visitors.

TRADE FAIR Unicera
WHERE Istanbul, Turkey
WHEN March 2012
DESIGNER Neo International Design
& Communications ☒ p.495
STAND CONSTRUCTOR Neo International
Design & Communications
CLIENT VitrA/Eczacıbası Building Products
MARKET SECTOR Sanitary ware
TOTAL FLOOR AREA 900 m²
PHOTOGRAPHER Halise Özel Mahmutogl

LIGH

Circo Modular by Rotor Group

ROLL UP, ROLL UP – THE
WORLD FAMOUS CIRCO
MODULAR IS IN TOWN.

'The greatest show on earth' needs the best lighting. That was the starting point for the architectural lighting brand Modular's presentation at the 2012 edition of the Light+Building trade fair in Frankfurt. When Rotor Group was commissioned to come up with a creative idea for the stand, the team once again chose a high entertainment factor as the most important goal of its approach, akin to the pinball booth that the group designed for the brand at the 2010 Light+Building trade fair. Seeking a presentation that emanated a great vitality and energetic vibe, the design team found inspiration in a circus theme, and so the 'World Famous Circo Modular' idea was born. The brief called for a movable booth with a conceptual design that would adapt well to criss-crossing the globe at different fairs, just like a travelling circus. An old trailer stood in front of a huge show tent, with an open and inviting design along the length of the presentation – aptly illuminated with Modular products. With inviting sights and sounds creating a colourful cacophony, visitors could hardly resist the urge to step inside and investigate what was going on. Authentic elements were dotted around the space, among them animal cages, real-life acrobats and a retro-style trailer, which served as the meeting room for VIP clients. In the middle of the tent there was a 360-degree bar serving refreshments, the design of which brought to mind a carousel, although the stand did not have any moving parts. Nor were there any wild animals allowed at the fair, so the cages remained mostly empty, although some clowns were spotted in the bar area. The circus is a place that is packed full of creativity and where surprises blossom, and this concept corresponded perfectly with what Modular stands for as a brand.

TRADE FAIR **Light+Building**
WHERE **Frankfurt, Germany**
WHEN **April 2012**
DESIGNER **Rotor Group** ◪ **p.497**
STAND CONSTRUCTOR **Rotor Group**
CLIENT **Modular Lighting Instruments**
MARKET SECTOR **Architectural lighting**
TOTAL FLOOR AREA **330 m²**
PHOTOGRAPHER **Philip Braem**

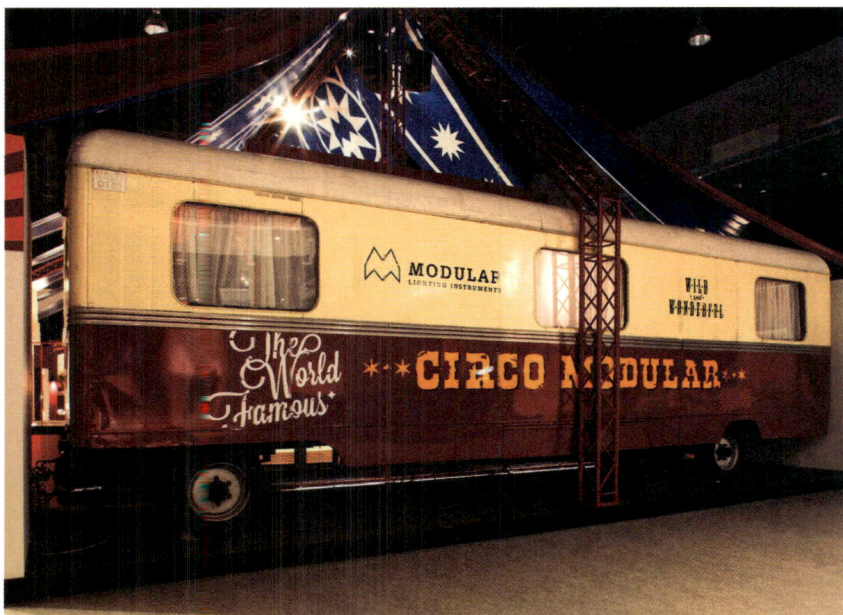

◪ The circus concept was introduced to present the latest high-end Modular lighting collection.
◪ Featured products illuminated the booth's interior and exterior.
◪ Inside the stand, visitors felt like they were in a circus big tent, ready to witness performers take to the stage.

Delta Light by Nice2C

A STRIKING BOULDER RESTING ON COLUMNS SET THE SCENE FOR A DEMONSTRATION OF LIGHT AS A FUNCTION OF ITS SURROUNDINGS.

TRADE FAIR **Interieur**
WHERE **Kortrijk, Belgium**
WHEN **October 2012**
DESIGNER **Nice2C** ☒ **p.496**
STAND CONSTRUCTOR **One Night Stands**
CLIENT **Delta Light**
MARKET SECTOR **Architectural lighting**
TOTAL FLOOR AREA **192 m²**
PHOTOGRAPHER **Delta Light**

Rather than the traditional product presentation stand, Delta Light wanted to bring an unrivalled lighting experience to the Interieur 2012 trade fair. The architectural lighting firm's design studio, Nice2C, came up with a concept for the stand as 'a structure like no other seen before'. That resulted in a monolithic boulder positioned above the exhibition space. From the exterior, the towering presentation looked like it was fashioned out of a chiselled rock face, supported by black metal columns. This stone-look facade hovered at a height of 1.86 m and rested on top of the pillars, with seemingly nothing else on the floor space. At first glance, there didn't seem to be much to see between the metal pillars that supported the monster stand. Passers-by may well have questioned this apparent emptiness. 'What exactly is this stand displaying?', they may have thought. And the next question would be, 'Why is everyone looking up?' It was only when they stepped into the sparse black and white environment that fair goers noticed the product placement overhead through a series of viewing holes punched through the low ceiling. These circular spy holes offered a clear line of site to the hollowed-out core of the boulder, revealing no fewer than 60 new Delta Light products. By wandering around the space and looking up through the nine openings, it was like visitors had access to several gigantic spyglasses that peered into differently illuminated scenarios. Each setting demonstrated how lighting could make a space warm or cold, how it could maximise or minimise a space, or how it could bring structures and materials to life.

☒ The imposing rock face was an impressive sight across the exhibition hall.
☒ Each circular opening had strikingly different product settings waiting to be viewed by visitors.

It was like visitors had access to spyglasses that peered into differently illuminated scenarios

Spherical shapes abounded beneath the boulder, from the columns and information podiums to the illuminated panels on the walls.
The openings in the ceiling all had different diameters.
The head-space within the stand was limited to contrast with the vast display space overhead, 'inside' the boulder.

Kreon by Kreon

LIGHTING PRODUCTS DISPLAYED WITH A LANGUAGE REFERRING TO PURE ARCHITECTURAL FORMS MIXED WITH NATURE.

The design of Kreon's lighting collections represents a way of thinking that reduces each product to its essential components without compromise. The brand's presentation at the 2012 Light+Building trade fair followed this premise, with an aim to show products as natural elements within the interior architecture of the stand. The booth design was conceived by Kreon, with the stand constructor Ueberholz ensuring all requirements were implemented in the presentation. Surfaces and spaces emphasised the lighting solutions, applied within a range of structured scenarios. A black and white colour palette created a homogeneous and clean-cut appearance, with metallic glints from the steel substrates catching the eye of fair goers. Such was the dominance of the square stand that it grabbed the attention of passers-by with an oversized white pelmet that wrapped around the top of the booth and featured a simple logo in black type on both sides to identify the stand to visitors. The elevated white perimeter appeared to float at times, but on closer inspection rested on matt-black columns on both sides of the booth. Other columns were set back to give the presentation an open feel. At two different junctures around the stand, a sense of nature prevailed owing to the birch tree trunks being positioned at an angle. The lighting concepts were subtly presented both here and inside the booth, where they formed an integral part of the architecture and engaged in a dialogue with the structure. Wall and ceiling panels overlapped, while niches, wall sections, walkways and seating areas were illuminated with an array of downlights, uplights and sidelights set harmoniously into the ceiling, floors and wall surfaces.

TRADE FAIR **Light+Building**
WHERE **Frankfurt, Germany**
WHEN **April 2012**
DESIGNER **Kreon** ⊠ **p.494**
STAND CONSTRUCTOR **Ueberholz**
CLIENT **Kreon**
MARKET SECTOR **Architectural lighting**
TOTAL FLOOR AREA **306 m²**
PHOTOGRAPHER **Frank Dora**

The black and white booth had elegant lines and a streamlined architecture.
At select points around the stand, tree trunks protruded from the floor and extended all the way to the ceiling.

Birch trees positioned on each of the stand's various patios had simple yet striking arrangements.

The architecture acted as if to frame the lighting concepts.

The product display areas were uncluttered and informative.

From the open edges of the booth, visitors could view the secluded seating areas within the interior.

Structured scenarios with a homogeneous appearance

Occhio by Drändle 70|30 and Martin et Karczinski

ELEGANT WHITE ARCHITECTURE SPLIT THROUGH THE CENTRE MERGED INTO A COHERENT UNIT FOR PRESENTING THE FUNCTION AND FUTURE OF LIGHT.

At Light+Building 2012 in Frankfurt, design lamp manufacturer Occhio presented its brand under the motto: 'future of light'. The stand was conceived, designed and built by Jürgen Drändle of Drändle 70|30 in collaboration with brand agency Martin et Karczinski, as well as designer Axel Meise from Occhio. The concept for the space was to create a luminous white stand that could display the entire product world of Occhio, divided into products of today, tomorrow and the future. A central walkway divided the elegant island into two distinct zones. The stand layout was symbolic: the public aisle of the exhibition hall doubled as the central aisle of the presentation. This open design invited visitors to enter the fascinating world of Occhio, which was equally divided between the product display area on one side and the communication zone on the other. These were flanked by a view of future developments in the Occhio family of lamps, to be introduced onto the market in 2013. The end walls of the elongated stand rose up to define the presentation. In the product area, glazed panels were set into the glossy white wall so that the 'future' innovations enjoyed an elevated pride of place, viewable to passers-by from every angle. On the ground level, four round islands presented current products, with corresponding circular canopies overhead reflecting the positioning of the podiums. An inviting arena and an illuminated water curtain positioned in the wall behind the bar dominated the generously proportioned communication area. The large, spherical-shaped canopy of the communication zone organically integrated io 3d spotlights that corresponded perfectly with the presentations in the two areas.

TRADE FAIR **Light+Building**
WHERE **Frankfurt, Germany**
WHEN **April 2012**
DESIGNERS **Drändle 70|30** ⊠ **p.491**
and **Martin et Karczinski** ⊠ **p.494**
STAND CONSTRUCTORS **Drändle 70|30, WSV Messebau**
CLIENT **Occhio**
MARKET SECTOR **Modular lighting systems**
TOTAL FLOOR AREA **360 m²**
PHOTOGRAPHER **Robert Sprang**

⊠ The helix motif in the water curtain symbolised the development of future Occhio products.
⊠ A crisp white decor created a relaxed air across the stand.
⊠ The client's name was simply stated on the exterior walls of the booth.
⊠ The circular podiums had a metallic treatment on one side, providing a sleek backdrop to the product displays.

Più Raumstrahler
Konzept 2013

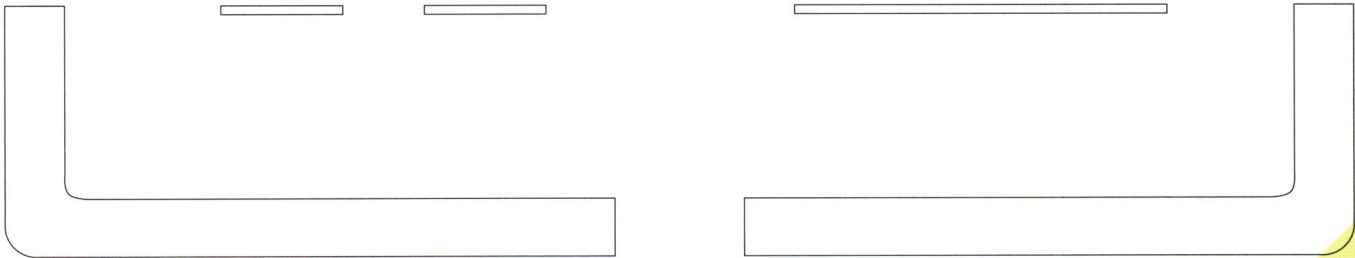

The concept encapsulated the client's motto: the future of light

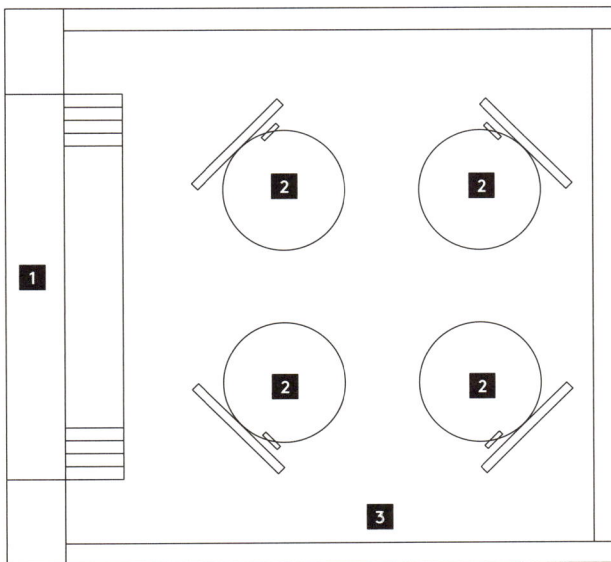

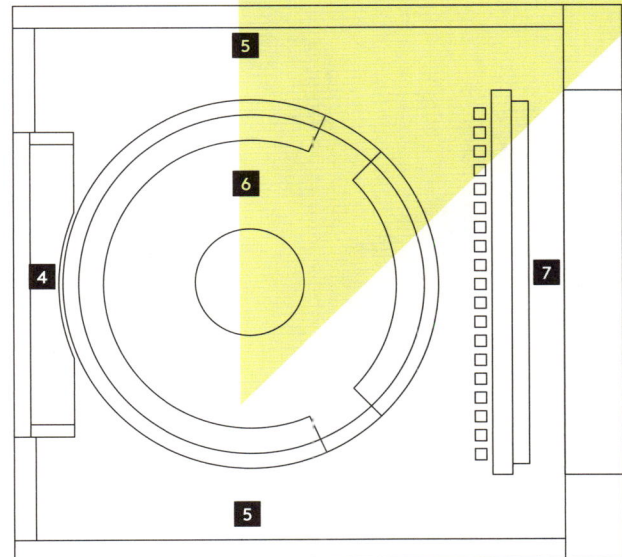

1 Upcoming products showcase
2 Current products showcase
3 Product sample area
4 Information desk
5 Infotainment area
6 Meeting lounge
7 Bar with water curtain

On the podium, visitors could get a closer look at the client's featured 'future' innovations.

Illustration of the entire stand profile with the suspended circular canopies overhead.

Off On by Ueberholz

SWITCHING ON THE LIGHT
FOR NEW LED TECHNOLOGY
IN A SHIPPING CONTAINER.

TRADE FAIR **Light+Building**
WHERE **Frankfurt, Germany**
WHEN **April 2012**
DESIGNER **Ueberholz** ☒ **p.499**
STAND CONSTRUCTOR **Ueberholz**
CLIENT **Off On**
MARKET SECTOR **LED technology**
TOTAL FLOOR AREA **22 m²**
PHOTOGRAPHER **Frank Dora**

At the Light+Building fair in 2012, Ueberholz was commissioned to develop a new presentation for Off On, a start-up company that creates and implements new lighting strategies with sophisticated design and high efficiency. The young company symbolises the dynamics of the LED market and its maxim is: 'Dedicated to light'. It develops energy-efficient LED technology, and the design team chose to highlight in the trade fair stand the first products the manufacturer created. The concept for the stand captured the firm's artistic and vibrant personality, and immediately captured the attention of fair goers as they approached. The setting featured two shipping containers placed side by side, with one positioned vertically to create a 10-m-tall tower that housed a bespoke chandelier made from 53 EQ T8 LED tubes. Here, visitors could adapt the different components of the contemporary light installation, changing the colours of the individual bulbs and finding out about the amount of energy consumption. The client's name symbolises turning off old behaviour patterns – in reference to currently available lighting devices – and turning on, opening the mind, to new lighting opportunities. One such opportunity is the everyday use of the firm's LED tube, which was the focus of the display elements in the second container. Here, colourful contexts were presented in the form of illuminated textile banners, integrated flat-screen monitors and light boxes to show the versatility in control and product ranges.

☒ The unusual set-up of the shipping containers presented the lighting firm as an intriguing and artistic entity.
☒ The booth was positioned in the open air, near the entrance of the exhibition hall.
☒ The vertical container with the impressive light chandelier rose to a height of 10 m.

ANSICHT SEITE-LK DLKSEITE.

INNENANSICHT

AUSSENANSICHT VARIANTE VORHANG

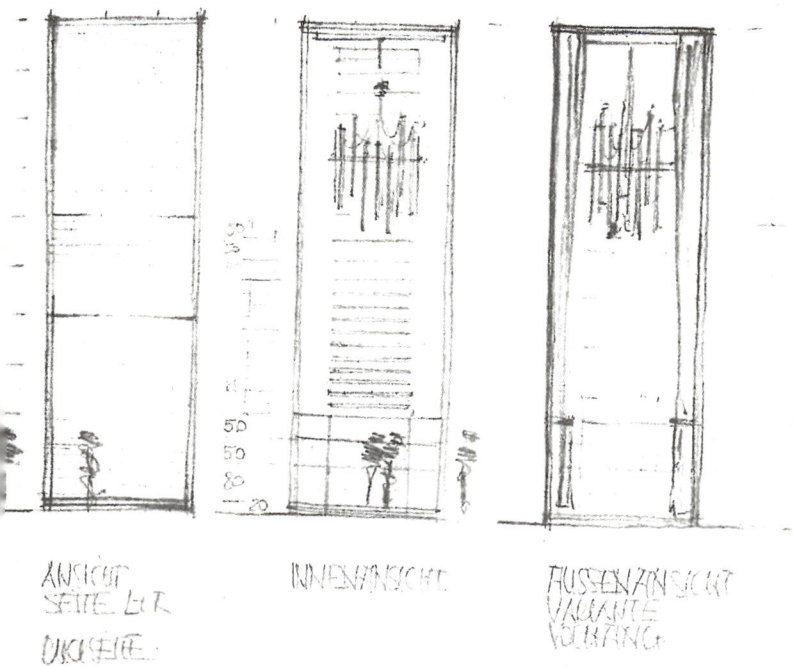

e show-stopping 10-m all tower housed a ontemporary chandelier

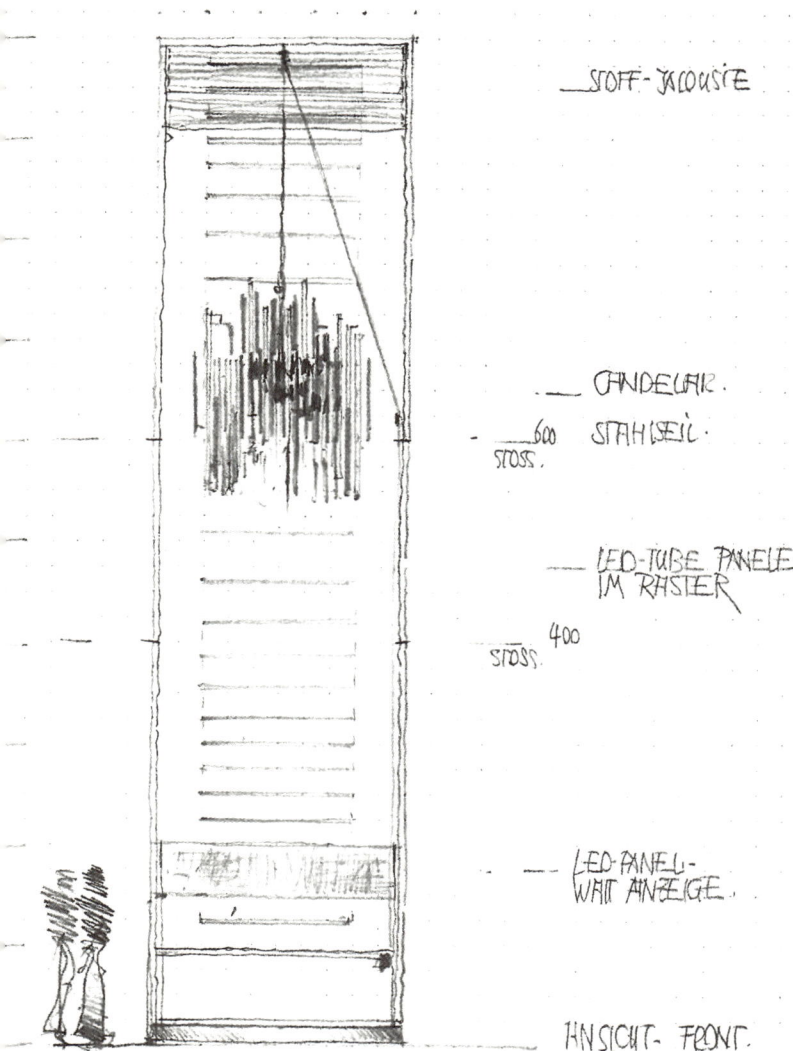

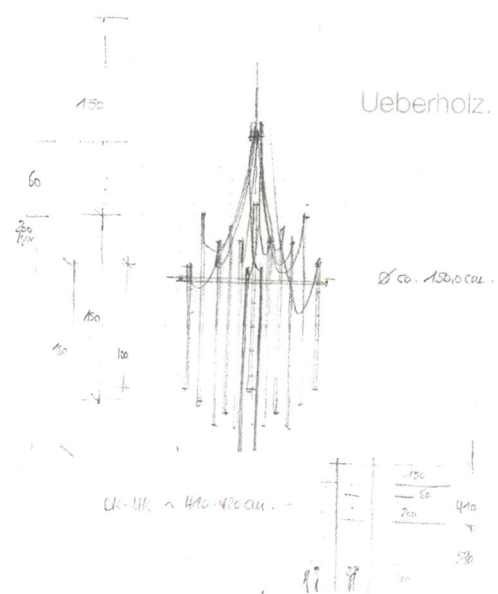

STOFF-JACOUSIE

CHANDELAR.

600 STAHLSEIL.
STOSS.

LED-TUBE PANELE IM RASTER

400
STOSS.

LED-PANEL-WATT ANZEIGE.

ANSICHT- FRONT.

Ueberholz.

⊠ As evening drew in, the dynamic light display really came to life.
⊠ Almost 100 LED tubes were used across the whole presentation.
⊠ Sketches of the vertical space with details of the various display elements.

⊠ The horizontal container displayed more examples of the client's innovations.
⊠ Information about everyday uses for the LED technology was available.
⊠ Visitors had chance to get up-close to the light source and handle the LED tubes in a 'lightsaber' fashion.
⊠ Dynamic media panels on the back wall communicated branded imagery.

The concept captured the firm's artistic and vibrant personality

Osram Opto Semiconductors by Bachmann.Kern und Partner

A SWEEPING BAND OF INSPIRATION HOVERING OVER EVERYDAY SCENARIOS HIGHLIGHTED LED USAGE FOR HOME AND WORK ENVIRONMENTS.

LED technology provides users with an abundance of lighting possibilities for both indoors and outdoors. The wide variety of uses inspired the Electronica trade fair presentation of Osram Opto Semiconductors, a leading manufacturer of LEDs. The stand was designed by architecture agency Bachmann.Kern und Partner to encapsulate the client's technology in terms of light, dynamics and speed. Five white bands, layered as waves on the back wall, represented the five product areas. One of the bands broke away from the surface to reveal glimpses of vibrant orange beneath, and this ribbon-like protrusion floated outwards from the wall and wrapped around and over the main area of the exhibition stand. Termed the 'band of inspiration', it optically connected the different areas used to present the wide range of applications. The exhibits were displayed in direct connection with the corresponding applications in mock-ups of living environments with highly abstract designs. The high-gloss black exhibits were presented in an almost sculptural manner, allowing them to stand out clearly against the matt-white backdrop. An Audi A8 car with a LED daytime running light was parked to one side of the stand under LED lamps and in front of an illuminated display window. A sketched-out floor plan provided the surroundings for the 'living' and 'working' areas, where LED technology abounded. In a black rotunda, four miniature everyday scenes portrayed by toy figures provided a fun example of the possible technical applications of Osram OS products. These scenes enabled visitors to use the integrated eyepieces to observe how, for example, a car-park barrier is opened using automatic number-plate recognition, or how the alarm system of a museum is activated when beams of light are crossed. An orange glow emanated from the hospitality lounge at the back of the stand, which revealed itself in the space thanks to the unraveling band.

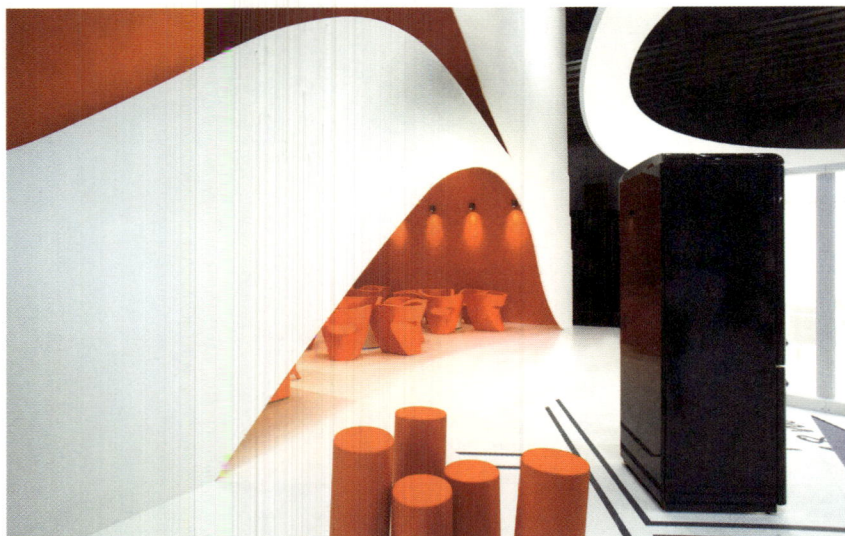

⊠ Where the white bands had peeled away from the back wall, the orange-hued hospitality lounge could be glimpsed.
⊠ The unravelling ribbon swept over the stand, visually connecting the different display zones.
⊠ The entire booth was positioned on a platform of white laminate flooring.
⊠ At the centre of the stand, LED technology that could be used in the living room was displayed.

TRADE FAIR **Electronica**
WHERE **Munich, Germany**
WHEN **November 2010**
DESIGNER **Bachmann.Kern und Partner** ⊠ **p.489**
STAND CONSTRUCTOR **Fruhen Messebau**
CLIENT **Osram Opto Semiconductors**
MARKET SECTOR **LED technology**
TOTAL FLOOR AREA **226 m²**
PHOTOGRAPHER **Marco Cormann**

Osram Opto Semiconductors by Bachmann.Kern und Partner

AN INTERLOCKING AND INTERCONNECTED BOOTH REPRESENTED A NETWORK OF PARTNERS FOR LED PRODUCTS.

Osram Opto Semiconductors was represented at the Light+Building 2012 trade fair as both a manufacturer of high-quality LEDs and the operator of its partner network 'LED Light for you'. Having previously worked with Osram at the 2010 fair, the architecture firm Bachmann.Kern und Partner was once again asked to design the 2012 booth for Osram and its network partners. The design focused on representing the network concept. Catchwords such as diversity, expertise, innovation and forum constituted the core in terms of both the content and design of the booth. The facade consisted of beams at different heights that intersected and overlapped. Converging in one line, the orthogonal beams became linear, horizontally extending into layers that formed a dividing wall to create an elliptical space called the forum. Here, the 16 partner companies could convene to present the LED network to visitors. At the front of the stand were circular podiums, which were segmented and divided up amongst the members of the network. Sharing a coherent and connecting visual image, the companies also had the opportunity to present themselves as independent entities within their own individually designed communication zones. An opening in the centre of the elliptical wall served as an access point to the lounge area at the back of the stand. Symbolically, this opening offered insight into the network and integrated visitors as active participants. The opening also referred to interlocking cogs, further underlining the network idea. Splashes of vibrant orange provided an attention-grabbing contrast to the overall white backdrop of the presentation. The criss-crossing beams allowed for glimpses into the interior, created a strong sense of depth, and drew visitors into the booth to linger a while.

TRADE FAIR **Light+Building**
WHERE **Frankfurt, Germany**
WHEN **April 2012**
DESIGNER **Bachmann.Kern & Partner** ⊠ **p.489**
STAND CONSTRUCTOR **Schmitt Messebau**
CLIENT **Osram Opto Semiconductors**
MARKET SECTOR **LED technology**
TOTAL FLOOR AREA **180 m²**
PHOTOGRAPHER **Frank Dora**

⊠ White was used as the base colour for the stand, with splashes of orange for the fittings and furnishings.
⊠ The criss-crossed beams represented the network concept.

Splashes of vibrant orange provided an attention-grabbing contrast

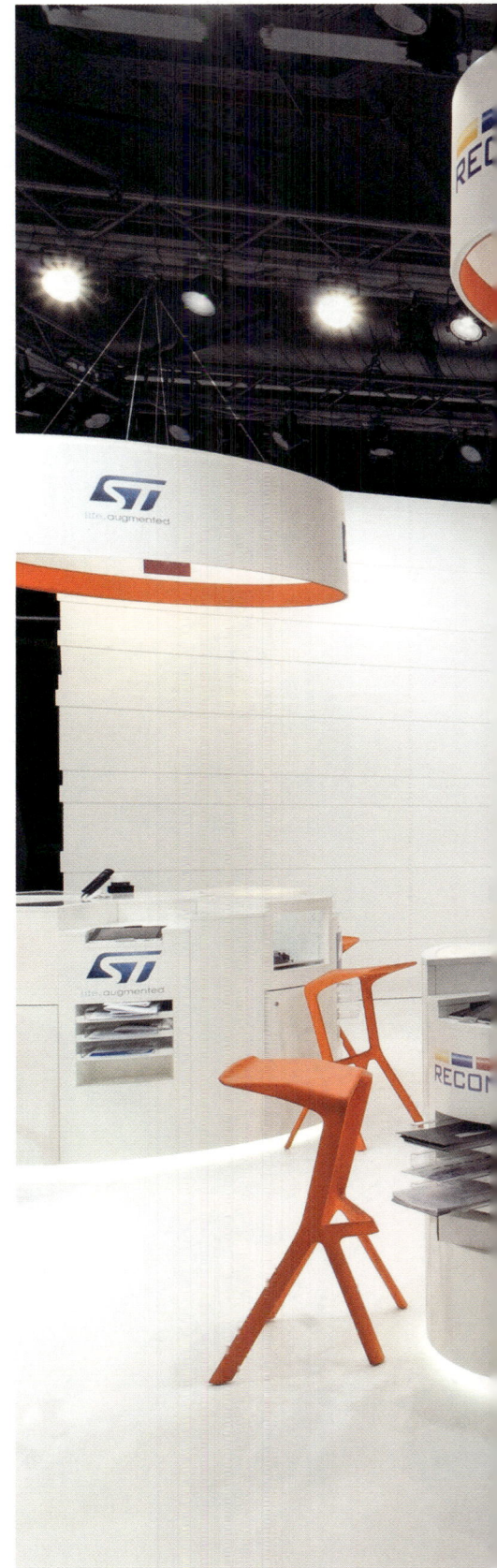

- ⊠ The positioning of the beams at the stand's corners meant passers-by could catch glimpses of the interior.
- ⊠ The exhibition area presented all partners equally while also highlighting their own individual strengths.
- ⊠ The semi-secluded meeting area at the back gave a sense of depth of the stand.

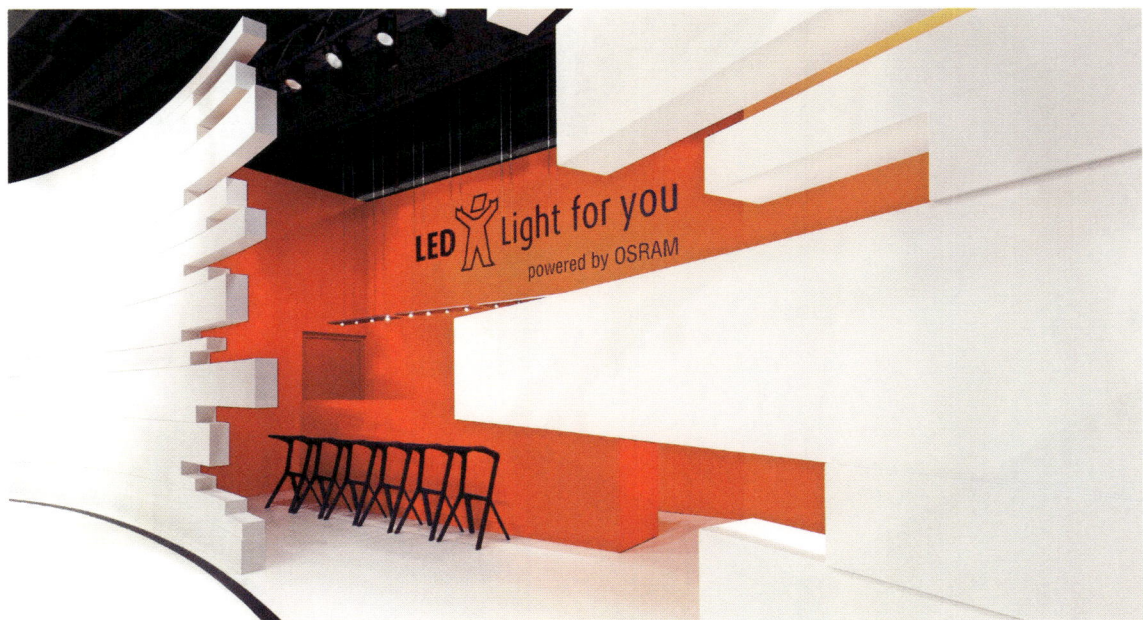

Prolicht by Arting

ARCHITECTURAL LIGHTING WAS ENCAPSULATED
WITHIN A MOUNTAIN-LIKE, ANGULAR STAND TO
CONJURE UP A FUTURISTIC INTERIOR.

Prolicht, the Austrian provider of innovative lighting solutions, wanted to create a branded space that sent strong signals about its products and design heritage to break through the competitive noise at one of the world's largest lighting fairs. At the same time, the stand had to showcase a broad selection of the company's fixtures, and create separate zones for getting up close and personal with the products, as well as for interacting with clients. Arting was in charge of the project and approached the challenge by first creating an architectural black envelope, pierced by fissures of light, to establish an intriguing facade that represented the essence of the brand. Ultimately, light cannot be contained or stopped, and through these luminescent cracks in the mountain-like exterior of the stand – recalling the client's Tyrolean heritage – visitors were attracted to catch glimpses of what was going on inside. That encouraged them to step inside and find out more. Upon entering the stand, fair goers embarked on a journey through a snowy white landscape of angled surfaces illuminated by a tasteful range of recessed, surface-mounted and suspended lights and spotlights. In this inner sanctum, guests were afforded the time and space to focus entirely on individual products, undisturbed by the noise outside. At the heart of the exhibition space was a secluded, cosy and elegant lounge. With its warm colours and natural oak surfaces, the hospitality area was the perfect place to unwind whilst subtly providing yet another showcase for additional featured products, this time in an intimate context ideal for the kind of relaxed negotiation that only occurs between confident and comfortable partners.

TRADE FAIR Light+Building
WHERE Frankfurt, Germany
WHEN April 2012
DESIGNER Arting ☒ p.488
STAND CONSTRUCTOR Arting
CLIENT Prolicht
MARKET SECTOR Architectural lighting
TOTAL FLOOR AREA 460 m²
PHOTOGRAPHERS Simon Fischbacher,
Steffen Stamp

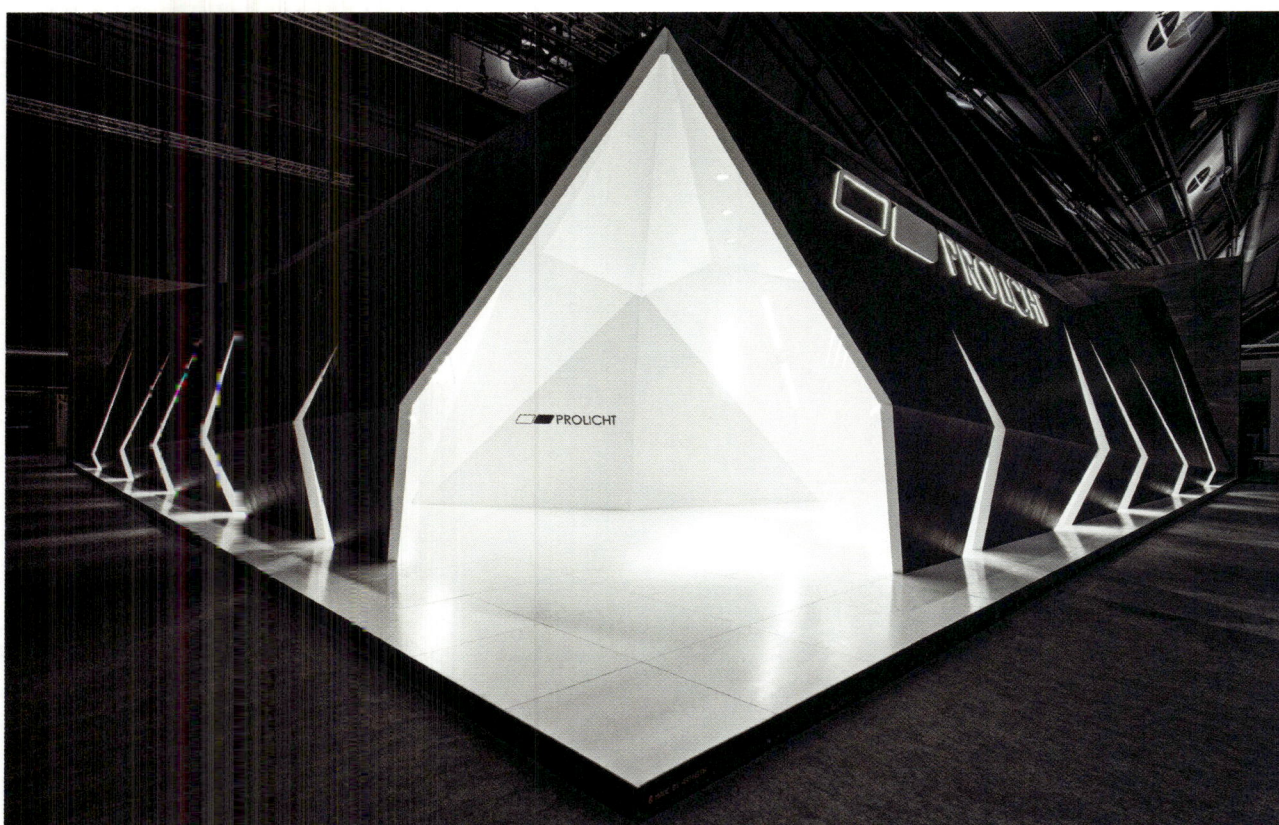

☒ The stand's facade restricted the view of the products inside, building suspense for fair goers.
☒ Strong contrast between the black exterior and the white corridors drew visitors into the light.

Journeying through a
snowy white landscape
of angled surfaces

LIGHTING

GRAND STAND

☒ Along the corridors, different product families were positioned.
☒ The black rock accommodated a meeting room and a water fountain.
☒ A sleek concrete wall added to the collection of natural materials that decorated the space.

The oak wood in the lounge area oozed warmth and cosiness.

The long wooden tables were illuminated with feature pendant lights.

Construction visuals of the angled walls taking shape.

Floor plan

Reception
Lounge area
Library wall
Bar
Kitchen
Meeting lounge
Storage

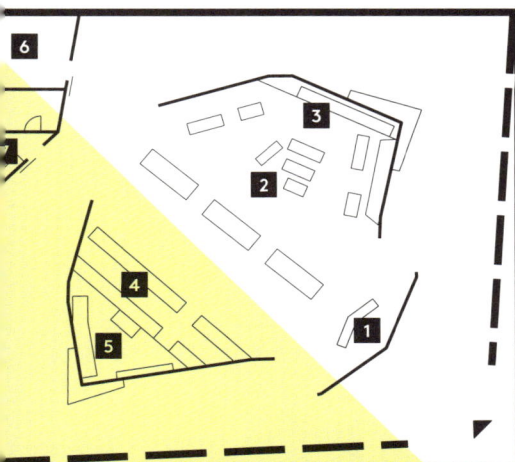

Vibia by Francesc Rifé Studio

LARGE ARCHITECTURAL VOLUMES CREATED AMBIENT SILHOUETTES AND INTERESTING PERSPECTIVES THAT ALLOWED DECORATIVE LIGHTING SCENARIOS TO SHINE.

TRADE FAIR **Light+Building**
WHERE **Frankfurt, Germany**
WHEN **April 2012**
DESIGNER **Francesc Rifé Studio** ✕ **p.491**
STAND CONSTRUCTOR **Montaggio**
CLIENT **Vibia**
MARKET SECTOR **Decorative lighting**
TOTAL FLOOR AREA **350 m²**
PHOTOGRAPHER **Fernando Alda**

Lighting firm Vibia aims to exert a large impact on its target market. That is why its trade fair stands are often large. To leave a lasting impression, the firm's presentation at Light+Building 2012 once again encompassed this philosophy in its design. Realised by Francesc Rifé Studio, the stand featured several large architectural volumes for the presentation of individual brand collections. When viewed from the outside, the long facade played with different levels and perspectives, as if it formed the skyline of a great city. Latticework applied to the exterior walls allowed fair goers to instantly see in a subtle way the novelties of the Vibia brand. As visitors approached the booth, they could easily distinguish the different products with illumination emanating from the various junctions in the framework of the stand. The presentation was large and impressive, but was light in character thanks to the textures and materials used. From shiny white to dusty mink to natural oak, the various materials created settings and highlighted specific product groups dedicated to home luminaries or outdoor scenarios. The large box-like volumes appeared as oversized window frames that emphasised the products glimpsed within. Rich fabrics also ensured a translucent display of the product inside, but to see everything in its entirety, visitors were enticed to enter the stand. Here, further box-like volumes were arranged as rooms with minimalist settings that allowed the decorative lighting modules to shine.

✕ The stand design was based on a cube concept, as were the interior volumes.
✕ The lattice wall attracted visitors, giving them a glimpse of the products inside which enticed them to enter and find out more.
✕ From the outside, the architectural volumes piled on top of each other looked like a contemporary apartment block.

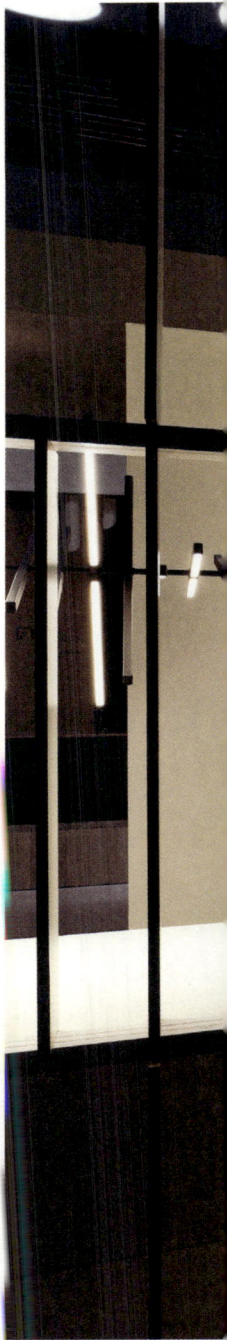

From shiny white to dusty mink to natural oak

⊠ The stand's rich materials were the perfect backdrop for the client's decorative lighting collection.
⊠ The individual volumes fitted together to create an enticing, glowing cube.
⊠ The geometric shape of the furniture complemented the light modules that adorned the ceiling and walls.

MOBI

ITY

Audi Ring by Schmidhuber and KMS Blackspace

THIS HAVEN FOR AUTOMOBILE LOVERS BOASTED A TEST TRACK THAT RACED THROUGH THE BUILDING LIKE A PULSATING ARTERY.

The central square on the grounds of the Frankfurt Motor Show 2011 set the stage for Audi's appearance at the fair. A freestanding building – the Audi Ring – was constructed as the brand's monumental trade fair stand, complete with driving track. The concept and architecture of the installation were developed by brand architects Schmidhuber, in cooperation with KMS Blackspace for communications and media content. The idea behind the spatial concept was the notion that 'cars have to move'. At the heart of the megastructure – which occupied a space of 100 x 70 x 12 m – was the integrated driving track capable of accommodating up to nine automobiles moving simultaneously on two levels. The layout played with variations between the interior and exterior: large openings allowed parts of the 400-m-long track to 'swerve' outside the stand via elongated openings in the facade, where they caught the attention of passers-by. The driving track formed the core of the architectural ensemble, which was characterised by flowing forms, curved lines and surprising transitions. Inside the building, all the design features were geared towards the experience of visitors as they toured the presentation alongside the latest Audi models. Unique encounters appeared at every turn, from the opportunity to control the holographic images projected onto acrylic vehicle models, to the first-hand involvement with the presentation by co-piloting the vehicles on display. At the end of the tour, two showcase cars were staged, accompanied by the multimedia brand show where real and virtual elements, spatial dramaturgy and communication were perfectly choreographed to blend into one.

TRADE FAIR **IAA**
WHERE **Frankfurt, Germany**
WHEN **September 2011**
DESIGNERS **Schmidhuber** ☒ **p.497**
and **KMS Blackspace** ☒ **p.493**
STAND CONSTRUCTOR **Ambrosius**
CLIENT **Audi**
MARKET SECTOR **Automotive**
TOTAL FLOOR AREA **8500 m²**
PHOTOGRAPHER **Andreas Keller**

A sense of motion filled the air as visitors got to experience the cars at first hand.

The free-flowing lines of the vast architecture dominated the trade fair's central plaza.

Dynamic illumination and media presentations created a high-tech show for visitors.

Flowing forms, curved lines and surprising transitions

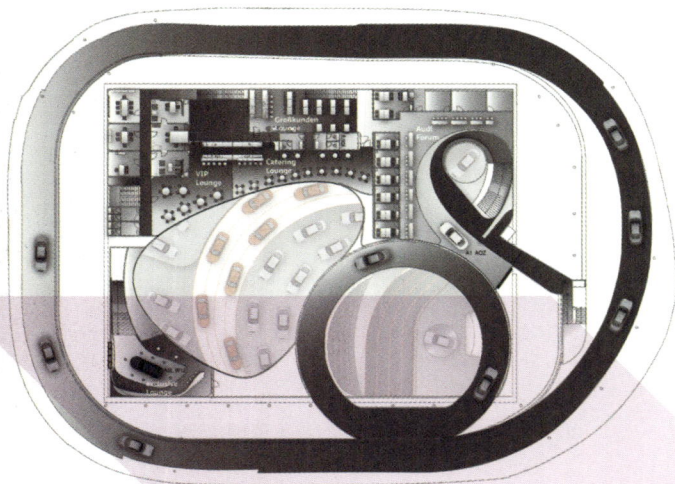

☒ First floor

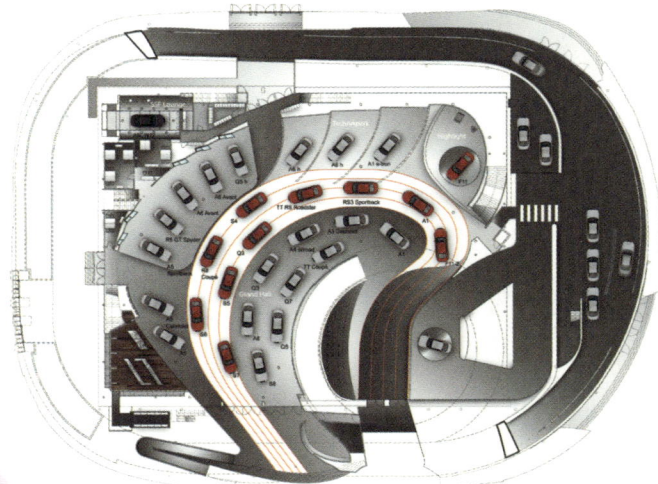

☒ Ground floor

☒ The staging and multimedia displays conveyed dynamism and innovation.
☒ Movement and flowing contours were discernible from every point of the booth.
☒ The showcased models could be encountered from multiple angles.

Colour One for MINI by Scholten & Baijings

LAYING BARE A VEHICLE'S ESSENTIALS AND PIMPING UP THE COMPONENT PARTS RESULTED IN AN ABSTRACT TAKE ON CAR DESIGN.

The concept Colour One for MINI, presented at the Salone del Mobile 2012, explored the world of a car in the area between objective fact and imaginative vision. The installation analysed the process of design and investigated the composition of a car, right down to the smallest details. The commission was instigated by Adrian van Hooydonk, senior vice president of BMW Group Design, when he approached Scholten & Baijings to formulate a new vision of MINI. He gave the designers an open invitation to do whatever they wanted. A statement about their relationship with the car, a product that somehow reflected the car, an installation around the car – everything was possible. The duo set about deconstructing the MINI One, which embodies all the hallmarks of MINI design, by stripping it layer by layer and extracting the essence of every component. Scholten & Baijings worked closely with the brand's own design team and enhanced the stripped parts with colour and texture to reveal an innovative view of car design. The core of the vehicle and its constituent parts was laid out in a paddock-like enclosure, surrounded by a three-dimensional roof structure and translucent walls. From the perforated fibreglass outer layer of the car through to the interior aspects that were treated as art exhibits on low-rise plinths – including the moulded fluorescent steering wheel, transparent rubber tyres and bright orange bumper – visitors could walk around the perimeter of the presentation to investigate the abstracted car parts up-close. Porcelain white was used as the basic unobtrusive colour accent for the presentation, with vibrant aspects added in the splashes of fluorescent colour, along with shiny textured materials and geometric patterns. Display cases visualised for fair goers the entire design process, showing the textiles and samples that were executed in the designer team's own atelier.

TRADE FAIR **Salone Internazionale del Mobile**
WHERE **Milan, Italy**
WHEN **April 2012**
DESIGNER **Scholten & Baijings** ☒ **p.497**
STAND CONSTRUCTOR **Scholten & Baijings**
CLIENT **BMW Group**
MARKET SECTOR **Automotive**
TOTAL FLOOR AREA **900 m²**
PHOTOGRAPHERS **BMW, Scheltens & Abbenes**

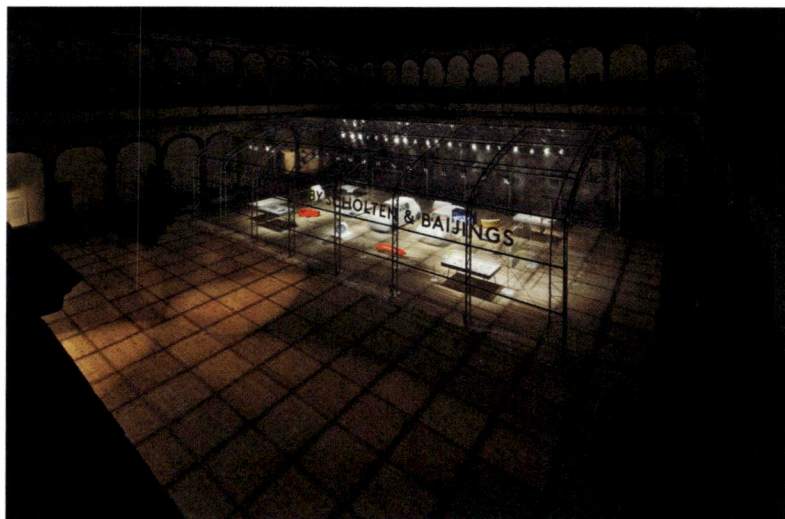

☒ The location was a paddock that afforded a view of the 18th-century courtyard of the State University of Milan.
☒ The sketch books gave visitors a real insight into the design process of the project.
☒ The research display cases also presented scaled models and design drawings.
☒ The presentation was laid bare, much like the constituent parts of the car.

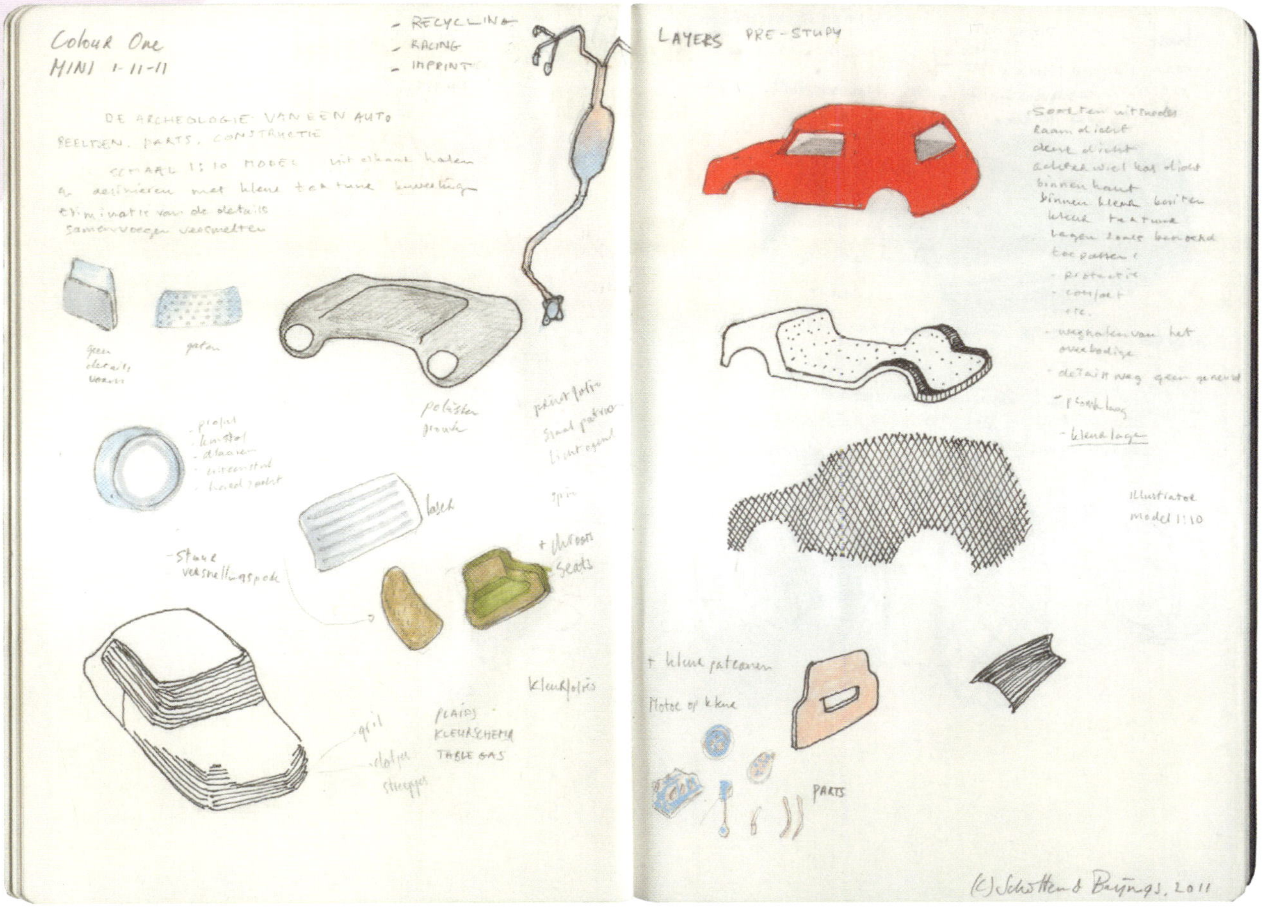
Colour One
MINI 1-11-11
- RECYCLING
- RACING
- IMPRINT
DE ARCHEOLOGIE VAN EEN AUTO
BEELDEN, PARTS, CONSTRUCTIE
LAYERS PRE-STUDY
KLEURSCHEMA
PARTS
(C) Scholten & Baijings, 2011

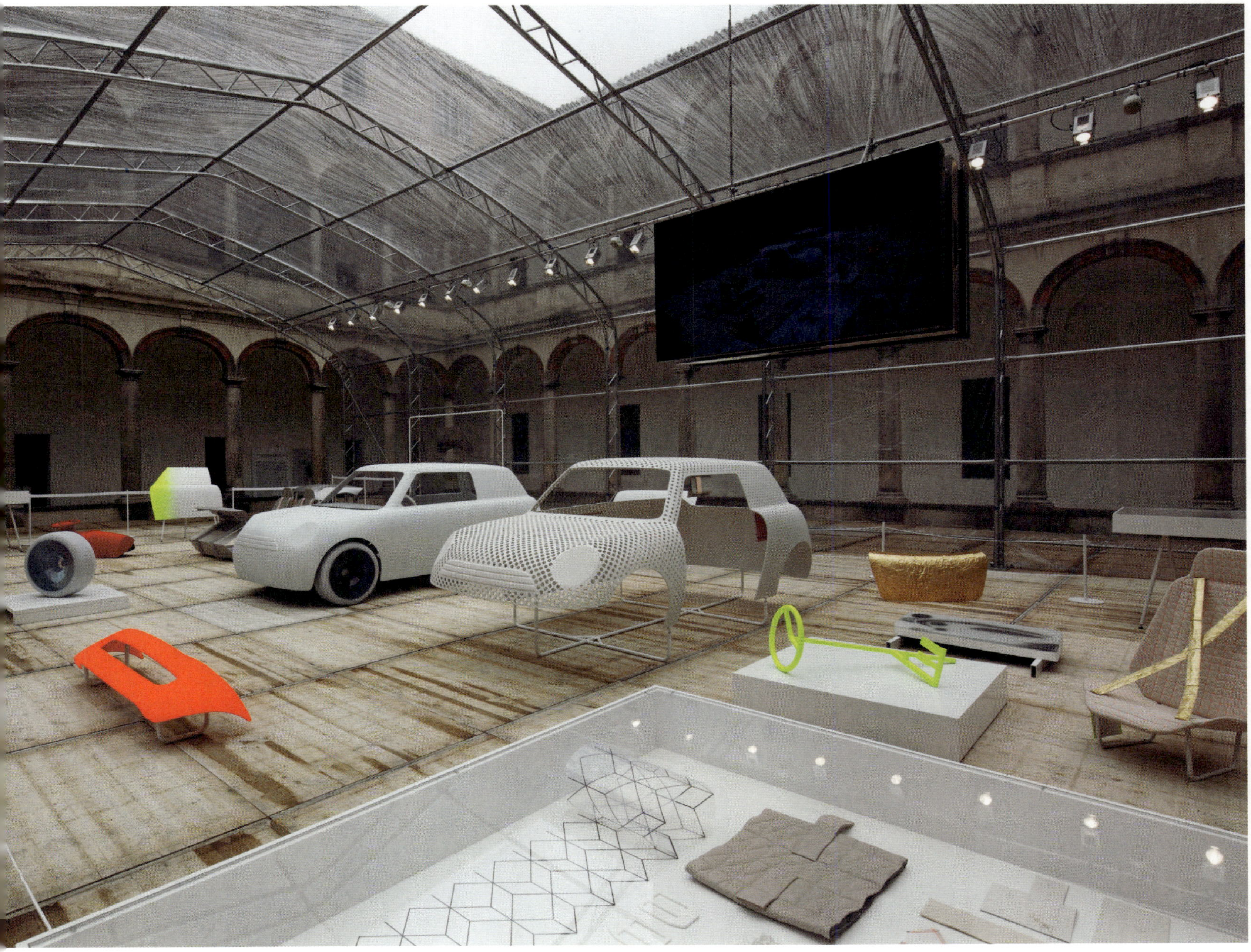

Interior aspects were treated as art exhibits

- ⊠ The outer shell was transformed with porcelain lacquer, perforated by a myriad of tiny little holes to create an organic system of ventilation.
- ⊠ The car's interior was lined with geometric patterns.
- ⊠ Steering wheel, doors, seats and the bumper were treated as works of art.

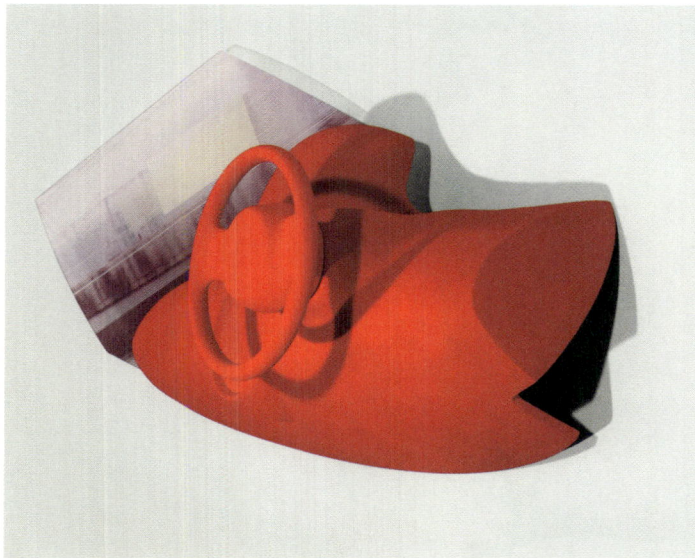

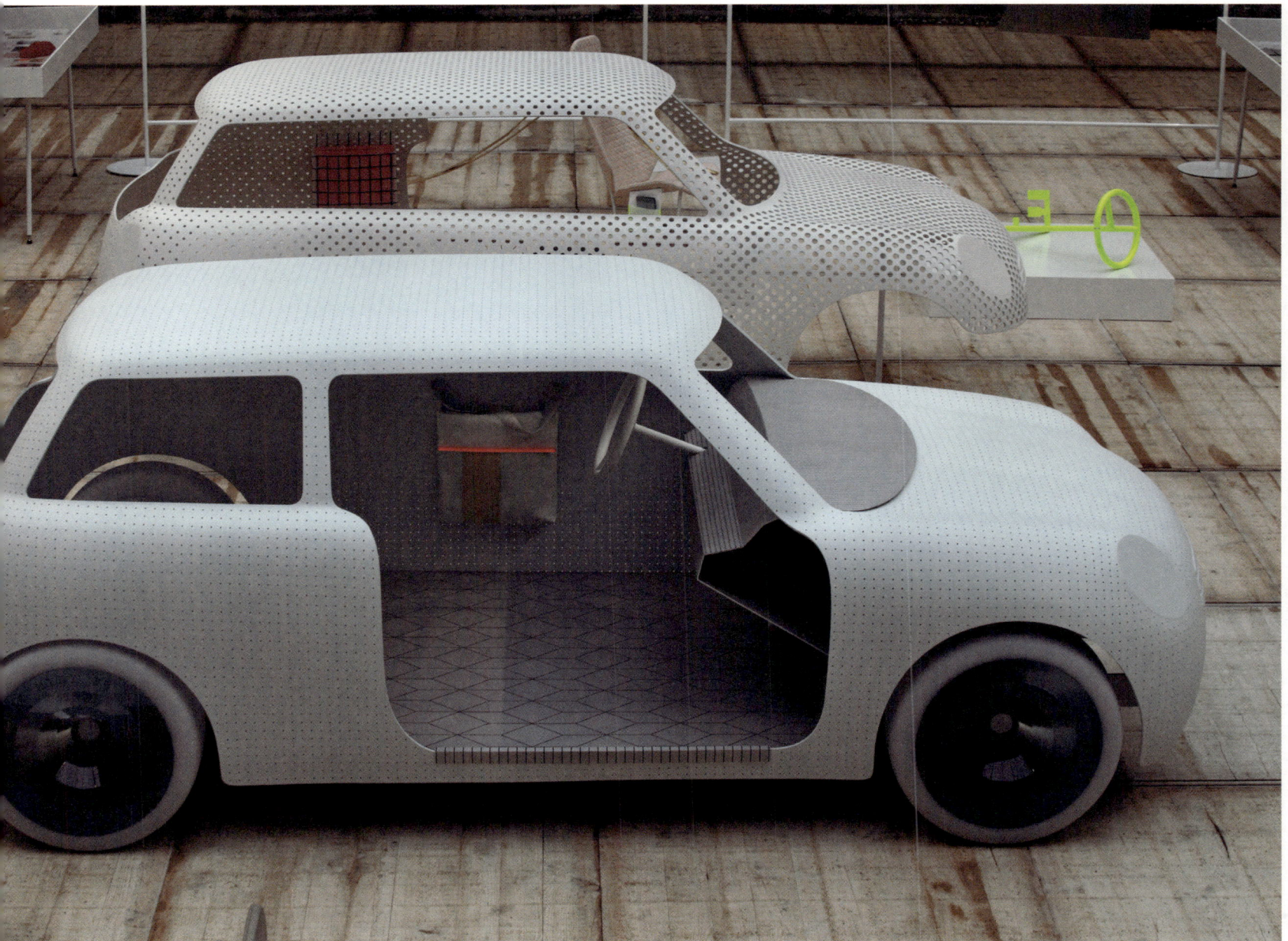

Mazda by Uniplan

A DYNAMIC CAR PRESENTATION THAT GAVE THE STAR OF THE SHOW THE RED-CARPET TREATMENT.

Tasked with realising the Mazda presence at the IAA motor show 2011 in Frankfurt, design studio Uniplan focused on the fact that Mazda's fleet of vehicles are fun to drive. This was the thirteenth time that the team had designed the client's stand at the IAA fair, and so it had already established a firm relationship with the automotive brand. The task on this occasion was to promote the fun of the Mazda brand with a concept that started out with the motto: 'defy convention'. The trade fair booth was a combination of the modular stand design developed for Mazda over the years, plus some new, surprising stand elements. A key highlight was the presentation of the world premiere of the Mazda CX-5. The car was displayed on a quartz granulate strip that sliced through the platform's white and grey stone floor tiles. Akin to a red carpet of the motoring world, the surface glistened like an ice-covered road. The LED design ensured an added dramatic aspect, with strips of light emanating from glass panels on the floor. The lighting strips were also integrated into the stairs immediately behind the vehicle and suspended from the ceiling as an eye-catching installation. The double-sided platform in the middle of the stand created two strong, media-charged stages for further vehicle display that flanked the central presentation. LED projections allowed for dynamic movement that gave the impression that the vehicles were actually moving. On the ground floor were areas for visitor interaction and information. Tucked underneath the raised platform, the 3D cinema showed the CX-5 in action at close range. Positioned next to it was the 'lab', where the engines and gear-boxes of the current Skyactiv generation were presented.

TRADE FAIR **IAA**
WHERE **Frankfurt, Germany**
WHEN **September 2011**
DESIGNER **Uniplan** ☒ **p.499**
STAND CONSTRUCTOR **Uniplan**
CLIENT **Mazda**
MARKET SECTOR **Automotive**
TOTAL FLOOR AREA **1880 m²**
PHOTOGRAPHER **Stefan Schilling**

☒ The central platform transformed the area beneath into a closed auditorium.
☒ The highlight vehicle was in a clear visual relationship with the flanking cars, demonstrating their shared origins.
☒ Media displays presented product highlights and innovations.

Mercedes-Benz by Phocus Brand Contact

AN IMPOSING BLACK BOX HOUSED A SUSPENSEFUL SPECTACLE IN THE RUN-UP TO THE PRODUCT LAUNCH.

AutoRAI, also called the Amsterdam International Motor Show, is a biennial motor show in the Amsterdam RAI exhibition centre. At the 2012 fair, Mercedes-Benz presented the first phase of the launch of its new city van – Citan – prior to the full market launch in autumn 2012. Phocus Brand Contact designed the exhibition stand with the goal of developing a truly innovative concept to attract as much attention as possible. The project needed to reflect the client's leading-edge image and not only convey the story of the new Citan and its high quality, but also generate buying interest among the fair goers. The challenge was to communicate and demonstrate all the benefits of the new vehicle without having the Citan on site at all. The chosen concept was that of a 'Black Box'. Within a dark, lustrous volume 7 m in height, a full-size model of the Citan was impressively presented via 3D projection mapping. The vehicle staging focused the dramatic presentation by using five projectors and LED technology on three surfaces – the floor, the backdrop, and a mock-up model of the van. An accompanying soundtrack and monochromatic visuals told the story of the new vehicle, vividly representing how the Citan cannot be held back by anything and rises to any challenge imposed on it by the city. A tiered seating area invited visitors to sit and watch a 4-minute show where in the abstract projections, urban scenes and accompanying suspense-packed soundtrack created a mesmerising spectacle. The eye-catching black box formed an impressive silhouette within the fair environment by itself, whilst the booming bass that spilled out of the branded space was an additional contributing factor in attracting passers-by to investigate what was going on inside.

TRADE FAIR **AutoRAI**
WHERE **Amsterdam, the Netherlands**
WHEN **April 2012**
DESIGNER **Phocus Brand Contact** ☒ **p.496**
STAND CONSTRUCTOR **Artlife**
CLIENT **Daimler**
MARKET SECTOR **Automotive**
TOTAL FLOOR AREA **222 m²**
PHOTOGRAPHER **Ludger Paffrath**

☒ A dark, mysterious multimedia created intrigue in the new product.
☒ The looped 4-minute-long show divided into four acts.
☒ The scenarios on screen linked wit visuals projected onto the van.

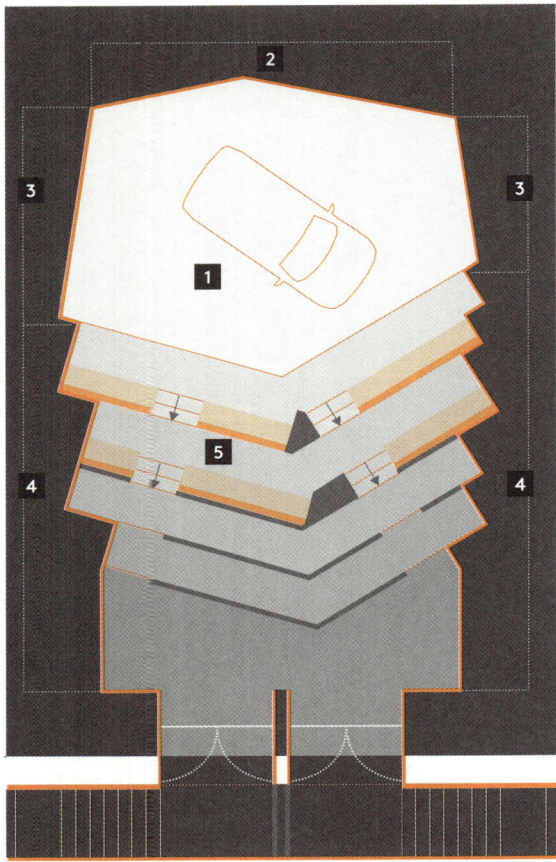

Floor plan

1 Stage
2 Projection screen
3 Mirror
4 LED elements
5 Auditorium

Dramatic presentation in a dark, lustrous space

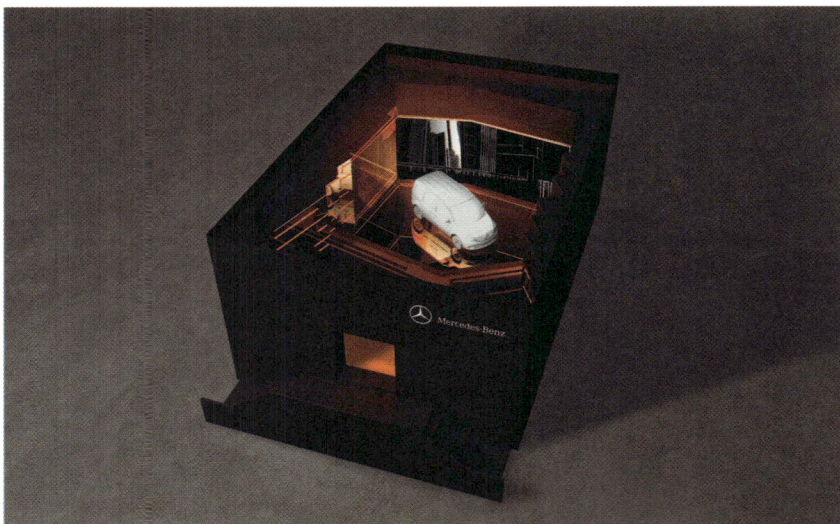

From the auditorium, the hi-tech visual show could be fully appreciated.

The exterior of the large Black Box was noticeably branded with the Mercedes-Benz trademark.

A monochromatic feel ran through the film until the van's covering was removed to reveal a citrus orange colour.

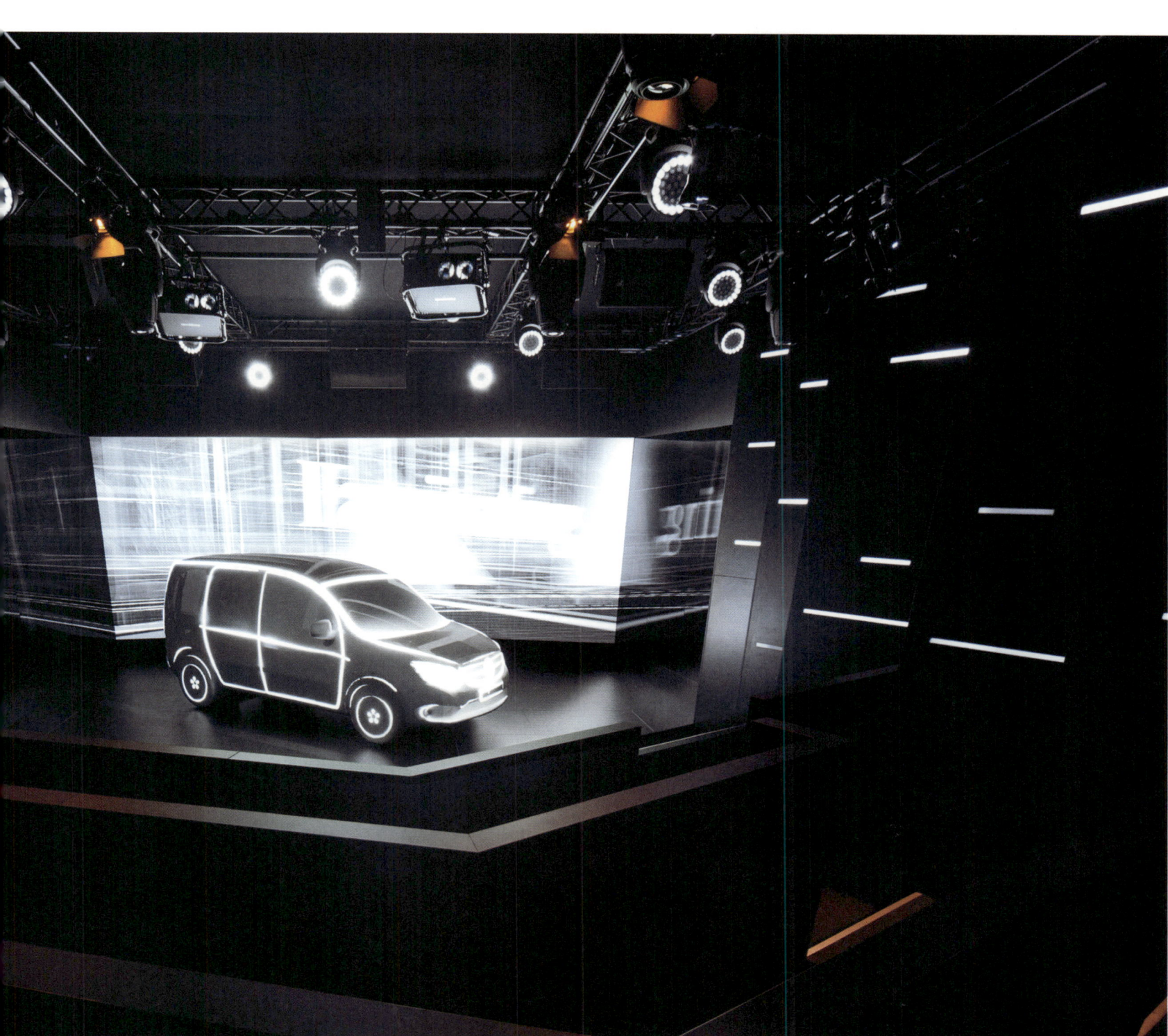

Always on the move...

Mercedes-Benz Geneva by jangled nerves

THE STAGE WAS SET FOR AN A-CLASS AUTOMOTIVE PRESENTATION IN GENEVA.

TRADE FAIR Geneva International Motor Show
WHERE Geneva, Switzerland
WHEN March 2012
DESIGNER jangled nerves ⊠ p.493
STAND CONSTRUCTOR Raumtechnik Messebau & Event Services
CLIENT Daimler
MARKET SECTOR Automotive
TOTAL FLOOR AREA 3800 m²
PHOTOGRAPHER Andreas Keller

The focus of the trade fair exhibition by Mercedes-Benz at the 82nd Geneva International Motor Show was the world premiere of the new A-Class. Its sporty and dynamic look is primarily designed to appeal to a younger target group. The main topics of the automotive presentation, which covered an area of 3800 m², were translated into a spatial brand experience by German creative firm jangled nerves. It integrated a striking 'brand ribbon' into the stand, which enveloped the space and caught the eyes of fair goers from a distance. With its distinctive silver polygonal surfaces made from brushed aluminium sheets, the band not only generated a unique look but also established all the necessary functional divisions within the exhibition space. Visitors were invited to walk in and around the space decked with dark wood parquet flooring as they circumnavigated the cars, displayed as if they were distinguished stars on a stage. Around the periphery of the stand, amidst the branded silver ribbon, were large staircases that invited fair goers to visit the upper floor where a lounge, cafeteria and VIP area awaited them. Appearing to float, the elevated level afforded a magnificent view of the exhibited vehicles and the entire hall. At the same time, the visitors themselves became part of the spectacle. The back office area was at ground level, shielded from the crowds by its discreet integration into the brand ribbon. A dynamic visual feature of the exhibition stand was an almost 100-m² LED wall that created a prominent space for communicating contemporary brand messages to the target audience. Dedicated areas for displaying technical information flanked both sides of the back wall, and visitors could also enjoy a 20-minute film that highlighted the specifications and characteristics of the new A-Class vehicle series. Architecture and media production merged to form a brand experience that blurred the distinction between real and virtual space.

◪ The LED wall allowed for dynamic branded imagery.
◪ Architecture and media production merged to form a unique brand experience for visitors.
◪ The upper level afforded fair goers magnificent views of the booth.
◪ Technical information was housed in enclaves on the back wall.

Mercedes-Benz SLK
by jangled nerves

FOR THE UNVEILING OF A SHINY
NEW AUTOMOBILE, THE STAR OF
THE SHOW WAS PRESENTED WITH
THE GIFT-WRAPPING PEELED BACK
AND THE TOP DOWN.

The excitement of Christmas, birthdays and any other gift-giving celebrations happening all at once – that was the feeling that the design team jangled nerves conjured up for the launch of the Mercedes-Benz Convertible SLK in Germany. The special exhibition set brought to mind the shiny wrapping paper that is ripped off a surprise present at the very moment you excitedly reveal what is inside. The peeled-back layers gave passers-by their first glimpse of what was inside – in this case, a sparkling new car. Painted MDF panels printed with branded messages and phrases were arranged at angles to one another, rising up at either end of the presentation and almost cocooning the pristine white vehicle. At the same time, they gave the impression that at any moment this new-born would be set free. The convertible nature of the premiere vehicle was also emphasised, with evocative stereoscopic images aimed at bringing to life that unique feeling of driving with the top down. Suspended above the SLK, as the focal point of the installation, were angled features covered with mirrored laminate. These elements created a cloud imagery that once again evoked the sensation of driving a convertible in the open air. The polygon-shaped clouds with reflective elements suspended from cables created an illusion of dynamism and a wide-open sky. The stand's modular structure allows the presentation to adapt to all kinds of exhibition spaces. It is even possible for a team to easily assemble the temporary display in a matter of hours, including the necessary suspension equipment and lighting elements.

TRADE FAIR **Mercedes-Benz Exhibition**
WHERE **Munich, Germany**
WHEN **March 2011**
DESIGNER **jangled nerves** ⊠ p.493
STAND CONSTRUCTOR **Raumtechnik Messebau & Event Services**
CLIENT **Daimler**
MARKET SECTOR **Automotive**
TOTAL FLOOR AREA **80 m²**
PHOTOGRAPHER **Andreas Keller**

⊠ The modular design allowed flexible adaption to different spaces.
⊠ The installation featured a blue colour scheme and cloud imagery to evolve the sensation of driving in the open air.

The excitement of every
gift-giving celebration
happening all at once

The set, structured by form TL, contained
all the necessary suspension equipment
and lighting elements.
Painted panels included branded
messages and phrases in mirrored writing.
The 'clouds' overhead reflected the
phrases the right way up.

Mercedes Next by Kauffmann Theilig & Partner and Atelier Markgraph

PULSATING ONSTAGE PERFORMANCES COMPLEMENTED PREMIERE VEHICLE PRESENTATIONS.

Frankfurt's Festival Hall once again played host to the most important trade fair presentation of Mercedes-Benz at the IAA, where the 'pulse' of a new generation of automobiles was on display. The design was the ninth IAA collaboration between Kauffmann Theilig & Partner and Atelier Markgraph for the brand and entailed a continuation of its year-long theme: '125 years of automobile'. The vast space of the exhibition hall was divided by a longitudinal axis into two sharply juxtaposed sides. To the south was a spacious stage for displays, performances and media events, while to the north were the exhibition zones that doubled as viewing areas for visitors. Overlooking the central area, both sides rose up and reached towards the suspended midnight-blue dome overhead. The stage was framed by a sweeping band made of anodised brushed aluminium. This 1200-m² silver sculpture surrounded a media-kinetic stage on which the staggered media surfaces, cars and people merged into a three-dimensional choreography. The presentation pulsated out from this stage: horizontal and vertical LED surfaces created spaces of surprising depth and achieved constantly changing dynamics through moving images in the fore- and back-ground and on the LED floor. The pulse defined the rhythm for both the visitor experience and the premiere vehicle presentations. At the entrance of the hall, visitors were directed to first rise to the top of the building by escalator. From there, they walked around the presentation along a circular route via the intimate, terraced spaces and various vehicle displays on all the tiered levels, before returning back to the ground floor. An optimal view of the media stage was incorporated into the entire experience. On every level, the glass railings, long edges and built-in seating areas opened up new vistas for fair goers, who could leisurely move between the show and the clearly arranged vehicle areas.

TRADE FAIR **IAA**
WHERE **Frankfurt, Germany**
WHEN **September 2011**
DESIGNERS **Kauffmann Theilig & Partner** ⊠ **p.493** and **Atelier Markgraph** ⊠ **p.489**
STAND CONSTRUCTOR **Display International**
CLIENT **Daimler**
MARKET SECTOR **Automotive**
TOTAL FLOOR AREA **10,800 m²**
PHOTOGRAPHER **Andreas Keller**

⊠ Seating was provided on all levels for visitors to watch the show.
⊠ Overhead was a midnight blue 'sky' with rings of spotlights.
⊠ The media stage provided a vast space for a visually dynamic show.

KAUFFMANN THEILIG & PARTNER
AND ATELIER MARKGRAPH

MERCEDES NEXT

- A silver anodised and brushed aluminium sculptural band surrounded the stage.
- Terraced spaces juxtaposed the media stage for a continuous view.
- On the top level, the show car Concept A-Class was exhibited.

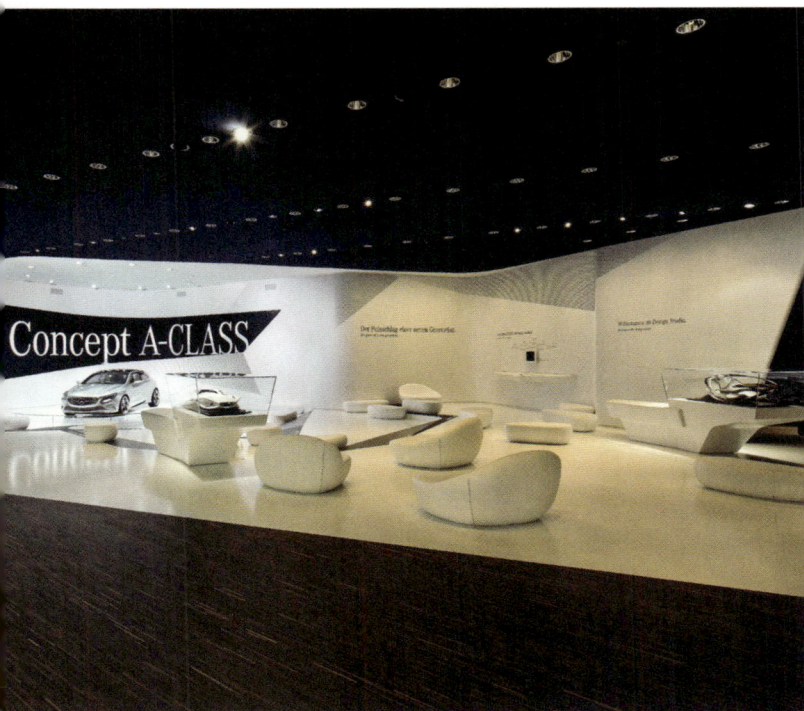

The animated pulse beat defined the rhythm for the presentation

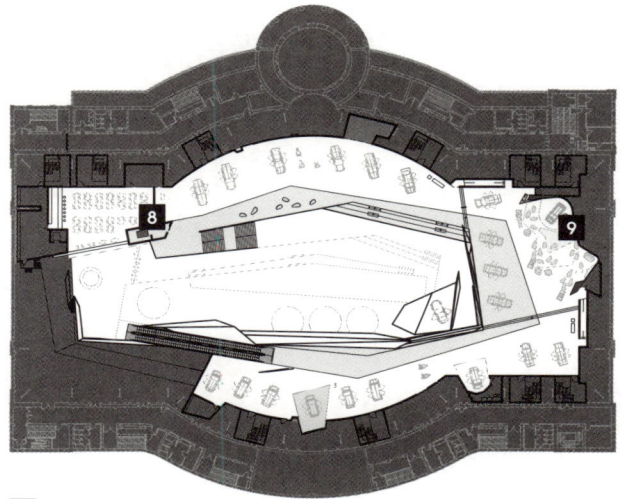

⊠ Second floor

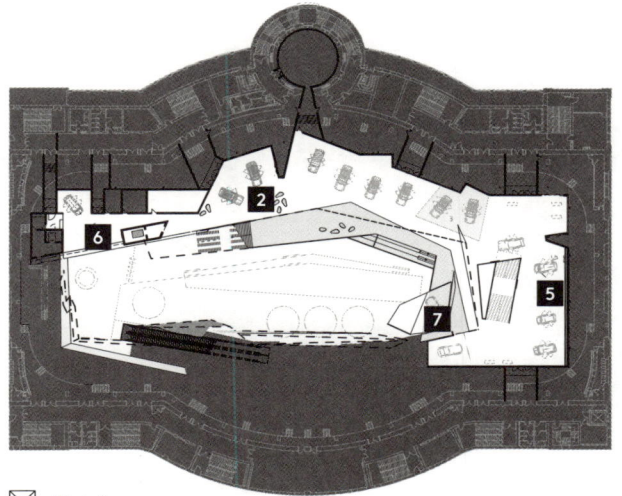

⊠ First floor

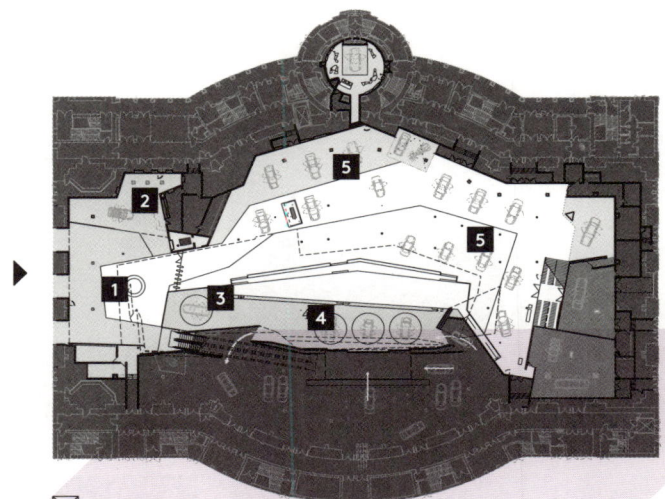

⊠ Ground floor

⊠ Floor plan

1   Reception desk
2   Shop
3   Show car F125
4   Stage
5   Display area
6   Key account lounge
7   World premiere SLS AMG Roadster
8   Cafe
9   Show car Concept A-Class

Every elevation ensured new vistas for fair goers

☒ On entering the hall, visitors were directed to travel up through the building by the escalator.

☒ Premium vehicle presentations were positioned on every level.

☒ Visuals on the dynamic media panels created an impactful backdrop for the real cars on the spacicus stage.

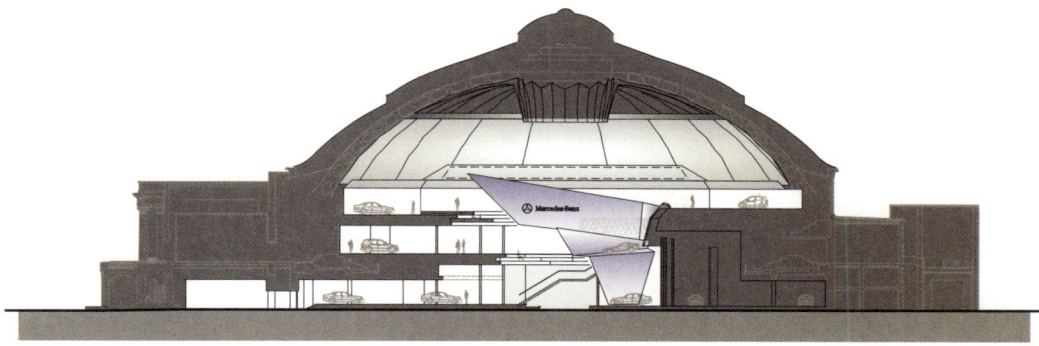

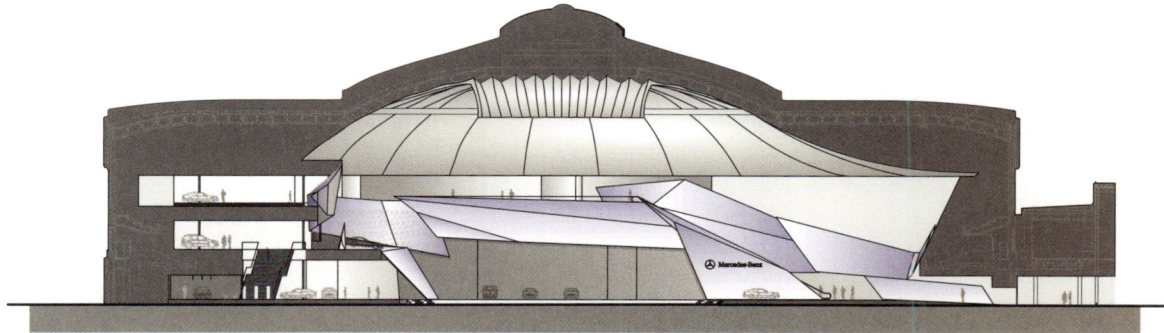

Longitudinal sections

MINI by Meiré und Meiré

A VIBRANT VEHICLE PRESENTATION THAT
GOT THE MESSAGE ACROSS: EVERY DAY
REALLY CAN BE AN ADVENTURE.

For the fourth time in succession, BMW commissioned Meiré und Meiré to lead the creation and design of the MINI brand presentation at IAA, the world's largest motor show, in 2011. In addition to a comprehensive redesigning of communication, Meiré und Meiré subjected the architecture to further radical development and highlighted the diversity of the MINI brand in an impressive and involving way. The design team opted for a concept with an open structure in which they shifted the orthogonal architectural grid slightly to provide an interesting angular aspect at the front of the presentation and to open up a large number of themes that caught the attention of fair goers. Combined with a grid-like facade, the resulted branded booth offered new insights and transparencies. The stand's skeleton consisted of a black metal grill structure. A 9-m-diameter rotunda – with a display surface spanning 360-degrees inside and out – staged the world premiere of the MINI Coupé. This rotunda constituted the stand's centre of energy, positioned at the very heart of the stand. The illuminated circular opening overhead sliced through the surface above, connecting with the product family presentations on the upper level. Visitors could experience all of the flanking highlights as they walked around the stand, with distinct topic areas directly and edgily juxtaposed. Blocks of colour and illuminated graphics delineated the different zones, one of which was an impressive double-height black space. Suspended cubes filled the ceiling void above and shared real-life stories about how to 'design your own MINI'. Throughout, each product presentation emphasised the strength of its positioning and substance by drawing on narrative and interactive elements, materials, dynamic light choreographies and sound. The signature elements were composed and coordinated, fitting together harmoniously in a coherent story for visitors as they passed through the stand.

TRADE FAIR IAA
WHERE Frankfurt, Germany
WHEN September 2011
DESIGNER Meiré und Meiré ☒ p.495
STAND CONSTRUCTORS Raumtechnik Messebau &
Event Services and Winkels Messe- und Ausstellungsbau
CLIENT BMW Group
MARKET SECTOR Automotive
TOTAL FLOOR AREA 1700 m²
PHOTOGRAPHER diephotodesigner.de

- The space was dedicated to infotainment systems with technical content conveyed by playful illustrations.
- Personal experiences of customers were portrayed in media streams projected onto the cubes hanging from the ceiling.
- The open-fronted stand enabled fair goers to view the full family of cars, with their individual characters and stories.
- When visitors stood in the circle next to the feature car, the floor vibrated to the sound of a club soundtrack.

ANOTHER DAY.
ANOTHER ADVENTURE.

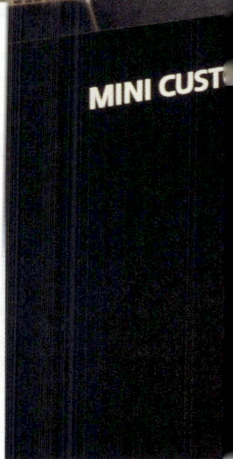

The thrill of driving the MINI Cabrio could be experienced in strong, windy streams, created by an array of wall- and ceiling-mounted fans.
A 6-m-high rack of accessories displayed the options for car customisation.
The stand design had a see-through architecture with contrasting material clashes and semi-transparent surfaces.
The racing sub-brand of MINI was set in a pit-lane garage setting: telemetry-tickers in the back, pulsing neon tubes on the ceiling and accessories on the walls.

A narrative of dynamic light choreographies and sound

SAF-Holland by mbco

VISUAL IMAGERY FORMED THE BACKDROP TO THE BOOTH AND EMPHASISED THE BRAND'S ESSENCE: KEEPING TRUCKS ON THE ROAD.

The global company SAF-Holland offers quality engineered components, systems and services to the commercial vehicle industry. For its presentation at the Mid-America Trucking Show in 2012, the brief to design studio mbco called for a booth that encapsulated all aspects of the brand. Aiming for a stand that could be adapted and used at other trade fairs across the globe, the design needed to be consistent with four main cornerstones: identity, flexibility, continuity and cost efficiency. The concept was based around a formal analogy between the axle of a truck and the client's logo, creating a framework that both defined the look of the booth and established the spatial order. A series of oval rings with elongated aluminium frames parallel to one another generated an open-fronted stand. The metal frames – with their curved ends edged in orange Perspex – were grouped in pairs, making room for product displays near the front of the booth and more secluded meeting areas towards the back. Integrated into the modular system were the graphics, lighting and information panels, all set against the golden glow that emanated across the presentation. The design team picked out one of the corporate colours with which to define the space, emphasised by the key brand imagery of a silhouetted long-haul lorry as the backdrop to the booth. A realistic and cost-effective practicability was one of the most important challenges for the design team in developing the modular system. In order to achieve this, certain elements were designed so that they could be produced close to the locality of each particular trade fair and be integrated into the specific booth design, with other elements offering flexibility in terms of layout to suit the requirements.

TRADE FAIR **Mid-America Trucking Show**
WHERE **Louisville, United States**
WHEN **March 2012**
DESIGNER **mbco**  **p.495**
STAND CONSTRUCTOR **EEI Global**
CLIENT **SAF Holland**
MARKET SECTOR **Automotive**
TOTAL FLOOR AREA **300 m²**
PHOTOGRAPHER **David Alan Wolters**

Products were positioned with a central alignment in front of the key visual.
Tinted Perspex provided a transparent perimeter at the sides of the booth.
The specular metal framework was an ideal platform for the machinery on show at the fair.

- The design had connotations with a truck's axle.
- An accessible and sturdy system was composed of oval rings.
- The design concept afforded an open and transparent stand for the products.
- The renderings indicate how the design could be adapted for different fairs due to the modular concept.

The elements offered flexibility in terms of layout

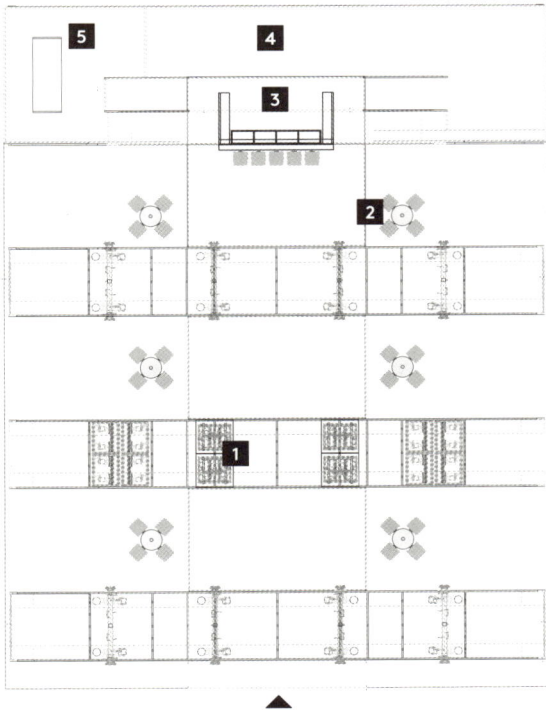

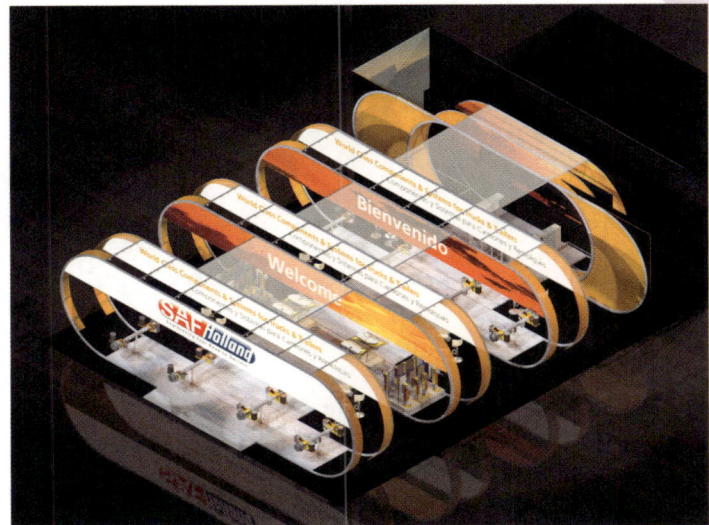

- Floor plan

1 Product display
2 Meeting area
3 Bar
4 Kitchen/storage
5 Meeting room

Shiny Treasure Chest by tisch13

AUTOMOTIVE CONCEPT CARS DISPLAYED IN A GLOWING OASIS.

TRADE FAIR **CES**
WHERE **Las Vegas, United States**
WHEN **January 2011**
DESIGNER **tisch13** ✖ **p.498**
STAND CONSTRUCTOR **A&A Expo International**
CLIENT **Audi**
MARKET SECTOR **Automotive**
TOTAL FLOOR AREA **325 m²**
PHOTOGRAPHER **Gabor Ekecs**

For Audi's first ever presentation at the CES electronics trade fair in Las Vegas, tisch13 was commissioned to create a place of calm and concentration in a field of visual chaos. With the concept of 'open for the future', the design team realised a treasure chest that, when opened, enlightened visitors and gave them an insight into the mobile future of the Audi brand. With the basic constructs of a backlit ceiling and a sheer, angled enclosure overhead, the booth exuded the atmosphere of a glowing oasis. The rectangular structure represented a dramatic accent with a rear-tapered interior and appeared as if a giant shiny box had been lifted up at the front to reveal a brilliantly bright and magical delight inside. Visitors were attracted from afar by the monolithic outer appearance of the presentation, clearly defined by the glittering, grand cube that enveloped and defined the brand's space. The looming large box literally glowed, enticing fair goers to step inside the sci-fi enclosure – gleaming white on all sides, geometric facets all around, from the floor, ceiling and walls to the furniture and installations. This futuristic setting was the perfect stage for the interactive exhibits and fascinating e-tron concept cars displayed at the fair. The bright white light was emitted thanks to the illuminated ceiling covered with a translucent membrane, 130 spotlights and exclusively high-gloss white surfaces throughout the interior. The overhead element consisted of a suspended timber construction cloaked with a silver mesh fabric on the outside. The materiality of the individual elements was key to the visitor experience and the different perceptions of internal and external aspects of the stand.

✖ The gleaming white ceiling was formed by a back-lit stretch film.
✖ The 'opened box' revealed to visitors the future of Audi.

MOBILITY GRAND STAND 4

Metallic mesh was applied on the outside of the cube.
The stylistic use of a light blanket created a crisp, optimal environment for the concept cars.
Visitors were lured by the glowing light emanating across the exhibition hall.

Fair goers were enticed into the sci-fi enclosure

smart City by Braunwagner

AN URBAN CONTEXT HIGHLIGHTED ELECTRIC MOBILITY FOR THIS AUTOMOTIVE BRAND.

'Let's not just build a booth. Let's build a city.' That was the client's brief to Braunwagner when commissioning the studio to design smart's presence at IAA in Frankfurt for the fifth time in succession. The challenge was not to look pretentious but confident, to present the smart as a strong urban brand with a high design standard. Braunwagner structured the marketing messages with an urban metaphor, with a city centre, business district and green areas in a motorised metropolis. Visitors first encountered the suburbs, which offered a sense of high-quality life. They could glimpse this through the glass walls of the fair hall, where an architecture called the 'smart sphere' framed the brand environment. A key highlight was the brand's electric drive research car: the smart forvision. The team had developed the smart cube – a design feature that could be used either alone or in clusters. An abstract city silhouette composed of stacked structures was generated and offered concentrated spaces for individual elements. Made of a white, high-gloss material, the cubes were of different sizes, with some abstract forms housing high-tech display screens and visuals. Against the white backdrop, colour coding and architectural characteristics helped identify the individual display areas. Electric mobility was highlighted at the very heart of the booth, with the brand's new generation of electric smart cars displayed next to the innovative e-bike. Continuing the theme of urban mobility, lanes and walkways made of authentic materials such as concrete and cobblestone directed visitors around the presentation, passing public spaces and parks positioned in an open architecture that featured green areas and benches. A high density of architectural elements, strong contrasts in materials, and lively media content underlined the vibrant atmosphere.

TRADE FAIR **IAA**
WHERE **Frankfurt, Germany**
WHEN **September 2011**
DESIGNER **Braunwagner** ☒ **p.490**
STAND CONSTRUCTOR **Klartext**
CLIENT **Daimler**
MARKET SECTOR **Automotive**
TOTAL FLOOR AREA **3370 m²**
PHOTOGRAPHER **Andreas Keller**

☒ Even the suburbs were part of the urban metaphor and welcomed the visitors to the open air area.
☒ Spaciousness, dynamic forms and colour-coded visuals were used to define the business area.
☒ The smart forvision, with research cooperation from BASF, visualised the mobility of 2020 in the exhibition area.

The smart sphere had an abstract city silhouette

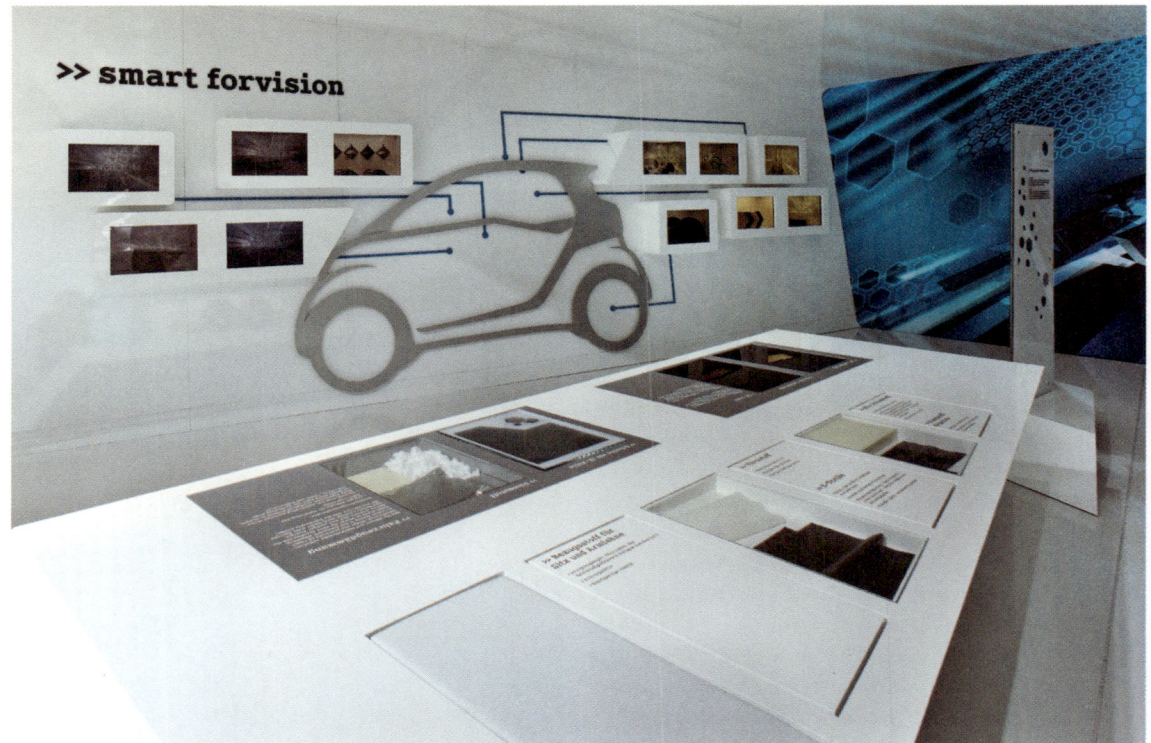

Urban life was reflected in a deliberate mix of styles.
Contrasting materials, sound, lighting effects and media productions reinforced the effect of a lively metropolis.
The Future City Lab exhibit outlined for visitors the innovations installed in the smart forvision.
The smart history was recalled at the front of the booth.

Staging Concept A-Class by Nest One

A SNOWY MOUNTAIN-TOP LANDSCAPE FORMED A PREMIER BACKDROP FOR THE MERCEDES-BENZ CONCEPT A-CLASS.

The Ski & Boarder week in Val Thorens is the largest 1-week winter sports event in the Alps. With guaranteed snow, Europe's highest ski resort is the perfect place for 5000 young visitors from five nations to party, compete and show off their skills. For Mercedes-Benz in 2011, it was the perfect environment to present the Concept A-Class to a new target group. The brand sponsored the event and set up the A-Lounge in the central square in Val Thorens, to present the premier vehicle. The design team at Nest One was called upon to create the concept for the display, which consisted of a presentation of the car inside a transparent hemisphere that resembled a giant snow dome and protected the car from the elements. Alongside this translucent, sometimes snow-covered bubble was a metal sculpture reminiscent of an oversized 'Aeolian harp' – an instrument that is played by the wind – expressing the Mercedes-Benz design statement 'shaped by the wind'. The central location of the stand in the town meant it formed the ideal meeting point so that after their gruelling races, visitors could chill out on 20 Fatboy beanbags and watch the latest snowboarding films on a large LED screen. Inspired by the tricks shown in the films, snow lovers could also use the frame railings positioned nearby as their own playground where they could perform tricks in front of the assembled audience. In the evenings, a visual highlight for the skiers and snowboarders alike were the giant laser images projected onto the side of the distant snow-clad mountains. Driving experiences on a nearby ice racetrack and après-ski parties in the lounge made for an intensive and emotional brand experience.

⊠ Light projections on a nearby mou[...] created a big impression.
⊠ LED spotlights illuminated the h[...] steel frame in different colours.
⊠ The 'car in a bubble' presentation v[...] draw for boarders.

TRADE FAIR **Ski & Boarder Week**
WHERE **Val Thorens, France**
WHEN **December 2011**
DESIGNER **Nest One** ⊠ **p.495**
STAND CONSTRUCTOR **Drei D Medienservice**
CLIENT **Mercedes-Benz**
MARKET SECTOR **Automotive**
TOTAL FLOOR AREA **250 m²**
PHOTOGRAPHER **Nest One**

Staging Concept Style Coupé by Nest One

DENMARK'S MUSIC FESTIVAL FOR EMERGING TALENT DOUBLED AS A STAGE FOR A NEW AUTOMOTIVE CONCEPT BY MERCEDES-BENZ.

The Spot Festival in Aarhus is one of Denmark's most important music festivals. Over the course of two days, new artists are showcased in this creative hotbed of new Scandinavian musical talent. Mercedes-Benz was a sponsor of the event in 2012, and it considered the festival to be the perfect place to introduce its Concept Style Coupé to a young target group. The vehicle's provocative lines and uncompromising sportiness makes a statement for avant-garde design and at the same time proves that only non-conformists take new paths. That mirrors the brand's objective to continually pop up with presentations in unexpected places. German brand communication agency Nest One was in charge of the design of the display, which was located in Godsbanen, one of the main festival venues. This is a dynamic new hub for art and culture which has emerged in the city between a landscape of historical freight train warehouses, and the design team wanted a stand that had a synergy with its surroundings for visitors to be able to experience the vehicle up close. Taking inspiration from the design of the concept car and building on the brand's existing presentation system, the designers came up with a free-form platform in black acrylic glass with illuminated inserts. An angular motif was incorporated around the car, positioned on a raised podium akin to the adjacent stages at the festival. The branded campaign was prominently displayed on a textile back wall, with LEDs arranged in a pixellated grid structure behind the print to give a dynamic, three-dimensional quality. Media content about the concept car flashed from an embedded screen, and the car was illuminated by coloured spotlights suspended from a rigging system supported by scaffolding columns, which aptly fitted in with both the industrial landscape and the festival architecture.

TRADE FAIR **Spot Festival**
WHERE **Aarhus, Denmark**
WHEN **March 2012**
DESIGNER **Nest One** ✕ **p.495**
STAND CONSTRUCTOR **Artec**
CLIENT **Mercedes-Benz**
MARKET SECTOR **Automotive**
TOTAL FLOOR AREA **150 m²**
PHOTOGRAPHER **Nest One**

✕ The bright green angular motif tied in with the neon colour scheme of the music festival.

✕ Bespoke cube-shaped seating was positioned alongside information about the brand, available on iPads.

Scaffolding fitted to the industrial landscape and the festival architecture

The Grid by tisch13

A NETWORK OF NEON TUBES CREATED
AN IMPRESSIVE ILLUMINATED
KALEIDOSCOPIC GRID OVER VISITORS'
HEADS IN THIS AUTOMOTIVE STAND.

At the start of 2012, Audi appeared for the second time at the world's largest electronics trade fair, CES in Las Vegas. The brand's presence at the trade fair symbolised the basic principles behind the guiding concept of 'Audi Connect'. This was the brief given to the design team at tisch13, commissioned to realise the brand's CES fair stand for the second year running. The tisch13 team opted for a vivid scenography based on the three elements behind Audi Connect: networking, interfaces and data streams. To symbolise this, the team chose the image of a tight grid, which in turn led to a cubic element that recurred in all elements of the design and layout of the trade fair stand. From afar, the branded booth caught the eye with a lattice-type network of illumination spilling out from the shimmering silver box positioned over the entire space. As visitors approached, they saw that this elevated perimeter was in fact constructed from a series of suspended square panels and, inside the stand, they immediately saw the source of the light. A seemingly never-ending myriad of neon tubes overhead emitted a bright white light in a kaleidoscopic fashion. There was no trickery or play with mirrors at work here though, just a glittering glow from the almost 2000 fluorescent lamps positioned over the visitors' heads to give a vibrant perspective. High-gloss materials and polished surfaces – including the cars themselves – afforded interesting reflections of the architecture, and the vehicles on display transported the 'grid' down to the visitors' level.

TRADE FAIR **CES**
WHERE **Las Vegas, United States**
WHEN **January 2012**
DESIGNER **tisch13** ⊠ **p.498**
STAND CONSTRUCTOR **A&A Expo International**
CLIENT **Audi**
MARKET SECTOR **Automotive**
TOTAL FLOOR AREA **325 m²**
PHOTOGRAPHER **Gabor Ekecs**

⊠ The high-gloss interior reflected the illuminated grid overhead.
⊠ The energised cube had bright light leaking out in a geometric pattern.
⊠ The glow from the myriad of neon tubes created a seemingly unending network.

MOBILITY GRAND STAND 4

Toyota & Lexus by Muuaaa

THIS DISPLAY OF ALTERNATIVE MOBILITY TECHNOLOGIES DEMONSTRATED ECO-FRIENDLY PRACTICES.

The Technological Rainforest Expo took place in Puerto Rico in April 2012 as part of 'Earth Month'. The aim was to show innovative ways in which automotive technologies support environmental preservation and protection. The joint presentation for Toyota and Lexus was designed by creative studio Muuaaa, who turned 1672 m² of unused retail space into a whole new brand experience. The brief outlined a requirement to promote alternative mobility technologies. Through visuals and an extensive display of hybrid vehicles, the exhibition included a series of elements that conveyed the overall concept for the design: the representation of nature through technology. A vital aspect for the design team was to stay true to the idea of a fusion between nature and the latest developments in automotive design, making use of innovative technologies and design techniques – such as digital representation, fabrication and form finding – to create bespoke components. From custom-made spec stands with a tessellated crystal-like formation to a small amphitheatre resembling a tiered landscape, visitors were directed through each of the distinct exhibition zones. They first encountered the Toyota display area, which featured curvaceous walls that framed the winding pathway and a colour scheme of blues and greens. Digital motion graphic projections alluding to artificial nature further enhanced the sinuous feeling. In order to achieve brand differentiation, the Lexus experience layout expressed minimal elegance. In this case, orthogonal lines substituted the organic forms within a more monochromatic scenography, turning the exhibited cars into gems exposed in a museum-like environment. Enhancing the illuminated black box, a series of custom light fixtures filled with glass crystals that refracted light served as a perfect metaphor of the box containing gems.

TRADE FAIR **Technological Rainforest Expo**
WHERE **San Juan, Puerto Rico**
WHEN **April 2012**
DESIGNER **Muuaaa** ⊠ **p.495**
STAND CONSTRUCTOR **Héctor Rivera Díaz Construction**
CLIENT **Comstat for Toyota & Lexus Puerto Rico**
MARKET SECTOR **Automotive**
TOTAL FLOOR AREA **1672 m²**
PHOTOGRAPHER **Kenneth Rexach**

⊠ The expo breathed life into a disused retail space.
⊠ Vibrant colours illuminated the Toyota presentation area.
⊠ An elegant monochromatic colour scheme decorated the Lexus zone.

Búsqueda por la Perfección

Lexus busca la perfección para que los clientes puedan disfrutar la vida apasionadamente si Lux se ha redefinido por Lexus, para que cada cliente pueda maximizar cada momento disfrutando de la travesía tanto como del destino.

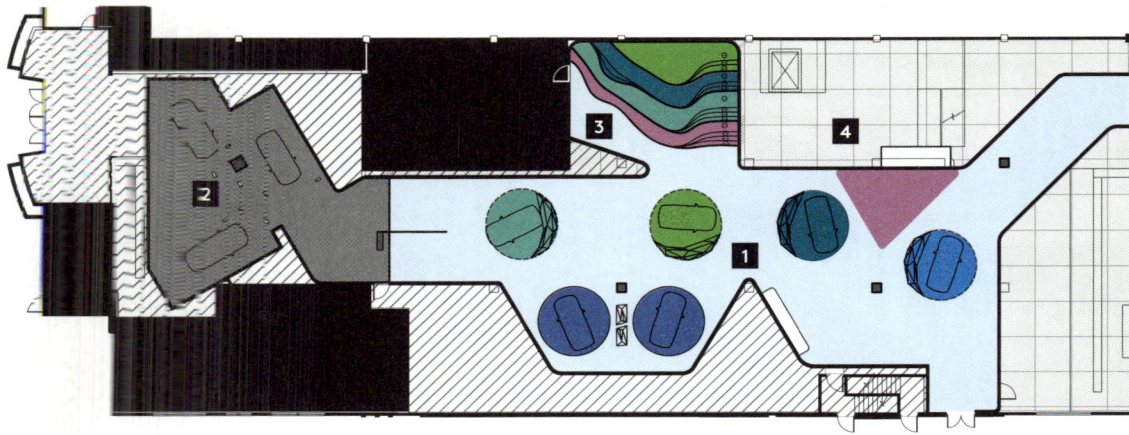

Curvaceous walls that framed the winding pathway

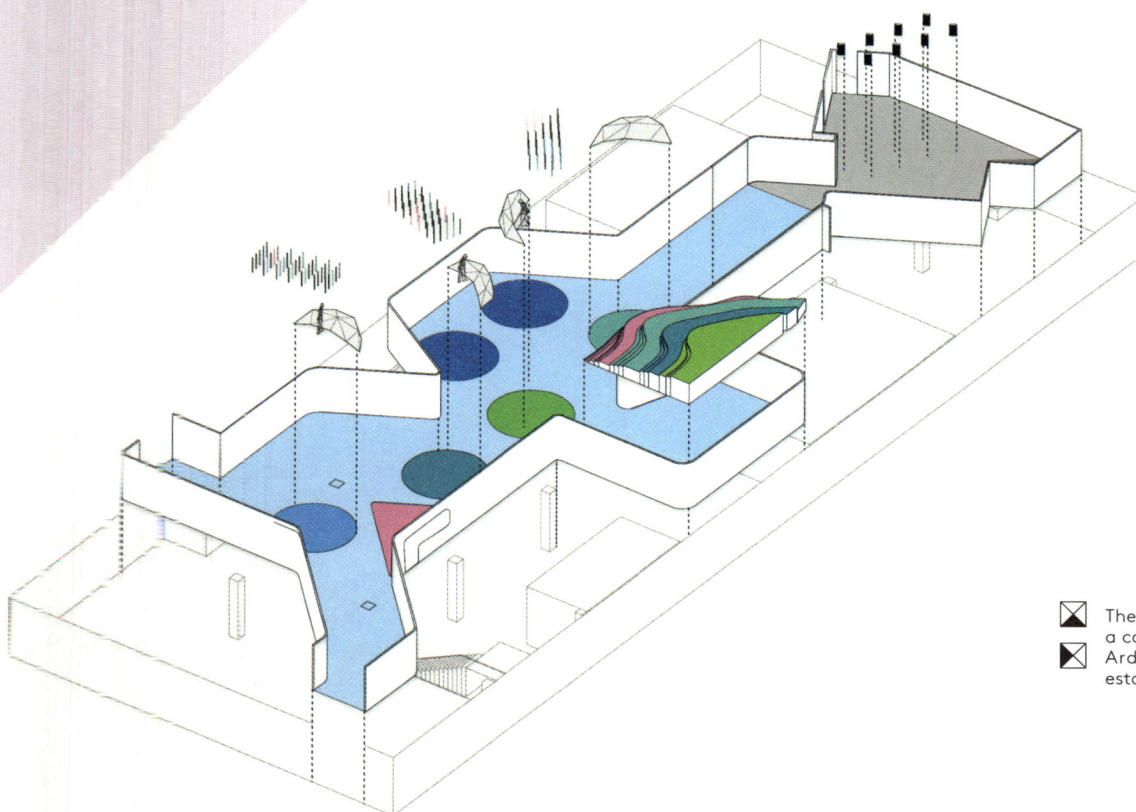

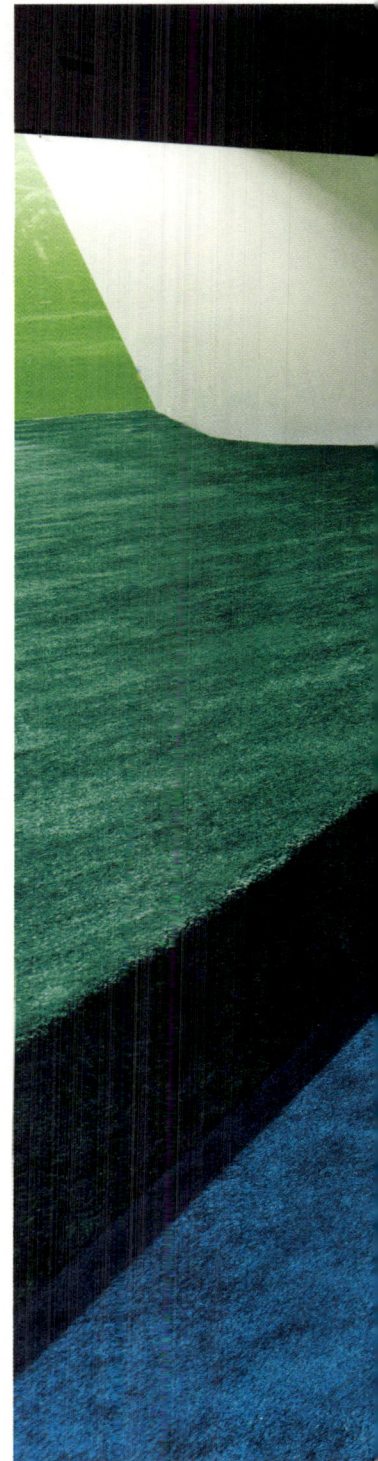

⊠ The tiered auditorium was decked out in a colourful, deep-pile carpet.
⊠ Arduino-programmed LED raindrops established focal points above each car.

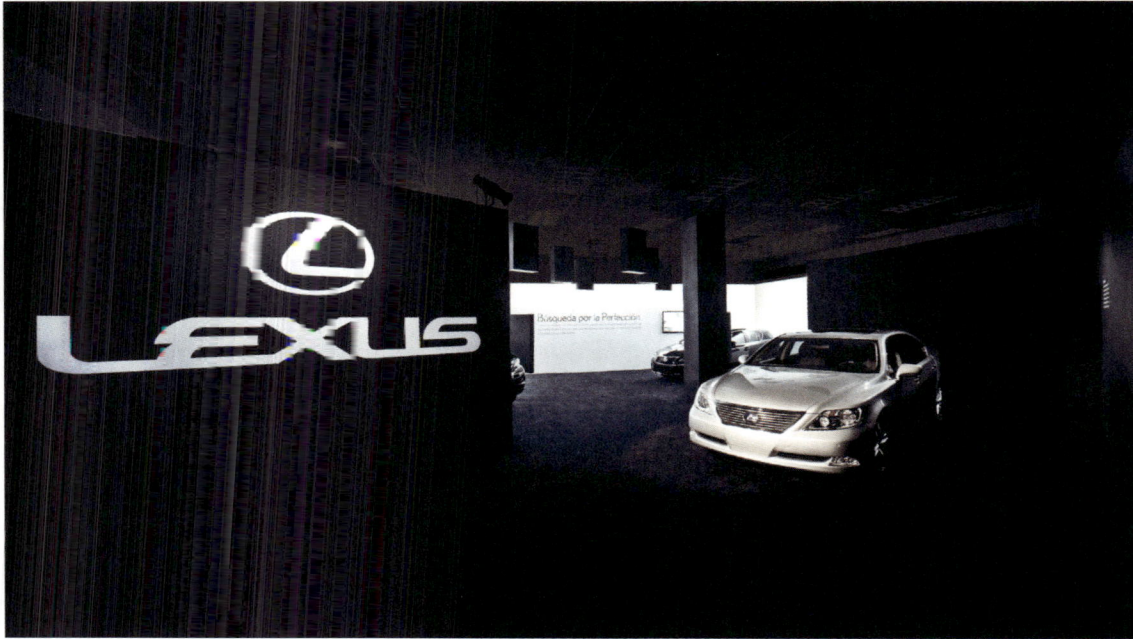

◪ Near the entrance was a reception desk and a sales area.

◪ The Lexus zone had a monochromatic decor with the cars positioned as works of art.

◪ Tessellated space displays resembled rock formations 'cut' in nature.

◪ Rendering indicating the positioning of the rainscreen above the car and the information panel alongside.

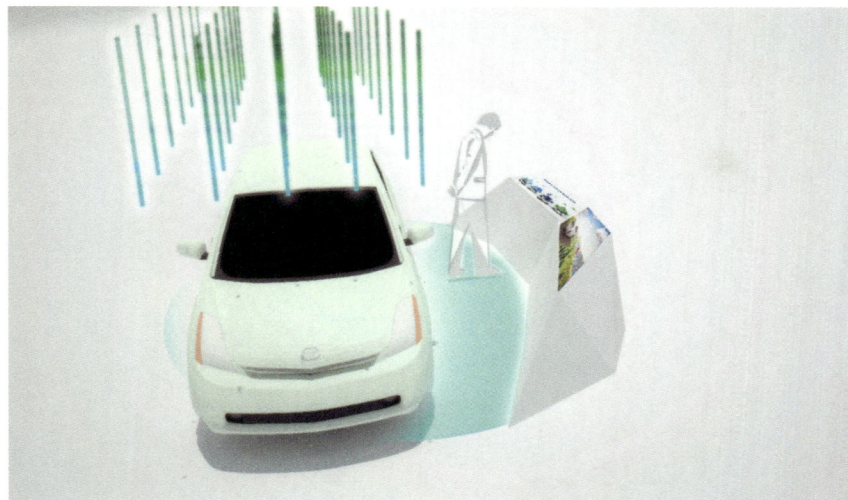

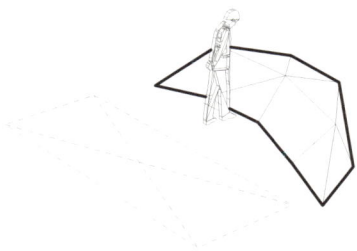

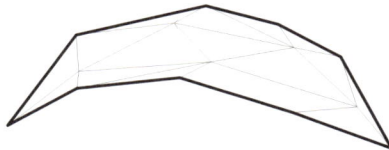

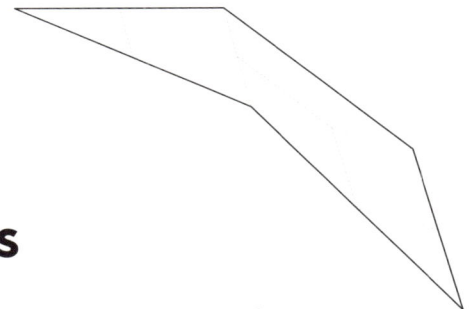

Organic forms versus orthogonal lines

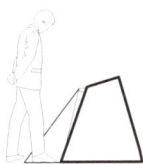

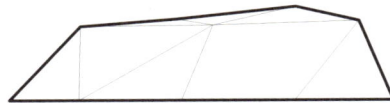

Volkswagen Beetle by Fugzia

REPRESENTING A VISUAL TIME LINE FROM CLASSIC TO CONTEMPORARY CARS, AKIN TO A HISTORIC MOTORWAY.

Design studio Fugzia was commissioned to realise the presentation for the Belgian launch of the new Volkswagen Beetle at Autoworld Brussels in 2011. The new vehicle, dubbed 'The 21st Century Beetle', is a reinvention of the original automotive icon, and the exhibition needed to reflect this. The Fugzia team aimed to create a unique historical overview, focusing on key aspects of the new car: how its exterior reinterprets the silhouette of the classic Volkswagen Beetle, combining stylistic elements borrowed from the original coupled with the latest technology. The design concept was that of a time line in the form of a 'priority expo lane' on which models of the car were positioned. The presentation began with the original Beetle design. The classic outline of the car was displayed in a framework form, exposing its inner-workings as an interesting spectacle for visitors. Sequentially, more modern models of the car lined up one in front of the next – from the original Volkswagen convertible, first launched in 1949, to the Volkswagen New Beetle, introduced in 1997. The most contemporary incarnation of the car was positioned at the head of the line. A twist in the road took on the contour of the car itself, in order to perfectly cocoon the latest creation beneath its surface. Interactive stations placed along the road's timeline attracted attention from visitors. The Fugzia design team, in collaboration with Engage BBDO, were also responsible for the special Beetle pop-up restaurant with its delicious meals served up by Michelin star chef Yves Mattagne. There was also a VIP area designed with a Beetle-inspired look and bespoke furniture placed alongside vibrant visuals.

TRADE FAIR **Autoworld Brussels**
WHERE **Brussels, Belgium**
WHEN **November 2011**
DESIGNER **Fugzia** ☒ **p.492**
STAND CONSTRUCTOR **Fugzia**
CLIENT **Engage BBDO/ D'ieteren/ Volkswagen Belgium**
MARKET SECTOR **Automotive**
TOTAL FLOOR AREA **1400 m²**
PHOTOGRAPHER **Eventattitude**

☒ The historical line-up of cars accentuated the iconic character of the VW Beetle.
☒ The undulating lane brought to mind recollections of the 'yellow brick road' in *The Wizard of Oz*.

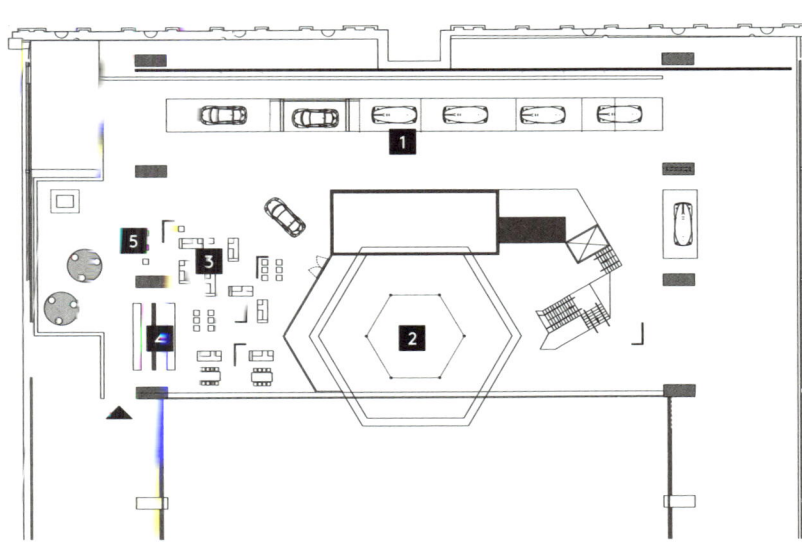

Floor plan
1 Chronological car display
2 Restaurant
3 Lounge
4 Bar
5 iPad display area

Reinventing the original automotive icon

Renderings showing the concept for the exhibition and the restaurant.
Urban imagery decorated the lounge seating areas.
The restaurant was fully decked-out with VW Beetle branding.
The historical expo had hands-on digital media aspects positioned alongside.

SERL

5AM by Five AM

A BUDGET-SAVVY BOOTH
THAT TURNED 1000
FLOWERPOTS INTO AN
EYE-CATCHING DESIGN.

TRADE FAIR **Bedrijven Contactdagen**
WHERE **Kortrijk, Belgium**
WHEN **December 2011**
DESIGNER **Five AM** ☒ **p.491**
STAND CONSTRUCTOR **Five AM**
CLIENT **Five AM**
MARKET SECTOR **Design services**
TOTAL FLOOR AREA **9 m²**
PHOTOGRAPHER **Olivier Caluwier**

Bedrijven Contactdagen is an annual 'get together fair' for local businesses in the Flanders region of Belgium. The corporate networking event takes place over two days in December and is divided into three main sectors: services, supply and industry. At the 13th edition of the fair in 2011, Belgian design studio Five AM made its very first appearance. The studio was only established in the same year and wanted to make its inaugural presence at the event – where its design services could be communicated – one to remember. There was just one problem: making an impression but with very little budget was going to be challenging. A resourceful solution was required, which was not a difficult thing for the creative design duo to realise. After looking at which cheap materials could be used without having to rely on big machinery to assemble the booth, the designers came up with an answer encapsulated by one word: 'flowerpots'. By utilising multiple quantities of an everyday object to completely cover the walls and the ceiling of the space, they ensured that the ordinariness of that item would fade away. Black plastic flowerpots were selected for their low cost and light weight. This meant there was no need to affix the pots to a heavy structure to support the ceiling, so recycled honeycomb cardboard could be used for the panelling. Variation and texture were incorporated into the design by screwing the three different sizes of flowerpot to the panels in a random pattern. With upturned pots making an appearance as pendant lampshades and stools, the resulting monochrome booth was eye-catching in its simplicity.

☒ Over 1000 pots in three different sizes were used to create a 3D pattern.
☒ The space was lit by large plastic pots that hung from the ceiling.

Absa by Flance

AN INTERACTIVE STAND THAT DISPLAYED THE ARTISTIC APPRECIATION OF A CORPORATE SPONSOR.

TRADE FAIR Design Indaba
WHERE Cape Town, South Africa
WHEN March 2012
DESIGNER Flance ⊠ p.491
STAND CONSTRUCTOR Scan Display
CLIENT Absa Group
MARKET SECTOR Art supplies
TOTAL FLOOR AREA 78 m²
PHOTOGRAPHERS Andre van Niekerk

Absa is the largest consumer bank in South Africa and one of the largest corporate art collectors in the world. Actively promoting the arts, Absa sponsors the annual Design Indaba fair hosted in Cape Town. The firm's stand at the 2012 event aimed to cross-leverage the Absa L'Atelier Art Competition for upcoming artists. A generic 'art child' was designed, manufactured and distributed to 26 individually selected artists, who in turn interpreted and reworked the sculpture to their own individual styles. This new generation of art 'children' was then displayed during the fair. The brief to design studio Flance called for a stand with an open and relaxed gallery-like feel. Flance collaborated with the Alwijn Creative studio to create a space to showcase individual pieces whilst maintaining a coherent impression of the group project.

An overall simple aesthetic was achieved with an uncomplicated layout and clear corporate colour palette. A base of white with exaggerated lines of red accompanied architectural elements. The regimented positioning of white plinths formed a minimalist backdrop to the focal display of artworks, aligned to maximise flow through the space and to encourage circulation through the stand. An additional interactive experience allowed visitors to come into close contact with the artworks. As a central point of interest, fair goers were invited to take part in the creation of the larger 'hero' art child. This 1.2-m-tall sculpture was an exact replica of the smaller versions, except this one was plain white at the start of the fair. It was positioned on a rotating podium and visitors were actively encouraged to draw on it to make a unique creation, which by the end of the fair had developed a personality all of its own.

⊠ Simple, white powder-coated steel plinths were used to display the individual works of art.

⊠ Painted MDF was used to construct the freestanding columns, as well as the angled shards that were suspended from the ceiling.

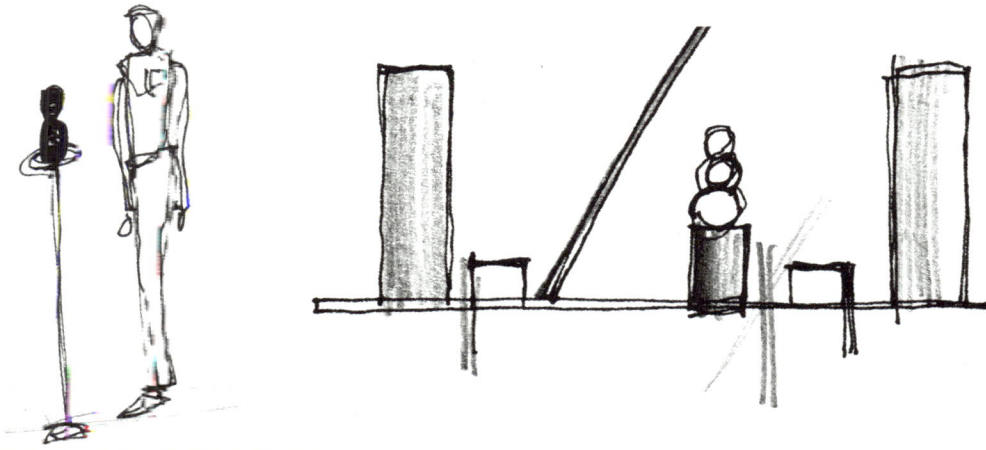

Visitors could draw on the 1.2-m-tall white sculpture

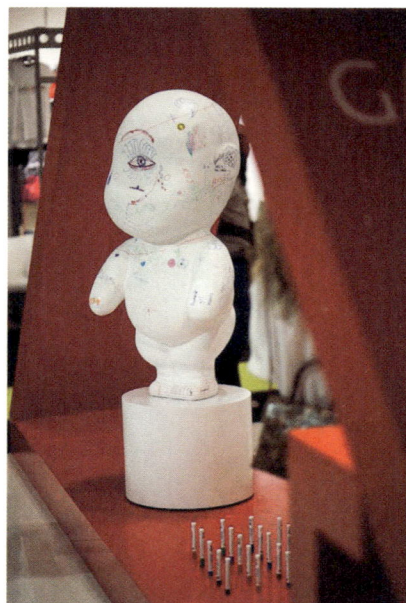

⊠ Sketches showing how the idea for the concept had inspiration from the client's logo.

⊠ At the centre of the stand, in the midst of the red architectural elements, was the rotating display unit used for the interactive art project.

⊠ The artists' displayed work (left) was a fraction of the size of the sculpture decorated during the fair (right).

⊠ From the rendering to the final execution, the stand maintained a high graphic quality through its simplicity.

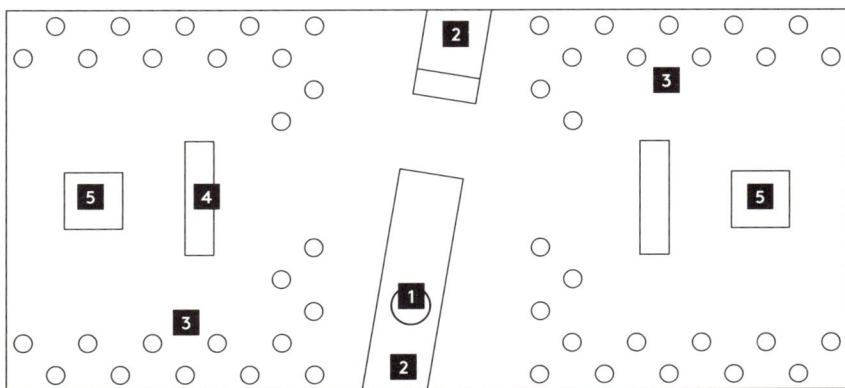

Floor plan

1 Rotating 'hero' art child
2 Red architectural panel
3 Display plinths
4 Seating
5 Media columns

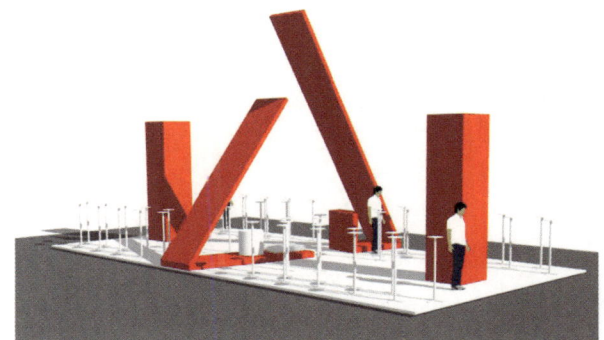

Algeria Pavilion by Totems

A PAVILION WITH TRADITIONAL ARCHITECTURE VISUALISED THE CULTURAL WEALTH OF ALGERIA FOR VISITORS.

Totems designed the Algeria Pavilion at the World Expo 2012 with the nation's incredible cultural wealth of several millennia and world heritage sites in mind. The rich history of Algeria takes a great deal from its location, bordered by the Mediterranean Sea to the north and the vast sand sea of the Sahara to the south. The design team proposed to tell the story of these seas with a concept that circumnavigated a north–south axis theme. The essence of the architecture was a traditional, two-storey building with columns and archways surrounding a central plaza, from where the designers integrated views of the golden-hued Sahara stretching out in one direction and of the deep blue Mediterranean Sea in the other. Individual exhibits focusing on different aspects of Algeria and its culture, costumes and history occupied the plaza. Entering the building from the west wing, visitors encountered an interactive pre-show gallery, followed by the exhibition in the plaza and open courtyard. The VIP area on the second floor overlooked the central space and offered stunning views of the exhibition below. Hexagonal tiles covered the floor and a star-shaped mosaic element in the middle overlaid with a large compass emphasised the north–south axis theme. The south side of the building contained large arched openings behind which a sand-strewn floor and a wide panoramic screen formed a presentation that focused on the Southern desert. Beautiful photos and imagery accompanied the media presentation. To the north of the compass, heavy wooden doors automatically opened every 5 minutes to give access to the main show feature space. Glimpses of a wide panorama of the Mediterranean enticed visitors inside, where a film in a static loop was laid out before them on an immersive large screen projection.

TRADE FAIR **World Expo 2012**
WHERE **Yeosu, South Korea**
WHEN **May 2012**
DESIGNER **Totems** ⊠ **p.499**
STAND CONSTRUCTOR **FM Communication**
CLIENT **Office of the Prime Minister of Algeria**
MARKET SECTOR **Information and education**
TOTAL FLOOR AREA **866 m²**
PHOTOGRAPHER **Totems**

⊠ The view to the north showed the Sahara desert exhibition area towards the rear of the pavilion.
⊠ When the large doors were opened from the plaza to the terrace, visitors entered into a wide panoramic film experience.

- The pre-show space offered a brief introduction to different aspects of the Algerian nation.
- Renderings showing the overall layout and the different exhibition settings.
- Traditional architecture was captured in great detail, from the blue and white ceramics, wood-cut panelling, twisted columns and traditional lantern-lighting.
- The terrace area offered a 12-m wide media experience.

The concept circumnavigated a north–south axis theme

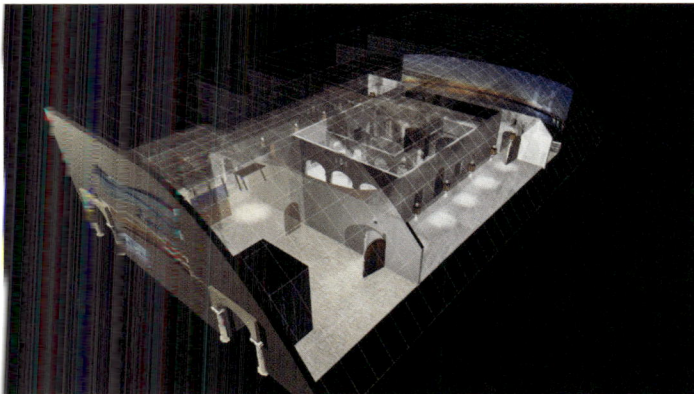

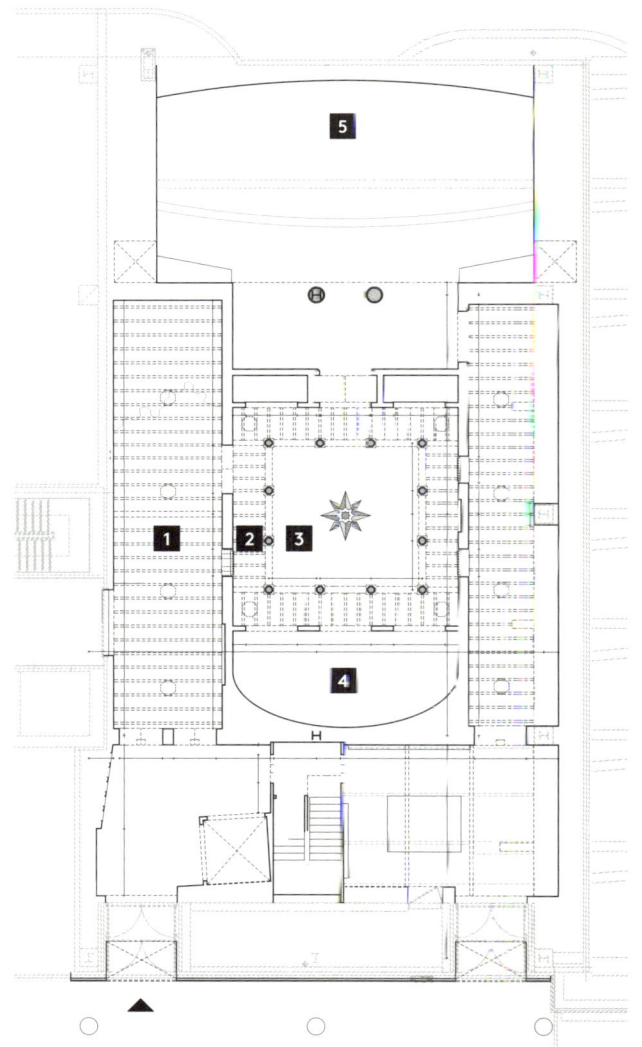

☒ Floor plan

1 Pre-show area
2 Exhibition area
3 Central plaza
4 Sahara south
5 Mediterranean north

Avocis by Delafair

THE ANGLED SURFACES OF A SCULPTURE COMMUNICATED THE STORY OF A NEW COMPANY THROUGH VIDEO MAPPING.

During 2011, six communications service providers united under a single brand umbrella called Avocis. To mark this union, Avocis seized the opportunity to present at the CallCenterWorld trade fair in Berlin, which offered an advertising opportunity for the new company name. Delafair was in charge of this project, the aim of which was to create an innovative, spectacular and publicity-enhancing representation of Avocis. The design team collaborated with video artists Sven Gareis and Ute Härtung to craft a unique concept. In order to elicit an emotional experience from visitors, the basic idea was to set a stunning sculpture in an empty space and to layer it with video mapping in order to unravel a story for the duration of the fair. Through a combination of changing object architecture and adjusted video animation, an atmosphere of suspense and intrigue extended from the announcement of the union on the first day to the unveiling of the new company name on the second day. To visualise the diversity and innovation of the company's services, a multifaceted diamond shape was used to represent its broad corporate spectrum and to offer many surfaces onto which to project the dynamic visuals. The 3-m-high angled structure was constructed from MDF sheets and had a total of nine projection surfaces. Four full-HD video projectors enabled the display of images on all sides. At the appropriate time, the front facet of the diamond was removed to reveal to the world the new company logo. The coloured projections on the spatial sculpture and the reflection of the brightly illuminated object in the mirrored floor together created a kaleidoscopic display that aroused the curiosity of fair goers.

TRADE FAIR CallCenterWorld
WHERE Berlin, Germany
WHEN February 2011
DESIGNER Delafair ☒ p.490
STAND CONSTRUCTOR Delafair
CLIENT Avocis
MARKET SECTOR Media and telecommunications
TOTAL FLOOR AREA 16 m²
PHOTOGRAPHER Lorenz Kienzle

☒ Light cut-outs in the interior of the diamond allowed for the unveiling of the company logo on the second day.
☒ The high-tech display afforded a striking visual attraction.
☒ The artist telematique developed software which enabled a synchronous, high resolution and accurate projection onto the diamond's surfaces.

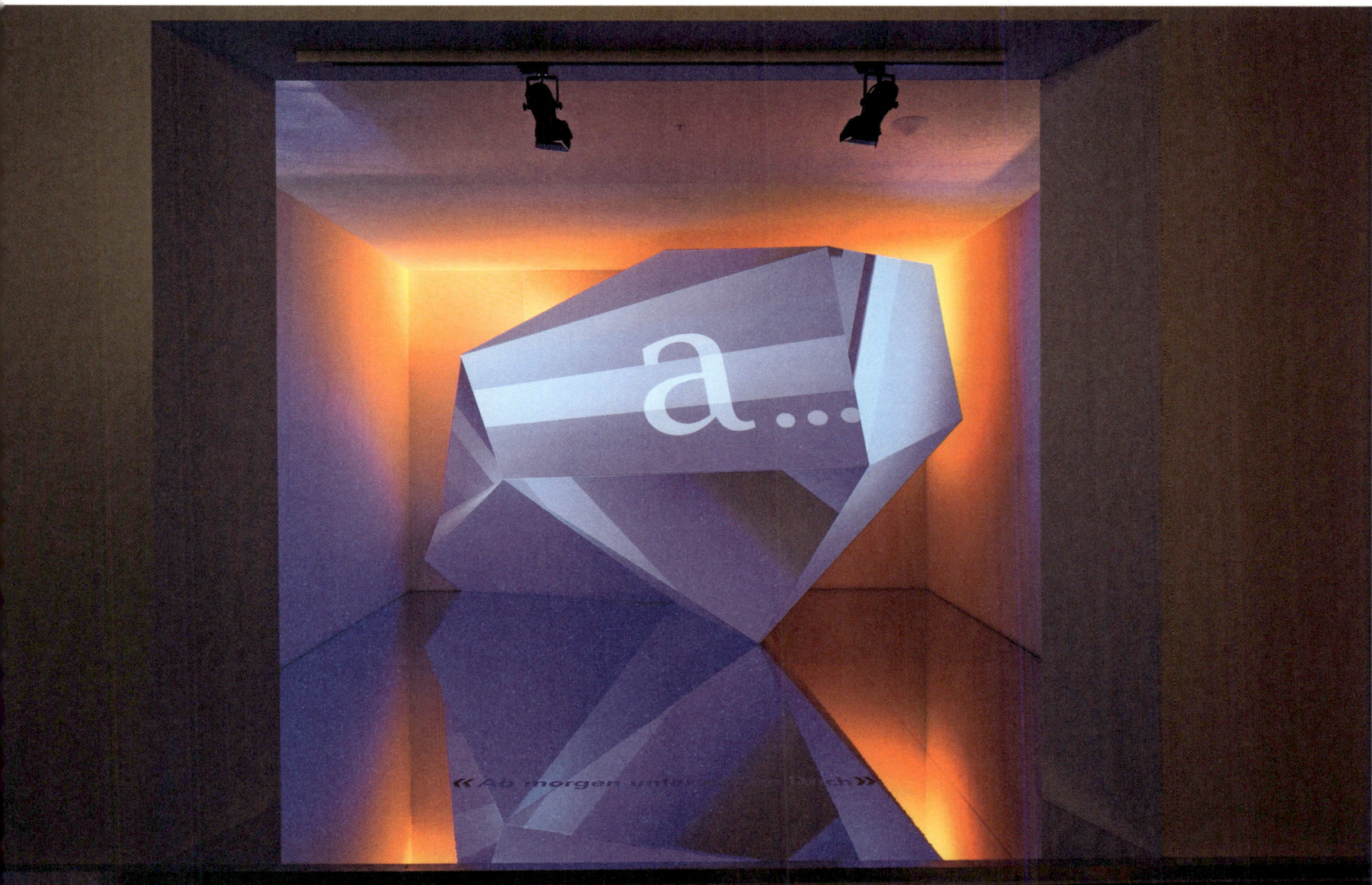

«Ab morgen unter einem Dach»

Bayer's Contrasts by Phocus Brand Contact

VISITORS WERE INVITED INTO A WORLD OF CONTRASTS THAT WOULD COMMUNICATE AND INFORM ABOUT PRODUCT FEATURES AND APPLICATION AREAS.

'Contrasts' was the motto of Bayer's brand presence at the European Congress of Radiology in Vienna. It was also the overarching creative concept of the healthcare company's exhibition stand, as designed by the team at Phocus Brand Contact. A glossy white backdrop, contrasted with blocks of brand colours, provided a clear external communication of the umbrella brand Bayer and its individual product brands. The interior space was imbued with the opulence of an interactive art café, providing visitors with an assured environment for meetings and technical discussions as well as a space for a spot of relaxation. Inside the stand, the contrasting concept was reflected in terms of both furnishing and media. Against the black and white decor, baroque style was juxtaposed with modern age and old-school chalkboards mingled with hi-tech tools. There was a true blend of communication methods and hands-on opportunities for visitors: on the one hand, they could write messages on the walls in branded coloured chalks and, on the other, they could use the iPads to artistically edit photographs and then transmit them to the art installation on the flat-screen TVs suspended overhead, thus becoming part of the brand presence. The iPads were positioned intermittently along the line of tall mirror-topped tables that ran down the centre of the stand. Two mirrored walls at either end added to polished presentation of the brand alongside its distinctive product range. The communicative atmosphere successfully allowed visitors to inform themselves about Bayer's latest developments in radiology.

TRADE FAIR **European Congress of Radiology**
WHERE **Vienna, Austria**
WHEN **March 2012**
DESIGNER **Phocus Brand Contact** ⊠ **p.496**
STAND CONSTRUCTOR **Schnaitt Internationale Messe- und Ladenbau**
CLIENT **Bayer HealthCare Medical Care**
MARKET SECTOR **Healthcare**
TOTAL FLOOR AREA **220 m²**
PHOTOGRAPHER **Britta Radike**

⊠ The stand's open architecture was eye-catching and inviting.
⊠ Hi-tech features in an art cafe setting created an inspiring atmosphere for in-depth communication.

Belgium Pavilion by Gielissen and Totems

A SERIES OF SPINNING CAROUSELS CONJURED UP A CHEERFUL IMAGE OF BELGIUM.

The Belgian Pavilion at the World Expo 2012 resulted from the creative partnership of Gielissen, Totems and NoA architects. The design team began by taking inspiration from Belgium's rich history of Flemish art – from the Old Masters to the expressionist and surrealist paints of the 20th century, to contemporary and comic culture. It is a country that appeals to the imagination as a colourful and outspoken leader. The presentation concept centred on a 'theatre of the imagination', taking visitors on a journey to a small carnival. The creative team, working collaboratively with NoA architects for the architectural design, crammed the pavilion full of striking visuals, fun elements and true impressions of the Belgian nation. On entering the 'fairground', visitors immediately experienced a convivial atmosphere thanks to the blinking light bulbs and spinning carousels presented before them. Candy-striped floors, fittings and furnishings added to the colourful pageantry, enhancing the main features of the booth: old-fashioned merry-go-rounds. The largest carousel recounted not only the history but also the current culture of Belgium. Here, visitors met with famous athletes and designers, as well as the nation's royal family, before moving on to spend time with master chocolatiers. In the far corner, a fantastic panorama of the Belgian coast opened up with scenes of dunes, waving grass, sandy beaches and the tempestuous North Sea. Along this vista, a number of smaller exhibits were positioned, with 'binocular viewers' available for visitors to point at an important aspect on the horizon and then watch a film relevant to the subject in view. A visit to the fair was not complete without Belgian fries, waffles, ice cream and chocolate, all available at the end of the tour in the themed restaurant and souvenir shop.

TRADE FAIR **World Expo 2012**
WHERE **Yeosu, South Korea**
WHEN **May 2012**
DESIGNERS **Gielissen** ⊠ **p.492** and **Totems** ⊠ **p.499**
STAND CONSTRUCTOR **Gielissen Interiors and Exhibitions**
CLIENT **Ministry of Economic Affairs (Belgium)**
MARKET SECTOR **Information and education**
TOTAL FLOOR AREA **1200 m²**
PHOTOGRAPHER **Totems**

⊠ The travelling theatre concept was likened to an annual fair located by the Belgian coast.
⊠ On entering the pavilion, visitors could walk to the 'ticket booth' where they could get their 'expo-passport' stamped.
⊠ The decor of the VIP lounge and the restaurant fitted in with the concept.

SERVICES GRAND STAND 4

Crammed full of blinking light bulbs and spinning carousels

- The carousel scenography was built up out of life-size 2D cut-out figures and LCD screens and was thoroughly tested in 3D design.
- When the carousels spun around, they added a dynamic aspect to an already magical fairground.
- The pavilion shop had tasty Belgian chocolate for sale.
- The three carousels were dedicated to chocolate, Belgian culture and ciamonds.

Cybersewing Atelier by Estudio Guto Requena

MERGING CYBER TECHNOLOGY AND OLD-FASHIONED SEWING ATELIERS, TWO DISTINCT UNIVERSES COLLIDED IN THIS ARCHITECTONIC SPACE IN SÃO PAULO.

TRADE FAIR **Mostra de Artes SESC**
WHERE **São Paulo, Brazil**
WHEN **November 2010**
DESIGNER **Estudio Guto Requena** ⊠ p 491
STAND CONSTRUCTOR **Cenotrak**
CLIENT **SESC/SP**
MARKET SECTOR **Information and education**
TOTAL FLOOR AREA **250 m²**
PHOTOGRAPHER **Fran Parente**

Cybersewing Atelier was a presentation designed by Estudio Guto Requena at one of the largest annual art events in São Paulo. Commissioned by the event organisers to display outfits that incorporated digital technologies, the space also hosted lectures and sewing workstations. The design team's scenography established a profound dialogue with the building that housed the exhibition – SECS Pompeia, one of the most architecturally relevant buildings in Brazil. A raw aesthetic imbued the apparently simple construction of the presentation of the technologically advanced content. A long, translucent surface unravelled through the space, with its dimensions, angles and proportions calculated to relate to its surroundings. The outfits were encased in a structure made from low-cost materials, with the transparent walls made of bubble wrap and certified pine wood to act as an interactive skin that responded to environmental stimuli. Thanks to the embedded sensors in the 'interactive membrane', movement was captured through sound. This acoustic stimuli resulted in the creation of different chromatic patterns and lighting hues in different parts of the space, adding a dynamic aspect the experience. Colours and distinctive graphic patterns invited the public to reflect on the way they occupy, walk and behave within the space. Cold shades (green and blue) indicated low levels of circulation and quietness, while warm hues (red and yellow) indicated more people, and hence noise, in the space. Alongside this, items of furniture such as worn-out chairs, decorative porcelain pieces, sewing machines and antique tapestries recalled the style of old-fashioned sewing ateliers. Modern elements, such as microchips microcontrollers, LEDs and transistors, were added to this temporal layer. The scenography and art direction of this project incorporated elements from apparently distinct universes that, like the advances of new information and communication technologies, seem to merge with each other: organic and machine-like, analogue and digital, natural and artificial, concrete and virtual.

⊠ Digital technology was incorporated into the garments on show, as well as in the architecture of the presentation itself.
⊠ The display booths were made from pine frames covered in bubble wrap.

Chromatic patterns
created dynamic aspects

☒ Floor plan

1 Reception
2 Workshop area
3 Exhibition zone
4 Artists' support area
5 Interactive membrane

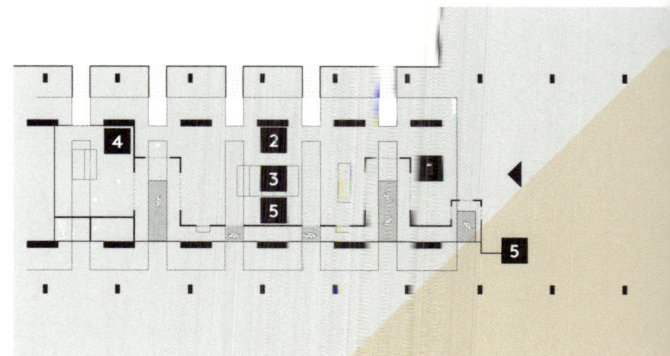

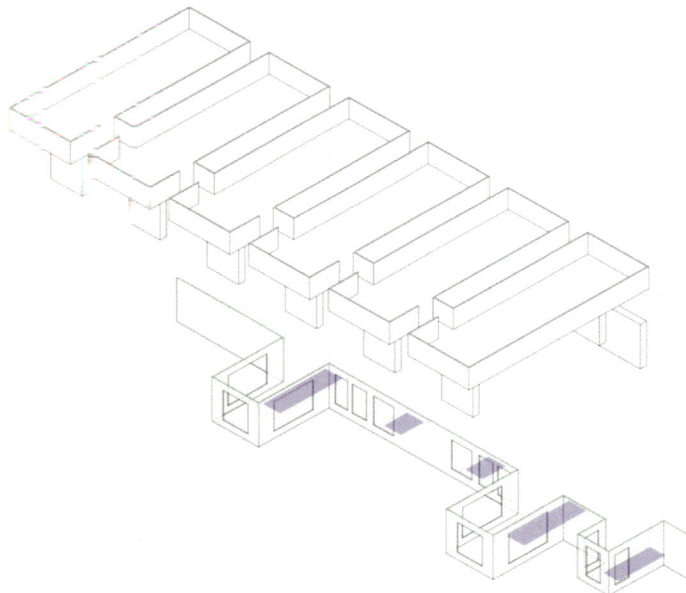

Exploded view

Dachser by mbco

COMMUNICATING LOGISTICS IN A STRIKING STAND WITH BLOCKS OF COLOUR AND A CANOPY OF CUBES.

'One world, one company, one network'. That was Dachser's corporate slogan for the transport logistic trade fair in 2011. Design studio mbco was in charge of translating this slogan into physical reality. The briefing from Dachser was to guide the visitors through the virtual stops within the IT network to reveal synergy with the physical network of hubs, trucks, trailers and containers. The presentation had to be warm and welcoming, both for existing clients and potential customers, whilst exuding the self-confidence and decidedness of the brand, all within a conceptual design. Cube shapes were at the core of the concept, decoded either as symbols of data packets or as packing devices. The 4-m² solid-blue cubes were positioned dramatically overhead – 8 m above the heads of fair goers – in precise rows. An attractive canopy was thus created above the entire area above the vast booth. Corporate colours were used to effectively split the presentation in a striking fashion: on the one side the all-blue communication zone and, on the other, the hospitality area with its sunny yellow glow. Full-height walls separated the two areas and created an impressive yet simple statement on the exterior of the stand. A vast expanse of solid colour, interrupted only by a strategically placed brand name, created a strong aesthetic and caught the attention of passers-by. A complete media system impressively demonstrated integration and logistics throughout the space. A total of 16 projectors located above the installation projected the company presentation and slogan from behind onto to the lower surfaces of the suspended cubes. Additionally, IT terminals with plasma touch screens displaying the different business segments of the client were installed in the communication area and a large plasma screen prominently displayed corporate messages. The ubiquitously visible 6 x 12 m wall of water in the blue zone was also an eye-catching feature, spelling out words and icons to supplement the client's slogan.

TRADE FAIR transport logistic
WHERE Munich, Germany
WHEN April 2011
DESIGNER mbco ☒ p.495
STAND CONSTRUCTOR mbco
CLIENT Dachser
MARKET SECTOR Logistics and transport
TOTAL FLOOR AREA 705 m²
PHOTOGRAPHER Peter Schaffrath

Cubes were decoded as symbols of data packets

☒ Setting the scene in the communication zone was the animated water feature (by watershow.de).
☒ The blue cube canopy also extended to the yellow hospitality area.
☒ The lounge, with its wood panelled floor and raised elevation, was referred to as 'the top deck'.

Deutsche Telekom IFA 2011 by q~bus Mediatektur

THE IDEA THAT SHARING STARTS AT HOME INSPIRED AN INTELLIGENT HOUSE TO BE PLACED AT THE HEART OF THE CONCEPT.

The integrated telecommunications company Deutsche Telekom commissioned q~bus to create the brand's stand at IFA 2011 based on the theme 'Life is for sharing'. The design team focused its concept on solutions for a connected and smart home. An intelligent two-storey building formed the pulsating heart of the vast presentation, which was swathed in a corporate magenta, instantly recognisable as the brand colour of the ICT service provider. The central white house had a sleek, contemporary architecture with natural wooden slats as a special feature. The construction consisted of a timber and steel framework and had one open gable end. Its side walls were sliced clean through, offering different entry points with smooth transitions between inside and outside space and giving visitors glimpses into the interior from different angles. Furniture and fittings ranged from design classics to much-loved items found at Berlin flea markets, which gave the interior decor a lived-in feel. Set up like a home of our everyday – and future – lives that showcased the client's products and solutions, the house had a hands-on role for fair goers. They could remotely control window blinds, lighting and kitchen appliances at the touch of a button, directly from the Pads and apps located around the building. If the home formed the hub of the connectivity concept, its garden and patio areas – spread out across the length and breadth of the exhibition hall – offered the space for a shared entertainment experience. With media platforms and performance stages dotted around, fair goers enjoyed plenty of opportunities for vibrant interactions. When it all got a bit much, they could rest for a while amidst the sea of sun chairs positioned on a tiered platform at one end of the hall to give them full view over the entire spectacle.

TRADE FAIR **IFA**
WHERE **Berlin, Germany**
WHEN **September 2011**
DESIGNER **q~bus Mediatektur** ☒ **p.497**
STAND CONSTRUCTOR **q~bus Mediatektur**
CLIENT **Deutsche Telekom**
MARKET SECTOR **Media and telecommunications**
TOTAL FLOOR AREA **3848 m²**
PHOTOGRAPHER **q~bus Mediatektur**

☒ The 'connected' house incorporated a natural design and intuitive features.
☒ Fair goers were invited to walk-in and try out the presentation modules.
☒ The fabric layered walls and ceiling were tinged with magenta illumination.

Smooth transitions between inside and outside space

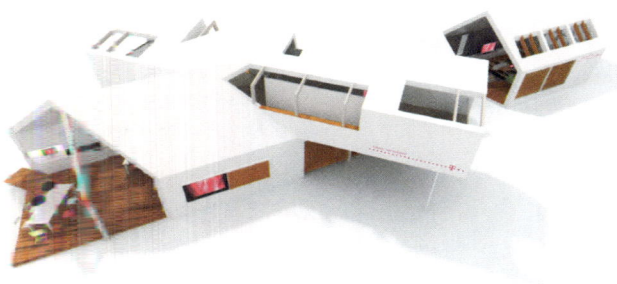

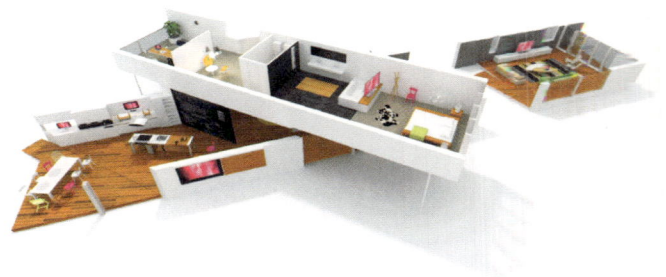

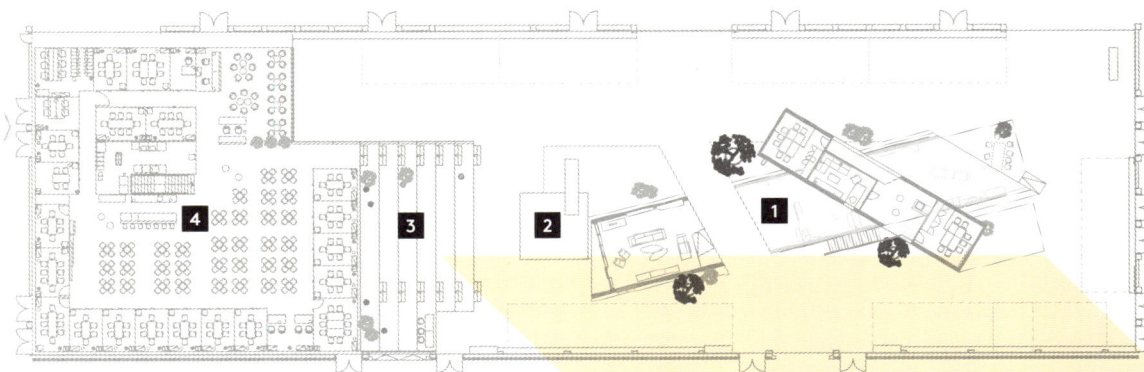

	Floor plan
1	House area
2	Stage
3	Tiered seating
4	Hospitality/meeting area

The tiered terrace gave visitors an optimum view of the stage.
Meeting rooms and VIP areas were situated behind the terrace.
Renderings of the house, showing its positioning in the hall.

Deutsche Telekom IFA 2012 by q~bus Mediatektur

A CONNECTED WORLD FILLED WITH ART, INTERACTIVITY AND INVENTIVE PURSUITS.

The strapline that underlined Deutsche Telekom's presentation at IFA 2012 read: 'Addressing the dynamics of a connected world'. The creative agency q~bus had the task of translating this slogan into a physical reality at the trade fair. The spacious exhibition hall has been dedicated solely to the services of one of the world's leading integrated telecommunication

companies. Here the design team developed a market-orientated concept that evolved over the course of the trade show. The idea of a 'network' served as a continuous visual feature, with threads of interconnectivity in the form of directional strips on the floor or lengths of magenta ribbon running through – and around – all the distinct spaces. Many elements evolved continuously over the duration of the fair, with as highlight the 20 x 5 m chalkboard wall put at the disposal of the Romanian artist Dan Perjovschi. He busied himself every day with images based on the theme of: 'Welcome to your connected world'. Beyond that, creative designers using tape art and knit art could also be seen creating new visual connections. Visitors were not only invited as spectators but also encouraged to take part in these inventive pursuits. Alongside the different display areas, glass-walled meeting rooms and hospitality hot spots offered further opportunities for interactivity. At the centre of the hall, a 40-m² sensitive and intelligent floor proved irresistible to fair goers who wished to connect with the beat of the fair. At the same time, the location hosted hourly shows and appearances by bands and other prominent guests. Berlin radio station FluxFM broadcast concerts live from the studio booth positioned adjacent to the stage. Overhead, bespoke lighting installations were suspended alongside the 'floating roofs', which provided angled canopies for the product demo areas around the perimeter of the presentation area.

TRADE FAIR **IFA**
WHERE **Berlin, Germany**
WHEN **September 2012**
DESIGNER **q~bus Mediatektur** ⊠ p.497
STAND CONSTRUCTOR **q~bus Mediatektur**
CLIENT **Deutsche Telekom**
MARKET SECTOR **Media and telecommunications**
TOTAL FLOOR AREA **3445 m²**
PHOTOGRAPHER **q~bus Mediatektur**

⊠ The white roofs formed a canopy over the display areas.
⊠ The artist's daily commentaries were illustrated on the chalkboard wall.

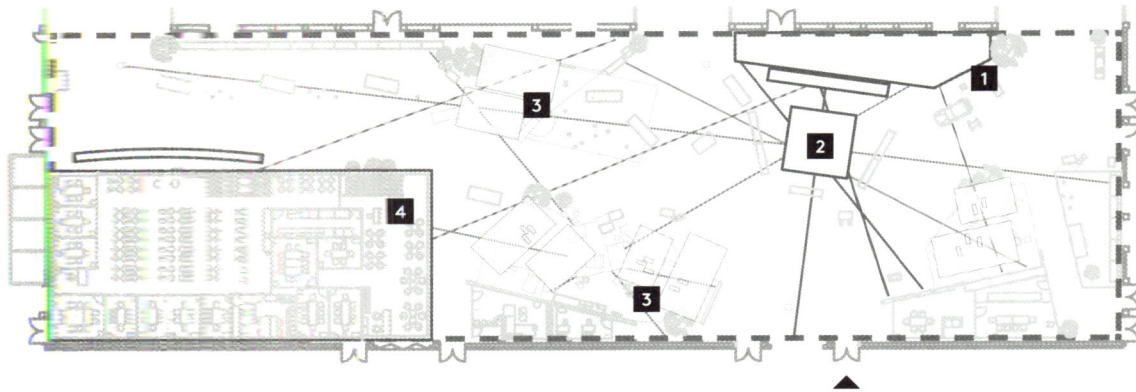

Floor plan

1   Chalkboard art wall
2   Stage
3   Product display areas under
    floating roofs
4   Hospitality/meeting area

Floating roofs provided angular canopies for products

☒ Angled lines on the floor reiterated the 'connected communication' theme.
☒ Visitors could relax alongside the product displays.
☒ The business lounge was located in one corner of the stand.

- Art and entertainment were embedded in the booth's design concept.
- Berlin radio station FLUxFM broadcast live from the studio next to the stage
- At the entrance, visitors were directed towards the performance area.
- Sketched ideas for the 'market place'.

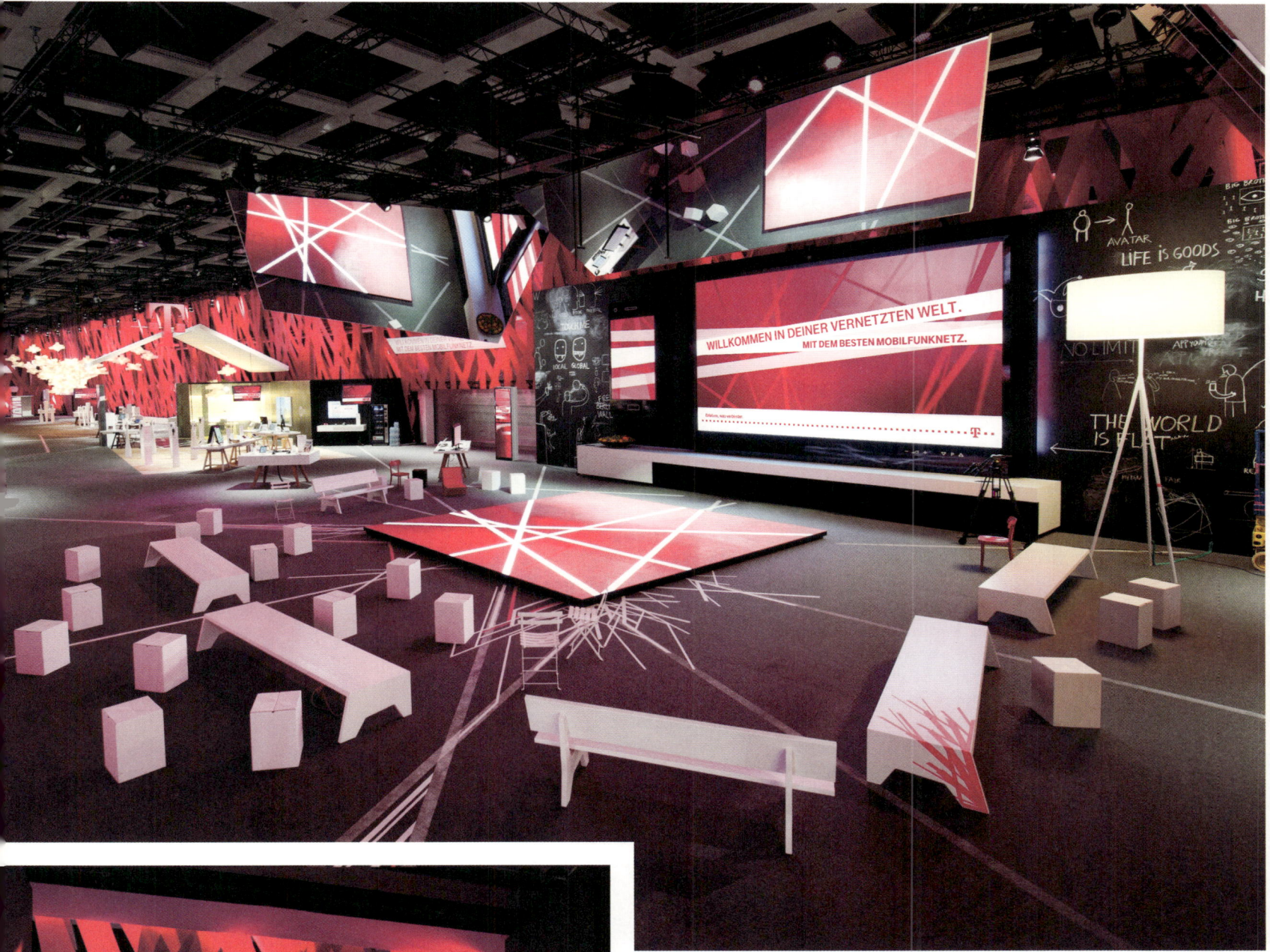

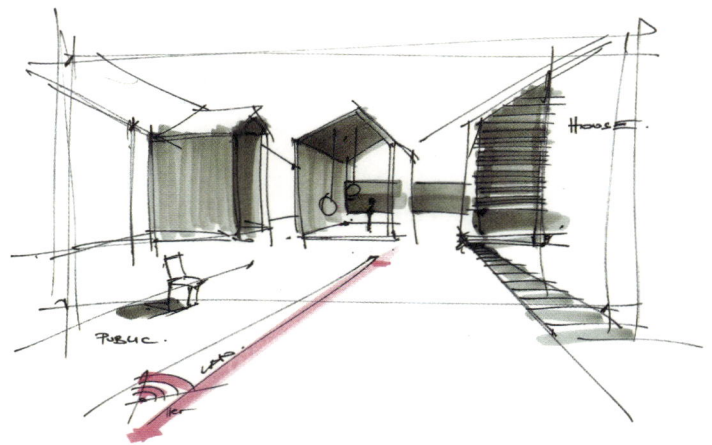

Dovetail by Mayridge

A FINANCIAL SERVICES BRAND FOCUSED ON PRECISION ENGINEERING WHILST COMMUNICATING A SOFTER EDGE.

At Sibos in Toronto, the largest exhibition of its kind for the financial industry, Dovetail called upon design firm Mayridge to communicate to fair goers its company slogan for its patented payment system: precision engineering. The brief outlined the need to create an environment that allowed for formal and informal interaction with delegates in a stylish and seamless way, whilst promoting the company's rebranding and new marketing direction. The design team focused on the large exterior frontage and maximised the impact and visibility of the stand. Its main aims included expressing the key message and conveying the simplicity, confidence and clarity of the brand as a mature and confident leader in the field. Graphics were kept to a minimum on the exterior, with a clean facade in the corporate colours of white, black and blue. Surface finishes were paramount in communicating an air of precision, right down to the choice of a black laminate with a subtle texture to mask the joints and lend it a flawless look. The timber-frame walls had a layered appearance. A black panel with an angular shape was positioned in front of the white back wall. The black surface was linked to the wall by two blue glazed sections at either end creating an eye-catching feature. The purpose of the blue transparent panes was twofold: to give passers-by a glimpse into the stand's meeting rooms, and to provide the interior with natural light. Secondary colours in the wallpaper, furnishings and bespoke furniture created a relaxed and homely ambience inside and communicated a softer image in line with the firm's rebranding.

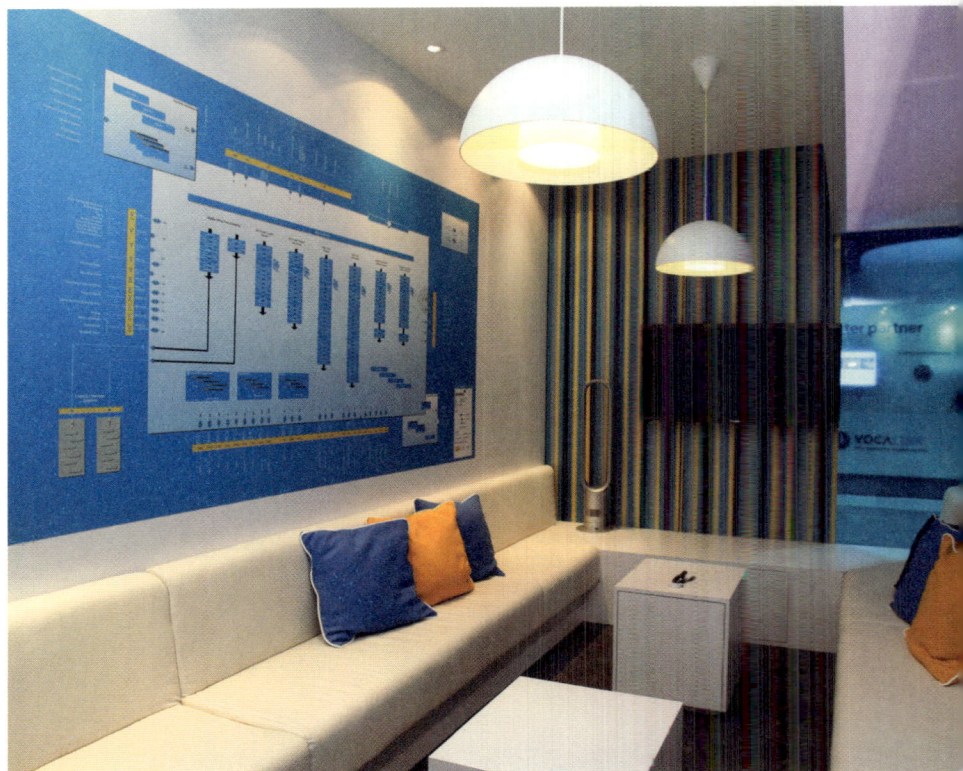

TRADE FAIR Sibos
WHERE Toronto, Canada
WHEN September 2011
DESIGNER Mayridge ☒ p.495
STAND CONSTRUCTOR Mayridge
CLIENT Dovetail
MARKET SECTOR Banking and financial services
TOTAL FLOOR AREA 48 m²
PHOTOGRAPHER Anthony Vallario

☒ The booth's architectural lines express simplicity and brand confidence.
☒ Key corporate facts were displayed the stand's dark exterior wall.
☒ The interior meeting rooms reflected softer, welcoming environment, w interpreting brand colours.

ELISAVA Stand Up Workshop led by Marcos Catalan and Stefano Coll

A CREATIVE CONSTRUCTION OF CARDBOARD BOXES COMMUNICATED A DESIGN SCHOOL'S ETHOS.

TRADE FAIR **Saló de l'Ensenyament**
WHERE **Barcelona, Spain**
WHEN **March 2012**
DESIGNERS **Marcos Catalan** ✉ p.494 **and Stefano Colli** ✉ p.498
STAND CONSTRUCTOR **M6 Grupo Empresarial de Proyectos**
CLIENT **ELISAVA Barcelona School of Design and Engineering**
MARKET SECTOR **Education**
TOTAL FLOOR AREA **60 m²**
PHOTOGRAPHER **Eugeni Pons**

Designers Marcos Catalan and Stefano Colli teamed up to create the presentation of the ELISAVA Barcelona School of Design and Engineering at the trade fair Saló de l'Ensenyament. This event is held annually in Barcelona with exhibitors covering the complete range of educational services on offer in the region. For four months in the run-up to the fair, the designers worked together on this project directly with the school, as well as getting the creative input from six of the school's students: Alberto Aranda, Bernat Bisbal, Marc Borrell, Francisco Javier Camino, Andrea Josende and Andrea Soto. The team created a cloud concept capable of communicating a great variety of values that define the school and the courses it offers. These values were arrived at through the help and advice of educational tutors and the collaboration of our business partners. The principal element of the project was a hollow cardboard construction, with multiples of this box-type unit used as building blocks for the stand architecture. Each of the illuminated 'bricks' contained information about the school and student projects. Creating a sheltered space inside the booth, the bricks were also permeable and visible to people passing the stand. This curved, corner platform captured its surroundings thanks to the large, illuminated red letters that spelled the school's name and caught the attention of visitors from across the exhibition hall. Clad on all surfaces – floor, walls and ceiling – with grey carpet tiles, the interior boasted a calm environment with a muted colour scheme. The design team realised a bespoke octagonal multi-level 'carpet table' that formed an attractive centrepiece of the stand. Visitors were invited to take a seat on the Vitra chairs and cork stools, taking time to gather further information about the courses and watch the branded film.

◩ The school's name was a metal framework with red textured paper, lit with LEDs.
◩ The tiered table was designed during the project.
◩ More information about the project and its collaborators at: bitly.com/elisava.

GE Healthcare by McMillan Group

INNOVATIVE ADVANCEMENTS IN HEALTHCARE SERVICES DOMINATED A STAND BUZZING WITH TECHNOLOGY.

McMillan Group provided the design of GE Healthcare's presence at the Radiological Society of America in 2011. The trade fair stand needed to provide brand and product continuity across its diverse businesses, with the main challenge to create a fresh new look and integrate a total of 12 different product areas into one unified presentation. To build on the launch in 2010 of the client's 'Healthymagination' initiative, which aims for better health for more people everywhere, the 2011 theme was: 'Working together for healthier lives'. A secondary theme incorporated technological aspects, with another important objective to ensure clear navigation, way-finding and product exploration for all visitors. One design solution to achieve the look and feel of a unified brand presence consisted of large portraits that wrapped around the stand. Along with smaller blue duotone pictures, these images of people from around the globe added an underlying warmth to the brand message. The visuals featured real-life situations and brought to the attention of fair goers the idea of 'people versus technology'. Technical equipment was positioned across the booth, with each setting outlining different medical scenarios. These were interactive spaces where visitors could also discuss their needs with the GE industrial design team. Immediate concepts for improved products were visualised on large screens. The large multi-media stage positioned at the front of the booth formed a focal point for presentations from industry experts. Dramatically edge-lit identifier signs, scaled at different heights and positioned to give the brand a visibility from across the exhibition hall, lined the perimeter of the stand. Each modality featured at least one new product supported by a monolithic graphic icon at each of the new product demo areas.

A pre-show theatre at the front of exhibition featured overviews by industry and GE experts.

A number of secluded suites illustrated environments for the products to be used for healthcare diagnosis.

TRADE FAIR **Radiological Society of North America**
WHERE **Chicago, United States**
WHEN **November 2011**
DESIGNER **McMillan Group** ⊠ **p.495**
STAND CONSTRUCTOR **Elite Exhibits**
CLIENT **GE Healthcare**
MARKET SECTOR **Healthcare**
TOTAL FLOOR AREA **3159 m²**
PHOTOGRAPHER **Jamie Padget**

GE Healthcare

Working together for
healthier lives

- Bold forms provided brand identity and theme messaging that literally surrounded the product areas.
- The interactive pavilion showcased emerging technologies.
- Various views of different product zones within the exhibition from the perimeter of the stand.

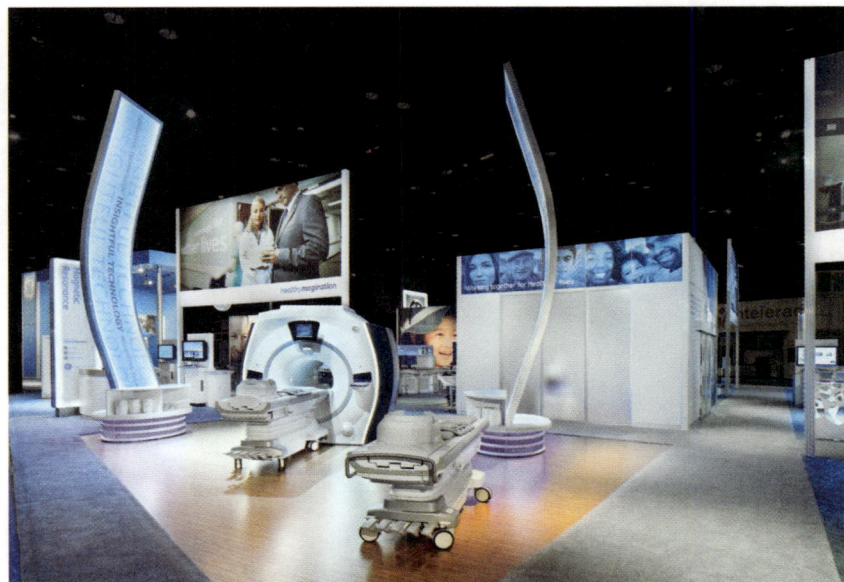

**Portraits provided
an underlying warmth
to the brand image**

goldgas by Nest One

A RICH DESIGN THAT LEFT VISITORS CONVINCED THIS ENERGY SUPPLIER'S PIPES WERE LINED WITH GOLD.

For its presentation at the E-World Energy & Water trade fair in 2011, the German gas supplier goldgas entrusted Nest One with the design of its trade fair stand. The brief called for the creation of a contemporary space with a tranquil air. The stand's concept revolved around a bespoke object in the space – the impressive light installation – inspired by the graphics in the energy supplier's logo, which represents the gas pipes that are such a vital aspect of the client s service. Circular tubes in differing dimensions were positioned within a larger, outer cylinder. All aspects of the chandelier were lined with fabric in cream and gold hues. This feature guaranteed wide-range visibility from across the exhibition space, whilst flooding the stand with a warm and golden glow. The palette of the presentation cited the colours and materials of the goldgas headquarters in Hamburg, Germany. Black lacquered walls wrapped around the booth to provide a rich feel to the space when combined with the shimmering golden accent colour. Wooden parquet flooring in an oak finish spread across the expanse of the stand's platform, with a circular carpet that broke up the striped effect of the floorboards positioned directly below the light feature. Bespoke furniture elements in black and gold incorporated metal pipework to create attractive tall tables and platforms. In one corner at the back of the stand, a screened-off area allowed for a secluded meeting room where the client could converse with customers away from the bustle of the fair. There was also a hospitality bar discretely positioned at the opposite back corner. Visitors were encouraged to stop and take their time, relaxing for a while in the designer chairs that furnished the seating area. The premium environment that was produced entirely represented the high standard of the brand.

TRADE FAIR **E-World Energy & Water**
WHERE **Essen, Germany**
WHEN **February 2011**
DESIGNER **Nest One** ⊠ **p.495**
STAND CONSTRUCTOR **Mehrblick**
CLIENT **goldgas**
MARKET SECTOR **Energy supplier**
TOTAL FLOOR AREA **80 m²**
PHOTOGRAPHER **Nest One**

⊠ Gold pipework was a recurring theme the booth's furnishings.
⊠ The bespoke light installation was a feature of the stand design.
⊠ The metallic gold colour used in fixtures and fittings was set again black backdrop.

HKIA Master Plan 2030 by Oval Design

AN AIRPORT EXPANSION PROPOSAL PROJECT COMMUNICATED A FRESH, FUN AND INTERACTIVE CONCEPT.

TRADE FAIR Hong Kong International Airport Exhibition
WHERE Hong Kong
WHEN June 2011
DESIGNER Oval Design ⊠ p. 496
STAND CONSTRUCTOR Oval Design
CLIENT Airport Authority Hong Kong
MARKET SECTOR Information and educati
TOTAL FLOOR AREA 450 m²
PHOTOGRAPHER Danny Yu

Hong Kong International Airport (HKIA) launched an exhibition in 2011 which outlined the airport's achievements, 'green' projects and expansion plans. It was also a platform to consult the public about specific options for future development. The idea for the space created by Oval Design started with a thematic representation of a 'tree' – the graphic symbol that HKIA had already used for its expansion phase. Oval's approach took on the appearance of a vibrantly growing tree that would attract visitors' attention from a distance. A space was carved out with intertwining arches and 'crawling' structures, resembling branches, with information displayed in demarcated, thematic zones. A fresh colour palette in shades of blue, green and orange was used across the presentation. This created an attractive concept for passers-by, enticing them inside to find out more. The entrance was designed as a runway with markings and lights, above which hovered a plane-shaped prop. Visitors were directed to follow a defined route around the booth ensuring all the exhibition content was viewed in a logical sequence. Two interactive models helped illustrate the possible directions of the airport's future development, specifically the two- and three-runway options. Projectors concealed in the ceiling of the stand projected animations onto the models made of translucent acrylic, enabling visitors to understand the various features of the two scenarios of future expansion: planes taking off and landing on a third runway; new road and rail links with moving traffic, new layout, etc. Before leaving the exhibition, visitors had the opportunity to give their opinion on the two options. Although the nature and subject matter of the exhibition was decidedly serious, the design ensured that visitors were not overwhelmed. The adoption of a fresh and flowing concept with attractive colours created an ambience pervaded with energy and fun.

⊠ A section of the booth structure was created as multiple vaults in reference to the familiar exterior of the airport terminal building.
⊠ Pictograms in a range of vibrant hues made for a colourful exhibition.

Intertwining arches and crawling structures resembled branches

Visitors used touch-screen monitors to view detailed information on the airport's future, as well as animations on proposed features on the model.

Renderings giving a bird's eye view of the route through the stand, which was formed by the 'tree branches'.

Walking through the entrance, visitors had the feeling of being on a runway with the plane overhead coming in to land.

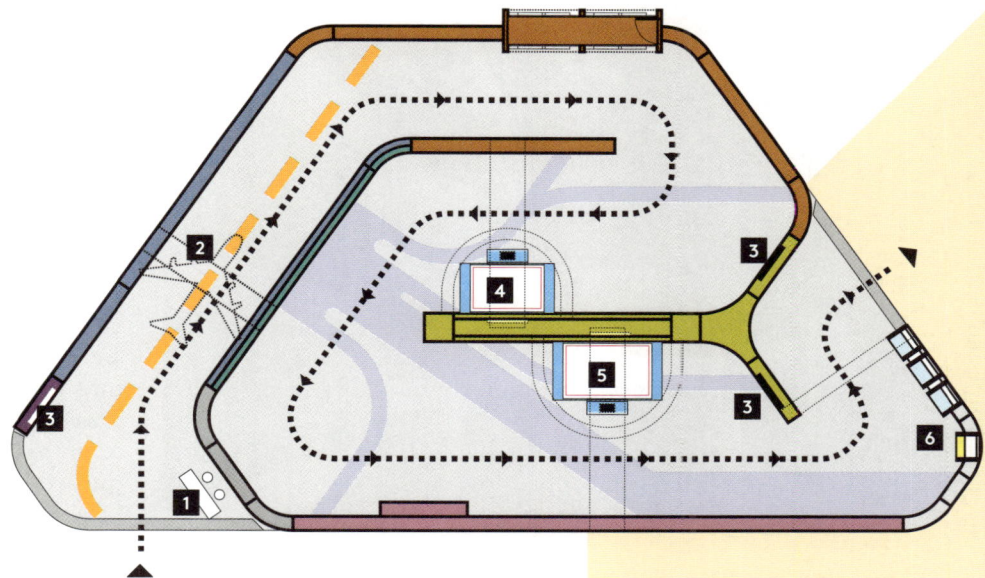

Floor plan

1 Reception counter
2 Plane prop
3 Video screen
4 Scenario 1 presentation
5 Scenario 2 presentation
6 Visitor opinion collection

Hong Kong Pavilion by Oval Design

VISITORS FOUND THEMSELVES IN A GREEN SANCTUARY WHERE THEY COULD ENJOY NATURE WHILE VIEWING THE EXHIBITS.

TRADE FAIR MIPIM Asia
WHERE Hong Kong
WHEN November 2011
DESIGNER Oval Design ⬆ p.496
STAND CONSTRUCTOR Oval Design
CLIENT Development Bureau,
Hong Kong SAR Government
MARKET SECTOR Information and educat
TOTAL FLOOR AREA 120 m²
PHOTOGRAPHER Danry Tu

The Hong Kong Pavilion at MIPIM Asia 2011, a leading international real estate trade show, was the Hong Kong SAR Government's showcase of its initiatives and efforts in building a green and sustainable future for the city. Themed as 'A Greener Hong Kong', the presentation featured three major areas: natural wonders; green architecture and building practices; and urban regeneration. The booth was created by Oval Design as a green sanctuary that combined the innovative application of the principles of recyclability, reusability and biodegradability. A number of eco-friendly ideas were implemented to create a highly sustainable exhibition. Potted plants of different species were mounted on reusable metal-grid structures to form green walls of varying sizes and shapes, cleverly providing display space for the exhibits. Visitors walked on real grass instead of carpets and were guided to the different exhibition zones along a pathway paved with eco-friendly bricks made from recycled glass bottles. Thanks to the moisture and cooling effect of the plants and grass, visitors also enjoyed a nice chill inside the booth. The potted plants and grass patches, even though biodegradable, were not discarded but returned to the nursery after the exhibition. Additionally, recycled plywood was used to build the wooden structures. The presentation also maximised the use of digital displays and interactive models, and energy-saving LED lights were used for general illumination. Even special PAR lights, which emit wavelengths conducive to photosynthesis, were added to enable the plants and grass patches to continue growing during the exhibition, a measure that improved air quality inside the exhibition booth. The stand had one of the smallest carbon footprints ever produced by an exhibition in Hong Kong thanks to the green measures suggested by an independent consultant and to carbon offset calculations.

☒ Created as a green haven, the booth design provided a relaxed setting for visitors to view the exhibits.

☒ Monitors suspended overhead showed images of Hong Kong's natural beauty and green infrastructure.

☒ Motion-detection technology enabled visitors to see images of neighborhoods before and after renewal by waving their hands in front of the sensor.

Masdar by 2LK Design

CURVED CONTOURS AND SPHERICAL SHAPES CREATED A HUB FOR RENEWABLE ENERGIES.

Masdar, an agency based in Abu Dhabi, United Arab Emirates, invests in the development and commercialisation of renewable energy and sustainable technologies. The organisation has hosted the European Future Energy Forum (EFEF) annually in different European cities since 2009, comprising a major conference and exhibition. At EFEF 2011, the host company wanted a platform to promote its work and commissioned 2LK Design for the realisation of its trade fair stand. Inspired by Masdar's core values – to be agile, commercial, sustainable and grounded – as well as its corporate identity and brand philosophy, 2LK Design created an architectural style for the stand that made it the 'hub' of the exhibition hall. Curved lines, rounded corners and bold shapes dominated the white space, clearly branded with a corporate blue hue. At the front of the stand, key corporate projects were given prominence, with interactive stations to attract the attention of passers-by. From across the trade fair, the Masdar brand was also clearly discernible thanks to the overhead banners that wrapped around the core of the presentation. A 'figure of eight' configuration made up of two circular arrangements linked together by a storage room delineated the zone dedicated to the company's five individual business units. With sustainable and eco-friendly materials, the vertical component was integrated with curved outer walls. Each sub-unit was individually colour-coded along the edges of its vertical curved wall, which featured video screens on the exterior and graphic case studies on the inner surfaces. When grouped together, these spherical enclosures created more secluded areas for fair goers to gather information and discuss the possibilities of renewable energy with the Masdar team.

☒ The curved fascia sweeps overhead creating a semi-enclosed area below.
☒ Core projects were displayed digitally around the perimeter.
☒ Integrated seating units furnished the discussion area.

TRADE FAIR European Future Energy Forum
WHERE Geneva, Switzerland
WHEN October 2011
DESIGNER 2LK Design ☒ p.488
STAND CONSTRUCTOR Push Studios
CLIENT Masdar
MARKET SECTOR Renewable energy and sustainable technologies
TOTAL FLOOR AREA 96 m²
PHOTOGRAPHER Steve Burden

Netherlands Pavilion by Gielissen and Totems

MAPPING A HISTORICAL TIME LINE FOR THE DUTCH NATION.

The creative teams of Gielissen and Totems worked together to realise the Dutch pavilion at the World Expo 2012 in Yeosu, South Korea. For a country with a flat, delta landscape, the concept presented a 'view from above'. Aerial photography and satellite images explained the layout of the land and offered visitors an impression of the water-veined countryside. Old and new maps also shed light on how the Dutch crafted the landscape out of water over the years by reclaiming new land from the sea through the construction of polders and dikes. A large, unfolded map formed the main feature of the presentation. Executed on a grandiose scale, the map transformed into the architectural landscape and occupied a central position in the entire pavilion interior, wrapping up the sides of the elongated booth. A central walkway that weaved its way through the stand like a meandering stream took visitors past a multitude of themed images projected onto the audio-visual map. This complete visionary experience included such juxtaposed themes as the past and future, people and technology, the Netherlands and the world, and problems and solutions. Two areas at either end of the map zone acted as pre- and post-show features. The entrance area created a cultural bridge to introduce the Netherlands to the local visitors. This took the form of an exhibition about a 17th-century Dutchman from the famous VOC trading company, who was shipwrecked and stranded in Korea as one of the first foreigners there. A series of illustrated stories depicted pages from his journal in the pre-show space, dominated by classical picture frames that filled the walls in a time line of that era. The post-show area saw visitors taking a leap forward to the present day, with information on numerous Dutch innovations communicated via wall-mounted iPads. At the end of the journey through the pavilion, visitors could buy the latest Dutch design products in the shop.

TRADE FAIR **World Expo 2012**
WHERE **Yeosu, South Korea**
WHEN **May 2012**
DESIGNERS **Gielissen** ☒ **p.492 and Totems** ☒ **p.499**
STAND CONSTRUCTOR **KBS**
CLIENT **Ministry of Economic Affairs (the Netherlands)**
MARKET SECTOR **Information and education**
TOTAL FLOOR AREA **650 m²**
PHOTOGRAPHER **Totems**

☒ A splash of vibrant orange lined the surfaces of the shop where Dutch design products were featured.
☒ The pre-show zone had the air of a gallery with historical artworks on show.
☒ The main display was depicted as a folded map, with 17 projectors used to create an immersive experience for visitors.

- The frames were filled with stills, graphics, painting replicas and LCD screens with media content.
- Renderings giving a bird's eye view of the whole presentation, clearly depicting the three stages of the pavilion.
- The audio-visual media projections created different scenarios providing information on the Dutch nation.

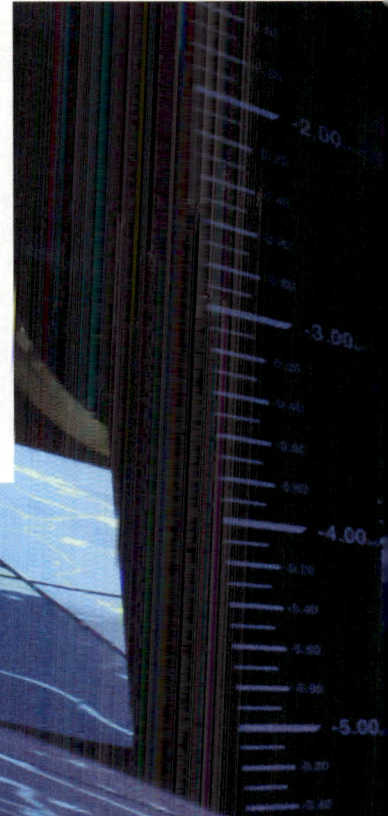

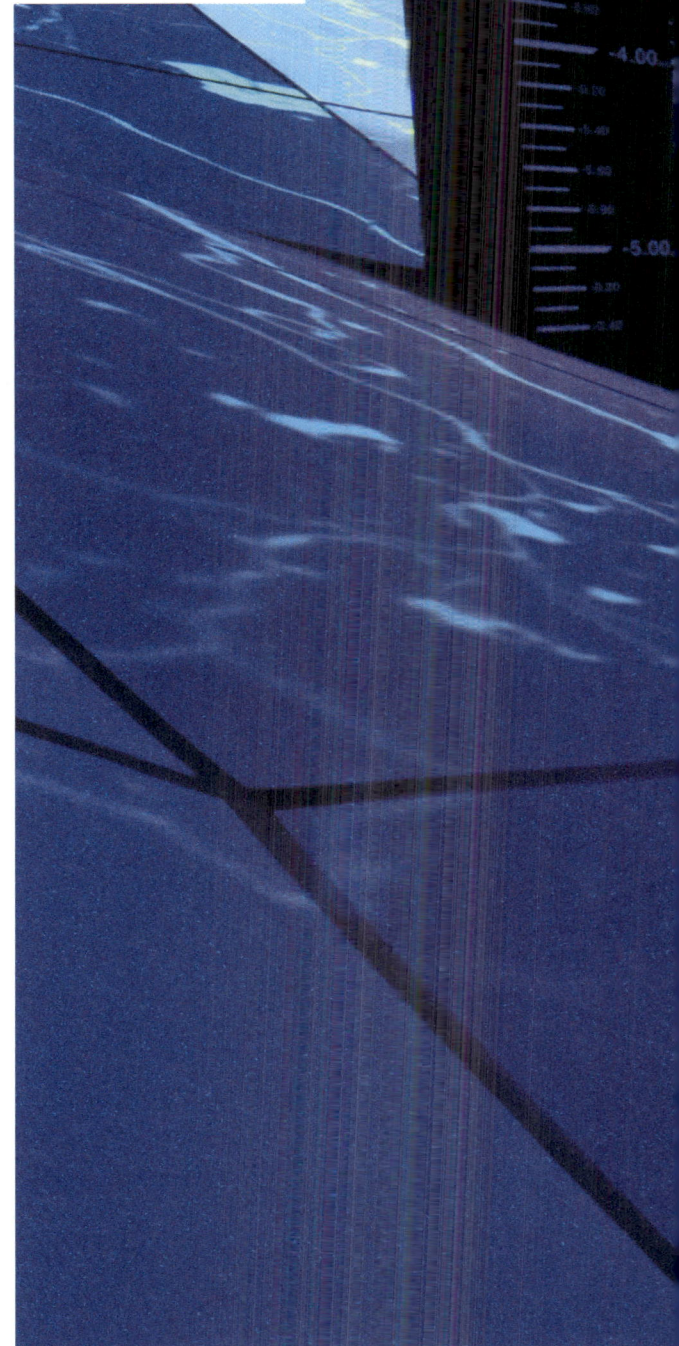

The central walkway was like a meandering stream

One by D'art Design Gruppe

STATIC SCENARIOS CAPTURED FROM DAILY LIFE IN A DESIGN STUDIO VISUALISED ITS COMPETENCIES IN SPATIAL COMMUNICATION.

For D'art Design Gruppe's seventh appearance at the retail trade fair Euroshop in 2011, the company wished to visualise its own core competencies and capabilities in the realm of spatial communication. Visitors were welcomed by a presentation that consisted of five architectural metaphors for situations taken from everyday life within the design studio. The creation of a stringent communication thread was the primary objective for the design team, and so the five scenarios were set out as interconnected spaces taking the form of elongated cubes that were open at each end. Two black boxes formed the side boundaries of the booth, their glazed walls turning them into oversized display windows. The mysterious air of these simple, dark spaces enticed fair goers into the stand, from where they could catch glimpses into the adjoining spaces. This stark and subtle arrangement was sufficiently intriguing for visitors to step forward and investigate further. The scenic, staccato-like sequences offered visitors not only sufficient scope to interpret what they encountered, but also enough tools to discuss the range of services on offer. The three interior cubes were uncluttered, bright and airy, with text graphics adorning the walls. The central room was architecturally neutral and featured a natural wood finish on the floor, walls and ceiling, as well as on the central counter. This space formed the hub of the stand, where visitors could discuss opportunities with D'art staff or just relax on the bar stools. This was also the only room with any seats, or at least seats that were actually meant for sitting on. In one interior space, chairs that were quirkily affixed to the walls could be seen alongside a white-painted angular panel that wrapped up and over the ceiling, morphing into gravity-defying workstations. This scenario, whilst instilling a sense of disorientation, succinctly expressed the design studio's sense of fun.

TRADE FAIR Euroshop
WHERE Dusseldorf, Germany
WHEN February 2011
DESIGNER D'art Design Gruppe ☒ p.490
STAND CONSTRUCTOR Projektpilot
CLIENT D'art Design Gruppe
MARKET SECTOR Design services
TOTAL FLOOR AREA 204 m²
PHOTOGRAPHERS Joerg Hempel Photodesign, Tobias Wille Photographie

☒ D'art Design Gruppe interpreted its work architectonically in five spaces that were interconnected.
☒ The title One was tongue-in-cheek, as there are actually limitless possibilities for services offered by the agency.
☒ The grey-hued room quirkily displayed integrated office tools to indicate the immediacy of the creative process.

Roteiro Musical da Cidade by Estudio Guto Requena and Atelier Marko Brajovic

A SCENOGRAPHY OF SÃO PAULO'S MUSICAL HISTORY WAS SET OUT TO DELIGHT VISITORS' SENSES OF SIGHT AND SOUND.

TRADE FAIR São Paulo's Anniversary Expo
WHERE São Paulo, Brazil
WHEN January 2012
DESIGNERS Estudio Guto Requena ✕ p.49
and Atelier Marko Brajovic ✕ p.489
STAND CONSTRUCTOR Fábrica de Milagr
CLIENT SESC/SP
MARKET SECTOR Decoration and
home equipment
TOTAL FLOOR AREA 300 m²
PHOTOGRAPHER Fran Parente

Roteiro Musical da Cidade de São Paulo ('musical tour of the city of São Paulo') introduced 100 years of history of Brazil's largest city from the point of view of music specially written for the municipality. Its scenography and art direction organised a multitude of documents, from audio files, rare records and LPs to musical scores, illustrations, photographs, news items, interviews, lyrics and songs. This collection is the result of 22 years of research into musical history by curators Assis Ângelo and Andrea Lago, and the design direction of the exhibition came about through a collaboration between the studios Estudio Guto Requena and Atelier Marko Brajovic. The design process contemplated the immersion and interaction of visitors by taking them on a musical ride through the history of one of the world's largest cities. The interior ambience suggested the allure of an old cabaret hall matched to contemporary aesthetics, decorated with lush carpeting, velour drapes and upholstered furniture in shades of rich red, burgundy and purple. After passing through a 17-m-long musical tunnel, with 2600 historic album covers creating a pixelated wrapping for all surfaces, visitors entered an area featuring 11 large, interactive lampshade-like domes overhead. Organised chronologically with historical content, each of the illuminated circular zones contained a musical summary of a specific decade. A typical 'boteco' (a popular bar in Brazil) was designed to house records and songs about the São Paulo football teams. Cabinets embedded in the walls housed part of the historic collection of objects, such as old radios and laser-cut rococo-style frames displaying photos and news items. The last space in the exhibition was hidden behind large theatrical curtains and featured a large interactive map on the floor. By walking on the different areas, visitors set off recordings of songs related to each neighbourhood, treating themselves to a unique soundtrack of the city.

✕ The bar area was decked out with the traditional São Paulo sidewalk mosaics, lights and poster-bombs.
✕ The circular installations were interactive, allowing visitors to appreciate the displayed set lists, texts and pictures.
✕ At the entrance, visitors were enticed into the musical passageway, which was dubbed the 'pixel-LP record explosion'.
✕ The decoration on all surfaces in the musical tunnel was meant to confound and confuse the senses of visitors.

ESTUDIO GUTO REQUENA AND
ATELIER MARKO BRAJOVIC

ROTEIRO MUSICAL DA CIDADE

SERVICES

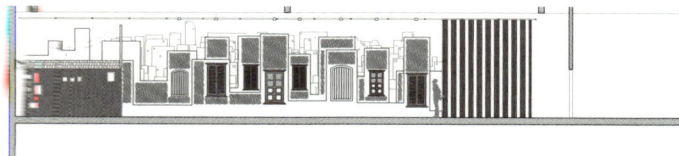

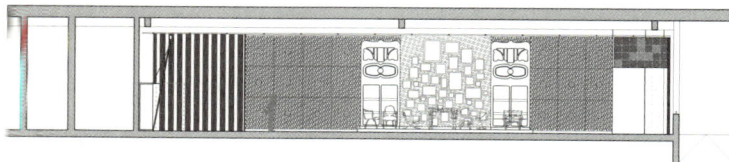

Section B

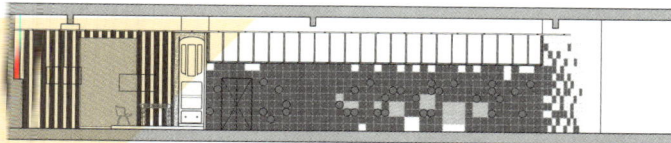

Section C

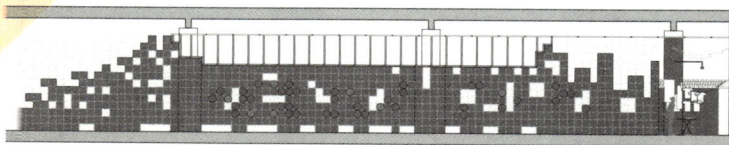

Section D

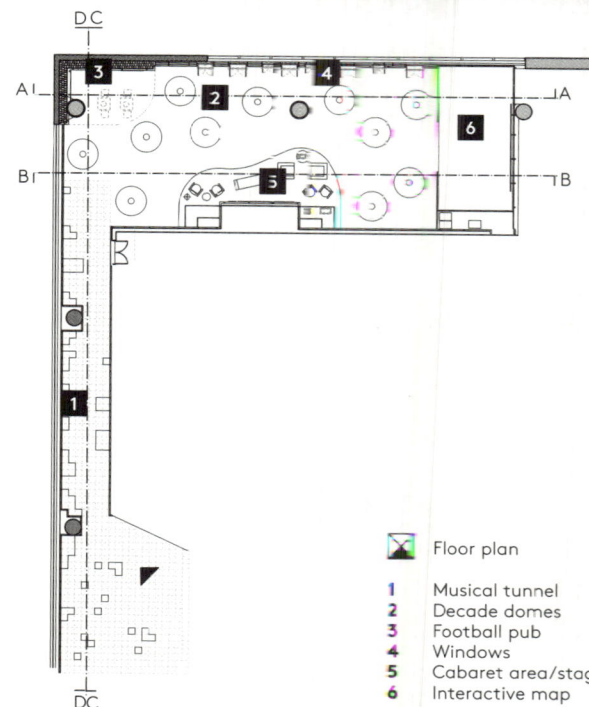

Floor plan

1 Musical tunnel
2 Decade domes
3 Football pub
4 Windows
5 Cabaret area/stage
6 Interactive map

Visitors were taken on a musical ride through the city

- The path through the collection was evocative of symbols of São Paulo; its skyline, sidewalks and street lamps.
- The colour palette of the exhibition was inspired by the installation *Desvio para o vermelho* (1967) by Brazilian conceptual artist Cildo Meirelles.
- The scenography took into consideration the concepts of universal design evoking of the Belle Époque era.

Sberbank by 4vida

A MULTIFACETED CRYSTALLINE FORM INSPIRED THE SCALE OF THE STAND AND WAS A METAPHOR FOR THE CLIENT'S CAPABILITIES.

Sberbank is one of the major financial institutions in Russia. In 2011, during the celebration of its 170th anniversary, the bank wished to communicate its vast heritage as well as its future vision at the International Economic Forum in St Petersburg. In charge of the bank's stand design for the fair was Moscow-based studio 4vida. 'Leadership reflected in the edges of history' was the main slogan for the stand, whose central symbol was a crystal. Elaborating the concept of a crystal that can be shaped, sharpened and transformed into a polished, gleaming gem, the design team found inspiration in the crystal's multifaceted nature that metaphorically represented the various activities of the client. The exterior architecture of the booth was angled and oblique, with the stand taking on a crystalline structure thanks to its metal framework. The aluminium skeleton was connected by various material finishes: composite panels, plastic, fabric and glass. Dynamic illumination turned the construction into an iridescent, pulsating object thanks to 300 LED screens that covered the facade. The stand was divided into distinct zones according to function, all the while engaging visitors in an all-round interactive experience. From the information and meeting areas to the hospitality and entertainment zones, an application of colourful lighting sequences gave the interior a contemporary air. At the heart of the stand was a multi-screen cubic space – a 3D cinema environment created by an assembly of 100 plasma display panels – that took forum members on a fascinating journey through the client's history. All the elements, including furniture, light fittings and demonstration equipment, were made exclusively for the stand to mirror the overall design concept, conveying a coherent and crystal-clear message.

TRADE FAIR **International Economic Forum**
WHERE **St Petersburg, Russia**
WHEN **June 2011**
DESIGNER **4vida** ☒ **p.488**
STAND CONSTRUCTOR **4vida**
CLIENT **Sberbank of Russia**
MARKET SECTOR **Banking and financial services**
TOTAL FLOOR AREA **350 m²**
PHOTOGRAPHER **Victor Zarudny**

Conveying a coherent and crystal-clear message

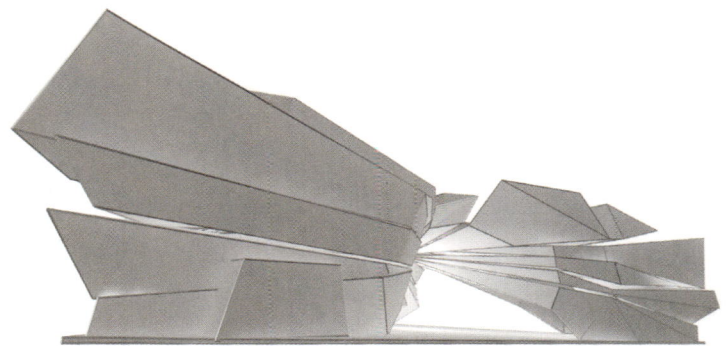

Colourful sketches depicted the vibrant hues used across the stand in the form of dynamic illumination.

Renderings showing the stand when viewed from different angles.

The shape of the stand combined numerous edges, representing the client's varied range of services.

The stand's cinema visually-related to fair goers the Sberbank universe.

Sikorsky by McMillan Group

ABSTRACT FORMS OF AIRCRAFT FUSELAGE COMMUNICATED AVIATION MESSAGES.

TRADE FAIR **Heli-Expo**
WHERE **Orlando, United States**
WHEN **March 2011**
DESIGNER **McMillan Group** ◣ p.495
STAND CONSTRUCTOR **The Taylor Group**
CLIENT **Sikorsky Aerospace Services**
MARKET SECTOR **Logistics and transportation**
TOTAL FLOOR AREA **390 m²**
PHOTOGRAPHER **Line 8 Photography**

Sikorsky Aerospace Services (SAS) is an aviation service company. At the Heli-Expo trade show in 2011, SAS needed to communicate its unique range of capabilities and expertise in aerospace engineering, from material support and integrated logistics to maintenance and overhaul. McMillan Group was the design team brought on board for this task. The client felt that previous booth designs had lacked a contemporary edge, even though seeing real helicopters at close range always impresses. The challenge was to make all areas of SAS of equal importance by unifying the multiple divisions with new acquisitions into one clear presentation. At the heart of the creative component lay a concept that evoked connotations of aviation. The team designed an abstract version of an aircraft fuselage, positioning different sections of it around one portion of the stand. Constructed from custom-fabricated aluminium, the interior of these hulls acted as presentation vestibules, enticing visitors to enter and discover detailed information about the client's services. This feature provided a visual statement just as powerful as the aircraft on display, particularly thanks to the dynamic illumination directed from overhead – in the shape of rotating helicopter blades – and in the interior in the form of changing digital imagery projected onto the walls. The look and feel of this new addition to the Sikorsky story complemented the existing brand image, both in technical aptitude and corporate identity, with a consistency in the materials and graphic treatment. For this SAS exhibition, the design team succeeded in creating a new brand icon that delivered a dramatic presentation as well as an exciting 3D mode of communication for a broad range of aviation services.

◪ Visitors walked along the 'runway' to discover the client's capability categories through dynamic projected images and product displays
◪ Shadows of the animated blades were seen on the sides of the 'hulls', which were also textured with corporate messages.
◪ The space had displays mounted in the context of an aircraft interior.

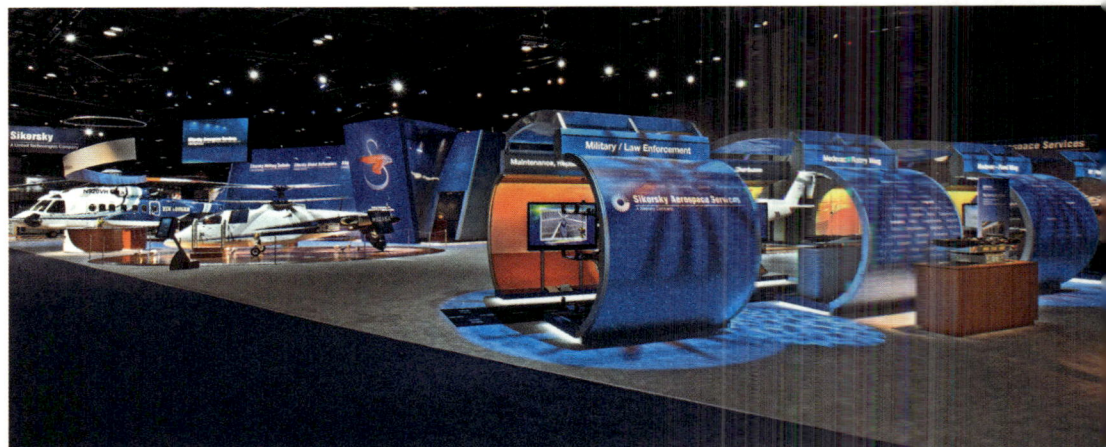

Software by Schmidhuber

AN OPTIMISTIC AIR OF CONNECTIVITY WAS WIRED INTO THE CIRCUITRY OF THIS BOOTH WITH COLOURFUL AND STREAMLINED GRAPHICS.

TRADE FAIR **CeBIT**
WHERE **Hannover, Germany**
WHEN **March 2012**
DESIGNER **Schmidhuber** ◪ **p. 97**
STAND CONSTRUCTOR **Walbert Schmitz**
CLIENT **Software**
MARKET SECTOR **Media and telecommunications**
TOTAL FLOOR AREA **1040 m²**
PHOTOGRAPHER **Joerg Hempel**

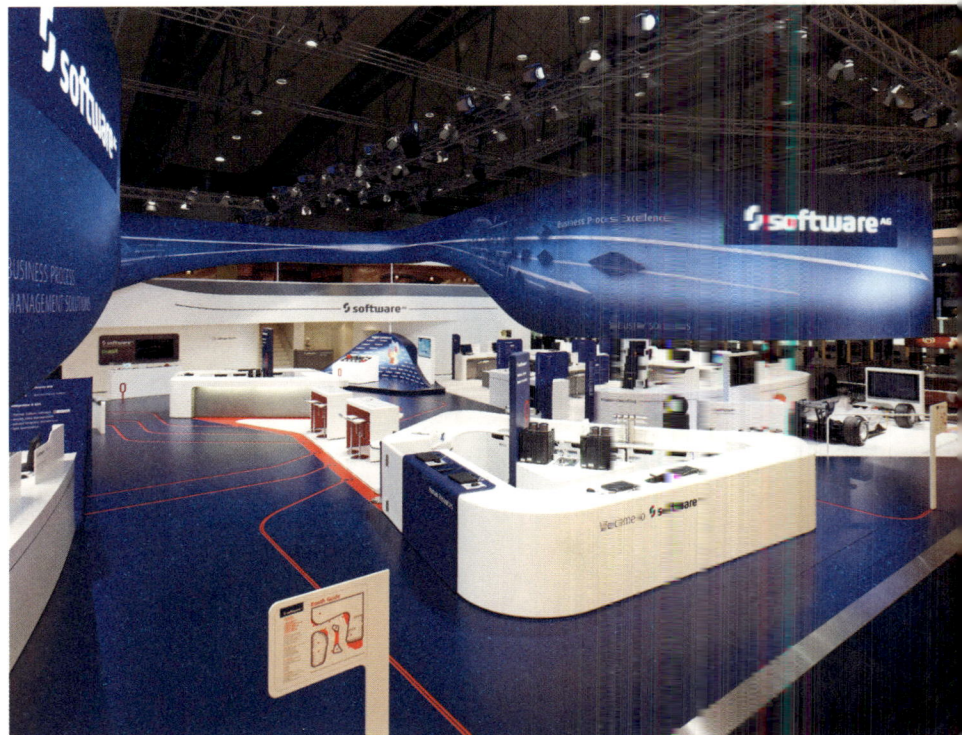

Software brought Schmidhuber on board to ensure its presence was felt at the CeBIT 2012 trade fair in Hannover dedicated to the digital world. The Munich-based design firm opted for a concept based on the technical specifications of a racing car circuit, replete with chequered flags and a real racing car. The bright, bold and blue booth also had another circuit engrained into the design, that of a printed circuit board. Used as a graphic element across the booth and stand fittings, this substrate for electronic components assumed a symbolic character: it connected countless interactive exhibits, showcases and customer testimonials to the information area within the central zone of the stand. Visitors entered the space through two channels demarcated with flag-like 'booth guides' that represented the layout of the stand visually. A thin red line on the floor then directed the route to the central information hub and, from there, on towards various 'experience spots'. These were specific showcases of the client's areas of expertise, IT solutions and optimised processes. The booth architecture created a prominent feature on the landscape of the exhibition hall, thanks to its blue canopy that wrapped around the space, including the curved two-storey rear enclosure and the adjoining product island. Within the stand, this overhead swathe of fabric that encircled the booth provided surfaces where brand messages could be presented. The bright blue graphics over a silhouetted city skyline created a fresh and optimistic air, communicating to fair goers the global nature of the client's business. Together with the printed floor graphics that doubled as a map to aid orientation and for selecting areas of interest, the topics of networking and connectivity were successfully visualised in an entertaining way.

◪ Long-distance impact was supplied by the undulating branded banner that wrapped the top of the stand.
◪ Colourful 'booth guides' and floor graphics ensured visitors were fully informed.

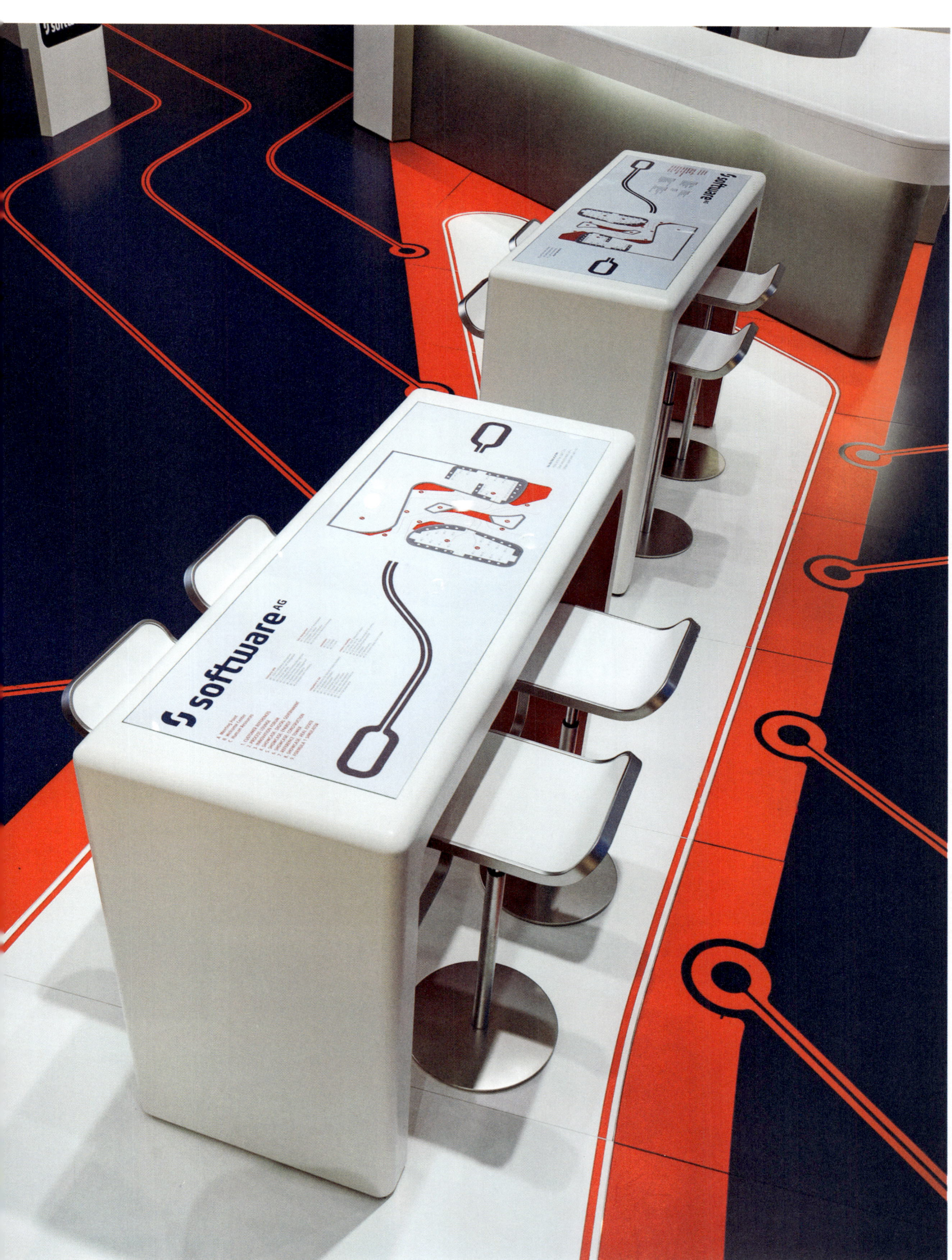

The central design element was the 'brand stream', with rectangles and rhombuses positioned as process symbols, taken directly from the language of IT.
The constant stream of visitors witnessed a fluent architectural design language, as well as displays depicting digital information flow.

Substrate for electronic components assumed a symbolic character

Spacedealer by Delafair

A NEST REPRESENTED A NETWORK OF COMMUNICATION CHANNELS AT THIS DIGITAL INDUSTRY FAIR.

Spacedealer is a rapidly growing, interactive marketing agency from Berlin. At the international trade fair for the digital industry – dmexco 2011 in Cologne – the company wanted to present itself as a reliable, sustainable and inspiring partner. Delafair was charged with realising the trade fair stand for the firm according to this brief. In response, the design team developed an eye-catching exhibition concept that linked the values of sustainability, growth, competence and peacefulness with the technical, creative, fast-paced and avant-garde advertising and media industry. The idea was to create a natural and atmospheric retreat, akin to a cosy nest in a forest, to establish an emotional relationship between the client and its visitors. Untreated wood was chosen as the primary construction material for the booth in combination with visual imagery that conjured up an oasis. A mural of a distorted birch forest ran along the length of the booth on the back wall. The square grid positioned over the image served as a link between nature and technology. The grid-like pattern recurred in the towering, curved side wall of the stand. This three-dimensional network of wooden beams – the nest – rose up as a symbol of well-being, housing and protection. Inside, an area of seclusion provided space for the client and its visitors to convene. The green landscape continued on the exterior of the branded facade, with a park bench positioned on a patch of grass. Taking a seat in front of a monitor nestled into the wall, visitors could take a break from the fair and watch a film showing a bird's eye view of Berlin. In all aspects the space was a symbol of naturalness that contrasted with the digital world.

TRADE FAIR dmexco
WHERE Cologne, Germany
WHEN September 2011
DESIGNER Delafair ➤ p.490
STAND CONSTRUCTOR Delafair
CLIENT Spacedealer
MARKET SECTOR Digital communications
TOTAL FLOOR AREA 45 m²
PHOTOGRAPHER Lorenz Kienzle

☒ In a well created of tension wood, positioned branded water bottles which visitors could take away.

☒ The stand had a mix of high-quality furniture and basic elements made of wood or leather to create a natural feel.

☒ The design of the booth echoed the client's green credentials.

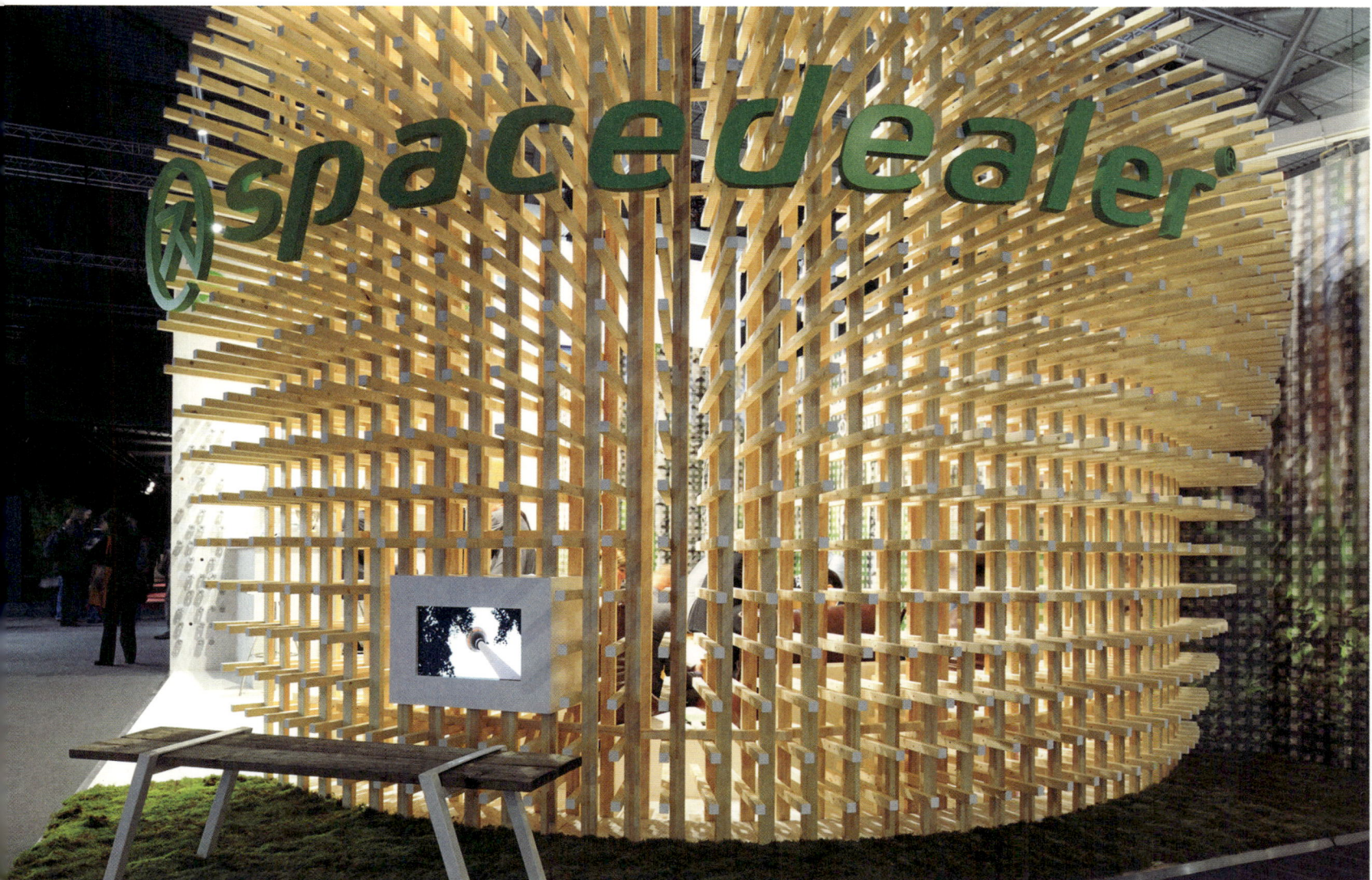

Floor plan

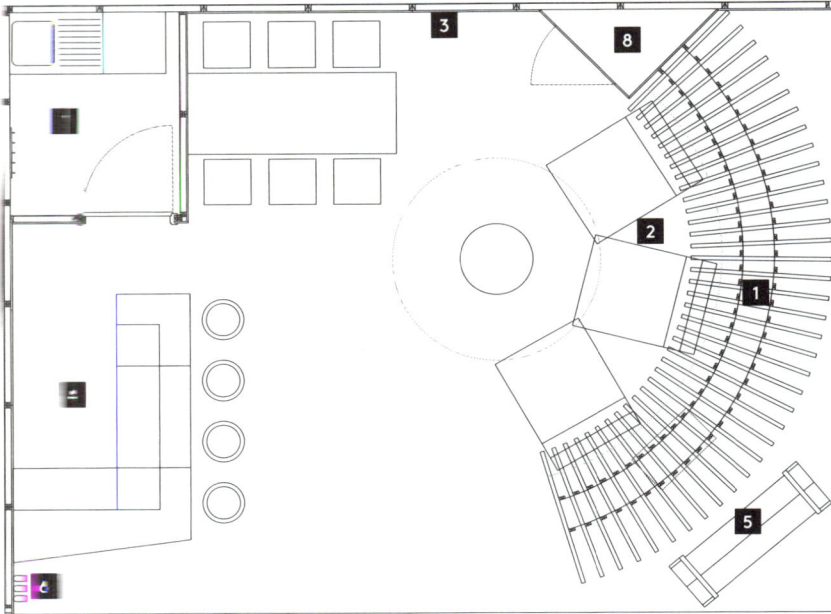

1. Curved 'nest' wall
2. Meeting area
3. Forest wall
4. Bar
5. Park bench
6. Water bottle feature
7. Kitchen
8. Storage

The feature 'nest' wall was a symbol for well-being, housing and protection.

Renderings depicting how the design provides a protective shell for quiet conversations within the booth.

The bespoke birch forest mural on the stand's back wall was overlaid with a grid of squares to instil a technical aspect.

Visual imagery that conjured up an oasis

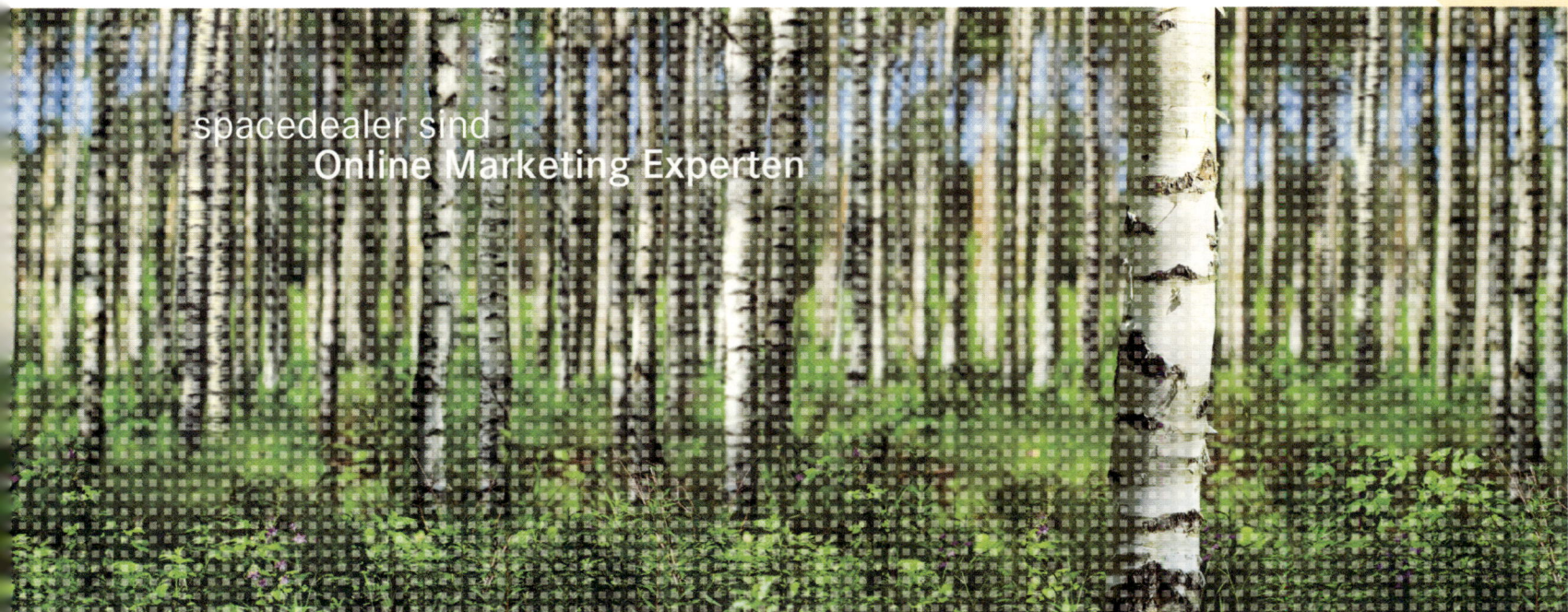

spacedealer sind
Online Marketing Experten

Superfarm by Hafsteinn Juliusson, Joana Pais and Rui Pereira

QUESTIONING THE FUTURE OF FOOD, THESE DESIGNERS PLACED A FARM IN AN URBAN SETTING.

TRADE FAIR **Salone Internazionale del Mobile**
WHERE **Milan, Italy**
WHEN **April 2011**
DESIGNERS **Hafsteinn Juliusson, Joana Pais and Rui Pereira** ⊠ p. 492
STAND CONSTRUCTOR **Cosmit**
CLIENT **Scuola Politecnica di Design**
MARKET SECTOR **Information and education**
TOTAL FLOOR AREA **60 m²**
PHOTOGRAPHER **Sabine Schweigert**

Scuola Politecnica di Design (SPD) was invited to take part in the '50 + 50' exhibition in Milan in 2011, celebrating the 50th anniversary of the Salone furniture fair. Provoked by the question, 'What will be the role and meaning of design in 50 years?', the school asked three of its master's degree students to create an exhibition stand in response. Hafsteinn Juliusson, Joana Pais and Rui Pereira came up with the idea of a Superfarm, betting on the power of design to change behaviour and lifestyle rather than to produce new objects. The designers were inspired by a quote from the movie The Social Network: 'First man lived on farms, then he lived in cities, now he lives online. What's next?' Re-imagining both farm and supermarket in ways that could potentially transform neighbourhoods, public health and humanity's connection to food, the Superfarm project predicts that farming in the city will play an increasingly active role in future food production. The collateral effect is the creation of a new urban ecosphere, an extensive green network developing throughout the city. This was all communicated in Milan at the fair's very own farm, which consisted of a greenhouse, courtyard and supermarket, all surrounded by a white picket fence. The grass-clad courtyard – with its life-size cut-outs of farmyard animals, authentic hay bales and flour mill –

elicited lots of interaction from visitors, always with the air of championing a revolutionary green mind shift. Offering products and information promoting a healthy lifestyle, this low-tech presentation contained a high added-value message. The booth's joyful colours inspired a convivial atmosphere, similar to that of a traditional farmer's market. With its red and white awning and the matching sails on the towering windmill, the booth caught the eyes of visitors far across the fair.

⊠ The supermarket area had a simple w podium in the centre displaying 'Wheel of nutrition' plate.
⊠ The playful depiction of a farm of future was communicating a m serious, underlying message.

Life-size cut-outs of farmyard animals in the grass-clad courtyard

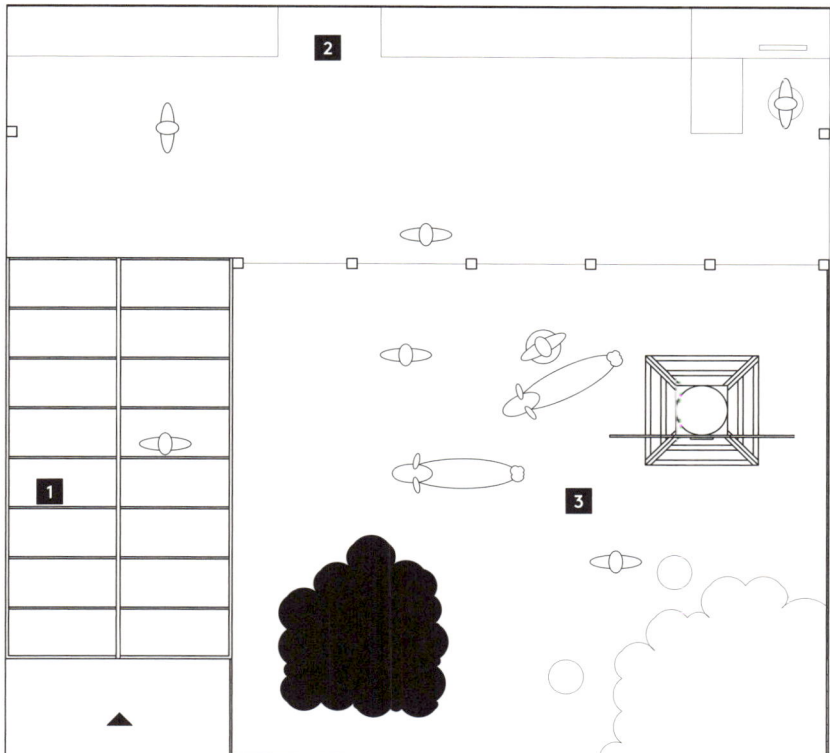

The 'farm field', with its happy animals, olive tree and mill, was designed so that visitors could interact with the displays.
The 2D animals that popped-up on the farm included a cow, chickens, sheep and pigs.
Sketches showing the studies for the outdoor and indoor scenarios.

Floor plan
1 Greenhouse
2 Supermarket
3 Courtyard

HAFSTEINN JULIUSSON,
JOANA PAIS AND RUI PEREIRA

SUPERFARM

Sustainable Vorarlberg by Kaleido and Tortenwerkstatt

A VILLAGE FORMED THE SETTING FOR THINKING ABOUT FUTURE PLANS FOR A FORWARD THINKING AUSTRIAN PROVINCE.

TRADE FAIR **Frühjahrsmesse**
WHERE **Dornbirn, Austria**
WHEN **March 2012**
DESIGNERS **Kaleido** ☒ p.495 and
Tortenwerkstatt ☒ p.498
STAND CONSTRUCTORS **Tortenwerkstatt, Tischlerei Ammann**
CLIENT **Land Vorarlberg**
MARKET SECTOR **Information and education**
TOTAL FLOOR AREA **280 m²**
PHOTOGRAPHER **Hanno Mackowitz**

Vorarlberg, the most westerly province of Austria, has always been a region with up-to-date attitudes about forward-thinking energy policy. In 2012, the state parliament took a political step towards establishing an autonomous future in energy consumption in the area, and presented this message at the Frühjahrsmesse 2012, a spring fair in Dornbirn. The design agency Kaleido and architecture studio Tortenwerkstatt took responsibility for creating the stand in the 'Building & Energy' zone, one of the main topics covered at the fair. In its 'Building Future' presentation, the design team wanted to communicate abstract energy concepts using the metaphor of 'togetherness' in a rural community and conveying the sense of cosiness within a small village. The whole stand was made of recyclable material, with the walls of the houses constructed from cardboard with a honeycomb filling. The building method, structures and layout of the space were simple and featured basic materials such as wood and cardboard to create new connections and contexts. The opened-ended houses were designed as display spaces to give shelter to the various partners in Voralberg who are working on autonomous projects in their own specific fields. Visitors to the fair became part of the village concept, as they walked over the zebra crossing or along the streets, past the trees and lamp posts, also shaped from cardboard. Open spaces offered plenty of opportunities for them to slip into conversations with the experts who were on hand. The concept combined modes of communication that unified thoughts about tomorrow in a familiar setting.

☒ An overall white colour palette was interrupted with splashes of red.
☒ The village square, equipped replete with trees and zebra crossing.
☒ The furnishings were made from same cardboard materials as the house.

KALEIDO AND TORTENWERKSTATT   SUSTAINABLE VORARLBERG

Water Cathedral by Gun Architects

A POINTEDLY GEOMETRIC INSTALLATION COOLED THE CROWDS UNDER CHILE'S HOT SUMMER SUN.

At the end of 2011, a cultural event in central Santiago saw the presentation of Gun Architect's Water Cathedral, the winning design proposal from the MoMA young architects programme. The studio conceived of the project as an outdoor installation built for public use during the Chilean summer. Laid out as a vast nave of 700 m², the presentation consisted of a field of fabric prisms suspended from steel frames with triangulated sections. The suspended structures resembled stalactites in a cave. The numerous components were arranged in clusters of variable densities and heights, some made of white fabric and others of clear plastic. A hydraulic network discreetly positioned above this system fed a water supply to the canopy and distributed it to each of the textile units in the overhead canopy. The water trickled down through the prismatic stalactites, slowly saturating the volume of little stones contained within them and seeping through the fabric seams. Through these tapering structures, water dripped gently at various pulses and speeds, adding sensory delights to this mysterious and playful space. The refreshing and shaded atmosphere was enhanced by the sound of droplets falling in different intensities. Concrete truncated prisms akin to stalagmites on the ground functioned as seating and water-storing elements. The dynamic process ensured precisely measured doses that optimised water consumption across the space, with amounts equivalent to the average daily use of a few families. Hundreds of visitors made the most of the cool climate in the hot afternoon sun whilst spending time in the space.

TRADE FAIR **Matucana 100**
WHERE **Santiago, Chile**
WHEN **December 2011**
DESIGNER **Gun Architects** ☒ **p.492**
STAND CONSTRUCTOR **Gun Architects**
CLIENT **Yap_Constructo**
MARKET SECTOR **Architectural services**
TOTAL FLOOR AREA **700 m²**
PHOTOGRAPHER **Guy Wenborne**

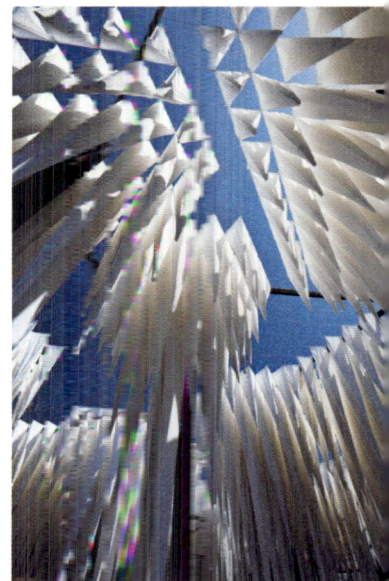

☒ The geometric shapes created a play of shadows that cooled in the Chilean sun.
☒ The stand was made from a structural steel frame, a network of metal grids and hanging fabric prisms.
☒ Water dripped through the prisms onto the concrete 'stalagmites' positioned around the edge of the booth.

Welltec by Arting

SPHERICAL MOTIFS CREATED A COSY ENCLAVE IN WHICH TO DISCUSS SOLUTIONS FOR THE OIL AND GAS INDUSTRY.

To stand out among 1400 companies at the semi-annual Offshore Europe conference and exhibition, held in 2011 in Aberdeen, United Kingdom, Welltec wanted a branded presence that would differentiate it from the crowd. Design studio Arting was commissioned to undertake the project, with a brief that called for a stand in which the client's service solutions for the oil and gas industry could be communicated in a memorable manner to a global audience of engineers and technical specialists. Furthermore, three functional spaces were required within the boundaries of the relatively small stand. Arting decided to create a strongly sculptural solution to reflect the precision engineering that embodies Welltec's devices. The design team found inspiration for the concept within the client's established graphic identity programme, which features three concentric circles in a corporate colour palette of lime green and crisp white. The transformation included removing these circles from their normal 2D context and reapplying them as 3D spherical openings within the framework of the stand: a footprint of 7.5 x 6 m, with a maximum height of 4 m. By playing with how the three spheres could be juggled within the stand's rectangular dimensions, the designers came up with a solution that was reminiscent of a church roof with criss-crossing trusses forming archways. The resulting interior was modest with a cosy atmosphere, yet it had rather a grand feel. The circular motif continued throughout the design, from the window shapes to the branding graphics on the walls. By cutting the first sphere through two of the freestanding walls, the designers created a welcoming entrance that led into the open interior, with walkways connecting to the different areas where visitors could sit and watch video presentations in the lounge area, or mingle, discuss and be enlightened within the information zone.

TRADE FAIR Offshore Europe
WHERE Aberdeen, United Kingdom
WHEN September 2011
DESIGNER Arting ⊠ p.488
STAND CONSTRUCTOR Arting
CLIENT Welltec
MARKET SECTOR Energy supplier
TOTAL FLOOR AREA 45 m²
PHOTOGRAPHER Simon Price

⊠ The circular cut-outs added a grand feeling despite the stand's small size.
⊠ The randomised joints of the archway made for dynamic detailing.
⊠ The circular shapes underlined the graphic identity of the client.

SHOE
ACCES

AND
ORIES

APM by Arquitect Studio

JEWELLERY DISPLAYED IN A LIGHT LOFT-STYLE SPACE STRONGLY CHARACTERISED BY THE USE OF TECHNOLOGY, ALL HIDDEN AWAY.

French jewellery design group and manufacturer APM commissioned Arquitect Studio to design its stand for the jewellery trade fair VicenzaOro in 2012. The design team took advantage of the favourable position of the booth by proposing a completely open design, with the basic idea to create a loft-style space. On the ground floor visitors were free to access the space from two sides, with the presentation visible from all angles of the exhibit on hol thanks to a white branded band that wrapped around the top of the stand. The jewellery showcased on the stand's lower level featured table displays that contained four windows, each set inside their tops. LED lighting was integrated into the windows themselves, while speakers and perfume diffusers were hidden within the structure of the tables. Glass showcases at the corners of the booth functioned as shop windows. The space had a sense of lightness thanks to the transparency of the design, the open entrances, the glass panels along the perimeter, and the all-white colour palette with lacquered walls and floor tiles. Along the back wall, two large video screens transmitted images of the client's advertising campaign, with other surfaces coated in resin to achieve a rustic brick effect and painted white to give the ambient atmosphere of a true loft. A staircase that had the same brick treatment on the walls led up a narrow passage to the first floor. Here, visitors entered a bar area, beyond which was an automatic sliding glass door. Secluded workstations with semicircular tables and recessed monitors provided APM employees and customers with space for meetings. At the very end of the top floor, another sliding door concealed a VIP room built for private meetings with the most important clients.

White lacquered surfaces adorned the interior and exterior of the booth.
The loft-style space on the lower level had five display tables and two video walls.
The stairwell was completely covered by the white brick-wall leitmotif.
The upstairs meeting spaces also had an elegant white finish.

TRADE FAIR **VicenzaOro**
WHERE **Vicenza, Italy**
WHEN **January 2012**
DESIGNER **Arquitect Studio** p.488
STAND CONSTRUCTOR **Arquitect Studio**
CLIENT **APM**
MARKET SECTOR **Jewellery**
TOTAL FLOOR AREA **120 m²**
PHOTOGRAPHER **APM**

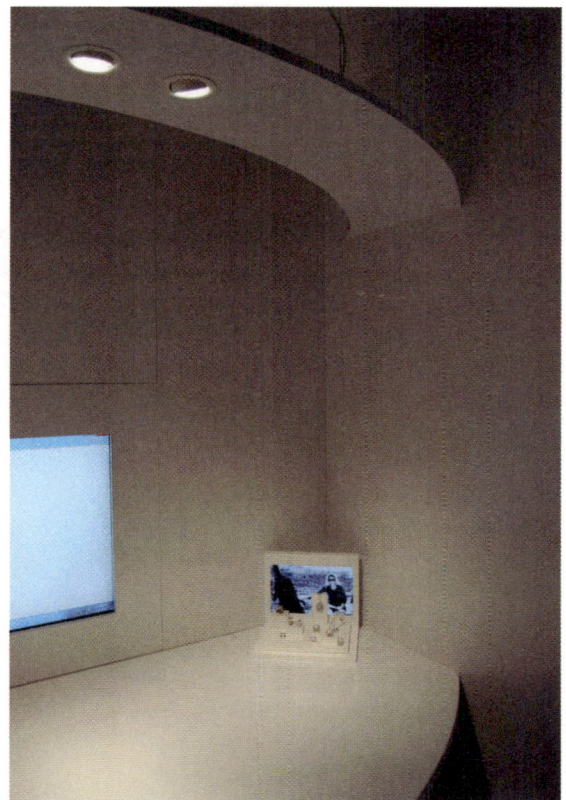

Atomic by atelier 522

A WINTER WONDERLAND FOR A TRADITIONAL BRAND IN SPORTS EQUIPMENT.

TRADE FAIR **ISPO**
WHERE **Munich, Germany**
WHEN **February 2011**
DESIGNER **atelier 522** ⊠ **p.489**
STAND CONSTRUCTOR **Stagegroup**
CLIENT **Atomic**
MARKET SECTOR **Sports equipment**
TOTAL FLOOR AREA **420 m²**
PHOTOGRAPHER **atelier 522**

At the ISPO 2011 trade fair, Atomic presented its product innovations for the upcoming season in a winter scenography made of architecturally unique ice cubes. Across the 420-m² space, the designers of atelier 522 created an individual stand based on a winter wonderland set against snow-covered mountainous terrain. The collections of Atomic were presented in customised 'ice cubes', each having a unique, angled shape that brought to mind a steep mountain landscape. The display vestibules were tailored to the interests of each target group with attention to detail. In the Freeski cube, concrete walls, raw lattice boxes, wooden stools as product displays and an old workbench transported visitors emotionally to an authentic room for waxing skis. The interior of the All Mountain cube was decorated with felt, which created a warm and cosy atmosphere. Visual imagery of skiers on high mountain peaks featured on both the back wall and a panel positioned prominently at the front of the stand behind the information desk. In a simple but stylish design, the newest products for the racer were presented on a concrete wall in one of the other cubes. And the new collection for the youngest ski fans enjoyed pride of place on a bed of colourful bubble shapes. The testing area, where the customers were able to try on the latest ski boots, was located in the centre of the Atomic-Ice-Cube-World surrounded by the display areas. For customer pitches, the designers created a conference area that was separated slightly from the main crowd. This area, with its traditional mountain touch, radiated the charm of a modern alpine chalet and harmonised perfectly with the whole stand.

The angled vestibule rose high above fair goers in the lounge, mimicking an overhanging cliff on a mountain top.

Each 'ice cube' was fitted with striking pendant lampshades.

The large-scale graphics enhanced the wintery atmosphere of the stand.

Botas 66 by A1 architects

A COLOURFUL AND PLAYFUL EXHIBITION SPACE FOR THE BOTAS 66 SNEAKER BRAND, ALL FOR A LIMITED BUDGET.

TRADE FAIR **Designblok**
WHERE **Prague, Czech Republic**
WHEN **October 2010**
DESIGNER **A1 architects** ✉ p.486
STAND CONSTRUCTOR **Entander**
CLIENT **Botas 66**
MARKET SECTOR **Shoes**
TOTAL FLOOR AREA **25 m²**
PHOTOGRAPHER **David Maštálka**

A1 architects had previously designed a well-received Botas 66 concept store in Prague. So it was no surprise when the team was asked to create a stand for the sneaker brand at Designblok10, Prague's design week. The project needed to present Botas 66 sneakers in a contemporary manner on a very limited budget. A1 architects responded with a simple concept based on a colourful soffit, with an eye-catching overhead feature made out of Botas 66 shoelaces. The vibrant array of laces that dangled above the heads of visitors went back into the production process after the exhibition, thus keeping the cost of the project low. The team encountered some limitations and challenges while designing the space. Doors and niches in three walls meant that just one wall was available for displaying sneakers. The raw, white decor that filled the rest of the room allowed visitors to move easily and fully appreciate the simple yet striking display. A bespoke Botas 66 wallpaper – a creation of graphic designers Jan Kloss and Jakub Korouš – lined the sneaker wall. The wallpaper graphics formed the starting point for the redesign of the 66 collection and structured a 'colour questionnaire'. Visitors were invited to draw on the black-and-white sneaker illustrations on the wall with the colours they would like to see in the future. The organic shape of the ceiling structure featured 1800 coloured shoelaces, arranged at different heights within a grid of 10 x 10 cm. This playful structure and the sneakers on show ensured that visitors entered a welcoming space at the Botas 66 booth.

✉ The 'shoelace cloud' was created by affixing the laces to a textile net normally used for a football goal.

✉ Visitors were invited to colour-in the wallpaper to create their vision for new Botas sneakers.

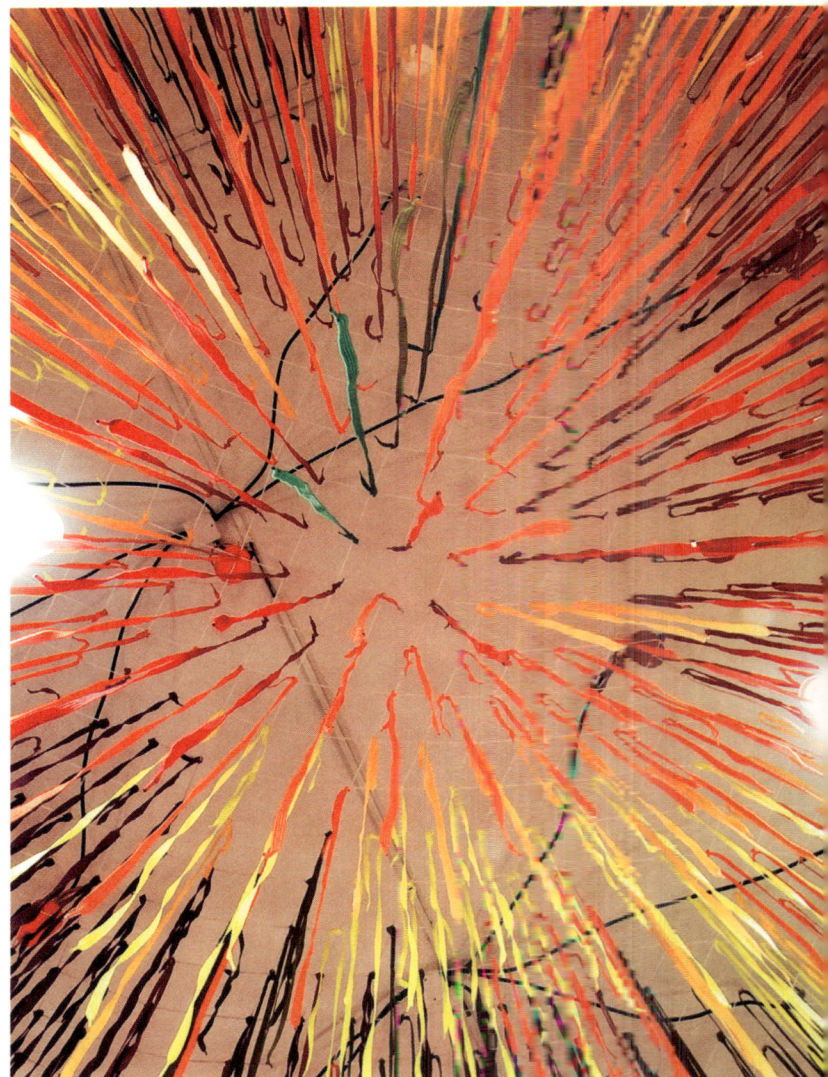

Hlasujte pro model, který se vám
nejvíc líbí, a navrhněte svůj vlastní
design botasek.

Bulgari by atelier oï

MIXING NATURAL PHENOMENA WITH
THE PRECISION OF WATCH-MAKING
PRODUCED A LIVING AND BREATHING
INSTALLATION WITH A MYSTERIOUS AIR.

The Italian fine jeweller and watchmaker Bulgari launched two new products specially for the jubilee of Baselworld, the international watch and jewellery trade fair, which celebrated its 40th anniversary in Basel in March 2012. When atelier oï was commissioned by the luxury brand to create a scenography for one of the new models presented in the Bulgari booth, the brief called for an open space that would attract visitors with a mysterious and memorable atmosphere. The approach that the atelier oï team took was based on Bulgari's new travel watch Bulgari Papillon Voyageur, which includes a second time zone. Taking inspiration from this feature, in which the alternate time is indicated by a central, teardrop-shaped blue hand that evokes the movement of a butterfly, atelier oï based the scenography on this element. The resulting booth was dominated by a vibrant, shimmering blue bespoke light sculpture that reminded fair goers of butterflies fluttering in the air. Dynamic light projections turned the initial impression of a static totem into what looked like a living and breathing object. A total of 16 elegant, elongated sculptures hanging from the ceiling were arranged in a circular formation around the main attraction. Two showcases in the middle of the installation displayed the Bulgari watches, making them the centrepieces of the booth. A solitary video screen positioned behind the display cases beamed images of incandescent butterfly wings, which tied in with the concept.

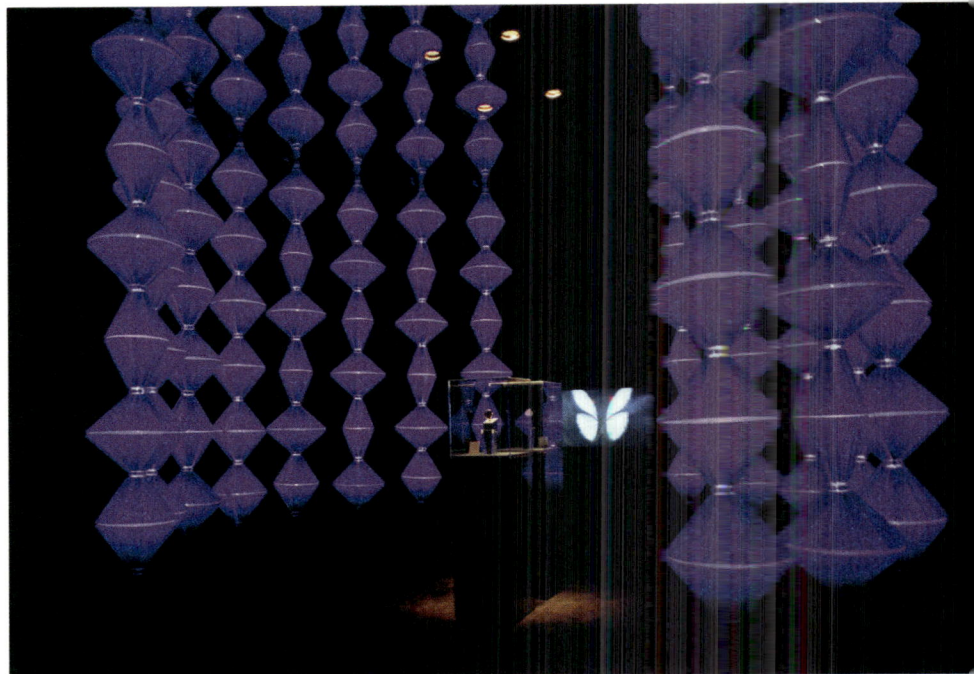

TRADE FAIR **Baselworld**
WHERE **Basel, Switzerland**
WHEN **March 2012**
DESIGNER **atelier oï** ☒ **p.489**
STAND CONSTRUCTOR **Expomobilia**
CLIENT **Bulgari**
MARKET SECTOR **Watches**
TOTAL FLOOR AREA **40 m²**
PHOTOGRAPHER **atelier oï**

☒ The circular set-up was created to showcase the Bulgari Papillon Voyageur.
☒ The illuminated blue hanging sculptures shimmered in the darkness, reminiscent of butterflies fluttering in the air.

Havaianas by Criacittá

A COLOURFUL, AUTUMNAL STAND FOR A FOOTWEAR BRAND ASSOCIATED WITH SUMMER.

TRADE FAIR **Bread & Butter**
WHERE **Berlin, Germany**
WHEN **January 2012**
DESIGNER **Criacittá** ☒ p.490
STAND CONSTRUCTOR **Double Europe**
CLIENT **Havaianas**
MARKET SECTOR **Shoes**
TOTAL FLOOR AREA **80 m²**
PHOTOGRAPHER **Álvaro Perez de Mocrid Carreras**

Havaianas is the master of creating a lust for life from colourful rubber. Naturally associated with summer, the footwear brand decided to celebrate autumn with a new collection of rain boots and asked Criacittá to design its booth for the trade fair in January 2012. Surprising the audience at Bread & Butter is always a challenge, given the number of brands and the multitude of stands and messages. In addition, the client wanted to link its new product, the rain boot, with its bestseller, the flip-flop, thus calling for a mixed concept that connected the fall/winter campaign with the spring/summer spirit of the brand. The design team drew inspiration from the client's motto: 'Even when it's cold or raining, if you wear Havaianas it's a warm summer'. Criacittá reinterpreted the footwear company's fall/winter campaign, imagining a 5-m-tall tree made of painted layers of plywood, with 800 flip-flops positioned as foliage alongside printed leaves. Besides the tree, visuals of huge, colourful rain boots made clear which product was the focus of the season. The design team imagined the stand as a park – replete with soccer field, playground, fountain and picnic area – with each zone corresponding to a specific product family. In the middle of the stand, a bright blue display table shaped like a huge puddle played host to the key product: the rain boot. Layered graphics created from Ultra Board, corrugated paper board with a printed front, decorated the stand together with real-life props such as street lamps and bicycles. A green band, representing the strap of a flip-flop, ran along the walls of the stand, connecting each product family. A real mixture of actual products and graphic elements gave the unexpected touch that the brand is known for.

☒ The colourful tree with its flip-flop foliage attracted visitors from across the exhibition hall.
☒ Aged and white-washed pine boards were used on all surfaces of the stand.

SHOES AND ACCESSORIES

TREE BOOTH

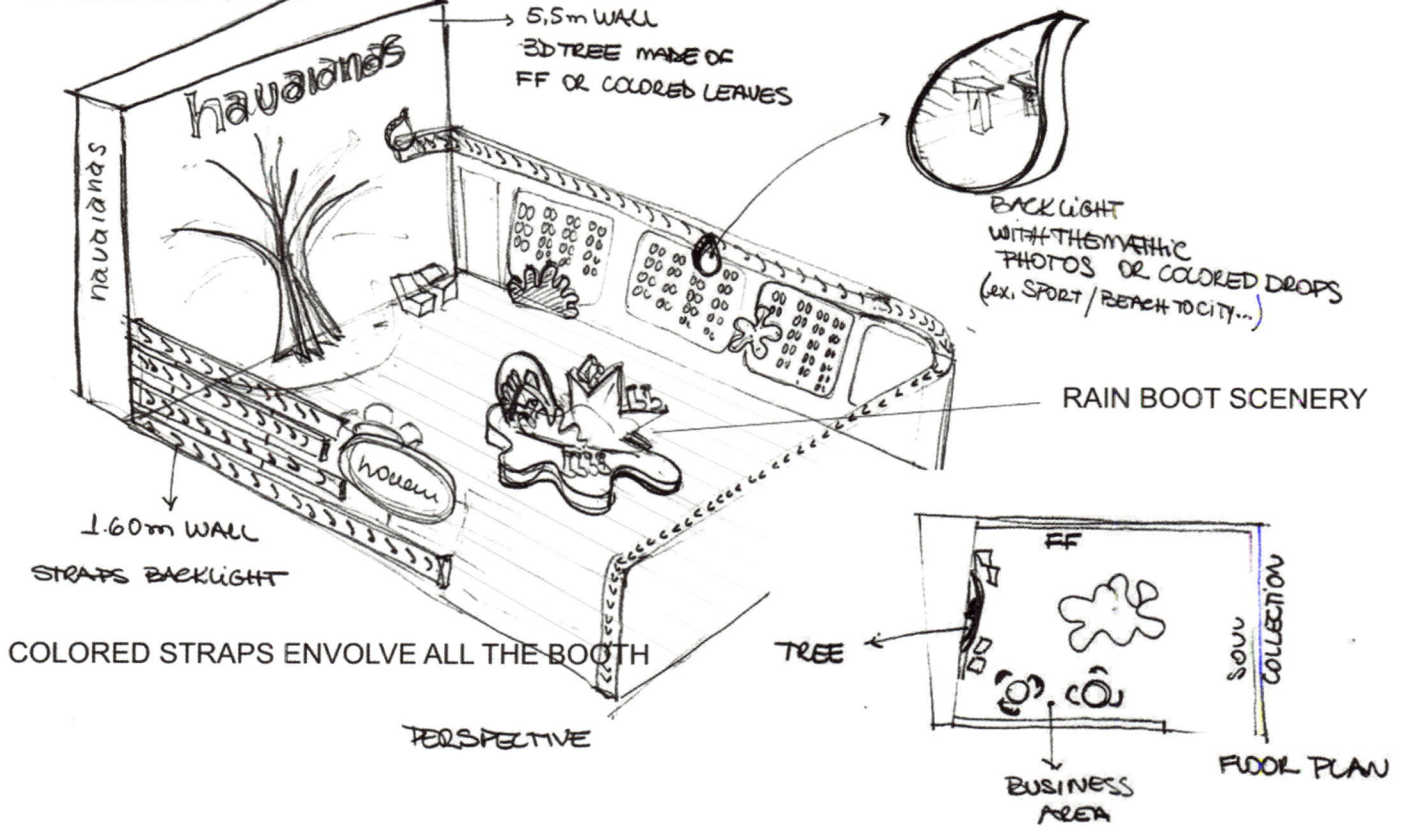

havaianas

navaianas

5,5 m WALL
3D TREE MADE OF
FF OR COLORED LEAVES

BACK LIGHT
WITH THEMATHIC
PHOTOS OR COLORED DROPS
(ex. SPORT / BEACH TO CITY...)

RAIN BOOT SCENERY

1.60 m WALL
STRAPS BACKLIGHT

COLORED STRAPS ENVOLVE ALL THE BOOTH

PERSPECTIVE

TREE

FF

SOUV
COLLECTION

BUSINESS
AREA

FLOOR PLAN

'Even when it's cold or raining, if you wear Havaianas it's always summer'

- ☒ Layered graphics were created from Ultra Board, a corrugated paper board with a printed front.
- ☒ The sketches outlined the design concept, with the tree forming the most impactful part of the design.
- ☒ From the early stages of the concept, the renderings encompassed the vibrant and playful lust for life of the client.

K2 Skis by mbco

A WEATHERED BARN, PACKED FULL WITH SKIING PARAPHERNALIA, VISUALISED '50 YEARS OF SERIOUS FUN'.

At ISPO 2012, there was a festive atmosphere at the presentation of K2 Skis. As the cult ski brand was celebrating its 50th anniversary, a special design was called for that incorporated the historical dimension. Inspired by the very first K2 Skis advertisement from 1962 'Chew K2', the design team from mbco created a concept that aimed to bring the ad's imagery of a farmhouse barn to life in the trade fair hall. The idea was to create a humorous design, interpreting the advertisement's original style whilst incorporating a contemporary edge. The stand needed to fulfil multiple functions, ensuring visitors were fully entertained and providing relevant product information. Artificially aged and weathered wooden planks were used to reconstruct a 3D version of the barn as the basis of the presentation. The booth was divided into two areas: an interior product display zone, and a separate outside area that featured an imitation water tower, flagpole and fenced courtyard. The long-range reach across the exhibition hall came from its double height presentation. A printed graphic wrapped around the top of the barn roof to create a mountain panorama that could be seen from all sides of the stand. An additional request in the client brief was to integrate the brand's newest product – one of the most durable and responsive pairs of skis on snow – as well as a real life BMW vehicle, with an ultimate image of sportiness. This latter point was realised with a four-wheel drive literally bursting through the wall of the building, framed by cracked fragments of wooden boards. Other eye-catching features, fun aspects and humorous accessories dotted around the stand ensured visitors could get up close to all the key products within a visually creative presentation.

TRADE FAIR ISPO
WHERE Munich, Germany
WHEN January 2012
DESIGNER mbco ☒ p.495
STAND CONSTRUCTOR mbco
CLIENT K2 Skis
MARKET SECTOR Sports equipment
TOTAL FLOOR AREA 400 m²
PHOTOGRAPHER Peter Schaffrath

☒ A 1960s-style farmhouse barn created the framework for the booth.
☒ The car appeared to have broken out of the barn at top speed.
☒ A visual fusion of product, brand and decorative accessories delighted visitors.

Construction details

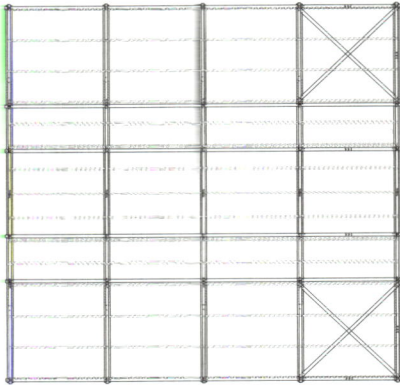

Barn outline

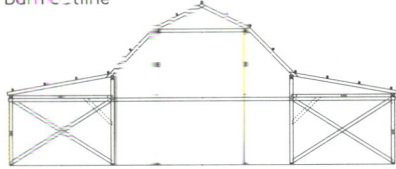

Front elevation

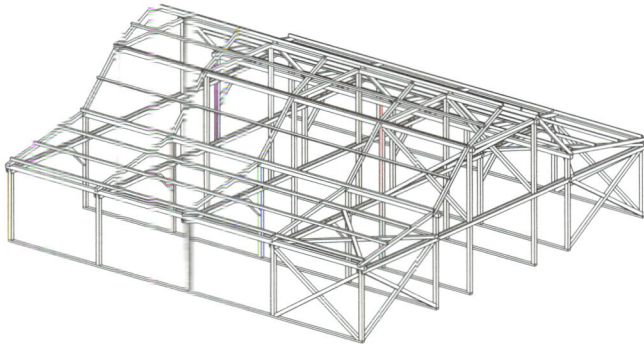

Barn framework

The renderings gave an all-round impression of the barn and the surrounding area.

Historical imagery of the brand was positioned in the rafters.

Inside the barn, skis and accessories were divided into distinct product groups.

The stand was a reinterpretation of the brand's first advertisement from 1962

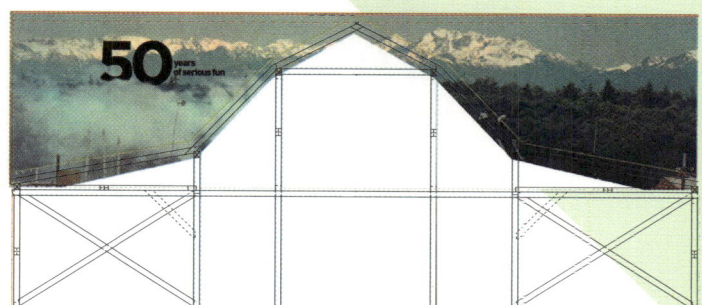

Facade elevations

K-Swiss by Werkstatt65

A RETRO, WOOD-CLAD BOOTH PRESENTED SPORTS FOOTWEAR WITH A CHILLED-OUT CALIFORNIAN BEACH VIBE.

TRADE FAIR Bread & Butter
WHERE Berlin, Germany
WHEN January 2011
DESIGNER Werkstatt65 ☒ b.500
STAND CONSTRUCTOR Werkstatt65
CLIENT K-Swiss
MARKET SECTOR Sports shoes
TOTAL FLOOR AREA 110 m²
PHOTOGRAPHER Marc Weemen

Sneaker brand K-Swiss gave design duo Alex Sijpesteijn and Bas de Graaf of Werkstatt65 just one short phrase when they were briefed to create a stand for the Bread & Butter fair in Berlin. The phrase was taken from the K-Swiss campaign and was made up of just two words: 'Go gonzo'. This tagline as well as the location of the client's headquarters – in sunny California – were the inspiration for the design concept. The team wanted to generate the feeling of a Californian lifestyle, and the stand also needed to be a crowd-stopper. Werkstatt65 took on a 'gonzo' approach which ended up as a collage of fun and a playground for modern youth. A retro feel pervaded the stand, which was bedecked with fittings and furniture that invited fair goers inside to have some fun. The booth was laid out like a beach-front bar or pool hall. At the back of the stand in one corner was a pinball machine and some old, leather-clad punch bags. Visitors could also just sit back and relax in the chill-out zone on the slouchy couches and poufs. From here, they could view the other offerings of entertainment space dotted around the space amidst product displays. Recycled wood was the main construction material used for the stand, with planks positioned to form the back wall alongside sheets of corrugated iron. A low-level platform at the front of the presentation featured a stage in one corner. Here, the design team had reworked some campaign visuals and reformatted them into 'pop-up scenarios' to create an intriguing 3D branded scenography. At allotted times during the fair, it looked like a pop-up book had come to life, with a story portrayed in the different scenes directed by the sports footwear brand. This was a popular feature amongst fair goers, with spontaneous rounds of applause heard from the K-Swiss booth on occasion.

☒ Passers-by were invited into the space to join in the fun and play some games.
☒ Vintage items set the scene and added to the chilled-out atmosphere.
☒ The back wall was made up of metal sheets, wooden planks, graphics and illuminated panel.

◪ Floor plan

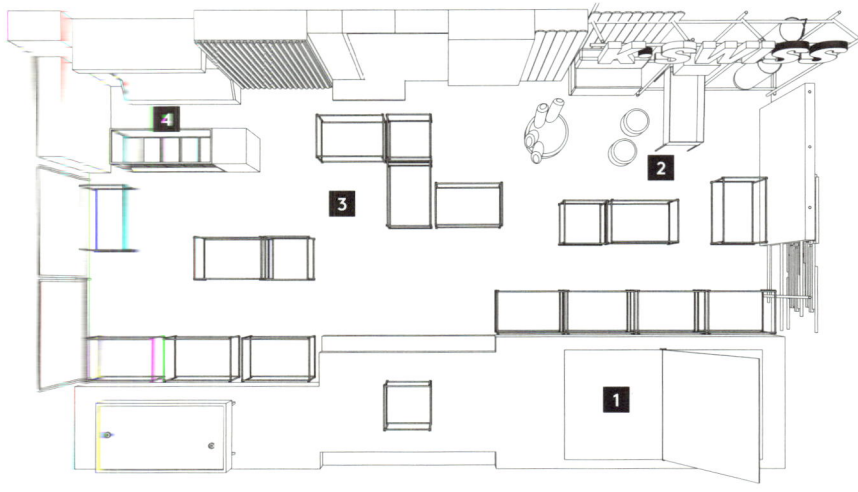

1 Pop-up stage
2 Chill-out zone
3 Product presentation
4 Bar

◪ Front elevation

◪ The space communicated the sportiness of the brand.
◪ The booth was a relaxed platform with a real surprise element embedded.
◪ Two campaign photos were reworked into 3D pop-up scenes that were changed by hand during the fair.

It looked like a pop-up book had come to life

MIDO by Francesco Pagliariccio

AN ORGANIC CLOUD MADE OF
4600 M² OF PARCHMENT PAPER
UNIFIED DIFFERENT COMPANIES
IN THE HUGE HALL.

For the MIDO trade fair, an exhibition where leading manufacturers in the eyewear industry showcase the finest brands and product lines, set designer Francesco Pagliariccio erected a lounge area in the centre of the exhibition hall. The main objective of the project was to unify the different companies and not overpower exhibitors at ground level. Pagliariccio therefore attached the project to the ceiling, overlooking the show space. Made of paper, the lightweight 'organic cloud' looked like it was in constant, slow motion and assumed different identities in dynamic fashion. Designed to resemble an iceberg, this alluring sculpture was constructed from almost 3000 pieces of paper. The installation wrapped around coloured lights that glowed from within. Constant changes in mood and colour lent the structure a sense of vibrancy. Below this dynamic glacial masterpiece, visitors could take a seat at the spiral-shaped lounge cubes, which were also lit from within. Located at one end of the lounge, the bar surrounded the only part of the installation that touched the floor. The construction time of the whole installation was another interesting aspect of this project. The paper pieces were all prefabricated and, thanks to precise planning, were assembled in just 24 hours.

TRADE FAIR **MIDO**
WHERE **Milan, Italy**
WHEN **March 2012**
DESIGNER **Francesco Pagliariccio** ☒ p.492
STAND CONSTRUCTOR **Nolostand**
CLIENT **MIDO**
MARKET SECTOR **Eyewear**
TOTAL FLOOR AREA **1750 m**
PHOTOGRAPHER **Davide Sala**

☒ The flowing, organic shape was created
with different lengths of paper strips
hung vertically.
☒ Coloured illumination transformed the
installation into a rippling canopy.
☒ The material was a fireproof paper
normally used for printing.

SHOES AND ACCESSORIES GRAND STAND 4

Pierre Cardin
by Kenan Pençe
Design Office

A MYSTERIOUS BLACK ENCLAVE
LURED VISITORS INSIDE TO EXPLORE
THE LATEST DESIGNER FASHIONS
FOR FEET.

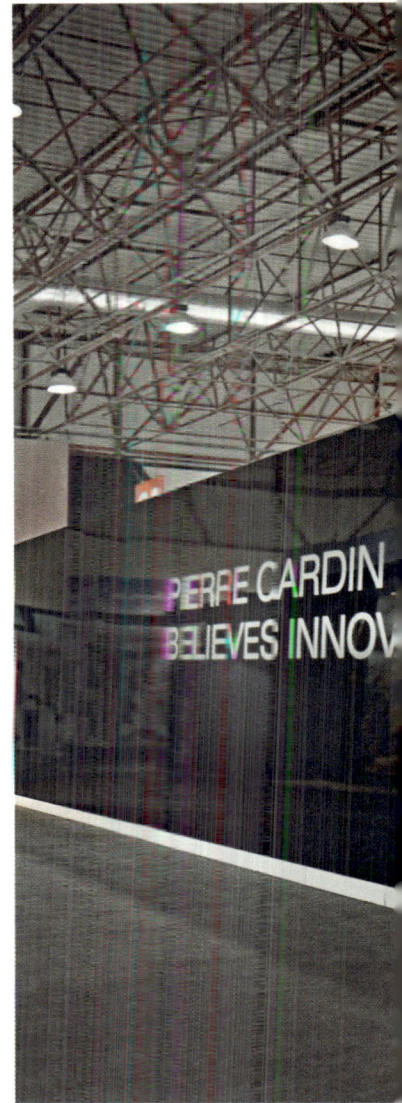

Pierre Cardin's stand for AYMOD 2011, Istanbul's International Footwear Fashion Fair, was realised by Kenan Pençe Design Office. In order to present the fashion designer's latest collection of shoes, bags and leather accessories, the design team created a concept that conveyed the brand's core values. The architecture, colour and graphics of the stand represented key words, such as innovation, art, handcrafted and passion. The stand incorporated the colours of the Pierre Cardin's logo: black and red. Pençe created the space as an abstract, contemporary sculpture, with geometric shapes cut out of the surfaces that were both functional – serving as doorways and shop windows – and aesthetic. These geometrical volumes were emphasised by a glamorous red colour. The monumentality of the stand conveyed the deep-rooted sense of tradition of the Pierre Cardin brand. In addition, the vibrant and reflective colours of the vast shiny surfaces expressed a dynamic vision of the brand. Graphics consisting of quotes from Pierre Cardin himself conveyed the brand's core values. Surrounded by these eye-catching and mysterious walls, passers-by were immediately lured into the stand to explore all the products on display. Inside, the display units positioned along the walls used repeated simple forms that made a surprisingly visual impact. At the centre of the stand, a rectangular display presented feature products, with bespoke furnishings designed following the same aesthetic principle.

TRADE FAIR AYMOD
WHERE Istanbul, Turkey
WHEN April 2011
DESIGNER Kenan Pençe Design Office ⊠ p.493
STAND CONSTRUCTOR Simart Mobilya ve Dekorasyon
CLIENT Aydınlı Group
MARKET SECTOR Shoes and accessories
TOTAL FLOOR AREA 400 m²
PHOTOGRAPHER Deniz Calisir

THINKING

"MY LIFE IS DRA WING
CUTTING AND S EWING WITH MY HAND"

Pierre Cardin

☒ The stand was a monument to the traditional and innovative roots of the fashion designer.
☒ The black and red colour scheme was also applied to the interior space.

THE ART OF

8 HALL

CENREXPO

Floor plan

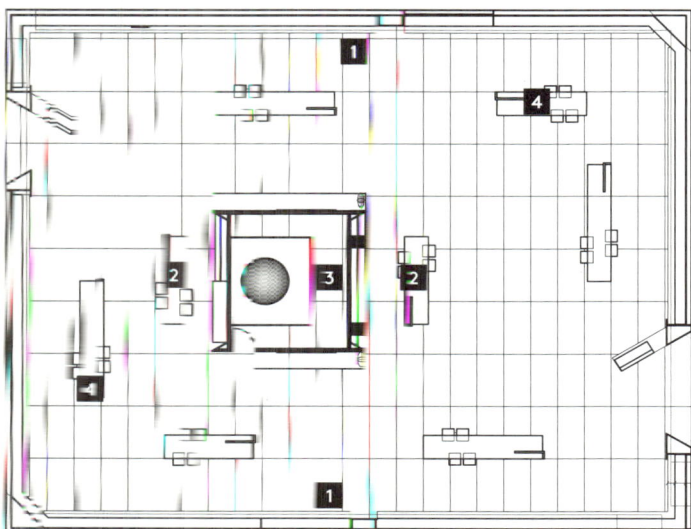

1 Display area
2 Sales desk
3 Storage
4 Seating are

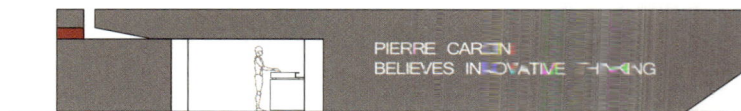

PIERRE CARDIN
BELIEVES INNOVATIVE THINKING

Front elevation

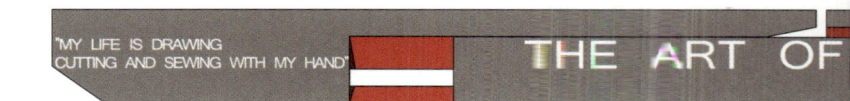

"MY LIFE IS DRAWING
CUTTING AND SEWING WITH MY HAND"

THE ART OF

Side elevation

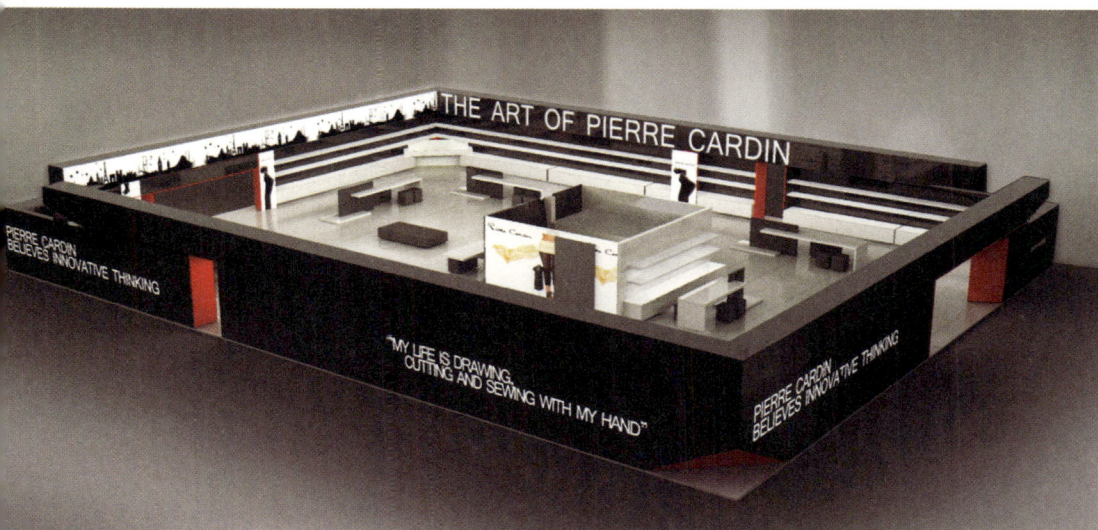

The entrance was a geometric shape cut out of the solid, shiny black exterior wall.
The display elements flowed around the interior space as a continuous unit.

Swatch by 3deluxe

THE WHITE, DELICATE PAVILION APPEALED TO THE VISITORS' EMOTIONAL PERCEPTION.

The Swatch pavilion for the Venice Biennale was conceived as an open-air living room for relaxed encounters in the middle of the Giardini park. Both the white colouring and the delicate unobtrusiveness of all the design elements communicated the Swatch brand philosophy in a fresh and contemporary manner. The pavilion architecture, designed by 3deluxe, consisted of an airy canopy supported by a number of slender pillars that rested on a wooden terrace-like platform. Moveable curtains suspended from the canopy roof allowed the pavilion to be closed, and their translucent lightness and movement in the wind emphasised the delicate nature of the design. The platform offered four seating islands to rest and relax, which turned the interior of the booth into a space for mellow lingering and contemplation. Two light installations were specially conceived for this project as an interpretation of time. The white back wall of the pavilion had a rectangular linear structure, with illuminated recessed panels positioned in the wooden panel. An array of LED strips of various lengths illuminated this from behind. The soft-flow programming, with irregular intervals, created a surprising effect on the plain wall surface that suggested the passing of time. Another light installation was integrated into a blossom-shaped arrangement suspended from the ceiling. Also incorporated into the back wall were a number of glass displays presenting Swatch products, as well as iPads that provided information about the product range, special events and the entire Swatch universe. The concept focused on addressing the visitors' emotional perception. Communicative content was to be 'felt' rather than rationally comprehended. Brand values were conveyed atmospherically in the form of a special place that emphasised a human touch, openness and harmony.

TRADE FAIR **Venice Biennale**
WHERE **Venice, Italy**
WHEN **June 2011**
DESIGNER **3deluxe** ☒ **p.488**
STAND CONSTRUCTOR **Gecco Scene Construction Company**
CLIENT **Swatch**
MARKET SECTOR **Watches**
TOTAL FLOOR AREA **150 m²**
PHOTOGRAPHERS **Jef Briguet, Sascha Jahnke**

☒ The ceiling panels had a DMX-controlled lighting system installed.
☒ Douglas fir floorboards with spar varnish created a natural platform for the booth.
☒ The fittings of the stand had a sinuous shape, following the contours of the steps in the park.

tallabé by KMS Blackspace

WITH ONLY A LIMITED SPACE AVAILABLE,
A CLEVER SOLUTION COMMUNICATED
EXACTLY HOW THIS PRODUCT WORKS.

TRADE FAIR **ISPO**
WHERE **Munich, Germany**
WHEN **February 2011**
DESIGNER **KMS Blackspace** ✕ p.493
STAND CONSTRUCTOR **e.venture**
CLIENT **tallabé**
MARKET SECTOR **Wellbeing**
TOTAL FLOOR AREA **8 m²**
PHOTOGRAPHER **Daniel Grund**

At first glance it may look like an ordinary sports cap, but tallabé is more than that – it is an ergonomic inlay for hats. The integrated weights improve people's posture and promote awareness of their bodies. As a finalist in the ISPO BrandNew Awards, which honour innovative products from new sporting goods companies, tallabé had a booth at ISPO 2011. The company was only given a limited amount of space for its first booth at the world's largest trade show for sporting goods and fashion accessories. It measured just 8 m² and had a height restriction of 1.5 m. At this point, KMS Blackspace came into the picture. The team's goal was to create an attention-grabbing installation that highlighted the benefits of the product and showed visitors how the product works – all within this very tiny space. Despite the restriction of the booth's dimensions, tallabé's stand was clearly visible from afar. Models, wearing the tallabé product on their heads, regularly patrolled the walls of the space, carefully negotiating the stepped side walls to reach the narrow catwalk along the back – a performance that required balance and concentration while walking. Circumnavigating the space in this way, they were easy to spot from a distance and created a sense of curiosity amongst fair goers. The catwalk on which the models demonstrated how to walk wearing tallabé was 3-m long and 1.5-m high and the beam was only 15 cm in width. As such, it made the best possible use of the limited space available. Visitors watched the models balance on the narrow beam while wearing tallabé, learned about the product and tried it out themselves. The trade show booth effectively communicated the idea of tallabé in an appealing way to people interested in improving their posture.

⊠ Visitors had chance to discover more about tallabé and try the product out for themselves.

⊠ The models stood tall whilst showcasing the product.

⊠ The unusual sight of people walking on the booth walls attracted attention from afar.

2LK DESIGN
The Courtyard, 17 West Street
Farnham GU9 7DR
United Kingdom
+44 1252 727 727
info@2lk.com
www.2lk.com

An owner-managed, multi-disciplined agency founded in 1994, 2LK Design combines architectural, experiential and communication creative disciplines with a wealth of project management experience. With 18 members of staff, and offices in the United Kingdom and the United Arab Emirates, the studio implements brands and marketing messages in both temporary and permanent exhibition environments, and across a breadth of media. 2LK Design has a global reach, handling projects for internationally-known brands.

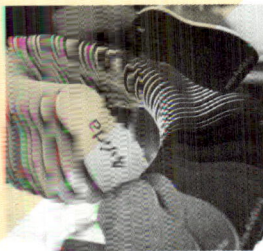

p.154, 412

3DELUXE
Schwalbacher Strasse 45
65183 Wiesbaden
Germany
+49 611 952205-0
inexterior@3deluxe.de
www.3deluxe.de

Founded in 1992, the 3deluxe studio today employs about 50 individuals from the fields of architecture and interior design, communication and graphic design, and motion and web design. The German firm has its headquarters in Wiesbaden, with additional offices in Hamburg and Shanghai. Headed by Dieter Brell, Andreas and Stephan Lauhoff, Sasch Koeth and Peter Seipp, the interdisciplinary team devises holistic design solutions ranging from graphic and interactive brand communication to media installations and architecture. The firm's spatial works reflect social and cultural tendencies and, at the same time, present visions for the future.

p.482

4VIDA
Parkovaya 16, building 27
105484 Moscow
Russia
+7 495 723 44 66
info@4vida.ru
www.4vida.ru

Design studio 4vida was established in 2003 by a group of ambitious designers from Russia. Over the years, the company has developed its own full-cycle production of exhibition stands using innovative materials and high-tech multimedia technologies. The aim of the studio is to develop new forms, images and way of exhibiting. While turning the most creative design ideas into reality, the team also realises industrial interiors, museums and demo-centres.

p.426

A1 ARCHITECTS
Dobrovského 8
170 00 Prague
Czech Republic
+420 775 903 277
info@a1architects.cz
www.a1architects.cz

Architects Lenka Křemenová and David Maštálka, who studied together at the Academy of Arts, Architecture and Design in Prague, started collaborative and independent projects in 2003. Two years later they jointly established a studio and creative workshop called A1 architects. In 2006, graphic designer Marta Maštálková joined the studio and, in 2012, architect Tereza Schneiderová completed the team. The studio focuses on client-oriented and tailor-made projects in which interdisciplinary communication and the search for unique solutions are the main characteristics.

p.456

APOSTROPHY'S THE SYNTHESIS SERVER
290/214 Ladprao 84
10310 Bangkok
Thailand
+66 846 851 662
aposssssss@gmail.com
www.apostrophys.com

Initiated in 2000 by a group of architecture students who set out to test their design skills, creative company Apostrophy's the Synthesis Server currently boasts a large number of international clients. Directed by Fontavith Lawaroungchouk, the multi-disciplinary design studio offers services that include visual design, motion graphics and lighting programming, as well as exhibition and architectural design.

p.038, 054

ARNO DESIGN
Bavariastrasse 6B
80336 Munich
Germany
+49 893 801 940
office@arno-design.de
www.arno-design.de

Arno Design was established in Munich in 1991. The studio concentrates on the design and realisation of trade fair booths, showrooms and stores. Led by Mirko Nassiri, Peter Haberlander and Claus Neureib, the design team works with intense creativity, concentration and personal contact to find the best possible solution for every project. Implementing diverse materials guarantees new and unexpected settings, with efficiency and ecology as the keywords that define the studio's design concept.

p.012, 116

ARQUITECT STUDIO
Contrà San Silvestro 40
36100 Vicenza
Italy
+39 347 5750945
studio@arquitect.eu
www.arquitect.eu

Architect Luca Biancoviso and designer Andrea Sovilla founded Arquitect Studio in 2010. The firm started off as an architectural office, but since 2012 the team has also worked on more project-management and construction projects. Arquitect Studio specialises in brand consulting, interior design and ephemeral architecture. The studio has four employees and is located in Vicenza, Italy.

p.452

ARTING
Artvej 1
7100 Vejle
Denmark
+45 7022 4048
dialog@arting.dk
www.arting.dk

Design company Arting was founded Danni P. Nicolaisen in 2002. The studio conceives, designs and builds exhibit solutions that give voice to brand architecture. The company strives surprising concepts that stretch the boundaries of what's possible while retaining a strong dedication to execution and craftsmanship. A team of experts in design, marketing and production work in the firm's headquarters Denmark as well as its office in New York.

p.278, 448

ATELIER 522
Fitzenweilerstrasse 1
88677 Markdorf
Germany
+49 754 4956 0522
atelier@atelier522.com
www.atelier522.com

Established in 2006 by Philipp Beck, atelier 522 is a creative agency made up of architects, interior designers, product designers, graphic designers and photographers working closely together to create buildings, retail interiors, products and more. The team always looks for new forms of expression, enthusiastic about the affiliation of sensual and skilled trade, in the traditional as well as forward-looking sense.

p.092, 232, 454

ATELIER BRÜCKNER
Krefelder Strasse 32
70376 Stuttgart
Germany
+49 711 500 0770
kontakt@atelier-brueckner.com
www.atelier-brueckner.com

Atelier Brückner was established in 1997 by architect and stage designer Prof. Uwe R. Brückner and architect Shirin Frangoul-Brückner. Now with more than 70 employees, the company is a leading studio for the creation of narrative spaces, guided by its philosophy 'form follows content'. The company works on the development and implementation of 3D communication for themed and branded environments, including architecture, scenography and exhibition design for museums and visitor centres, as well as for trade fairs, events and expo pavilions. **Photo: Reiner Pfisterer**

p.222

ATELIER MARKGRAPH
Ludwig-Landmann-Strasse 349
60487 Frankfurt am Main
Germany
+49 6997 9930
contact@markgraph.de
www.markgraph.de

Based in Frankfurt, Atelier Markgraph is an agency that specialises in spatial communication. This interdisciplinary design and planning provider creates tangible experiences for companies and brands for clients all over the world. Using cutting-edge technologies, the studio produces surprising spatial productions at the interface of business, culture and science, from exhibitions through media productions to corporate architecture.

p.316

ATELIER MARKO BRAJOVIC
Rua Apinages 440
05017-000 São Paulo
Brazil
+55 11 2371 9206
marko@markobrajovic.com
www.markobrajovic.com

Architect Marko Brajovic founded his atelier in 2007 in São Paulo, Brazil. The multidisciplinary team of architects and designers operate as a 'hands-on' workshop, implementing a strategic design process to achieve the most valuable and coherent results. The ateliers portfolio of projects includes architecture, product design, interior design, scenography and interactive installations, and covers all stages of the process: concept, development, testing, presentation and installation/building.

p.194, 420

ATELIER OÏ
Route de Bienne 31
2520 La Neuveville
Switzerland
+41 32 751 5666
contact@atelier-oi.ch
www.atelier-oi.ch

Since it was established in 1991, Swiss design studio atelier oï has been striving to dissolve barriers between genres and foster cross-disciplinary creativity. Founded by Aurel Aebi, Armand Louis and Patrick Reymond, the studio works on intertwining projects in architecture, interior design and set design for an international clientele. A multidisciplinary approach, team spirit and intimate rapport with the material are the watchwords of the studio. Born of an intuitive and emotional affinity with the act of shaping different materials, atelier oï's projects have been recognised all over the world. **Photo: Frederike Baetcke**

p.458

ATELIER SEITZ
Birkenstrasse 28
85467 Niederneuching
Germany
+49 812 393 050
info@atelierseitz.de
www.atelierseitz.de

For over 50 years, Atelier Seitz has been designing, creating concepts and constructing exhibition stands, events and showrooms for clients across the globe. The team of architects develops innovative and custom-made concepts, constantly seeking ways to reduce waste and increase recycling in trade fair projects. Working from a 4000-m² facility with over 40 qualified staff, the studio is a full-service partner for the duration of any project, from the rough sketch to the final touches.

p.094, 130

AUTOBAN
Mesrutiyet Cad. 99/1
34430 Istanbul
Turkey
+90 212 243 8641
info@autoban212.com
www.autoban212.com

Established in 2003 by Seyhan Özdemir and Sefer Çaglar, Autoban is a design studio operating in the fields of interior design, architecture and product development. Inspired by the chaos of Istanbul, contrasts, contradictions and the co-existence of otherwise autonomous elements are all trademarks of Autoban projects and products. The studio, with a team of 35 members, is located in Beyoglu, a lively district of Istanbul. With solid foundations based on architectural principles, a modernist twist is often complementary to traditional components that find life in new interpretations and contexts.

p.170

BACHMANN.KERN UND PARTNER
Gasstrasse 10–18
42657 Solingen
Germany
+49 212 556 6900
Info@bkp-architektur.de
www.bkp-architektur.de

Founded in the year 2000, architecture and design agency Bachmann.Kern und Partner has its headquarters in the German city of Solingen. The conceptualisation, mediation and realisation of interior architecture is the firm's focus, in particular in the realms of exhibition, shop, event and trade fair design. The principal tools that the firm makes use of are creativity, competence and enthusiasm, along with a network of stand constructors and trade fair-related agencies.

p.228, 270, 274

BRAUNWAGNER
Krefelder Strasse 147
52070 Aachen
Germany
+49 241 401 0720
info@braunwagner.de
www.braunwagner.de

Braunwagner is a design agency that focuses on environmental, product and communication design, as well as architecture and consulting for strategic brand development. Since its foundation in 1999, the firm has realised a wide range of trade fair stands for clients from diverse industries. Led by Prof. Manfred Wagner and Marina Franke, the 25-strong creative team emotionalises corporate identities and transforms brand values into spatial communication, with creativity, know-how and enthusiasm.

p.336

COMO PARK STUDIO
Joris Ivensplein 94
1087 BP Amsterdam
the Netherlands
+31 6 122 6454
info@comoparkstudio.com
www.comoparkstudio.com

Como Park Studio specialises in interior architecture, from concept and design to execution. Established by Kenneth Jawor in 2000, the studio has a broad portfolio of projects in the realms of shops, hotels and trade fairs. The company's mission is to design not only for who its clients are but also for who they would like to become.

p.014, 028

CONFETTI
Sevillaweg 132
3047 AL Rotterdam
the Netherlands
+31 104 762 726
info@confettireclame.nl
www.confettireclame.nl

Confetti is a Dutch design studio headquartered in Rotterdam that was established in 1989 by Monique Morks and Eric Zijffers. The company works on projects in many different disciplines, including interiors, retail and exhibition stands, as well as product, furniture and graphic design. The Confetti team works to provide inspiring solutions with a young, fresh and innovative approach, aiming to create unique concepts based on an 'atmospheric experience'.

p.160

CRIACITTÁ
32A Rue du Faubourg Poissonniere
75010 Paris
France
+33 637 521 506
info@criacitta.fr
www.criacitta.com

Criacittá has been creating brand experiences in Brazil since 1998. The rest of the world discovered Criacittá's work through its collaboration with the Havaianas brand. The company is structured into four business units: Set Designs, Retail, Special Products and Factory. Besides Havaianas, the Criacittá portfolio includes clients such as AB InBev, TAM and Audi. The firm has its headquarters in São Paulo and opened a second office in Paris in 2007.

p.460

D'ART DESIGN GRUPPE
Am Zollhafen 5
41460 Neuss
Germany
+49 213 140 3070
info@d-art-design.de
www.d-art-design.de

Spatial communications firm D'art Design Gruppe was established in 1991 and consists of interior architects, communication and product designers, project managers, PR and marketing specialists. The studio's approach is one in which creative design skills merge with interdisciplinary expertise. Located in Neuss, Germany, the company works in the field of retail and exhibition design, creating brand experience and adventure spaces for global clients.

p.066, 136, 418

DCUBE
Rampe de Chevant 16
1232 Confignon
Switzerland
+41 227 713 196
infodesk@dcube.ch
www.dcube.ch

Davide Oppizzi is the founder and owner of dcube, an architecture and design firm established in 2001 in Geneva. The studio works at an international level across the fields of fashion, interior design, commercial layout, lighting design, bathroom design and green technologies. Oppizzi creates objects using nature as a source of inspiration. Uninterested in mass-production, he prefers the approach of the artisan in striving to find new high-quality ways of working with materials.

p.200

DELAFAIR
Schwedenstrasse 9
13359 Berlin
Germany
+49 30 2977 3330
mail@delafair.com
www.delafair.com

Delafair is a Berlin-based enterprise that has been creating temporary architecture since its establishment in 2001. Creative director Kristina Schipper, together with her team, develops innovative concepts for international clients for trade fairs, exhibitions or promotion. The company has a broad-ranging portfolio and high standards in terms of performance, combining creative variation and professional know-how. Design, project management and modern production techniques are optimally linked to often exceed clients' expectations.

p 370, 436

DFROST
Hauptstätter Strasse 59A
70178 Stuttgart
Germany
+49 7116 6481 711
info@dfrost.de
www.dfrost.com

Founded in 2008, visual marketing firm dfrost focuses on the creation and realisation of target-oriented design and solutions for the retail sector. From shop fitting, stand construction and window displays to communication tools and point of sale activities, every project is taken on by an interdisciplinary team with great focus on attention to detail. The Stuttgart-based firm is headed by Nadine Frommer, Christoph Melzer and Fabian Stelzer.

p.028

DITTEL ARCHITEKTEN
**Rotenwaldstrasse 100/1
70197 Stuttgart
Germany
+49 711 4690 6550
info@d-arch.de
www.d-arch.de**

Dittel Architekten was founded by Frank Dittel in 2005. The interdisciplinary design company has a team of 23 architects and interior and communication designers working from its Stuttgart and Berlin offices. The company creates, defines and different ates brands in consultation with its international client base. Developing distinct spaces across a wide range of projects, the firm executes its own unique approach from concept to completion.

p.030

DOSHI LEVIEN
**49 Columbia Road
London E2 7RG
United Kingdom
+44 20 7739 363*
mail@doshilevien.com
www.doshilevien.com**

Progressive and forward-looking studio Doshi Levien was established by Nipa Doshi and Jonathan Levien in 2000. The Anglo-Indian husband-and-wife team takes a hybrid approach to design that allows them to combine various cultures, industries technologies and craft techniques. The London-based studio likes to tell stories, working across disciplines and industries to establish criteria that are based on extracting as much richness as possible out of an idea.

p.188

DRÄNDLE 70|30
**Etterschlager Strasse 6
82237 Steinebach am Wörthsee
Germany
+49 815 3997 0350
info@draendle7030.de
www.draendle7030.com**

Drändle 70|30 is committed to making the brand visible and tangible in a three-dimensional manner. The company's range of services includes consulting, planning and conceiving spatial brand experiences for trade fairs and store branding projects. All solutions are based on the concept of combining brand messages, materials and creative effort into one effective statement.

p.258

EINS:33
**Dreimühlenstrasse 19
80469 Munich
Germany
+49 894 6153 6517
info@einszu33.de
www.einszu33.com**

Founded in 1999 by Hendrik Müller in Stuttgart and relaunched in Munich in 2005, eins:33 is a studio offering full scale architecture and design services worldwide, as well as creating tools for brand identity and communication. The team of architects and interior designers works on projects ranging from showrooms, retail stores and exhibition concepts to corporate architecture. The studio's name refers to the scale 1:33 which is a significant aspect in architectural teachings although it is only rarely used in the planning process these days; it nevertheless has an important meaning at the interface between architecture and interior design.

p.142

ESTUDIO GUTO REQUENA
**1996 Rua Oscar Freire, Pinheiros
05409-011 São Paulo
Brazil
+55 11 2528 1700
contato@gutorequena.com.br
www.gutorequena.com.br**

Founded in 2010 in São Paulo, Estudio Guto Requena was formed by architect Guto Requena, associate architect Paulo de Camargo and five collaborators. The studio reflects cyberculture and digital poetic narratives in its work. Encompassing a varied portfolio – objects, interiors, buildings and cities – the team develops products and designs residential, commercial and exhibition spaces. Photo: Victor Affaro

p.212, 378, 420

FIVE AM
**J Vandaleplein 3
8500 Kortrijk
Belgium
+32 5674 4132
question@fiveam.be
www.fiveam.be**

Design atelier Five AM was established in 2011 by interior designers Mathieu Bellens and Olivier Couwier. Creating interior and exhibition spaces for semi-public organisations and private companies, the Five AM portfolio also extends into product design. The studio's aim is to generate a moment of astonishment in the process of realising an inspiring result. With simplicity as a starting point, each design needs to interact with the user and build up naturally until the story is complete.

p.360

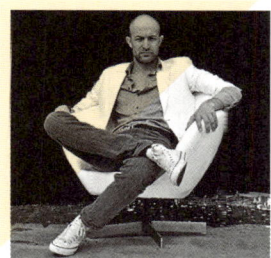

FLANCE
**73D Rose Street, Bo-Kaap
8001 Cape Town
South Africa
+27 21 422 4006
mayor@flance.co.za
www.flance.co.za**

Flance is an independent studio under the creative leadership of Eugene Meyer. It is a small and ambitious design and brand development studio based in Cape Town. A broad range of industry experience between the four studio members enables the team to take on a diverse range of projects, from corporate identity design and packaging to branding, signage and way finding systems. Always combining honesty within the design, the studio sets out to tell a unique and relevant story for each client.

p.362

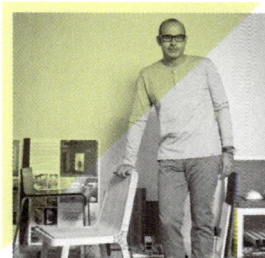

FRANCESC RIFÉ STUDIO
**Escoles Pies 25
08017 Barcelona
Spain
+34 934 14 12 88
f@rife-design.com
www.rife-design.com**

With a degree in interior and industrial design, Francesc Rifé began his professional career as an undergraduate with independent commissions for various design and architecture studios, while at the same time undertaking his own projects. He established his own studio in 1994 in Barcelona, where he now leads a team trained in various fields of design. The studio specialises in commercial and private projects that encompass spatial order and geometric proportion with a portfolio covering interior and industrial landscapes.

p.284

FRANCESCO PAGLIARICCIO
via Maroncelli, 14
20154 Milan
Italy
francesco@pagliaricciodesign.com
www.pagliaricciodesign.com

Francesco Pagliariccio is a set designer who started his career more than 20 years ago. Since then, he has developed an expertise in many areas of communication. The interaction between different 'languages' is the main path of his creative activity and research, and occupies the core of each new challenge along with the constant aim to experiment. Among his main clients are the largest communication agencies in Italy, television production companies, and numerous international brands.

p.474

FREESTATE
4 Goodge Place
London W1T 4SB
United Kingdom
+44 20 30 5 7990
info@freestate.co.uk
www.freestate.co.uk

FreeState was founded in 2002 by Charlotte Boyens, Ben Johnson and Adam Scott. Along with the chairman David Gilbert and the core London team of 12 entrepreneurs, designers, architects and strategists, FreeState also has an office in Singapore. Working with a global client base, the team has expertise in architectural and 3D design, creative conceptualisation, branding, graphics, digital, retail, content creation, production management and business development.

p.162, 164

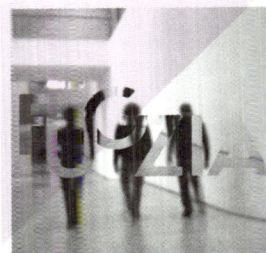

FUGZIA
Vaartkom 35/1
3000 Leuven
Belgium
+32 1623 0803
info@fugzia.be
www.fugzia.be

The Belgian design firm Fugzia has over 20 years of experience in creating three-dimensional projects. Working with worldwide clients to find new perspectives, the studio has an extensive portfolio that includes exhibition stands, retail interiors and showrooms, as well as visitor centres. From concept to fabrication, all projects are supported by custom-made interactive tools and applications, utilising natural and sustainable materials as far as possible.

p.354

GIELISSEN
Freddy Van Riemsdijkweg 21
5657 EE Eindhoven
the Netherlands
+31 40 2353 37
info@gielissen.nl
www.gielissen.com

Gielissen Interiors & Exhibitions has been in the trade show, interior and exposition business since 1937. The company has a rich history working on a diverse range of projects: retail solutions, trade show exhibits, expos and convention management, as well as big or small events. The firm has 10 offices worldwide, with a global team of 300 professionals who design and realise projects in any form and size. Consultation and cooperation are central to activities. Gielissen is associated with renowned creative partners.

p.374, 414

GUN ARCHITECTS
Avenida Santa Maria 0346, apt 715
Santiago
Chile
+56 981 881 167
info@gunarq.com
www.gunarq.com

Gun Architects is a Chilean–German design office founded by architects Jorge Godoy and Lene Nettelbeck. Based in Santiago since 2010, the firm engages in architectural and urban projects that are deeply connected to local environmental and cultural realities. Recent works include the construction of a monostructural bamboo pavilion, and the master-plan for a self-sufficient community near Tongoy Peninsula in north-central Chile, which includes developing infrastructure, energy systems, orchards and housing typologies in an area that is shifting from farming to tourism and housing.

p.446

HAFSTEINN JULIUSSON, JOANA PAIS AND RUI PEREIRA
Langahlid 19
105 Reykjavik
Iceland
+354 695 8550
h@hafsteinnjuliusson.com
www.hafsteinnjuliusson.com
www.joana-pais.com
www.rui-pereira.com

A collaboration between industrial and interior designers Hafsteinn Juliusson, Joana Pais and Rui Pereira began when they met in 2010 while studying for their master's degrees at the Scuola Politecnica di Design in Milan, Italy. During that time, the trio designed several projects together, from retail concepts to kitchen appliances. Since graduating, they have all started their own design studios, though they occasionally develop some projects together.

p.440

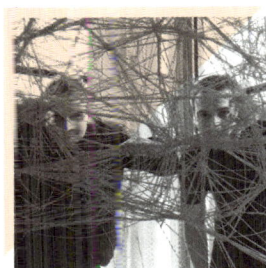

HIPPOS DESIGN ARCHITECTURE
Chorvatska 12
101 00 Prague
Czech Republic
+420 271 732 251
hippos@hipposdesign.com
www.hipposdesign.com

Designers Radim Babák and Ondrej Tobola founded their own studio, hippos design architecture, in 2003 in Prague. The firm concentrates primarily on product design, interior design and architectural projects. Fundamental to the studio philosophy is a constant search for a story, a context, that is elemental to creating the character of an object or a space. Questioning common proportions and details, the hippos team often digs to the very core of a given problem to find a new starting point.

p.218

HW.DESIGN
Türkenstrasse 55-57
80799 Munich
Germany
+49 892 025 755
info@hwdesign.de
www.hwdesign.de

The Munich-based agency hw.design was founded in 1995 and focuses on communication design, interactivity and architecture projects. With a team of over individuals, the agency advises, designs and implements strategies that allow organisations and brands to liven up their identity, both visually and in terms of content. The company also welcomes and supports the desire of its global customers to seek sustainable communication and design solutions.

p.060

IPPOLITO FLEITZ GROUP
Augustenstrasse 87
70197 Stuttgart
Germany
+49 711 993392 330
info@ifgroup.org
www.ifgroup.org

Ippolito Fleitz Group is a multidisciplinary, internationally-operating design studio based in Stuttgart, founded by Gunter Fleitz and Peter Ippoliti. Currently, the company presents itself as a creative unit of 37 designers, each contributing specific skills to the alternating, project-oriented team formations. Providing creative solutions for its global clients, the studio covers a wide field of design disciplines, including interiors, products, graphics and architecture.

JACK MORTON WORLDWIDE
16–18 Acton Park Estate
London W3 7QE
United Kingdom
+44 20 8735 2000
experience@jackmorton.com
www.jackmorton.com

Jack Morton Worldwide was established as a start-up company by founder Jack Morton in 1939 on the basis of 'bringing top entertainment to corporate events'. Today, the global brand experience agency comprises 700 people in 22 offices around the world, promoting breakthrough ideas about how experiences connect brands and people – in person, online, in retail, etc. For powerful and effective solutions that engage customers and consumers, the company successfully creates experiences to launch products, align employees and build brands.

JANGLED NERVES
Hallstrasse 25
70376 Stuttgart
Germany
+49 711 550375-0
info@janglednerves.com
www.janglednerves.com

Stuttgart-based jangled nerves was established in 1998 by Thomas Hundt and Ingo Zirngibl. The company operates in the public and private sectors on projects for museum and exhibition architecture, brand experience, and trade fair and event design. The office consists of an interdisciplinary team of, on average, 35 employees and 20 freelancers. Merging the sensibilities of a conception agency, a planning office, and a film and media production firm, jangled nerves has created an entirely new way of working in the field of spatial communication.

KALEIDO
Austrasse 50
6832 Sulz
Austria
+43 699 1711 2008
office@kaleido.cc
www.kaleido.cc

Karoline Mühlburger and Silvia Keckeis founded Kaleido in Sulz, Austria in 2008. The duo works together as a complementary unit on a range of projects, products and strategies. The studio creates beautiful forms, shapes and figures with a portfolio that covers graphic design, branding, editorial work and publications, as well as interior and exhibition design.

KAUFFMANN THEILIG & PARTNER
Zeppelinstrasse 10
73760 Ostfildern (Stuttgart)
Germany
+49 711 45 122 0
info@ktp-architekten.de
www.ktp-architekten.de

The office Kauffmann Theilig was established in 1988 and became Kauffmann Theilig & Partner in 1995 with Prof. Andreas Theilig, Dieter Ben Kauffmann and Rainer Lenz as business partners. The office plans and realises variously sized projects for global clients in all fields of building construction, as well as corporate architecture and exhibition design. KTP has cultivated an intensive collaboration between experts and engineers to achieve integrated architectural solutions.

KENAN PENÇE DESIGN OFFICE
Poyracik Street, Yasemin Apt 1/3, Tesvikiye
34360 Istanbul
Turkey
+90 212 296 2351
kenanpence@gmail.com
www.kenanpence.com.tr

Kenan Pençe graduated from the Department of Interior Architecture at the Mimar Sinan University in Turkey in 1993. After working as a designer for several years, he established his own interior design firm, Kenan Pençe Design Office in 2002 in Istanbul. The office is involved in a wide variety of projects, specialising in shop, office and stand design. The company's philosophy is based on following human needs and sensations to create new aesthetics and concepts.

KMS BLACKSPACE
Tölzer Strasse 2c
81379 Munich
Germany
+49 89 490 411 0
info@kms-blackspace.com
www.kms-blackspace.com

KMS Blackspace creates and designs fascinating brand experiences and their touch points. More than 50 employees focus on activating brands through the disciplines of space, motion design and customer experience design. The results are successful brand experiences, trade shows and events, shops and showrooms, corporate headquarters, exhibitions, museums and crossover activities for companies of any size and sector. KMS Blackspace forms, together with KMS Team and KMS Mindshift, Germany's largest owner-managed branding agency group, with more than 120 employees under one roof and more than 25 years of experience in activating brands.

KNOCK
Kungsgatan 5
103 87 Stockholm
Sweden
+46 8 21 74 84
info@knock.se
www.knock.se

Knock is a concept, design and brand experience agency that focuses on creating unique experiences where the brand and target group are given an opportunity to interact. The company is based in Stockholm, Sweden and was founded by Jesper Kjaergaard in 1994. The studio's mission is to develop design concepts and produce events that are highly creative, relevant and credible to the target group.

KREON
Industrieweg Noord 1152
3660 Opglabbeek
Belgium
+32 8951 9631
mailbox@kreon.com
www.kreon.be

Kreon, a Belgian company represented all over the world, has been developing and producing interior lighting and metal ceiling systems since 1982. The basis for Kreon's design is a clear and characteristic visualisation of the company's philosophy: purity and simplicity. Architects, designers and engineers implement lighting concepts at the planning stages of the design process. Typical applications for the studio's portfolio include residential, hospitality, retail, display and office interiors.

p.254

LABORETWANG
Bartning-llee 2
10557 Berlin
Germany
+49 171 6321694
info@laborotwang.de
www.laborotwang.de

Carsten Bauer, Fabio Dornhege, Christoph Franz and Sven Temerling began collaborating professionally under the name of Laborotwang at the University of the Arts in Berlin. The Laborotwang 'laboratory' keeps each client's brand, product and message at the centre of its concept. Completed projects include trade fair stands, showrooms and retail solutions.

p.020, 022

LIGANOVA
Herdweg 59
70174 Stuttgart
Germany
+49 711 6522 0201
info@liganova.com
www.liganova.com

Liganova is a specialist in integrated brand retail marketing, founded in 1995 by Michael Haiser and Bodo Vincent Andrin. With 200 employees working in interdisciplinary teams, the firm is well known for its intuition and seeking out the zeitgeist. The studio creates cutting edge brand experiences without losing sight of the individual identities of the brands. Blurring the boundaries between classic brand communication and point of sale marketing, the result is the creation of meaningful solutions across all channels in the fashion, lifestyle, automobile and luxury goods industries.

p.008

LITTLE
17-3 SPBS Kamiyama-cho Shibuya
150 0047 Tokyo
Japan
+81 354 650 577
saorimiwa@gmail.com
www.little-i.ne.com

Saori Miwa is an experienced designer based in Japan. After working with Tonerico for more than 5 years, she established her own interior design studio Little in Tokyo in 2010. The studio has already built up a portfolio that includes a range of interior design projects, including restaurants and cafes, offices and exhibition stands, and shops and retail spaces.

p.226

LUCILLE CLERC
416 Kingsland Road
London E84AA
United Kingdom
+44 758 120 1821
info@lucilleclerc.com
www.lucilleclerc.com

Graphic designer, illustrator and communication designer Lucille Clerc founded her studio in London in 2009 after graduating from Central Saint Martins. She is specialised in editorial design and illustration, occasionally also realising interior and exhibition spaces. Mainly working for the creative industry, her clients include David Kohn Architects, Jotta, Laurence King Publishers, Magma, Son of a Stag and Suzanne Goodwin (www.suzannegoodwin.com). Her detailed approach to illustration as well as her passion for printing/folding techniques and type illustration characterise her work.

p.234

MACH ARCHITEKTUR
Kanzleistrasse 18
8004 Zurich
Switzerland
+41 442 483 650
mach@macharch.ch
www.macharch.ch

Mach Architektur is an international architecture and design practice based in Zurich. Founded in 2000 by architects David Marquardt and Jan Fischer, the studio has carried out a wide range of corporate projects for global brands. The 10-member team believes that form should not only follow function but also add lasting value, from enhancing customer experience to increasing profitability.

p.242

MARCOS CATALAN
Rbla. Catalunya 98bis, 7° 3ª
08008 Barcelona
Spain
+34 600582361
marcoscatalan@gmail.com
www.marcoscatalan.com

Marcos Catalan graduated with a degree in interior design from the School Elisava – University Pompeu Fabra in Barcelona, Spain in 1997. He worked in various architectural offices until in 2006 when he founded his own design studio, Marcos Catalan interiorismo, developing integrated projects in the field of design and architecture. He currently combines his studio activities with lecturing project courses at ELISAVA Barcelona School of Design and Engineering.

p.398

MARTIN ET KARCZINSKI
Nymphenburger Strasse 125
80636 Munich
Germany
+49 897 464 690
info@martinetkarczinski.de
www.martinetkarczinski.de

Established in 2001, Martin et Karczinski builds brands for companies and institutions. Working in the fields of corporate identity, corporate design and corporate branding, the firm combines communication strategies with high-quality design. The company has an international client base working with such companies as Occhio, Audi and Alape.

p.258

MAYRIDGE
Burleigh House, Evesham Road
Evesham WR11 8SP
United Kingdom
+44 1386 871 400
marketing@mayridge.com
www.mayridge.com

Mayridge delivers measurable success for international clients through a creative mix of dedication, passion, energy and focus, but above all, knowledge and 35 years of experience. With established offices in central Europe, the Middle East and the United Kingdom, the firm provides an integrated approach to live events worldwide, which engage audiences in interesting and dynamic ways to achieve measurable return on investment. The company's services include design and build, project management and campaign marketing.

p.396

MBCO
Franz-Joseph-Strasse 10
80801 Munich
Germany
+49 89 380 1901
info@mbco.net
www.mbco.net

Munich-based studio mbco is dedicated to providing new contexts for personal encounters in the realms of trade show and exhibition design. Since its foundation in 1996, the firm has been demonstrating its comprehensive range of expertise across a broad spectrum of contrasting styles, realising temporary trade fair presentations all over the world. The 25-member team encapsulates corporate identities with enthusiasm, conceptual clarity and attention to detail, using a flexible approach to create individual solutions with a sustainable edge.

p.328, 382, 464

MCMILLAN GROUP
25 Otter Trail
Westport, CT 06880
United States
+1 203 227 8696
info@mcmillangroup.com
www.mcmillangroup.com

The founding partners of McMillan Group are Charlie and Nancy McMillan. The firm, which is located in Connecticut, United States, was founded in 1985 and specialises in the realisation of museum exhibitions, corporate business centres and exhibitions. The design capabilities of the studio include master planning, exhibition design, architectural and interior design, graphic design, interactive and media creative direction, lighting design, construction engineering and project management.

p.400, 430

MEIRÉ UND MEIRÉ
Lichtstrasse 26-28
50825 Cologne
Germany
+49 221 5777 0100
info@meireundmeire.de
www.meireundmeire.de

Meiré und Meiré has been working for German and international brands and companies for 25 years at the interface between culture and design. Over 50 employees in Cologne develop character-defining media for analogue and digital communication. As art director, Mike Meiré excels at corporate branding whilst Marc Meiré manages the strategy and consulting divisions. The studio also works on projects in the areas of editorial design, culture projects, public relations, brand coding and architecture.

p.164, 322

MIKS KONZEPTE
Strassenbahnring 15
20251 Hamburg
Germany
+49 40 3575 840
info@miks.co
www.miks.co

The interior design agency Miks Konzepte has been developing and realising the creative presentation of German and international brands since 1999. Managed by brother and sister duo Michaela and Christoph Kruse, the firm's team of 20 people generates innovative, interactive and event-oriented design for shops, showrooms and trade fair appearances.

p.106, 108

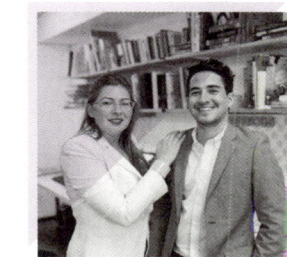

MUUAAA
605 Ave Corcado San Alberto
Bldng Ofic 719
00907 San Juan
Puerto Rico
+1 787 721 8756
info@muuaaa.com
www.muuaaa.com

Muuaaa is a creative studio specialising in design, cultural events and effective branding in the fields of art, architecture and design. Founded by architect Miguel Miranda Montes together with his partner Celina Noguera Cuevas, the multidisciplinary team is made up of opinion leaders, visual narrators, strategic thinkers and cultural forecasters. By combining branding and architecture, the studio creates evocative spaces that provoke experiences and sensations and create tighter bonds between people and brands

p.348

NEO
Atasehir Bulvarı, Ata 3/3 Plaza, 48 Atasehir
34758 Istanbul
Turkey
+90 216 456 8486
info@neo.com.tr
www.neo.com.tr

Founded in Istanbul in 2005 by Cenk Gün and Halise Özel, Neo International Design & Communications is active in the field of stand design and believes in creating presentations that reflect its clients' values and standards. The firm's work also extends into the realms of design and implementation of product displays and subsystems, as well as corporate identity, visual communication and graphic design.

p.244

NEST ONE
Mittelweg 22
20148 Hamburg
Germany
+49 40 2223 3438
kontakt@nest-one.com
www.nest-one.com

Nest One is a brand experience architecture agency based in Hamburg, Germany. The company was founded by Holger Pütting in 2000 to create stories that ultimately become experiential spaces through people and encounters. The company's 25-member team – strategists, architects, designers, trend researchers and consultants – likes to be inspired, working with a creative energy and enthusiasm to develop new formats unique to individual brands to transform ideas into designs and spaces.

p.340, 542, 404

NICE2C
Kantinestraat 4
8800 Roeselare
Belgium
info@nice2c.be
www.nice2c.be

Nice2C was founded in 2007 by Paul Ameloot (founder of Delta Light), and Maarten Demunster joined in 2008. As the main designers of the Delta Light collections, Nice2C has proven its ability to provide innovative lighting designs. Since it was first founded, the studio's approach has always been to focus on form, functionality and technology, with innovation being the driving force behind the business.

p.250

OURSTUDIO
Beurhausstrasse 58
44137 Dortmund
Germany
+49 231 53 0957
info@ourstudio.de
www.ourstudio.de

Ourstudio was founded in 2005 by Prof. Luis Ocanto-Arciniegas and Prof. Armin Rogall. Located in Dortmund, Germany, the studio boasts a wide-ranging project portfolio covering all areas of architectural design, energy consulting, marketing and communication. An interdisciplinary team of qualified architects, designers and engineers ensures that the office is competent to handle all aspects of projects, with a special strength in realising innovative concepts.

p.056

OVAL DESIGN
22D Legend Tower
7 Shing Yip Street, Kwun Tong
Kowloon
Hong Kong
+852 2802 2033
info@ovaldesign.com.hk
www.ovaldesign.com.hk

Established by Dennis Wong and Dominic Kam in 1991, Oval Design is a communication-focused creative agency specialising in spatial design and production of high-end exhibitions, events, commercial interior design and multi-media installations. The studio provides quality one-stop solutions to meet the communication needs of its clients. Built up over 20 years of continued growth, the Oval team comprises 30 designers and project executives at the company offices in Hong Kong and Shanghai.

p.406, 410

PAOLO CESARETTI | ARCHITECT
Via Oxilia 23
20127 Milan
Italy
+39 022 680 9419
contact@paolocesaretti.it
www.paolocesaretti.it

Paolo Cesaretti is an Italian design consultant and art director who explores the concept of designed space as a communication tool. After a period at Amsterdam-based UNStudio, in 1998 he became co-partner of vc a | vannini+cesaretti in Milan, specialising in exhibition and experience design. Paolo Cesaretti is also a lecturer at the Scuola Politecnico di Design Milano and a guest professor at the Domus Academy and Politecnico di Milano.

p.084, 086

PHOCUS BRAND CONTACT
Bartholomaeusstrasse 26F
90489 Nuremberg
Germany
+49 911 9334 225
contact@phocus-brand.de
www.phocus-brand.de

Founded in 1998, Phocus Brand Contact is an agency for active communication. More than 40 creative minds work in interdisciplinary teams to bring inspiring projects to life. The studio orchestrates exciting communication avenues: direct interaction between people and brands. The company's strategy is to make tangible and perceptible what is at the core of those brands and companies. The experienced team members constantly strive to create experiences that generate enthusiasm at the point of contact and which remain unforgettable long after they are over.

p.304, 372

PINKEYE
Hessenplein 2
2000 Antwerp
Belgium
+32 3290 6273
info@pinkeye.b
www.pinkeye.b

Pinkeye, founded in 2006, creates total concepts that grab the consumer's attention from three angles: form, function and feeling. The team members take pride in their geek status mixed with a world class. Product designers mingle with software programmers, interior architects, textile designers, artists and trend forecasters. The studio's speciality areas include custom-made concepts for interiors, events and brands.

p.110, 122

PLAJER & FRANZ STUDIO
Erkelenzdamm 59–61
10999 Berlin
Germany
+49 30 616 5580
studio@plajer-franz.de
www.plajer-franz.de

Berlin-based plajer & franz studio is an international and interdisciplinary team of 50 architects, interior architects and graphic designers. The company carries out all stages of projects from concept to design to roll-out. Dedicated teams work on interior and building construction projects and on communication and graphic design.

p.070

PLS DESIGN
Via Aretina 161
50136 Firenze
Italy
+39 055 265 8353
info@plsdesign.it
www.plsdesign.it

PLS design of Florence, Italy is an international design studio dedicated to architecture and interior design. It was established in 2002 by architects Lino Losanto and Lorenzo Peri after their shared experience as partners at Nardi Associates. PLS design is composed of a team of 15 architects and designers which carries out projects internationally. The firm has a diverse portfolio divided into professional sectors, including architecture, luxury retail, residential and hospitality design, branding, communications, event planning and packaging design.

p.006

PROJEKTTRIANGLE DESIGN STUDIO
Humboldtstrasse 4
70178 Stuttgart
Germany
+49 711 6200 9314
mail@projekttriangle.com
www.projekttriangle.com

Projekttriangle is a design studio for applied and artistic projects from all disciplines of visual, interaction, information and graphic design. Operating in the crossover zone between design, research and art, the firm executes international projects for corporate clients as well as media installations for industry, research and culture. The studio was founded in 1998 in Stuttgart by Prof. Danijela Djokic, Martin Grothmaak and Prof. Jürgen Späth.

p.078, 206

PUBBLIK
Sassenheimstraat 51-H
1059 BC Amsterdam
the Netherlands
+31 6 22485046
info@pubblik.nl
www.pubblik.nl

Founded in 2009 and headed-up by Marjolein Langma, Pubblik is an Amsterdam-based design firm working mainly on hospitality projects, as well as retail, offices, exhibition stands and public spaces. The company's design approach aims to combine contemporary elements with authentic materials in order to create a unique identity and flawless atmosphere. Bearing in mind the visitor's point of view at all stages of the design process, the company offers a full range of services, from concept development to interior design and graphic identities.

p.102

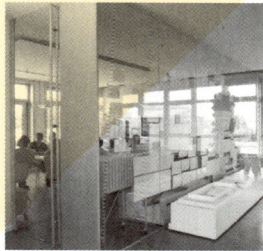

Q~BUS MEDIATEKTUR
Salzufer 14a/D
10587 Berlin
Germany
+49 30 390 489 0
info@q-bus.de
www.q-bus.de

The design agency q~bus Mediatektur is an owner-managed company, established 1995. Aiming for the integration of communication, architecture and technology, the firm implements a working method called 'ambient intelligence'. Transcending the boundaries of individual projects, q~bus integrates talents and specialists from different backgrounds such as communication design, architecture, software development and system integration. This interdisciplinary approach enables the agency to develop and realise pervasive concepts for wide-ranging projects, from brand environments to software solutions.

p.384, 390

ROTOR GROUP
Populierstraat 73
8800 Roeselare
Belgium
+32 5125 2725
post@rotorgroup.be
www.rotorgroup.be

Rotor Group designs corporate identities in the broadest sense of the word. The studio creates corporate stories for its clients and then narrates them through showrooms, packaging, websites, artwork, gadgets, fairs, cars, advertising, booths and products. Rotor Group prides itself on not following trends. Instead, it creates corporate worlds fitted out with ice-cold igloos, non-existent fairy tales, botanical gardens and amorphous ski-sheds.

p.198, 248

ROW STUDIO
Palmas 1145
11000 Mexico City
Mexico
+52 55 4753 9565
info@rowarch.com
www.rowarch.com

ROW Studio is an architecture and design firm that is a partnership between by Álvaro Hernández Felix, Nadia Hernández Félix and Alfonso Maldonado Ochoa. Established in 2005, its name derives from the term used in economy to refer to global phenomena (ROW: rest of the world). The team works in the realms of interior architecture and also expands its portfolio to other disciplines, such as sociology, psychology, economy and marketing.

p.112

SCHMIDHUBER
Nederlinger Strasse 21
80638 Munich
Germany
+49 89 157997 0
info@schmidhuber.de
www.schmidhuber.de

Established in 1984, Schmidhuber is a Munich-based design studio with a passionate team of over 70 architects, interior designers and designers. Linked with an interdisciplinary network of partners, the team implements visionary concepts and moving brand experiences in the realms of trade shows, exhibitions, events, shops and showrooms. Openness, respect and reliability are the main pillars of the studio's successful cooperation with its international client base, fostering a continuous redefinition of and refreshing approach to each new project.

p.204, 290, 452

SCHOLTEN & BAIJINGS
Westerdoksdijk 597
1013 BX Amsterdam
the Netherlands
+31 204 208 940
info@scholtenbaijings.com
www.scholtenbaijings.com

Scholten & Baijings is a design studio based in Amsterdam. Stefan Scholten and Carole Baijings have been designing together since 2000, filling their own niche within the world of Dutch product design. The duo's work is minimalist yet richly detailed and expressive, thanks to its skilful finishing and well-considered and powerful palette of colours. With its finesse, entrancing hues and subtle use of materials, the work has received considerable attention around the world from a range of international clients.

p.296

SMD+PARTNER
Juelicher Strasse 91b
52070 Aachen
Germany
+49 241 609 140
info@smd-partner.com
www.smd-partner.com

Set up in 1981, smd+partner design and architecture is a global player renowned for its outstanding conceptual designs and superb translation of the client's requirements into tangible presentations. Owned by Doris Bültmann and Mario Niessen, smd+partner has designed and realised a complete range of highly diverse projects from stands and exhibitions to large-scale office complexes.

p.090, 124

STANDARD STUDIO
366 Clementina Street
San Francisco, CA 94103
United States
+1 415 647 1700
hello@standard-studio.com
www.standard-studio.com

Standard Studio was founded in 2002 by Michael Dolan and Monina Johnson. Working from the precept that every business occupies space, whether inside a store, on the web or ultimately in the minds of customers. Standard helps people and businesses discover optimum ways to fill their space, both physically as well as experientially and emotionally. Combining environmental, industrial and communication design with brand expertise, the studio helps individuals, companies and organisations to compete more successfully.

p.132, 148

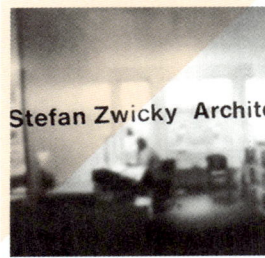

STEFAN ZWICKY
Zweierstrasse 15
8004 Zurich
Switzerland
+41 44 202 34 00
mail@stefanzwicky.ch
www.stefanzwicky.ch

After studying interior architecture at the School of Applied Arts in Zurich, Stefan Zwicky established his own studio there in 1983. The practice now has a team of six employees with an international portfolio that focuses on architecture, interiors, exhibitions and product design. In addition to appearing in Basel and Dusseldorf as a guest lecturer, Zwicky is also active as a publicist.

p.182, 208

STEFANO COLLI
Carrer Regas 3
08006 Barcelona
Spain
+34 932 225 090
stefano@stefanocolli.com
www.stefanocolli.com

Stefano Colli graduated with a degree in architecture from Politecnico of Milan. Since 1991, he has been working in Barcelona in his own studio specialising in corporate interior design and architecture. He currently combines his studio activities with lecturing project courses at ELISAVA Barcelona School of Design and Engineering.

p.398

STUDIOMFD
Tussen de Bogen 40
1013 JB Amsterdam
the Netherlands
+31 20 7704069
info@studiomfd.com
www.studiomfd.com

Martijn Frank Dirks founded studiomfd in 2006 in Amsterdam. The agency positively contributes to its clients' lives through the design of 2D and 3D environments, interacting open-mindedly in order to develop intuitive and deep-rooted creative concepts. This leads to authentic designs that reflect social themes. Form, style, colouring and the reuse of materials all consistently match the concepts, so that the final results are a reflection of the personality of clients.

p.100

STUDIO NITZAN COHEN
Naupliastrasse 103a
81545 Munich
Germany
+49 89 2032 8681
mail@nitzan-cohen.com
www.nitzan-cohen.com

Nitzan Cohen, who graduated from the Design Academy in Eindhoven in 2002, worked at Konstantin Grcic Industrial Design for a number of years before establishing his own studio in Munich in 2007. He has a research-oriented attitude towards conceptual design and an ability to translate this into a new visual language, objects and spaces. The studio has a multidisciplinary approach, with projects ranging from industrial products, furniture and spaces to art direction and strategic consultancy.

p.216

THE INSIDE
Teugseweg 13
7418 AM Deventer
the Netherlands
+31 570 656255
info@the-inside.nl
www.the-inside.nl

The Inside was founded by its owner and chief executive Michael Hermans in 1996 in Deventer, the Netherlands. Over the years, the design studio has developed into a nationwide company offering a range of services, including trade fair stand and exhibition design and construction, interiors and events. The firm's name symbolises the idea that the team of 60 employees works more productively by fully understanding the inside workings of every client.

p.076

TISCH13
Liebherrstrasse 5
80538 Munich
Germany
+49 89 1678 589 0
post@tisch13.com
www.tisch13.com

The Munich-based design firm tisch13 is an agency for two- and three-dimensional brand communication. Founded in 2001 by managing partners Heidi Buecherl and Carsten Roehr, the company has its core competencies in the realms of space, print, film, motion design, interactive exhibits and installations, as well as in mobile and web applications. The interdisciplinary team draws upon a large network of international specialists to tailor solutions for its customers and to offer cross-media solutions.

p.332, 344

TORTENWERKSTATT
Neurauthgasse 6a
6020 Innsbruck
Austria
+43 512 315577
info@tortenwerkstatt.net
www.tortenwerkstatt.net

Nikolaus Skorpik and Martin Mackowitz are part of Tortenwerkstatt which is an architecture collective and workshop in Innsbruck, Austria. Founded in 2009 by architecture students who collaborate on projects ranging from furniture to architectural designs, the collective works on sustainable architecture and new ways of thinking about materials.

p.444

TOTEMS
Pedro de Medinalaan 67
1086 XP Amsterdam
the Netherlands
+31 20 509 1311
amsterdam@totems.com
www.totems.com

Totems was established in 1997 in Amsterdam by the founding partners Gerard de Gorter, Florian Gerlach and Peter van Lier. Its multidisciplinary team comprises architects, interior architects, content developers and copywriters, as well as exhibition, media and graphic designers, all working together to turn stories into spatial experiences. The firm's approach is to connect the brand, theme or experience in a manner that encapsulates lightness, colourfulness and surprising perspectives. Totems is represented in Amsterdam, Dusseldorf, Stuttgart and Shanghai.

p.366, 374, 414

TULP
Gotzinger Strasse 52
81371 Munich
Germany
+49 891 259 4600
info@tulp.de
www.tulp.de

Tulp was founded in 1999 by designers Maik Schober, Alexander Striegl and Michael Zanin after they studied industrial design together at the School of Design in Pforzheim, Germany. The studio interprets and stages the ideas, attitudes, characters or content of its clients at trade shows and exhibitions, as well through interior and product design. The company's motto is 'think, reduce, create'.

p.050

UEBERHOLZ
Warndtstrasse 7
42285 Wuppertal
Germany
+49 202 280 96 0
info@ueberholz.de
www.ueberholz.de

Established in 1987, Ueberholz is led by architect and communication designer Nico Ueberholz. The company develops creative and innovative solutions for all strategic and operational aspects of temporary architecture. With expertise in the fields of trade fair and exhibition design as well as retail construction, the firm also provides event services for international brands encompassing all-round multi-sensory experiences.

p.172, 254, 264

UNIPLAN
Schanzenstrasse 39 a/b
51063 Cologne
Germany
+49 221 8456 90
uniplan@uniplan.com
www.uniplan.com

Uniplan is one of the leading agencies for live communication and creates brand promotions for events, trade fairs, showrooms and roadshows. Uniplan's customers include leading companies and brands such as adidas, Audi, BMW, Daimler, Deutsche Bahn, Deutsche Post DHL, Sony PlayStation, Toshiba and ZDF. The company is based in Cologne and has a workforce of 650 employees across its 12 branches worldwide.

p.120, 302

VC A | VANNINI+CESARETTI
Via Oxilia 23
20127 Milan
Italy
+39 022 680 9419
info@vc-a.it
www.vc-a.it

The design company vc a | vannini+cesaretti is a team of architects and designers specialised in exhibition and experience design, with a strong emphasis on innovation and research. Founded by Cristiana Vannini and Paolo Cesaretti in 1998, the firm focuses on enhancing spatial experience and brand identity, designing architecture for commercial spaces and exhibitions, permanent and temporary, and defining the identity of companies and institutions. Paolo Cesaretti and Cristiana Vannini are lecturers at the Scuola Politecnica di Design Milano and guest professors at the Domus Academy and Politecnico di Milano.

p.086

VIA2V
Laan van Mecklenburg 22
4818 GD Breda
the Netherlands
+31 5 280 5888
info@via2v.nl
www.via2v.nl

Via2V is an integrated supplier of interior architecture and project management, established by Hein Verberne in 2006. The firm offers technical and strategic advice, as well as supervising design processes. Utilising an integrated approach, the design team implements interiors in the realms of retail, office, hospitality and showroom projects, as well as trade fairs.

p.076

VON M
Rosenbergstrasse 93
70193 Stuttgart
Germany
+49 711 62 6 975 0
info@vonm.de
www.vonm.de

Von M was established by Matthias Siegert in 2004 and now is directed by three associate partners and has a 10-member team working in the fields of architecture and media design. The studio's portfolio covers interior and building construction projects as well as video and space installations. Characteristic of all its work is an open-minded and unbiased approach, concentrating on the essentials to achieve clear and effectively simple solutions. Within this exciting area of tension between architecture and interior design, mutual cross-references emerge again and again in the realisation of multi-facetted projects.

p.078, 206

WALBERT-SCHMITZ
Gut-Knapp-Strasse 8–14
52080 Aachen
Germany
+49 2405 600 20
info@walbert-schmitz.de
www.walbert-schmitz.de

Walbert-Schmitz was established in 1966 and is a family-owned company based in Aachen. Specialising in exhibition and stand construction, the firm offers a wide range of expertise in the field of three-dimensional brand communication – strategy, conception, design and architecture – as well as in production, installation and dismantling. The company employs more than 100 members of staff and maintains worldwide partnerships with specialised suppliers.

p.090, 124

WERKSTATT65

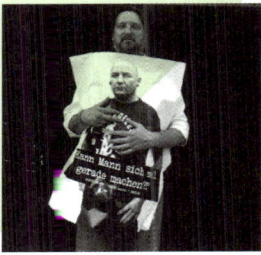

Lange Lakenstraat 2
2011 ZC Haarlem
the Netherlands
+31 650 201835
contact@werkstatt65.nl
www.werkstatt65.nl

Dutch creative agency Werkstatt65 was founded by Alex Sijpesteijn and Bas de Graaf, who joined forces in 2010 after graduating from The Royal Academy of Art in The Hague and the Gerrit Rietveld Academy in Amsterdam, respectively. Werkstatt65 works mainly for fashion related clients, as well as non-fashion companies. The studio's portfolio includes exhibition design illustration and graphic design, realised by the in-house team together with an extensive pool of freelance workers that are selected according to the requirements of each specific project.

p.468

WINK

Hooghiemstraplein 15
3514 AX Utrecht
the Netherlands
+31 30 247 0301
info@welcomewink.nl
www.welcomewink.nl

Located in the Netherlands and offering a complete 360-degree service, creative agency Wink designs made-to-measure event environments and happenings for and with its clients within the fields of fashion and hospitality. Wink helps to build and maintain brand identities worldwide, while remembering, 'The aim of the game is to feel real good'.

p.032

TRADE FAIRS

Credits

GRAND STAND 4
Design for Trade Fair Stands

PUBLISHER
Frame Publishers

EDITORS
Carmel McNamara
Marlous van Rossum-Willems

COPY EDITOR
Billy Nolan

GRAPHIC DESIGNERS
Barbara Iwanicka
Naama Goldschmid (intern)
Georgia Saltouridou (intern)
Marieke Vonk (intern)

PREPRESS
Edward de Nijs

PRINTING
D'Print

TRADE DISTRIBUTION USA AND CANADA
Consortium Book Sales & Distribution, LLC.
34 Thirteenth Avenue NE, Suite 101
Minneapolis, MN 55413-1007
T +1 612 746 2600
T +1 800 283 3572 (orders)
F +1 612 746 2606

DISTRIBUTION REST OF WORLD
Frame Publishers
Laan der Hesperiden 68
1076 DX Amsterdam
the Netherlands
www.frameweb.com
distribution@frameweb.com

ISBN: 978-90-77174-72-2

The Koninklijke Bibliotheek lists this publication in the Nederlandse Bibliografie: detailed bibliographic information is available on the internet at http://picarta.pica.nl

Printed on acid-free paper produced from chlorine-free pulp. TCF ∞
Printed in China

987654321